A JURAN INSTITUTE REPORT

Quality Wars

The Triumphs and Defeats of American Business

JEREMY MAIN

THE FREE PRESS
A Division of Macmillan, Inc.
NEW YORK
Maxwell Macmillan Canada
TORONTO
Maxwell Macmillan International
NEW YORK   OXFORD   SINGAPORE   SYDNEY

The Free Press
A Division of Macmillan, Inc.
866 Third Avenue, New York, N.Y. 10022

Maxwell Macmillan Canada, Inc.
1200 Eglinton Avenue East
Suite 200
Don Mills, Ontario M3C 3N1

Macmillan, Inc. is part of the Maxwell Communication Group of Compa-nies.

Printed in the United States of America

printing number
  2 3 4 5 6 7 8 9 10

Library of Congress Cataloging-in-Publication Data

Main, Jeremy
    Quality wars: the triumphs and defeats of American business / Jeremy Main.
        p.   cm.
    Includes bibliographical references and index.
    ISBN 0–02–916684–5
    1. Total quality management—United States—Case studies.
  I. Title.
  HD62.15.M3465   1994
  658.5′62′0973—dc20   93–42422
                                                   CIP

To Mary Main
Who Showed Me The Way

Contents

Foreword

The incredible growth of world-wide competition in the past 30 years, led first by U.S., then German and then Japanese companies, has shaken modern business to the very core. People around the world, especially Americans, have access to the best possible products at continually decreasing relative costs.

Industry after industry struggled with the onslaught of high-quality, reasonably priced products from Japan, Europe, Southeast Asia, and now China. Industry after industry in America collapsed. Many high-tech products are no longer made in the United States, or made by American companies in the United States, or made by American companies at all.

But some leading American companies have shown clearly and dramatically that it is possible to make things virtually without error, with few failures over time, at increasingly competitive prices. In the past 15 years we have seen companies reduce defects by 10 times, by 100 times. We have seen a company that used to take six weeks to manufacture a high-tech device now take the order, custom-design hardware and software, produce, and ship it in 1 hour and 45 minutes.

Finally, someone with both the experience and the necessary skills has taken the time to document the tumultuous times of the past 15 years of America's quality revolution. Jeremy Main has an unusual skill of writing clearly and engagingly about complex topics—and total quality management is a most complex topic.

Although there is definitely no shortage of books on quality management, unfortunately most fall into two categories, neither of which is fully useful. The first category consists of easy-to-read, entertaining collections of quality anecdotes. Inspiring perhaps, these quality ''lite-bites'' may leave the reader eager to get started but unsure of what to do and even less sure of how to do it.

In the second category you find well-meaning but often turgid books explaining in great technical detail the tools and methods of total quality, and even the road maps for change. Written by quality professionals or senior executives describing their own experiences, these books often overwhelm, frequently confuse, and sometimes mislead even the most dedicated reader.

Juran Institute recognized the need to create an objective documentation of America's quality revolution and, as it happened, that is just the kind of book Main wanted to write.

In *Quality Wars* Main has broken new ground. He covers major events that have transformed the management of business in fundamental ways. He describes them with a brisk, almost novelistic pace that sometimes leaves the reader breathless, but never bored or confused.

The breadth of topics Main covers is staggering. He starts with the beginning, sometimes emotional experiences that pushed many companies into action. He follows with a chapter on the leaders, what they did, and what they think now about their mistakes and successes. The author continues with a wonderful chapter, "The People: How Hard It Is." He then goes into intriguing detail to explain the rediscovery of the customer and the almost fanatical customer focus emerging across the country.

Main examines the tools of quality management, a subject most unusual for a book of this type. He pulls no punches here. After reading so many books by tools salespeople, I am delighted to see proponents and opponents given equal time and to see both the values and the misuses highlighted and discussed.

He then comes back for a second pass, this time in more depth. By devoting a chapter to each of several critical industries, Main allows himself time to explore the specific changes in the management of specific companies. He starts, naturally enough, with the automakers. These companies have been shaken to their very cores by incredibly strong competitors. In this chapter, Main's many years at *Fortune* shine through. The coverage is thorough but fresh. New insights jump off every page.

Main follows with two intriguing chapters on the pacesetters—the true leaders of the quality revolution—and the fumblers—those hard-working, well-intentioned companies who somehow lost their way. For many readers, the lessons of failure may be painfully familiar. For others, the lessons may come just in time. If you have no time to read anything else, read these two chapters. If you do, I'm sure you'll quickly go back and read the rest.

The author concludes with chapters on the railroaders, service companies, the professions, and even government. He describes a wonderful variety of approaches, of philosophies, but an even more wonderful wealth of similarities, of commonalities, of willingness to learn from each other.

Much has happened to American industry in the past 15 years—and to Canadian, and Mexican, and European, and Australian industry—and on around the world. Better than anyone else, Main has captured the essence of this quality revolution and packaged it so we can understand it. The book is about change:

- Change based on modern statistical methods and a revolutionary concept called total quality management.
- Change that yields incredible reductions in waste, that results in a new respect for the customer, that draws out the creativity and ability of every member of an organization.
- Change so profound that a new CEO announces he will not focus on short-term profits despite intense pressure to do so from institutional investors because he must also serve customers, suppliers, employees, and the community.
- Change so surprising that three second-graders serve on a quality improvement team with teachers, administrators, and custodians to improve recycling in their school.
- Change so unexpected that members of Mustang clubs throughout America participate with Ford in the design of a new model, working by fax and E-mail with a design team that includes suppliers, machinists, assemblers, market researchers, and engineers.
- Change that has spread through manufacturing companies and services around the world and now is beginning to impact our hospitals, our local, state, and even federal governments, and our educational systems.
- This book describes the key events, players, concepts, and methods that have created so much change and provides an extremely useful guide for others embarking on the same journey.

A. Blanton Godfrey
Chairman and CEO
Juran Institute, Inc.

Preface

This is not a how-to book or a book of theory. Nor is it an evangelical treatise or an act of worship. Too many books of those kinds have already been written by the advocates of what is known most generally as total quality management or TQM. They sometimes damage their case with an excess of zeal. They have seen how well TQM works, and they cannot wait to convince you, and they forget to talk about the failures and frustrations. What I have set out to do is to tell stories about companies and other organizations in the United States that have adopted some version of TQM. TQM is tough because it is not just a way of delivering better products and services; it is also a way of changing how we think, work, and relate to other people. It involves improving everything an organization does. Therefore it is stressful and demanding, full of surprises and problems, constantly challenging—especially for the CEO, who has to learn to lead in a new way. It has turned out to be one of the most difficult and rewarding realignments ever attempted by American business. Some companies have achieved levels of quality unimaginable a few years ago. Many have been disappointed. Adopting TQM amounts to much more than the formal steps that the textbooks outline. It seemed to me that to tell these stories, and to tell them as much as possible in the words of the crucial players, the CEOs, might be both useful and interesting.

The academic might be inclined to sniff at my approach as merely anecdotal. However, through these stories you might get closer to the reality of total quality management than you could through any number of surveys, theories, theses, symposia, and texts. Sometimes examples teach more than theory.

Quality boffins may be surprised to find that there is not a chart, diagram, graph, table, or other illustration to be found in this book. Most books on this subject are full of graphics. The practitioners of TQM seem to be unable to express themselves without propping themselves up with slides, blackboards, or illustrations. I cannot begin to count the number of diagrams purporting to explain some theory of quality or other that I have studied from every angle and found meaningless or just dressing on a banality. Here, in this book, the reader will find unadorned thought, fact, and interpretation and, therefore, my shortcomings will stand in plain view.

I regret that I could not tell more stories. I should have said more about Corning, General Electric, and Procter & Gamble, and have written about American Express, Federal Express, Harley-Davidson, Johnson & Johnson, 3M, Texas Instruments, Wal-Mart, Whirlpool, and many other companies, particularly the smaller ones. But so much is happening in so many places in the quality field that it would have been impossible to fit all the interesting stories into one volume.

Today there are few leading corporations which will admit that they do not practice total quality management, or that it is not paying off. I have tried as much as possible to find out what went wrong as well as what went right, because failure can be at least as instructive as success. But no doubt there are instances where I did not see through the screen of happy talk. If, as a result, I mislead a reader, I apologize.

I first became interested in the subject of quality in the 1970s when William S. Rukeyser, then managing editor of *Money* magazine, asked me to examine the adage, "They don't make things the way they used to." I found out that they don't—thank heavens. This was before Detroit woke up to the quality gap between its cars and the Japanese cars. Even so, the Detroit cars were clearly better than they had been. So were other products. In 1981 I became aware of the evolution of formal quality-improvement methods when I contributed to a series of articles in *Fortune* entitled "Working Smarter," which subsequently became a book (Viking, 1982). Through the 1980s I had the opportunity, thanks to *Fortune*, to study TQM on many occasions, and to listen to, talk to, and travel with the late W. Edwards Deming, Joseph M. Juran, and some of the other leaders in the quality field. When the Juran Institute offered to support the book I wanted to write and The Free Press to publish it, I grabbed the opportunity. The modern approach to quality improvement seems so rational, so sane, so successful when it is done right, that I had to write about it.

Jeremy Main
Ridgefield, Connecticut
September 1993

Introduction
"A Slight Problem"

S outhern Pacific's "Extra 7551 East" crested El Cajon pass at 25 miles per hour and started the long run down to San Bernardino, 2,000 feet below and 24 miles away. It was 7:03 A.M., May 12, 1989. At the head of the train, Engineer Frank Holland radioed Lawrence Hill, the engineer operating two helper locomotives at the rear, to ask if he had dynamic braking power. Hill replied, "Yeah, I'm in full." It was the only time they had spoken since the beginning of the trip. The dynamic brakes on a locomotive work like the gears on a car when the driver uses the weight of the engine to slow down. Holland knew that one of his four head-end locomotives was dead—no power and no brakes—and another had only intermittent brakes. But with dynamic braking from the two other head-end locomotives and the two helpers, plus the pneumatic shoe brakes on the 69 cars he was hauling, Holland could hold the train. The cars carried trona, a grayish mineral found in evaporated lake beds and used for making fertilizer, to be shipped from the Port of Los Angeles to Colombia. Extra 7551 East's computerized profile listed the train's total weight as 6,151 tons. If the information given to Holland was correct, he had ample braking power to control the train's descent, starting from El Cajon at 25 m.p.h.

As Holland expected, on the downgrade the train's speed picked up 5 miles per hour and Holland put 10 pounds per square inch of pressure into the pneumatic brake cylinders. The train held briefly, then started accelerating. Holland added a bit more pressure, and again the train held its speed briefly and then began going faster. Each time he applied a bit more brake power, the train held, then accelerated. Still Holland thought he had the train under control. When the train entered a straightaway, he released more air pressure into the brakes and thought the train "should start bogging down." It did not and he went to maximum braking power, 26 p.s.i. By 7:30 A.M. the train was rumbling downhill at 45 m.p.h. and Holland realized that "this train wasn't going to stop." At the bottom of the hill, in San Bernardino, the

1

train would enter a curve flanked by a housing development where people were getting up and going to work.

At the controls of the helper engines, Hill, without talking to Holland, threw the pneumatic brakes on full emergency. But by now they were smoking and overheated, so they had little holding power. Hill's action automatically blocked out the dynamic brakes, but they could not make much difference at that speed anyhow. The train began to surge forward. Everett Crown, the conductor, got on the radio to the yard at West Colton at 7:33 and said mildly, "We have a slight problem. I don't know if we can get this train stopped." Overhearing Crown's understatement, Hill put out a Mayday call over his radio. Then he braced himself on the floor of the engine cab with his back and head against the control panel. At 7:37 Crown called in: "Mayday, Mayday . . . we're doing 90 miles per hour, nine zero, out of control, won't be able to stop . . ." Holland and Crown remained in their seats. There was nothing they could do at this point to stop the train. When it hit the curve in San Bernardino less than a minute later, it was probably doing 110 m.p.h., but the train recorders do not register above 90 m.p.h. The entire train—six locomotives and 69 cars—flew off the tracks and piled up on the right of way and into the houses beside it. The leading cars lay side by side, like neatly stacked logs. The others were scattered randomly. Over everything lay a thick blanket of trona. Crown and the head-end brakeman died, as did two small boys in the houses. Somehow Holland survived. So did Hill and his brakeman. Five of the six engines and all 69 cars were totally destroyed and so were seven houses. (Thirteen days later, a cleanup crew ruptured a gasoline pipeline under the site of the wreck, setting off an explosion and fire that killed two more people and destroyed eleven more houses, but that is another story.)

The National Safety Transportation Board investigators amassed the details of what happened in the hours, minutes, and seconds before the wreck. They found that when the Southern Pacific clerk accepted the bill of lading from the shipper, the Lake Minerals Corporation in Owens Lake, California, he didn't notice at first that the weight had not been entered on the forms. Later, he tried calling Lake Minerals, but couldn't get their number, so he estimated the weight of the trona at 60 tons in each of the 69 cars. He testified later, "I figured these cars were lighter than cement cars and I knew cement cars weighed 75 tons." He wrote the total down on the bill of lading, but without noting that it was an estimate. Had he so noted, the billing office in Los Angeles would have double checked. But it didn't and thus drew up a train profile on the basis of 60 tons per car. In fact, as Lake Minerals assumed the Southern Pacific people knew, the 69 cars each carried 100 tons of trona. Adding to these 6,900 tons the weight of the train itself, Extra 7551 East started down from El Cajon weighing 9,000 tons, not 6,150 tons as Holland thought.

When Holland was making up his train he discovered that one of the locomotives would not start. It was dead. But he left it in the string of four engines because nobody told him what to do with it. Assigned to help Holland, Hill picked up the two additional locomotives and heard from the engineer he relieved that one of these locomotives had no dynamic brakes. He assumed that the engineer had already reported this failure, so he did not report it. Nor did he tell Holland. They did not discuss the weight of the train, either. Hill and Holland came from different yards, different chapters of the Brotherhood of Locomotive Engineers, did not know one another, and had very little communication over their radios at each end of the train. When Hill told Holland as they crested El Cajon, "I'm in full," he was referring to the one additional locomotive that did have dynamic brakes. Holland thought he meant both of them.

Extra 7551 East weighed 50% more than Holland thought and had a lot less braking power. Of the six locomotives, two had no dynamic brakes, and a third had only intermittent power. All these facts were known piecemeal to someone, but no one knew them all, certainly not Holland, who was driving the train. The investigation later revealed that the fourth engine might also have had only intermittent braking power.

The National Transportation Safety Board listed the probable causes as the failure to determine and communicate the accurate weight of the train, the failure to communicate the status of the train's dynamic brakes, and Southern Pacific rules that provided inadequate directions to engineers about downhill braking and speed. It did not address the question of whether Holland applied the brakes too slowly and in increments too small to bring the train under control.[1]

The NTSB findings addressed only the immediate causes or symptoms. The investigators did not ask the questions that might have gone to the roots of the accident. "The accident was caused by multiple failures," says Lloyd Simpson, Southern Pacific's vice president for quality. "The root cause was the total lack of a quality system. It all came together in one train." At the time, Simpson was SP's general manager for the Western Region.[2] Had the NTSB probed more deeply, it might have asked how SP could have put together a six-engine train with one locomotive dead and two if not three others malfunctioning. What was SP's locomotive maintenance program? How could such a critical item as the weight of the train be underestimated so grossly? And why wasn't the mistake discovered? Why didn't the five-man crew on the train act as a team and talk to each other? Why weren't the crew and the clerks and the dispatchers trained in the importance of knowing and communicating weights and other vital information? The questions go on and on. Above all, what were the management failures that led to this accident? Why didn't management attack the root causes? Why did it not create the tools, the practices, and the atmosphere that would have avoided the accident?

It is not as if the San Bernardino crash was an isolated incident. Southern Pacific was notorious for derailments, as well as for late trains, misplaced loads, decrepit engines, inaccurate accounting, and a management totally insensitive to the customers' needs. SP was spending $100 million a year to pay for the costs of derailments, which happened to be just about what it was losing every year. Since the San Bernardino crash, SP has, like other railroads, mounted an enormously difficult, risky, complex effort to improve its quality in every sense—to get at the root causes of those accidents and the railroad's other problems. However, like the rest of us, SP has a long, rough road to travel.

THEY DIDN'T LISTEN

We are surrounded by quality failures that are appallingly costly in money lost, opportunity wasted, work scrapped, grief incurred. Our lives are full of mundane personal failures. When I spend an hour looking for a file or a tool I have mislaid, when I go shopping and forget an item because I did not consult my list and therefore have to make a second trip, when I am late for an appointment or forget to pay a bill on time, then my personal quality control has failed because of my lack of a systematic way of doing things right the first time.* The suppliers I deal with often disappoint me with their quality failures: the cable television company that cannot send a bill to the right address or that sends an installer who drills through a power cable; the metal tongue on the can of corned beef that always breaks off before I have finished opening it; the new bathroom cabinet that arrives with a cracked mirror. Anyone who has to wait three hours to see a doctor or to be admitted to a hospital is the victim of a quality failure. So is the airline passenger who waits in line to check in, then stands in a

---

* The reader who thinks his personal quality needs improvement might want to read *Quality Is Personal* by Harry V. Roberts, a professor at the Graduate School of Business at the University of Chicago, and Bernard F. Sergesketter, an AT&T vice president (New York: The Free Press, 1993).

crowded waiting room, then stands in more lines at the gate and at the plane's door, then squeezes into a tiny seat, and then has the choice of going hungry or eating an execrable meal.

I recently made intimate contact with the construction industry by building a house. Although the house as a whole came out very well with minimum stress (I have to acknowledge here that the builder was my son-in-law), some of the subcontractors made me wonder how much they had to overcharge to make enough money to cover their mistakes and stay in business. A supplier of built-in fittings delivered library shelves and cabinets of light maple when the order plainly said dark oak; he brought kitchen cabinets with doors out of square; and he forgot the kitchen-counter tops altogether. Both the bathtubs installed by the plumber immediately leaked, one of them in three places: at the faucet, at the drain, and around the edge of the tub where caulking was missing. (Since I wrote the last sentence a fourth leak has developed.) The shower in that bathroom did not work because there was no device to divert the water from the bath faucet up to the shower head—which was just as well, because the shower would have leaked into the kitchen. The other shower worked, but the hot and cold pipes were reversed. We all have our quality horror stories, which we are eager to tell.

The impact of poor quality can be momentous. Ask the makers and recipients of the 86,000 Bjork-Shiley heart valves manufactured by Shiley Inc., a subsidiary of Pfizer Inc., and installed between 1979 and 1986. Because of fractures in the struts that hold a disk that closes the valve, 295 of these devices failed, resulting in 178 deaths. A second model, sold overseas but not approved for sale in the United States by the Food and Drug Administration, failed 94 times, resulting in 70 deaths.[3] Throughout the 1980s and into the 1990s the cost of these fractures and potential fractures hung over Pfizer. The company took a charge of $300 million in 1991 to pay legal claims and agreed in 1992 to pay $75 million into a research fund to identify valves at high risk.[4] Patients wearing the valve had to make a life-or-death choice: whether to leave the valve in place and run the risk of a failure with a two-thirds likelihood of death, or to have it replaced in a costly, risky operation. Just why the struts fractured may never be known because Pfizer has settled these suits out of court, heading off detailed public testimony. However, a report on the valve by Congressman John Dingell's Subcommittee on Oversight and Investigations said that Pfizer had marketed the valve ''aggressively'' even though it knew serious manufacturing problems existed.[5]

The spectacular explosion of the space shuttle *Challenger* with the loss of all of its crew on January 28, 1986, might have seemed like a freak, random accident. In fact, it had the classic pattern of a specific failure arising out of a flawed system that could have produced failure in many ways. The presidential commission that investigated the *Challenger* tragedy focused, as most such bodies do, on the immediate cause: the O-rings on one of the booster engines that allowed gases to escape through a joint in the booster. The launch occurred after a night of frost, on a day colder than that for any other shuttle launch, and the rubber O-rings lost their resilience and failed to set a tight seal at the joint.

But unlike the National Transportation Safety Board, which looked only at the immediate causes of the Southern Pacific wreck, the presidential commission looked into the root causes of the failure—perhaps not deeply enough, but more than most investigations. The commission found that the original design of the seal was flawed, that engineers at Morton Thiokol, which built the booster, and at the Marshall Space Flight Center, which was responsible for the booster and main engines, had for years warned of flaws in the performance of the seals. On previous launches, especially in cold weather, the O-rings were eroded by burns and marked with soot. But top management never listened to the warnings. NASA acted like a manufacturer such as an auto plant, with management demanding that it "push metal" out the door—and fix whatever problems might show up later. NASA was under pressure from Washington and the media to send more shuttle missions into space, but NASA had no way of fixing the shuttle's problems "later." The engineers well knew that *Challenger* should not fly right after a freeze, but NASA management did not get the message. So little frank communication existed among the NASA units and their contractors that potential problems did not get aired. Four months before the accident, Robert Ebeling, the head of a task force at Morton Thiokol appointed to study the O-ring problem, sent what he called a "red flag" message to his boss. He reported that the work of the task force was being delayed by "every possible means" available to seasoned bureaucrats and that the people in manufacturing, quality, and procurement whose help the task force needed "are generating plenty of resistance."[6]

Thus, a lot more than faulty O-rings caused the *Challenger* accident. The total failure of management, in business and government, to create both a system and an atmosphere that would allow the expert opinion of engineers on the spot to reach whatever level they needed to reach quickly was the root cause. In spite of the emphasis on safety, redundancy, and reliability, NASA was primed to fail. The loss of an Atlas Centaur rocket with an $83-million military satellite aboard the following year, the flaws in the Hubble space telescope launched in 1990, not to mention cost over-runs and general confusion, all emphasized the underlying weakness of NASA.

The reaction of Congress and federal functionaries to something like the *Challenger* disaster can almost be guaranteed to produce a result opposite to what they intend. Instead of giving NASA or whatever body happens to be the target of the official blame-seekers the incentives and ability to do better, the government encumbers it with more regulations and oversight, which are usually part of the problem in the first place.

Congress itself, of course, is a national model of poor quality, of a collapsing system. While its proliferating staffs and committees fall over each other to pester the administration and to find things to do that are good for us, Congress grinds out junk legislation. Recall Superfund, which has poured billions of dollars more into the hands of litigators than into actually cleaning up toxic waste dumps; or the futile efforts to balance the budget; or the tax reforms. In every year but two from 1981 to 1990 Congress passed a so-called tax reform bill. The net result was that the average American paid about the same in taxes at the end of the 1980s as at the beginning (although the very rich paid a lot less and the poor somewhat less). The total tax burden, including social security taxes, basically did not change. But the "reforms" did keep changing the structure of the taxes, the deductions, the incentives. Savings deposits were not taxable one year; the next year they were.[7] Stability would have helped more than reform. Our laws, like our factories, often run better when left to themselves than when humans constantly meddle with them.

THE COSTS OF FAILURE

Congress and NASA, plumbers and cabinetmakers, hospitals and airliness, railroads and cable TV—they all afflict us with poor quality, and we add to it by our own frequent failures to do things right the first time in our personal lives. The burden that poor quality imposes on society is probably incalculable. When corporations are asked what poor quality costs them, they guess around 5% or 7% of sales. But when they actually calculate their costs they find that it is more like 20% to 30%.

Hewlett-Packard decided at the end of the 1970s that it had to make better products. So it studied the cost of poor quality in two hardware divisions. Hewlett-Packard asked, if all their products were perfectly designed and perfectly manufactured, how much could the company save? The answer was 25% of sales, and most of that was coming right off profits. That number packed a kick that helped launch Hewlett-Packard on a campaign which is held up throughout U.S. industry as an example of how to do it right. Yet in 1992 when I asked Craig Walter, then Hewlett-Packard's corporate quality director, what the cost of quality would be today, he said it would probably still be 25% or 30% (although it has not been recalculated formally). He did not mean that Hewlett-Packard's efforts for the past 13 years have failed; rather, the company's expectations have risen: ''We've peeled another layer off the onion and we can see a lot of things now are obvious that were hidden before, a lot more opportunity.''

Hewlett-Packard's early calculations focused on hardware, and did not take into account the costs of failures in business processes like accounting and order fulfillment, or the costs of mistakes in software design. But in 1990 Hewlett-Packard sampled the costs of errors in software research and development during the year. The answer, $400 million, shocked Hewlett-Packard into a whole new effort to eliminate mistakes in writing software. The $400 million waste, half of it spent in the labs on rework and half in the field to fix the mistakes that escaped from the labs, amounted to one third of the company's total R&D costs. Or put another way, mistakes in software design were lopping $2 per share off the company's earnings. Since the earnings amounted to $3 per share that year, perfect software development could have increased earnings by almost 67%.[8]

The burden of poor quality that we carry, imposed and self-inflicted, should not blind us to the fine quality that we do enjoy. To err may be human, but it is not inevitable. Many things made and done in America are excellent and have been all along. Our jet aircraft are world leaders. Our airlines may provide dreadful service, but their safety records are astoundingly good. Our integrated circuits and our software are world class. Foreign visitors love to buy our sheets and towels, our sports and casual clothing. American fishing rods and other types of sports equipment are excellent and moderately priced. Our washing machines and dishwashers are unbeatable at the price. American-built construction and agricultural machines are as honest as the soil they work. In spite of the dismemberment of the Bell system, the United States enjoys superb telephone service. The list of good things made in America is long. Moreover, the United States of America remains the most productive country in the world and therefore, if productivity is the other side of the quality coin, our products and services cannot all be bad. But if you are making a lot of production mistakes, with high scrap rates, warranty costs, design corrections, returns, and repairs, then productivity is bound to suffer.

WHAT IS QUALITY, ANYWAY?

Sometimes we exaggerate the things gone wrong because our view of quality is muddled by nostalgia. We like to say, "They don't make things the way they used to. Remember the 1940 Lincoln Continental? A beautiful car. Beginning at the sculptured grille, the lines flowed back, clear, simple, and elegant. A classic. Show me a car built like that today!" Well, to be unsentimental about it, the Lincoln Continental was an oil burner. Like most cars built before the 1960s, it needed greasing every 1,000 miles and an oil change every 2,000. Any car today can run 5,000 miles or more between oil changes. The old Lincoln would need a valve job and perhaps a whole new engine by 40,000 miles or so. Today's engines are unlikely to need a valve job before 70,000 miles—if they ever do. The Lincoln had a primitive transverse spring-leaf suspension similar to what you would have found on a Model-T. Today's car might have independent four-wheel suspension with coil springs and an anti-roll bar. The Lincoln's tires and tubes would wear out at about 20,000 miles, and probably would go flat several times before getting there. Today's tubeless steel radials last 40,000 miles or so and grip the road a lot better. The comparisons go on and on. With its safety belts, air bags, collapsible steering column, crash bars in the doors and other safety features, today's car is much safer than the Lincoln. It emits a fraction of the old car's pollutants.[9] No, they don't make things the way they used to, thank God!

When we become nostalgic about quality, we are probably thinking about the kinds of exceptional things the privileged have always had: a Rolls-Royce, dinner at a three-star restaurant in Paris, the Oriental Hotel in Bangkok, the beautiful tapestries or fine steel produced by the secretive guilds of the Middle Ages, or the bank manager who knew your name. Quality of this kind has always been expensive, exclusive, within reach only of the few. Or else we are thinking about the work of skilled and caring hands, the armchair made by a grandfather, the way a farmer could scythe a field, the goodness of fruit fresh from an orchard. This kind of quality still exists, though perhaps mainly in the home (cooking) and in hobbies (fly-tying), but let's call it "old quality."

Fit for Use

The kind of quality at issue today, the kind that pits the Japanese economy against America's, produces good things at reasonable prices for everyman. The consumer determines what is good. Quality is "fitness for use," in the definition favored by Joseph M. Juran, one of the founders of the quality movement. Modern quality can be be found in a Ford Taurus, a pair of Levi Strauss jeans, a visit to Disney World, an Intel microprocessor, a Boeing jet, or even a Big Mac at McDonald's. The Taurus is well designed and built, comfortable, affordable, and durable. Levi jeans are sturdy, stylish, durable, and economical; they meet the wearer's requirements. Disney World employees are helpful, friendly, wholesome, and must never be seen in a soiled uniform. The Intel chip packs an incredible amount of power into a tiny space and almost never fails. The Boeing jet is a marvel of safety, speed, and reliability. The Big Mac is always the same; it is cheap; it is served by cheerful people in a clean, bright place; and at least to a child is a good hamburger. The customer always gets what he expects and wants.

The difference between old and new quality is that the old is the work of craftsmen and the new is the work of a system. The old quality was made by a few for the few. New quality is made by many for the use of the many. The first is expensive, in labor if not cash; the second reduces cost. The first is created mostly by skilled hands, the second mostly by intelligent minds. Old quality still matters because it produces beautiful things. But new quality can drive the economy by making business competitive and by serving the whole population with a general standard of products and services never before achieved.

This book is about the new quality. The way to achieve it goes by many names. *Total Quality Management*, or *TQM*, is the most common. TQM is a way of running a company or other organization that focuses its efforts in a systematic, disciplined fashion on improving continuously the quality of everything it does. It is not a management tool, to be added onto others, but an overall way of managing. It is not a cure-all for the problems of business, but the levels of quality it produces are becoming a requisite for staying in business.

The means for achieving the new quality are quite simple and common-sensical, but using them successfully is enormously difficult because they require fundamental change in the way we work. New quality demands painstaking, even fanatical, attention to improving all the time every activity in an organization. It demands patience and endurance because the effort never ends and sometimes the obstacles seem overwhelming. It requires workers with both the incentive and the training to examine everything they do and everything done around them to see whether it can be done better. It requires managers willing to break with the autocratic traditions of American management and encourage the will and the ideas of their people to flow upward. It requires leaders who are willing, even eager, to let their organizations change, who pay more attention to production and process, less to finance and staff, more to the long term and less to the short term. Above all, the new quality demands devotion to the needs of the customer. A fanatic attention to the wants of the customer mark a true TQM effort. TQM is a term much abused by organizations who think they are practicing it, or would like their clients to think they are practicing it. They adopt a fragment of TQM, or employ the jargon; but for them the results are bound to be disappointing.

GOOD ENOUGH ISN'T

Look at what happens when a company really lives up to the demands of new quality. In the days when "good enough" was good enough, a company expected that as much as 7% of the parts it received and 7% of the goods it shipped out would be defective; and that figure does not include the number of defective parts caught by inspectors and not shipped. Now some of the best quality companies no longer count the number of defects per hundred but the number *per million*. Corning Glass Works supplied the first glass to Alan Dumont when he invented television in the 1930s, and Corning used to consider itself preeminent at making TV tubes and the glass panels that go in front of them. A TV set manufacturer who bought glass from Corning could reject a panel if it had a bubble in it only 20 one-thousandths of an inch (.0020″) in diameter. Customers were rejecting only one in a hundred, or 1%. Then in the 1970s the Japanese came along and raced off with the television market, including the market for TV glass. Four of Corning's five glass plants in the United States closed. "We thought we were darned good," recalled Jamie Houghton, chairman of Corning. "But our customers were talking in parts per million—and 1% is 10,000 parts per million. It wasn't nearly good enough."[10] Houghton, the great-great-grandson of the man who founded the company in 1851, made quality improvement the focus of his tenure when he became chairman in 1983. By 1987 Corning's one remaining TV-glass plant at State College, Pennsylvania had improved its performance tenfold and was throwing out only 1,000 parts per million. Sony, with some condescension, now began buying glass from the plant, rejecting fewer than 100 out of a million pieces.

One thousand rejects per million parts, or 0.1%, is no longer good enough in some industries today—and remember that 7% was okay up to the 1970s.

In 1987 Motorola set the goal of achieving a level of quality designated as Six Sigma by 1992. *Six Sigma* is a statistical term meaning that Motorola wanted no more than 3.4 failures per million parts—in all its activities. The company did actually achieve the goal in some areas. Its semiconductors are produced at a Six Sigma level, which means in effect that it is almost impossible to buy a defective one. And Motorola wants to keep on improving. The company has set a goal of improving tenfold every two years until the end of the century, which would bring failures down to one per billion parts. Intel has also achieved striking results. It shipped about 20 million microprocessors in 1992, the 386s and 486s that are at the heart of most personal computers. The number of failures could be counted on the fingers of one hand, according to Craig Barrett, the company's executive vice president.[11]

With such striking results, why hasn't Total Quality Management now become the *only* way to run a company? Well, most executives who try TQM do not get those kinds of results. They are more apt to be disappointed. Disenchantment with TQM has shown up in a number of surveys. In a Gallup survey of Fortune 1000 executives in 1989, only 26% felt that they had achieved significant results from quality improvements, although 28% were pleased with the results of their programs. A similar sample of executives polled by the Opinion Research Corporation for Arthur D. Little, Inc. late in 1991 found that although 93% of the companies contacted had quality programs, just 36% believed their quality efforts had had a significant effect—but 62% believed the effects would be significant in the future. A survey of quality practices in four countries conducted by Ernst & Young for the American Quality Foundation concluded that "companies have experienced mixed results." The authors of the survey said that "we sense a growing disenchantment in the business community" with the axiom that overall performance will follow automatically from quality improvements.[12]

Other, more recent surveys are more optimistic about TQM's results and its future. After studying survey questionnaires returned by 106 members of the Business Roundtable, the Delta Consulting Group concluded in 1993 that "TQM is clearly alive and well and having a positive impact on the performance of a number of companies." "Contrary to the reports in the press and the assertions of critics of TQM," Delta said, the heads of a significant number of corporations see TQM as a powerful, positive tool and are committed to implementing it in the future. Another survey, jointly performed by *IndustryWeek*, Development Dimensions International, and the Quality & Productivity Management Association, reported in 1993 that 56% of a sample of 536 North American companies practiced TQM, and of that portion only 24% had been doing it for more than three years. In other words, TQM, far from waning, "is still an emerging business strategy." Substantial numbers of companies reported high levels of success.[13]

A CRITICAL POINT

Certainly we can say that the euphoria has gone and been replaced by some degree of disenchantment. One reason may be that TQM does not guarantee immediate and everlasting success. American executives like solutions that can be installed and forgotten, like an electric switch. But TQM does not work that way, and it cannot carry a company all by itself. Some of the leading companies in America that were in the quality movement all through the 1980s were profoundly troubled in the early 1990s. General Motors, IBM, and Westinghouse all have divisions that won the Malcolm Baldrige National Quality Award and pushed corporate-wide efforts to improve their products, but GM had to fight for its life, IBM lost its way, and Westinghouse staggered away from the losses in its credit unit. Employees and investors in all three companies were hurt badly. The directors of all three corporations forced out their chairmen in 1992 (GM) and 1993 (IBM and Westinghouse). Marketing mistakes, bad luck, fluctuations in exchange rates or changes in government policies can overcome the positives of a quality effort. (Obviously the absence of TQM does not doom a company either, or there would have been no successful U.S. companies before the 1980s. Many companies have embraced the essentials of quality without formally adopting a quality process, or even knowing there was such a thing. L. L. Bean's devotion to the customer long preceded any theorizing about quality. Intel is one of a number of relatively young companies that excel in quality, and other areas, without adopting the usual quality formulas.)

However, the disenchantment has a cause deeper than the realization that TQM will not solve all our problems: it is that most of us have not yet practiced TQM very well. Companies that think or say they have adopted TQM have perhaps only captured a portion of it, or are going through the motions, counting the number of people trained and the number of teams created, instead of continually measuring the outcome of these activities. The enormous efforts expended to improve quality in the 1980s and early

1990s in the United States were largely wasted. Juran has warned for some time that the results of quality efforts in America were disappointing, and that upper management was making the "fatal error" of delegating responsibility for quality. Juran says ". . . the great majority of those initiatives in the 1980s failed. We lost close to a decade groping for a road which would lead us to world-class quality."[14]

B. Joseph White, dean of the Business School at the University of Michigan, is one of a number of quality experts (he used to head the human resources function at Cummins Engine) who believe the movement has reached a critical crossroads. The reasons: it has been oversold; it is not magic; alone it does not guarantee business success; the huge consulting industry that has grown up around it includes too many opportunists; Americans' short attention span will not tolerate the long effort it took Japan to learn to make things well. Japan started in 1950 and did not become really competent until the mid-1960s. White fears that collectively U.S. business may give up the total quality effort, although individual companies will stick with it.[15]

Some argue that the United States is incapable of producing the kind of quality that has become routine in Japan. The late Kaoru Ishikawa, one of Japan's most distinguished quality gurus, wrote that the United States was culturally incapable of matching Japan's success. He said that only people who had gone through the agony of learning *kanji*, the Chinese script used in Japanese writing, had the necessary discipline. A multiracial, multilingual country could not match a homogeneous nation like Japan. Finally, he argued, the Eastern philosophies were more in harmony with quality control because they believe in the goodness of mankind, whereas the Christian religions believe that man is inherently evil (and therefore Westerners cannot be counted on to work well unless strictly supervised).[16] Ishikawa's foolish bigotry marred an otherwise superb book on quality, simply written and full of good sense.

Cultural differences may dictate some different approaches in the United States. Quality circles failed in the United States whereas they succeeded in Japan. But our country is not doomed to poor quality, even if it has been disappointed so far. "During the 1980s a few exceptions—perhaps 50 companies—did attain world-class quality," says Juran. "The fact that they did so proves that *world-class quality is attainable within the American culture.*"[17] Go to a place like the Saturn complex in Tennessee. Saturn makes a car that is very nearly as good as competing Japanese cars—so close that most owners would never know the difference. The car is produced in plants where labor is fully the partner of management, and sometimes even seems like a senior partner when it goads management to better efforts. The car is sold in dealerships which exceed even the Japanese in consideration for the customer. The owner is protected by a concept of warranty so generous that Detroit would have considered it madness a few years ago. Who else but a Saturn dealer would have his customers come to a barbecue party while he replaced a defective seat latch in their cars?

Saturn is one case that proves world-class quality is attainable in the United States. Hewlett-Packard, Intel, Milliken, Motorola, and several dozen other companies are proof that it is not only attainable, but profitable. They stand out, but they may be typical of companies that deliver high quality. The PIMS program (for Profit Impact of Market Strategy), a study over many years of what governed the performance of 450 companies, assigns the key role to quality. "In the long run, the most important single factor affecting a business unit's performance is the quality of its products and services, relative to those of competitors."[18] The analysis found that in the short term companies ranking in the top third in relative quality could sell their goods or services at prices 5% to 6% higher than those in the bottom third. In the long run, high quality proved to be the best way to grow and gain market share. *Business Week* calculated that had you invested in each of the Baldrige Award winners (or their parent companies) at the time the awards were announced you would have shown cumulative capital gains of 89.2% by the end of 1993, in spite of the dismal performance of GM, IBM, and Westinghouse. Identical investments made in the Standard & Poor 500-stock index would have yielded only 33.1%.[19]

The results of good quality can be extraordinary, and not simply because it captures market share and lifts profits. Total quality can transform a company: the relationship between manager and employer becomes open and democratic, the supplier becomes an intimate partner, the customer a satisfied long-term cheerleader. Work becomes worthwhile. Good quality lies at the heart of American competitiveness. Customers' expectations, already raised by some remarkable improvements, will demand better and better. The quality wars will continue on several fronts—against Japan and some others, especially Germany; against the resistance within our companies to the wrenching changes that TQM demands; and against the weariness that saps enthusiasm for the long-lasting battle for total quality. Those who lead the fight, the CEOs, the quality directors, and others, have no doubt they are at war. It is their difficult duty to persuade everyone else in their organization that they are doing things the wrong way and must change fundamentally how they work. That often makes them unpopular, the focus of an organization's hostility. But they are convinced their cause is right.

Free enterprise makes sense. It works. But it does not win hearts. It has no rousing philosophy. Even the most dedicated corporate raider can hardly be moved by a call to "maximize shareowner wealth." Quality does provide a battle cry. It gives meaning to work. It gives a company a mission. It gives you and me a reason to go to work with a will. These words are carved in a block of stone in front of the headquarters of the Newport News Shipyard, put there in 1917:

> We shall build good ships here,
> At a profit, if we can,
> At a loss, if we must,
> But always good ships.*

---

* These often-quoted words are written on a monument to honor Collis Huntington, who founded the shipyard in 1886, and presumably they reflected his views. However, there is a story that the words were adapted from a contemporary ad for a bourbon distillery. The words were reproduced in the manual printed by the U.S. occupation forces in Japan in 1947 to launch the Japanese on the road to good quality. Now the Japanese build good ships and Newport News, like all other U.S. shipyards, is out of the business of making commercial ships, but it does still make aircraft carriers and submarines for the U.S. Navy, good ships all.[20]

Part One

1

The Beginning
An Emotional Experience

In the beginning came disbelief. Then denial. Then terror. American executives who visited Japan came home in shock, trying to grasp the implications of what they had seen, and unable at first to get the people at home to believe their stories. Great American corporations that bestrode the world—Chrysler, Ford, Xerox, among others—began to think the unthinkable, that they could be driven out of business. They did not say it out loud then, but they knew it in their hearts. By the late 1970s, Japan had pulled so far ahead of them in quality, in productivity growth, in developing new products, and in understanding the market, that some American businesses were no longer competitive even in their home market. In Japan the quality movement was born out of the destruction of its economy in World War II and the island nation's absolute need to live by exporting, which forced Japan to discover new ways of working. American business, so sure of itself, so set in its ways, so successful for so long, could never have embraced total quality management without also experiencing a profound emotional experience.

Of course, America did not wake up solely because of the alarm set off by Japan. Many saw total quality as a weapon to overcome other competition, other problems. The railroads saw it as a way of beating trucks. Banks and other financial institutions which did not compete with Japan saw it as a way of winning and keeping customers. Hewlett-Packard was convinced by the discovery that it, like most U.S. companies, wasted 20% to 30% of its output because of poor quality. In the first edition of his *Quality-Control Handbook* in 1951, Joseph Juran called avoidable costs of quality "gold in the mine." He cited the costs of scrappage, repairs, extra inspection, the additional space and labor needed to compensate for defects, the discounts for seconds, the customer complaints, the warranty costs, and the intangible costs of lost business and good will, and the friction within a company caused by poor quality.[1] Philip Crosby, for 14

19

years a vice president and director of quality at ITT, made much of the cost of defects in *Quality Is Free*, a well-timed book that became a best seller in 1979. Roger Milliken, chairman of Milliken & Co., took a copy of *Quality Is Free* to his ski chalet in Vail for the Christmas holiday in 1980 and returned to work convinced.[2]

Motorola, recalls its retired chairman Robert W. Galvin, woke up to a clarion call from one of its most respected executives, Arthur Sundry, at a meeting of company officers in April, 1979. Sundry announced he had something more important to say than anything on the agenda—which was, as he put it baldly, that Motorola's quality "stinks." "You can be motivated by all manner of approaches," says Galvin.[3] But the threat from Japan lay under all the other motivations.

IN THE BEGINNING WAS INSPECTION

To put these stirrings into some perspective, we have to go back to the fledgling American Telephone & Telegraph Company in the late 1800s. AT&T realized that the huge and complex network of lines, telephones, and switchboards it was building would need to rely on systematic quality control rather than sheer craftsmanship. Therefore it created an elaborate, expensive inspection system under the inspection department of the Western Electric Company, AT&T's manufacturing arm, to make sure that the parts it received from suppliers were good, and that the equipment it sent out to the field was good. Quality control expanded to cover design and installation in addition to manufacturing as the telephone equipment grew more sophisticated.

Work to advance quality theory continued in the inspection department, soon to become part of the newly created Bell Telephone Laboratories. In 1924 a physicist in the department, Walter A. Shewhart, passed his boss a one-page memo that opened an entirely new phase of quality control. The memo suggested how a statistical control chart could track the variations in a manufacturing process and provide the basis for reducing those variations.[4] Quality could be achieved not by inspection but by monitoring and improving the process. Not only did this approach reduce the need for quantities of inspectors, but it assured better quality at a lower cost by eliminating defects at the source rather than after they had been made.

It took a long time for the new concept to win acceptance. World War II helped because so many inexperienced industries and workers were assigned defense tasks that the Army and Navy procurement agencies put quality-control clauses in their contracts and encouraged a burst of quality training and research. The spectacular performance of American equipment in World War II owes some debt to statistical quality control.*

The next beneficiaries of what the United States had learned were the defeated Japanese. To control the country effectively, the U.S. occupation forces needed good communications with the populace. The Civil Communications Section of allied headquarters brought in three American engineers, including Frank Polkinghorn of Bell Labs, to help the Japanese repair and improve their shattered communication systems. The three found corporations like the Nippon Electric Company (NEC) deplorably lacking in engineering and management fundamentals, not to mention buildings and equipment. They found potential, however, in a small company called Tokyo Communications, despite the fact that its executives sat at their desks with open umbrellas when the rain came through the roofs of the sheds where they worked. Tokyo Communications changed its name later to Sony. To help the Japanese improve, the Americans produced a modest textbook, *CCS: Industrial Management*, and started giving courses in statistical process controls.[6]

Ranging across the world's markets with little competition, and freed of the military demand for quality control, American industry pretty well forgot about the principles that had been developed here. However, a few Americans continued, in some obscurity, to elaborate and explain their ideas. In 1950, Armand V. Feigenbaum, General Electric's chief of quality, published *Total Quality Control*, which argued that quality was the responsibility of everybody, not just the quality department. The next year, Joseph Juran, who

---

* Anyone familiar with the lumbering procurement process in today's Pentagon might have difficulty imagining this, but in World War II Grumman test-flew the F6F Hellcat for the first time in June 1942, began delivering the plane the next January, and the Navy sent it into combat in August 1943. A simple, robust plane, the Hellcat wiped out the threat of Mitsubishi's Zero. Not only did Grumman take the Hellcat from test flight to combat in 14 months, it also built the factory to build the plane in that time, partly from scrap steel scrounged from the remains of the Second Avenue "El" in New York City. The plane was built largely by women who had never worked in a factory before. The Grumman plant at Bethpage, Long Island, was decades ahead of its time. A "green car service" was available to solve almost any small problem that might keep a worker from the job, like fixing a flat tire or turning the oven off at home. The plant had a day-care center for the children of working mothers. Grumman even practiced a rudimentary form of just-in-time manufacturing long before Toyota invented it. A visitor to the Bethpage plant asked his guide how they maintained an adequate supply of the hose clamps he saw in a barrel beside the assembly line. The guide dug out some of the clamps and showed the visitor a line painted part way down the inside of the barrel with these instructions: "See Joe."[5]

had worked for years before the war at Western Electric, edited and published the *Quality Control Handbook*, an authoritative reference work. Both books have been revised and updated repeatedly. The late W. Edwards Deming, who also worked at Western Electric during his summer vacations in the 1920s, had already been to Japan twice to advise the occupation authorities on statistical sampling. He was invited back at the end of 1950 by the Japanese Union of Scientists and Engineers to lecture business leaders on statistical process control. Juran followed in 1954 with a series of seminars that introduced the idea of "total" quality control as a management tool. From these books and lectures a view of quality much broader than statistical controls began to emerge: that it was the responsibility of everyone, especially top management, that it should encompass not only a company's products and services but all of its activities, and that improvement should be continuous.

Deming, Juran, Feigenbaum and others wrote and consulted in the United States, in some obscurity, but the message was beginning to get through. Crosby's 1979 book *Quality Is Free* reached a wide audience.

An easily understood and convincing call to arms, Crosby's book unfortunately left the impression that quality is easy as well as free. It is not. But for those just beginning the journey it was perhaps just as well not to know how hard it was going to be. Many saw the 1980 NBC documentary, "If Japan Can . . . Why Can't We?" which explained (very roughly) how Deming, then unknown in America but famous in Japan since the 1950s, could reduce failures through statistical controls. The more cerebral might have gotten the message from the so-called PIMS studies, which gave convincing evidence that quality was the key to growth and greater market share.

But for nearly three decades Japan had had the almost exclusive use of the new theories of quality and in practice had refined them to a level that astounded the West. One industry after another—autos, cameras, electronics, shipbuilding, office equipment, steel, construction—delivered world-beating products.

The oil crises of the 1970s maintained the sense of urgency created in Japan by the need to rebuild after World War II. Today, with no crisis and with a surfeit of praise from foreigners, Japan may be losing its passion for quality. The crisis of quality in Japan is that there is no crisis, laments Noriaki Kano, a professor at the Science University of Tokyo and a consultant to Japanese and American firms.[7] He even suggests slyly that Americans are trying to lull Japan with praise and deference. However, the downturn the Japanese economy experienced at the beginning of the 1990s may provide a new impetus, if not a crisis.

THE UNBELIEVABLE DATA

Thomas J. Murrin remembers how the tenor of his visits to Japan changed on many trips made he for Westinghouse over the decades. Murrin, who played tackle for Vince Lombardi at Fordham University, spent some frustrating years pushing for quality at Westinghouse and then more of the same in the government as deputy secretary of Commerce. Now, as dean of the business school at Duquesne, he has taken on the task of bringing quality to academe. Talking of his dealings with Japan when he was at Westinghouse, he says,

> "I started going there about 30 years ago on technical exchange agreements. They'd almost bow to the floor. You'd say hello and they'd write it down. Well, when I go now, shit, they just nod at you and immediately start lecturing you. 'What are you dumb lazy people doing?' It's been an incredible transformation. One of the things I was doing in the 1970s was studying their financial reports and we couldn't believe the data because it seemed to say that their big companies, which were similar to ours, had an annual real productivity gain of 8% or 10%. It was unbelievable. It was embarrassing. First of all, you know, we kind of looked at each other and we said, 'Well, so what?' 'What do you mean, so what?' 'Well, we must be doing the same thing.' We didn't know what the hell we were doing. We never ran those numbers. So we got our comptroller guys and they ran the numbers and they said, 'Hell, you know, you've got a couple of small units that do maybe 6% or 7% but your average is like 1% or 2% or 3%. And the country was like 0%. So we said there has to be something wrong with the Japanese numbers. . . .' "

Like others confronted with what the Japanese were achieving, Westinghouse managers tried to deny the facts at first. But the evidence held up. An entirely different persuader helped motivate the senior managers. After hours, over drinks, the Westinghouse brass used to brood over the difference between them and the GE brass. It seemed to them that many of the GE brass retired rich with stock options, but that didn't happen to them. Westinghouse had to change. Murrin represented a small group of convinced executives who went to the chairman, Robert Kirby, an unnerving experience.

> "He was so goddamned smart, he didn't have to grind these things out. He'd have the radio playing and he'd be making the most intricate

geometric pattern and you might have worked for six months on this Goddamned thing and you'd say, 'Bob, this is really important.' 'Huh,' he'd say. 'Go on, go on.' The son of a bitch would understand everything you said and he'd ask a few of the most penetrating questions and if you gave him the right answer, he'd say go ahead.''

If he wasn't carried away by Murrin's concepts, Kirby did at least approve. The annual management council meeting at the Tamarron in Durango, Colorado in 1979 recognized the importance of raising productivity and gave Murrin $2 million to start. As Murrin tells it,

> ''We doled out several hundred thousand here, several hundred thousand there, to any part of Westinghouse. No formality, no calculation, but we quizzed them. The fellow said, 'I'm the one who's going to spend this and this is what I'm going to do.' And we kind of said, 'Buddy, if you squander this we're going to shoot your nuts off.' I mean this is the way we talk in Pittsburgh.''

Murrin grew up on New York's East Side and he remembers his father, a structural steelworker, telling him what a ''dumb ass'' his foreman was. So Murrin liked the idea of quality circles, of using the brains as well as the brawn of workers. The construction group, one of the units under Murrin's supervision, started to work with quality circles in 1980. Westinghouse established a productivity center to lend a hand to anyone in the company who wanted to improve productivity. The quality circles failed (see Chapter 3) and it turned out that what Westinghouse needed was not so much higher productivity as better quality, so the center's name and aim were changed. It became the Westinghouse Center for Quality and Productivity. That is how Westinghouse stumbled into the era of quality. The company is still stumbling and its executives still have good reason to be envious of GE, but it did well enough so that its Commercial Nuclear Fuel Division won a Baldrige prize in 1988, the first year of the award.[8]

"YOU CAN'T BE THAT BAD": XEROX AND HP WAKE UP

Xerox, like Westinghouse, woke up with a start to what it also perceived as a productivity crisis. The decade of the 1970s opened with Xerox owning 90% of the U.S. market for photocopiers, which it had invented. By 1976, Xerox's share was down to 85%, and it kept dropping, bottoming out at 13% in 1982.[9] In 1979, as Xerox began to see its mortal danger, Peter McColough, the chairman, called Frank Pipp home from Rank Xerox in Europe to be chief of manufacturing. Unlike many modern manufacturing executives, Pipp knew the inside of a factory. He had been a foreman in a GM plant and had worked in Ford and Xerox plants. He also spoke his mind. He came home about when Xerox introduced the 3300 small copier, an unreliable machine that stank, scorched documents, and jammed the paper. It was another in a long line of terrible copiers made by Xerox. The faults of one would be repeated in the next model, for Xerox relied on a huge field force to fix the machines rather than fixing the causes of the problems before the copiers left the factory. Juran recalls being invited to talk to the company's senior managers at the time that "sales began to hemorrhage." He found that Xerox had plenty of information about why its copiers were failing but was not acting on it. When he asked for a list of the ten most common causes of failure of one popular model, in order of importance, Xerox provided it promptly. Then he asked for the same list for an earlier model. He put the two lists side by side and they were identical. In other words, Xerox had learned nothing from its failures. Product managers required their design engineers to focus on new product features and gave no priority to fixing old features known to be failure-prone, although they "posed a threat to the very survival of the company."[10]

Pipp discovered from Yotaro (Tony) Kobayashi, head of the Fuji-Xerox joint venture in Japan, that it already had experienced its productivity and quality crisis. In response to the enormous price increases in Japan caused by the Mideast oil embargo in 1973, relates Kobayashi, "we first tried raising prices and that didn't work because we were clobbered in the market, especially by Ricoh, which had practiced Total Quality Control. We decided to do something very fundamental and thanks to TQC in two years we had better quality than Ricoh." Fuji-Xerox produced a high-speed copier that was only one third the size of Ricoh's, which until then was the fastest in the world.[11]

Pipp talked to Kobayashi at a long-range planning meeting in the summer of 1979 and found that through Kobayashi he could get to the bottom of the Japanese success. Xerox people were speculating about how the Japanese were able to sell a copier in the United States for less than it cost Xerox to make one. The answer had to be dumping, they figured. Pipp put together a team of line managers and took them to Japan. What they found was so "shocking and nauseating," says Pipp, that he had to send over a second team of staff engineers before anyone at Xerox headquarters in Stamford, Connecticut, would believe their findings. It turned out that Ricoh and other Japanese firms could design and ship a copier in half the time and at half the cost required by Xerox. The Japanese were selling at a profit in the United States at a price below Xerox's manufacturing costs. "You can't be that bad," McColough said to Pipp. "I am," said Pipp.[12]

That was the starting point for the extraordinary transformation of Xerox, which led it step by step into one the most successful quality efforts mounted by any U.S. company (see Chapter 7). It was not until nearly a decade later that Xerox fully understood what it had to do, but as early as 1982 it began to recover market share.

Hewlett-Packard's rude awakening, which reverbated through the electronics industry, also came in the late 1970s. HP used 4K and 16K random access memory chips in its computers and until 1977 had bought them solely from American suppliers. In that year the U.S. vendors ran short of capacity, and so HP turned cautiously to a Japanese supplier. HP engineers still thought of Japan as a producer of junk, so they put the Japanese chips through rigorous tests. To their surprise, the Japanese chips passed very well. When another crunch came in 1979, HP bought more chips from Japan, this time from three suppliers. They were tested again. Richard W. Anderson, manager of HP's Data Systems Division, shook up the U.S. chip industry by going public with the findings. Comparing three Japanese and three American vendors, none identified, Anderson reported that not a single Japanese chip failed inspection on arrival, while 50 to 100 U.S.-made chips out of every 50,000 failed. In the field, the worst American chip was 27 times as likely to fail as the best Japanese chips. Anderson stated that the Japanese suppliers had lower scrap costs, lower rework costs, fewer production interruptions, lower warranty costs, and, most important, happier customers.[13]

Like Xerox, HP had an outrider in Japan, Yokogawa-Hewlett-Packard, a joint venture established in 1963. In the 1960s, "we were learning everything from the U.S. and we were very successful," recalls Katsumi Yoshimoto, quality manager for HP Asia Pacific. But in the 1970s, as HP's product lines changed, YHP began to have real quality problems and "we were really concerned whether YHP would survive." In 1977, the YHP management went to a quality seminar at the Japanese Union of Scientists and Engineers, which had worked with the U.S. occupation forces three decades earlier to start the quality movement in Japan and which had become the focus of that movement. YHP accepted JUSE's total quality control as the way to improve and sent its executives and most of its managers for training there. YHP led the way for its U.S. parent and in 1982 won the Deming prize for quality, administered by JUSE.[14]

HP headquarters in Palo Alto swallowed Anderson's findings and YHP's lessons more readily than Xerox did Pipp's findings. "HP had always been a high quality company," says John A. Young, the president and CEO then and for the next decade. As a high-tech company with a culture that encouraged diversity and innovation, HP was more open to change than others. Still, the mandatory trips to Japan to see YHP and Japanese companies were eye-openers. "They were doing things better than we were," says Young. "Boy, what a shock! The good news was that they weren't doing anything we couldn't do. There was no magic."

Young could also see new requirements coming. "I was persuaded that the expectations of our customers were going to be very much different in the future than in the past and that unless we changed our methods of doing things, we weren't going to be able to meet our customers' expectations," he recalls. HP's product lines were changing. The company was selling fewer small-volume, stand-alone instruments used in labs, and more high-volume items such as computer terminals that had to mesh with whole systems. The new markets required higher productivity and better quality, Young believed. "I was persuaded even then there was nothing cheaper than doing it right the first time and that was certainly not common wisdom." The studies of two HP divisions showing that the cost of poor quality amounted to 25% of their sales made it still more evident that the company had to change. So in 1980 when Young drew up a list of things that he thought were going to be important for the decade ahead, he put quality in the list. HP set a goal of improving quality tenfold in ten years.[15]

THE UAW HELPS SAVE WINDSHIELDS

Watching General Motors's elephantine and unsuccessful struggles to get it right all through the 1980s and into the 1990s, it seems hard to imagine that GM had begun to move in that direction 20 years ago. However, the initiator was not the corporation but the union, the United Auto Workers. And total quality was not the original objective. Not even product quality. The scholarly Irving Bluestone, former UAW vice president in charge of the GM division, persuaded the UAW convention of 1968 to adopt a resolution supporting what was called Quality of Work Life, or QWL. "I didn't know about quality then," says Bluestone. "My objective was that workers be treated with dignity and given credit for intelligence." The idea was to set up teams of workers who would discuss ways of improving work conditions. The UAW put a quality of work life proposal on the table in its negotiations with GM in 1970 and got an agreement in 1971. It turned out that quality was one of the things that most concerned workers.

GM's Tarrytown, New York plant was to have been shut down in 1973 because of its wretched performance. Quality was low and the backlog of grievance cases high. But the union and management decided to see what the team concept could accomplish. They started with one of the worst sections of the plant, where windshields and backup lights were installed. Quality was so poor that this section scrapped 60% of what it made. Teams formed, studied problem-solving techniques and cut the scrap rate to 2%. Absenteeism and grievances dropped and the team concept spread through the plant.[16] (GM decided in 1992 to put an end to Tarrytown's long and troubled story, announcing that it would close the plant in 1995.)

Ford discovered employee involvement in the 1970s when it sent managers accompanied by UAW officials to Japan. They returned convinced that the success of Japanese companies was based on waves of employee ideas, "accumulated drop by drop." In 1978, at a conference of 60 plant managers, Ford called for volunteers to try employee involvement. Just four volunteered their plants, with lukewarm support from the UAW locals. Within months, the plants began to show improvement; employee involvement won the support of Philip Caldwell, Ford's CEO, who endorsed employee involvement in one of the company's rare policy memos.[17]

The quality of Ford's cars had become a serious issue. Hertz, the biggest user of Ford cars, reported that Japanese cars were performing much better than Ford cars. Prior to a management meeting in 1978 Caldwell jotted down a note, "quality—number one," at the top of a list of priorities.[18] He told the meeting that from then on quality would be Ford's top priority. From that meeting came Ford's well-known slogan, "Quality is Job 1." To an automaker, if not to the auto owner, the slogan had strong symbolism because "Job 1" in auto talk is the first car of a new model that comes off the line. For reasons lost in history, meeting the date set for Job 1 had become sacred to Detroit.[19] What the choice of priority said to the worker was, "Don't worry what the car is like, just get it out on time." For a while, Ford's quality effort consisted of little more than the slogan, which was derided inside and outside the company. Its quality was the worst among the Big Three in terms of "things gone wrong" per car, and its market share was collapsing.[20] Ford was still asleep. Why worry? Ford made a profit of $1.2 billion in 1979 and had cash reserves of $2.2 billion.

"HOW SCARED WE WERE"—THE BIG THREE

The second oil crisis struck the auto industry in 1979. Chrysler lost $1.1 billion that year and its reserves fell so low that no bank would lend it money. Japanese cars, so much more fun to drive and better made than small

American cars, began to move on the market—without the premiums that dealers had had to offer before. The imports' share of the market shot up from 21.2% in 1979 to 26.1% in 1980. After making big profits in 1979, Ford began to hemorrhage money: $1.5 billion in 1980, $1 billion in 1981, and $700 million in 1982. Now the auto industry, or at least Ford and Chrysler, had the emotional experience that had been lacking before as motivation.

GM, with 46.3% of the North American car market, earned $2.9 billion in 1979 and had a colossal cash reserve of $3 billion. GM did lose $800 million in 1980, but was profitable once more in 1981 and 1982. In a sense, it was GM's loss that it did not lose more money then. It might have woken up sooner.

Chrysler and Ford were terrified. Chrysler was on the verge of bankruptcy. A Ford executive vice president remembered: "You can never underestimate how scared we were in 1980–81. We really believed Ford could die. From top executives through middle management down to the hourly employees, a lot of people got religion. It enabled us to deal with the turf, the egos, and the 'not invented here' attitudes that were killing us."[21] One particularly disturbing piece of news came from a Department of Transportation report based on studies by James E. Harbour, president of Harbour & Associates, Inc., a consulting firm in Troy, Michigan. Harbour estimated that the Japanese could build a subcompact for $1,500 less than the Americans in 1981. In 1982, he raised the difference to $1,750.[22]

Like others, the automakers reacted at first with disbelief and attempts to protect themselves. They pooh-poohed the Harbour report. They sought and obtained a quota limiting Japanese imports—which only allowed both U.S. and Japanese automakers to raise prices, giving the Americans a breathing spell and the Japanese fat profits that allowed them to finance their transplant factories in the United States. The U.S. consumer paid more for his car. Lee Iacocca, who ironically became a symbol of the entrepreneurial spirit, got a government loan guarantee to save Chrysler's neck.

However, Detroit was also catching on to the idea that quality could save it. Chrysler and GM were slow to get it. Chrysler was too busy saving itself and arrogant, insulated GM had too much money for its own good; it thought it could buy its way out of its difficulties by spending to automate. Ford, in the middle, was the first to find the right answer. The earlier employee involvement efforts at Ford blossomed into an extraordinary relationship between Ford's director of labor relations, Pete Pestillo, and Don Ephlin, the UAW official in charge of employee relations. Neither was exactly an organization man. Pestillo had come in from B. F. Goodrich and believed in employee participation. Ephlin, who had been the UAW regional director for New England during the Tarrytown experiment, had the same faith, although it was not shared by most of the UAW's leadership. Together they took a group of Ford managers and union members on a tour of Japan. Ephlin remembers: "We saw they weren't working their people to death. People had talked about all the robots in Japan. But it was not that really. Their automation wasn't much greater than ours. The trip dispelled the myths about Japan. There was no magic. They were just doing the job and doing it very well. We were impressed by the cleanliness of the plants, by the way the work was organized. We realized we were competing with them on the same basis, but their quality was much better. Some of that, maybe 30%, was in assembly, but most of the quality was in design."[23]

Ford in 1980 stood on the edge of a social revolution. Although many workers remained skeptical of the sincerity of management's quality pledge and would remain skeptical for some years more, employee involvement, in the words of one participant, produced "a tremendous upwelling of initiative from the ranks. Somehow we channeled it constructively." Ford management was examining itself too. North American Automotive Operations established a Blue Ribbon Committee to look at ways of breaking down the notorious "chimneys" at Ford which turned the functional divisions of the company into warring fiefdoms. Ford began to force its suppliers into the quality movement by telling its own subsidiary, Diversified Products Operations, which made a whole range of parts, to meet Japanese standards or be shut down.[24]

Ford was now ready for W. Edwards Deming, the avenging angel of the quality movement. The new president of Ford, Donald E. Peterson, invited Deming to Detroit at the beginning of 1981 and Detroit was never quite the same again. Deming had been so important in helping Japan launch its quality efforts more than three decades earlier that Japan named its premier quality prize after him. But Ford was the first really big U.S. company to seek his help. By now aged 80, Deming had built up quite a head of steam during the intervening years. Although he was gentle with blue-collar workers and students, he was the scourge of the managers at Ford and the other companies he advised. He told them in his deep, rumbling voice that they were of negative value, a drag on the American economy.

A group of Ford vice presidents and general managers met him at Ford's world headquarters, expecting to be handed a silver bullet that would solve their quality problems, but the first thing Deming did was ask, "Do you have constancy of purpose?" "What the hell does he mean?" they thought. "We've been in the auto business since 1903."[25] Sometimes, after an all-day session with his Socratic approach and his blunt opinions, he left the automakers climbing the walls. But he made them think profoundly about their jobs and their business. He told them that they had to build in quality, not inspect it in. He said they had to remove the barriers between the people in the different parts of the company and at different levels, and to drive out fear so that they could deal with each other frankly. He told them to develop long-term relationships with a few good suppliers, rather than switching suppliers whenever they could cut the cost a bit. He told them to institute training. And he talked to them about the statistical discipline that had opened his eyes to quality improvement, statistical process control.

With all these elements in place—committed leadership, involved employees, the teachings of Deming, and the fear of imminent ruin—Ford began a remarkable recovery. By 1985, Ford's quality was the best of the Big Three and its market share was growing. In each of the next three years, Ford's profits were greater than GM's, by a total of nearly $2 billion. Ford was on its way. For a time, Chrysler's crisis was masked by the enormous success of its minivans, and GM's crisis did not come until much later, when the futility of its vast spending on new plants and equipments was exposed at the end of the 1980s. But gradually both of them got on the road taken by Ford.

MOTOROLA'S LUCKY BREAK

Even when there was no direct threat from Japan, American companies heard a strong message from across the Pacific. Motorola may have been awakened by Art Sundry's cry that Motorola's quality "stinks." "That was a lucky break for us, that we had someone who had the guts to do that and caused all the rest of us who were sitting there to say, 'if Art says that, maybe there's something to it,' " Bob Galvin states. "There was no denial or rejection of Art Sundry's message [and] the following Monday morning, everybody came to work and had some, at least subliminal intent, 'I will do it a little better today.' "[26] Motorolans may have been preconditioned to Sundry's words by what what had happened to their old Quasar plant in Franklin Park, Illinois. Before Matsushita bought the plant from Motorola in 1974, the TV sets coming off the line had 140 problems per 100 sets. By the end of the decade Matsushita, with the same work force and management, had reduced the problems to 7 per 100 sets.[27] (In justice to Motorola, we should note that it already had decided to quit the television business and was not giving the Quasar plant the resources it needed.)

Although Roger Milliken's textile company was not directly threatened by Japan, he had sent three plant managers to Japan in 1979, figuring that they would find some secret to the equipment the Japanese were using that made them more productive. The team reported back that the Japanese were using equipment two to three generations older than Milliken's, but their "off-quality" output was one-tenth of Milliken's and their productivity three and a half times higher. The company sent a second larger team to Japan to check out the first team's findings and it came back saying the first group had underestimated the achievements of the Japanese.[28] So when Roger Milliken read Crosby's *Quality Is Free* in Vail during that Christmas vacation in 1980 he knew his company could do better. It was easier to accept Crosby's claim "that it was possible to bring a lot of otherwise wasted money to the bottom line if people in a business did everything right the first time."[29] On his return to headquarters at Spartanburg, South Carolina, Milliken ordered 300 copies of the book and distributed them to his executives.

WITHOUT PRODDING: DURACELL AND FPL SEE THE LIGHT

In the 1980s, once American managers began to see that it was not an immutable law of nature that a certain proportion of what they did had to be done wrong, that things could be made better without great expenditure and with improved productivity, the reasons for joining the quality movement multiplied. It just made good sense. Even those not directly threatened by Japanese competition began to see in total quality a way out of their difficulties. After a decline of nearly 50 years when they lost nearly half their business to trucks, America's seven major freight railroads finally roused themselves in the 1980s and found a new life in total quality. By 1993, only 31% of the companies surveyed by the Delta Consulting Group said they had felt a great or very great urgency about implementing TQM, and an equal 31% said they started although they felt little or no urgency.[30]

With a hold on nearly half of the U.S. and European markets for alkaline batteries, strong sales in other parts of the world, and batteries better than most, Duracell would not seem to have any compelling reason for turning to total quality. Indeed, Duracell's reputation for quality was a disadvantage when C. Robert Kidder, the CEO, began bringing in outside consultants to help. People in the company did not see the need for help. But when Kidder instituted quality audits around the world in the mid-1980s, the company found that its products and processes did not compare so well with others', and that there was indeed plenty of room for improvement. Every consumer wanted longer-lasting batteries. What could be done about that? Why did

Duracell have to tie up capital and space to let every battery age for 21 days to see if it leaked before it was shipped? Was it necessary to continue to use a dangerous toxin like mercury in the batteries? Why were the company's capital forecasts written in an almost incomprehensible English?[31] Obviously, Duracell had reason for adopting total quality, without any prodding from the outside. (Duracell has lengthened the life of its batteries by 50% in a decade, reduced battery aging time to zero and taken all the mercury out of its batteries. But writing the forecasts in English, that is a *really* tough problem.)

The regulated utilities would seem to be immune to the sort of threat that faced the auto and electronics industries. However, in 1981 Florida Power & Light Company linked its survival to its quality, which was not good at the time. FPL was hurting from the high cost of oil after two oil shocks, rising bond interest rates, customer complaints, and government regulation, and electricity rates were going up faster than the cost of living.[32]

Marshall McDonald, FPL's chairman at the time, explained,

"... we had been looking at the horse from the wrong end—and it was not a pretty sight. We had been concerned with keeping rejects down, instead of quality up. We had been busy keeping imperfection under control, rather than trying for perfection. We had sometimes burnt the toast and then scraped it clean, instead of fixing the toaster. Some of us even learned to like burned toast."[33]

Although FPL had no competition from Japan, it looked to Japan for help. FPL was predisposed to Japanese quality methods because the people who built and operated one of its units, St. Lucie 2, a nuclear power station, saved time and money by using quality improvement teams to figure out how to do the job better. Whereas the notorious Shoreham plant on Long Island, New York cost $11 billion and never was licensed to operate, St. Lucie 2 cost $1.4 billion, as originally estimated, and was built and licensed 30% faster than the average U.S. plant.[34] At first, when they visited Kansai Electric and other companies in Japan, the FPL people did not quite understand what they were looking at, but they certainly understood the results. In 1986 FPL compared the number of its "scrams"—temporary shutdowns of nuclear stations, usually caused by faulty instrument readings rather than by any real emergency—with Kansai's. FPL averaged seven shutdowns a year at each of its four nuclear stations. When John Hudiburg, who had succeeed McDonald as chairman, was told that Kansai had had *no* scrams in a year among nine nukes, he assumed at first that the interpreter had made a mistake. It was no mistake.[35] Finally, when FPL decide to compete for a quality award, it put itself in the hands of consultants from the Japanese Union of Scientists and Engineers and applied for Japan's Deming Prize, which it won in 1989.

Quality efforts rippled through American industry, from client to manufacturer to supplier. The pressure from big companies on their vendors forced thousands of companies to take up TQM. Ford had its Q-1 award and GM its Mark of Excellence to recognize the best suppliers. Hewlett-Packard, IBM, Motorola, Xerox, and other big companies rode hard on their suppliers. They in turn also heard from their own customers. For example, as U.S. banks installed more automated teller machines, they told IBM that its computers had to be more reliable since the public was now directly affected when the machines went down.

Analog Devices, a successful Massachusetts maker of the electronic links between analog and digital equipment, found itself facing new demands. Ray Stata, the founder and head of the company, says,

> "The first blush of TQM at Analog Devices goes back to the 1983–84 period, the beginning of the serious quality movement in the electronics industry, which was triggered by HP and IBM when they began to put pressure on their vendors. Everybody ran out to acquire TQM literacy. I would have to say that from 1983 through 1986 the flute music of TQM which I was preaching did very little to change the substance of the way we were managing."

Then came a second impetus in the late 1980s as the market for integrated circuits flattened out and the customers' quality demands got tougher. Analog Devices found itself with a dwindling military clientele and a need to expand into new markets. Stata had been accustomed to record growth and profits. The motivation for improving had been just that "we can do better than we've done." Now the motivation became, "If we don't do better than we've been doing, we're not going to survive." Quality became more than flute music.[36]

PRIORITY AT AT&T: "DO WE KNOW HOW TO RUN A BUSINESS?"

What was happening all the while at AT&T, the birthplace of modern quality? The answer should be sobering to quality fanatics who forget that quality alone does not guarantee success. While the seed planted by Bell

Labs in the 1920s had by now grown into a sizable tree with branches pointing in many directions, AT&T itself was not among the first TQM companies. It had developed an elaborate and well-practiced quality control system. Ample capital and the best in technology allowed AT&T to track the performance of each of its 20 divisions (before the 1984 breakup) on the basis of 130 criteria. AT&T knew exactly where and when customers were having trouble getting a dial tone in more than the permissible three seconds, or how well installers were keeping appointments, or the quality of voice transmissions. In the 1970s, AT&T began surveying its customers regularly to see how the service looked from the outside. But then, as the TQM movement gathered strength in the 1980s, AT&T was distracted by another matter. On January 1, 1984, by order of the courts, Ma Bell split off its seven operating companies, retaining only its long-distance service, manufacturing, and the famous Bell Labs.

AT&T was not driven by a quality crisis. "In fact," says Phillip M. Scanlan, head of AT&T's corporate quality office, "in 1985 we were much more focused at the top on, Do we know how to do marketing? Do we know how to do financial planning? Do we know how to do business management? Do we know how to create a company that is organized and runs properly? We had a lot of real serious fundamental issues to deal with. If you don't have the basics, quality can't get you anywhere."

Those issues gave AT&T a perspective on the importance of quality that other companies missed. After some false steps at the start, AT&T did become a successful, well-planned, market-oriented business. (It is interesting, if idle, to wonder now what the outcome might have been if history were reversed and the government had won its antitrust case against IBM and failed in its attempt to break up AT&T. Would IBM, or its parts, now be the agile, competitive force and AT&T the blundering giant?)

But AT&T was not practicing total quality management in the modern sense. In 1983 Bell labs had initiated a study of quality in software, in the reliability of design and products in the field, and in the quality of components. In 1985, the late James Olson, chairman of the newly divested AT&T, presided at a quality forum. The AT&T people who attend the forum came away thinking, "Hey, we're not really doing this new TQM." As a result AT&T formulated a new quality policy, allowing the business units and divisions to develop the specifics within a framework of satisfying the customer and empowering its people.[37] The results became clear in 1992 when two AT&T units won Baldrige Awards—and the stock reached a level nearly triple what it was at divestiture.

THE PULITZER PRIZE OF BUSINESS: THE BALDRIGE

The Baldrige Award itself gave the quality movement an unexpectedly strong boost when it was created in 1987. Unlike many government and industry prizes, which are hardly more than promotional stunts and deserve their obscurity, the Baldrige quickly established itself as a prize so well conceived and administered that simply applying for the prize forces a company to examine itself rigorously against an excellent set of standards. Winning the prize became a sought-after honor, the Oscar or Pulitzer Prize of business. The applicants numbered only in the hundreds in the first five years of the award, partly because of the difficulty of winning, but the companies using the criteria numbered in the thousands. Some major corporations, including Motorola and IBM, insisted that their suppliers hew to the Baldrige criteria and others, such as Westinghouse, made the Baldrige the model for their annual internal awards.[38] Leon Gorman, chairman of L. L. Bean, was so inspired at the unveiling of the Baldrige in 1987 in Washington that he went back to Maine determined to make Bean a total quality company and to apply for the prize the first year.[39] (Bean had a head start on other newcomers to TQM because of its tradition of stretching itself to serve the customer. Bean finished near the top in the competition for a Baldrige in 1988, but did not win.) State-wide quality prizes proliferated and attracted more competitors, ones that might have been scared off by the Baldrige.

The success of some companies, the pressure from large corporations on their suppliers, popularity of the Baldrige prize, the growing awareness that poor quality was extremely costly, and the need to match competitors who had improved their quality created a rush to TQM in the late 1980s and early 1990s. It spread from manufacturing to the service industries, and from big companies to small companies. TQM moved from the banks to the insurance companies to the hospitals. It began to interest the universities and the professions. Even law firms took notice, which was remarkable in that the law is perhaps the only line of work that can profit from its own incompetence and sloth. Here and there TQM appeared in the federal government: in the Internal Revenue Service and the Patent Office, and in the armed forces. State and local governments launched quality efforts, particularly in Arkansas, where Governor Bill Clinton showed an interest and understanding of total quality, which he took with him to Washington. All the newcomers to the field have the advantage of drawing on more than a decade of experience in the United States in total quality. They do not have to learn their lessons from a strange and distant culture. Unless the newcomers are to suffer the same disappointments that most of their forerunners experienced, they need to look at what other Americans have already learned about the practice of TQM. The following chapters will examine that experience.

CONCLUSIONS

Sheer survival got the quality movement going in the United States (just as it had in Japan about three decades earlier), but as the movement matured, American businesses accumulated other compelling reasons for adopting TQM. In rough chronological order, they were:

- The discovery that the costs of poor quality in many good companies amounted to 20% or 30% of total sales.
- The need to improve productivity, which led to the discovery that better quality meant higher productivity.
- The realization, through benchmarking or other methods of comparison, that other companies were doing things much better than ''we'' were.
- The growing awareness that better products and services were the critical competitive weapon.
- The pressure from big companies on their vendors to adopt quality management methods.
- The example and stimulus of the Baldrige Award.
- The increasing complexity of products that demanded higher levels of quality.
- The recognition in government that TQM might be one way to deal with the budget crunch.

Large segments of U.S. business have come to realize that TQM is a good way to run a business, that in many markets high quality has become the ticket that gets you in the market, and that customers now expect it.

2

The Leaders
The Wrong Stuff

The First Take on Quality: If it was poorly made, it had to be the workmanship, right? That loose bolt rattling around in the door panel and driving you nuts was left there by some union guy who just did not care. Maybe it was sabotage. You will never get Detroit to stop turning out lemons until the blue-collar worker learns how to do a real day's work. Good workmanship equals good products.

The early visitors who went to study Japan's industries came back with the news that quality circles were the secret of their success. So the quality movement in the United States focused at first on the factory floor, on reforming the blue collar worker, conveniently leaving the boss unchallenged and undisturbed.

The Second Take on Quality: Quality circles and other reforms on the factory floor worked no magic, in fact they hardly helped at all if used on their own. So maybe the problem was not the workers, but management. Maybe the reason the bolt was left in the car door was poor design. The door was so awkward to assemble that the worker could not help but drop some bolts inside it, and they were hard to get back out. It did not matter how much the worker cared, for he had no control over the system. As Juran had been saying for years, 80% of the defects in a process are controllable by management. The workers were responsible for only 20% of the mistakes. So poor quality must be the middle managers' fault. After all, top management was sold on quality; if workers had no control over the process, then those middle managers must be the problem. They are an obstructive bunch anyhow, scared of change, set in their ways, fearful of losing their prerogatives. Send them off for training, shake them up with a few veiled threats about getting on board, let the message about downsizing sink in. Tell the vice president for quality that he is responsible for seeing that middle management gets aboard. That should take care of quality, the chairman says to himself.

By now the bolts have stopped showing up in the door panels and maybe the hoods and trunks fit a little better. But the cars just are not exciting and they still have more defects than those imports. The new models are late and poorly designed. The dealers still treat the customers like rubes come to the city fair. The billing and receiving clerks are making as many mistakes as ever. The quality effort has stalled. Then the market slumps and there is a crisis. Suddenly the company reverts to the old ways: cut costs, lay people off, move product, and don't bother me about that quality stuff right now: it was not working anyhow.

The Third Take on Quality: Who, me? The CEO discovers that *he* is the key player and he has been missing until now. He needs the workers and the managers, but they are watching what he does before they commit themselves. Maybe he believes in quality, but he has not proved it, and until he does, quality just will not take. Once in a while a plant manager or division manager lifts his unit up without the help of the chief executive, but the effort will last only while that manager holds that job. Until the people at the very top of a company seal by their actions the commitment to quality, the rest of the company is likely to regard TQM as another management fad, like zero-based budgeting or management by objectives, something that the top asks the rest of the company to do—for a while.

THE CEO: LEADER, MANAGER, SELF-SEEKER, OR . . . ?

When Philip Caldwell announced to a Ford conference in 1978 that henceforth quality would be Job 1, nothing much happened. That was just talk. Two years later when he closed the Mahwah, New Jersey assembly plant, which was notorious for poor quality, that was commitment. All the other Ford plants then got a strong message that had them striving for good quality ratings. Robert Galvin, the former chairman of Motorola, maintains that "the CEO has to embrace quality with intensity and a sense of proprietorship that is very first person, and then of course he has to help to engage everyone else along the line."[1] The CEO needs to improve his performance even in a personal way, preparing for meetings more carefully, being on time, giving clear instructions to his secretary.

If TQM were just a set of tools, the CEO could delegate the job to someone else, but if TQM is a different way of running a company, if it is a transformation, then obviously the CEO has to lead. He cannot delegate the job. The CEO changes along with the company. But think of what has come to be expected and demanded of our chief executives: they are supposed to be tough and decisive, they are General Patton leading the tanks, they have "the right stuff," whatever that is. They want others to fix problems fast, they are happiest making deals, and they have not much time for the soft stuff. They spend their time with lawyers and accountants, rather than with engineers, workers, or customers. They look for magic pills to solve their problems. They know the numbers, but not the products.

Robert McNamara and the Whiz Kids set a pattern at Ford after World War II that crippled the company for years. His idea of cost effectiveness, which was just as destructive later when he applied it to the Pentagon, meant that an argument had to be quantified in dollar terms or it would carry no weight. The result, says James Bakken, former vice president of quality at Ford, is that

> "You build a cheaper wiring harness that has the potential to short out on a rainy, foggy morning and the car won't start. The common denominator for effectiveness could not be customer satisfaction. It had to be quantified in dollars and cents. The engineering and manufacturing people couldn't measure or articulate the effectiveness of a better harness in quantifiable terms. So it became Cost A vs. Cost B. The low-cost alternative was almost always selected."[2]

While paying scant attention to what was really required of them, chief executives got in the habit of taking very good care of themselves. The lavishness of executive pay became one of the business scandals of the 1980s, coinciding awkwardly with the years of the great downsizings. In 1990, when the median price of a share dropped by 7.7%, the average CEO wangled a 9.4% raise in total compensation.[3] The average weekly earnings of production workers went up 2.6% the same year. Eizo Watanabe, a counselor to the Japanese Union of Scientists and Engineers and at 78 an elder statesmen of quality, argues that one of the big differences between Japanese and American chief executives is that the Japanese return profits to the company while the Americans take as much as they can. He believes that "with that mentality you cannot achieve high quality."[4]

The inadequacies of heads of companies came under fire from a number of directions. They were not leading their companies to quality, they lacked the vision to see where their companies should go, they lacked the vigor to transform their companies, and they lacked the agility to compete in new world markets. It all came down to a lack of leadership. Chief executives were managers, deal-makers, bean-counters maybe, but not leaders. The U.S Army puts leadership training ahead of all other training for officers. The business schools did not even teach the subject; they taught the tools of running a business, not the heart of it.

The issue of leadership vs. management arose in the *Harvard Business Review* in 1977, in an article by Professor Abraham Zaleznik. He asked whether management and leadership were different and concluded that they were. Subsequently he occupied the first chair in leadership at the Harvard Business School. The Wharton School also began to teach leadership. Books on leadership in business began to pour out of business school faculties in the middle and late 1980s—from John Kotter at Harvard, Warren Bennis at the University of Southern California, and Noel Tichy at the University of Michigan. Tichy, who wrote *The Transformational Leader*, found his ideal in John F. Welch, the head of General Electric since 1981. Welch did the usual things like cutting jobs and getting rid of low-growth businesses but, more important, he fostered a radical spirit that got GE people to question what they were doing, to improve what was already good, and to take risks. He created the famous "work-outs," off-site meetings of groups of employees from all ranks who meet to "work out" their problems without their boss, and then tell him what they want to do. His was not a formal total quality campaign, but it contained many of the right ingredients.

Family Affairs

When it comes to leadership in quality, one might be tempted to say that family connections count most. Some of the companies that have improved their products and processes the most are either family owned or run by the descendants of the founders. Roger Milliken, chairman of Milliken & Co., is the grandson of Seth Milliken, who established the company in Portland, Maine in 1865. Leon A. Gorman is the grandson of L. L. Bean, the outdoorsman who founded the store for the outdoors in 1912 in Freeport, Maine. Both companies are still family owned. James R. Houghton is the sixth member of the Houghton family to run Corning Glass Works since it moved to Corning, New York in 1868. The company has gone public, but the family still owns 15% of the shares. Motorola, also publicly owned, undertook its quality drive under Bob Galvin, son of the founder: his son Christopher is now president of the company. Another publicly owned quality company, Hewlett-Packard, remains 26% controlled by the Hewlett and Packard families; David Packard did not announce his retirement as chairman until 1993.*

---

* In Japan, the Toyoda family founded and still presides over the auto company widely believed to have the best quality system in the world. But Soichiro Honda, who started the company that bears his name in 1946, took his relatives with him when he retired in 1972. His son was forbidden to work for the company. Toyota and Honda are upstarts in a country where companies endure like bonsai trees. Takenaka Corp., one of the big five construction companies in Japan, was established in 1610 by a shrine carpenter, Tobei Masataka Takenaka. Toichi Takenaka, his 17th generation descendant, now runs the company. It won a Deming Prize for quality in 1979, and a Japanese Quality Award, for which only Deming Prize winners are eligible, in 1992.[5]

Family ownership or management clearly confers one attribute on a company that it needs to excel: the continuity of long-term leadership. When the family name is involved it tends to make the clan chieftain care about what goes out under that name. Whether it comes from the family or not, continuity is essential to qualify because TQM is not something a chief executive can create and forget about. It will take years, even a decade or two, to make all the fundamental changes that raise a company to world-class quality. Even then, TQM requires constant attention because performance is never static. It either gets better or it gets worse.

Push Management versus Pull Leadership

Leading a transformation of this scope is difficult enough of itself, but it puts a special demand on the leader because he has to lead in a different way. "Corporate leaders don't know how to manage transformation," says Dan Ciampa, president of Rath & Strong, a consulting firm that focuses on quality and organizational culture. "The mandate is to inspire, to invoke commitment, to enable employees to form a different concept of the organization in which they believe deeply, and to change without being threatened." Ciampa talks of the "push" approach to management and the "pull" approach to leadership. The prevalent style of push management uses tools like budgeting and management by objectives, which control people but also restrain them. But people need pull as well as push. The leader needs to create a vision that will excite and inspire the employees to drive themselves.[6] The old-style boss imparts a murky vision and follows that up with nit-picking supervision, changing his mind several times about essential matters. The leader creates a clear vision and goals and then stands aside to let others do it.

But the new leader faces a dilemma. On the one hand, he has to make sure his people adopt total quality, but on the other hand he cannot order them to do it, or at least he cannot order them how to do it. The essence of quality is to draw out the best in everyone, but that only happens when people believe they have some control over their work. They must find their own way, under the leader's guidance. Each leader needs to find his own balance.

Mike Walsh, the chairman of Tenneco and before that the leader of a quality effort that made Union Pacific the benchmark for other railroads, explains his approach this way:

> "I suspect you've all heard of my so-called 'collegial' style of management. I run my Monday morning meetings that way. We talk. We argue. But, we also act. They aren't debates, they're business meetings.

I say that because I don't want you to misunderstand the concept. There is a big difference between collegial management and consensus management, and the difference is critical. Listening to people's views doesn't mean you always follow them. Not every idea is a good one. Not every opinion is valid. And being open-minded doesn't mean that you let your brains fall out. You have to use judgment. That's the mark of a leader.''[7]

Another railroad man, James A. Hagen, chairman of Conrail, used his leadership differently, in a way more suited to his style and character. Hagen is a quiet fellow; if you attended a Conrail board meeting he is probably the last person in the room you would pick out as the chairman. Hagen worked at Conrail for many years and in 1985 went off to CSX, where he took part in the start of a quality process. Four years later, he came back to Conrail as chairman. He liked the quality concepts and wanted to bring them to Conrail. His managers assumed he would, but he did nothing at first.

''The railroads are relatively hierarchical, militaristic just about, and if I'd come back and said, 'Okay, we're gonna have a quality program,' well, we'd have had one, but we wouldn't have had one. It would have been in name only, just because the chairman wants it. I didn't say anything to anybody for a while and finally a group of the top officers came to me and said, 'Why don't you want to have a quality program?' And I said, 'Who said I didn't want a quality program?' 'Well, you had one down there and you've never mentioned it since you've been back.' I said, 'Let me turn the question around. Do you want to have a quality program?' They did, so we started looking around. The next test I gave them was, 'Well, who do you think ought to run this? Give me your list of candidates and tell me who are the best ones out of your departments.' The reason for that test was that if they put somebody on there who was temporarily out of a job who they thought was a good guy or was having a problem running his job now and they wanted to put somebody else in there, then I would doubt their sincerity. They all passed that test because they came up with some of their best people.''[8]

The End of Autocracy: Milliken of Milliken

Roger Milliken makes little of his own transformation, but others who have known him for some time obviously think it was essential to the transformation of the company. By the time Milliken came to the new quality in

1980, he had been running the company for 33 years. A tall, rumpled, courtly Southern gentleman, Milliken became president at the age of 32 when his father, Gerrish, died—of a heart attack, as the two of them played golf—in 1947. For more than three decades he was boss, in the old style. When a South Carolina mill voted to unionize in 1956, he shut the mill the next day and then fought the workers' claims for 24 years before settling for $5 million. He never reopened the plant. Thomas J. Malone, the company president, who probably has as much to do with its excellence as Milliken himself, describes the old company as "very hierarchical, very top-down, but very good, very strong, and very positive." An executive a little further down the line describes the old paradigm: "In 1980 we were autocratic. Milliken made all the decisions and we like good soldiers did what we were told. Since people at the top were autocratic, we emulated them." He describes what he called a "whack-a-mole" culture: when any of the little moles in the company stuck their heads out of a hole, they got whacked. He remembers a two-day meeting of the managers of 60 plants at which the manager of one plant that had a bad safety record got so savagely whacked that he threw up on the projector and cried. In those days, they kept score of the number of messengers who got shot.

It was more a revolution than a transformation that carried Milliken & Co. and its restless, energetic CEO from the whack-a-mole mode to the participative mode that would allow self-managed teams to work in the plants without supervision. In one respect, Milliken had a head start on other CEOs because he had always pushed the quality of the company's textiles and he knew the whole process intimately. He was an ebullient booster of the company, which he wanted to look good in every way. He was obsessed with being the best.

After returning to Spartanburg from that Christmas vacation in 1980, Milliken sent 300 copies of Phil Crosby's *Quality Is Free* to his executives and two weeks later announced they would all be attending a four-day meeting with Crosby at Calloway Gardens, Milliken's conference center in Georgia. "We absolutely hated Phil," one of the participants remembers. "One of the division presidents was shaking his fist in Phil's face, shouting, 'Look, we're different,' and we were taking bets as to who would strike the first blow." But they did not come to blows, and Tom Malone led two groups of executives down to Winter Park, Florida to attend Crosby College. "We heard examples that stunned us," Malone recalls. "We came back with a real conviction." One factor that helped: To prove those huge estimates of the cost of quality wrong as far as Milliken was concerned, some executives calculated for themselves the company's cost of quality, but they came up with a sobering answer: 25%.

While Crosby was encouraging the troops, he was restraining Milliken. Milliken's natural inclination was to rush out and create quality. As he acknowledges now,

> "We were cautioned by Crosby not to try to adopt a procedure and force it down the organization but to try to let it come through the people to whom we were trying to communicate a vision."

Malone explained how he and Milliken changed:

> "He couldn't drive it the way he did before. That was Crosby's major contribution, and he said it over and over again. Every time I wanted to move into the mode of 'I'm gonna drive it now,' Crosby said, 'If you do, you're reverting back to your old top-down way and it won't work. This is a change in thinking and culture of the management team and they've gotta be given time to do that. They'll do it at different rates and you will drive it by looking for results rather than telling people what to do.' It was a very, very big change, and was probably possible only because of Milliken's commitment to change anyway."

Deprived of his usual managerial weapons, Milliken slipped quality into the company's day-to-day thinking through a side door that other CEOs such as Motorola's Bob Galvin have used. He made quality the first item on the agenda for a half day at the start of the regular meeting which top managers held every four weeks. That, he feels, showed "we were really serious."

The role of cheerleader fitted Milliken more easily. He is emotional and ebullient and he knows how to arouse the troops. He recalls how at a meeting of 400 managers in 1982, he was appalled when one of them said to him, "There are only five managers in this room who know how to listen." Milliken believed him and at the end of the meeting (with a little practice) he jumped up on a chair, raised his right arm, and asked the others to raise theirs and repeat after him:

> I will listen;
> I will not shoot the messenger;
> I recognize that management is the problem.

Milliken believes that was a breakthrough moment.

"That day we started to commit—unfortunately, not quite all of us—and to embark upon an entirely new approach to quality: one of leadership through listening and coaching. . . . Without realizing the magic of what we were about to do, we were indeed beginning to enable and empower each and every one of our associates to do what they know and can do best."

Malone saw it this way:

"The approach we had [formerly] was, if you had a problem, you assigned somebody ownership of it, and they used whatever resources they could, and if they were really good they would get it solved. If you didn't give ownership to an individual, nothing happened. And all of a sudden we were talking about forming teams to solve the problems and the members of the team being the people doing the work and not management. That was really new and different."

Milliken likes to say you have to "walk the talk," to demonstrate what you are saying. He also literally walks the talk in the sense that he has no office at corporate headquarters. He does have a little office in his house, but when he comes to the office he just walks around seeing people. If he drops by to see Malone everybody knows it, because Malone has no private office either, just a corner of a huge open office area. The whole company knows that Milliken walks the talk. A company executive describes how Milliken gets the message across.

"Milliken is obsessed with quality, from the way we write memos to the guest quarters. Once I picked him up at the airport and he asked me how long it would take to drive to the guest house. I said 12 minutes. He said, 'OK, you've got 12 minutes to tell me what you have done this week to improve quality.' "[9]

A Cerebral CEO: Stata of Analog Devices

While Milliken was taking care of the "soft" side of quality, that is, the acts of leadership that transform a culture, Ray Stata at Analog Devices was focusing on the "hard" stuff, the machinery and structure of quality improvement. As others have learned, the soft stuff can be harder than the hard stuff. Analog is a $537-million-a-year company that makes integrated circuits which translate the real or linear world of temperatures and speeds, for example, into the digital world of computers for use in aviation, medicine, and many other fields. The company makes a huge variety of products for markets that change fast. Its customers, companies like IBM and Hewlett-Packard, are demanding. Over the years, Analog has done extremely well, increasing its sales by 300% in a decade.[10]

In some respects Stata had a head start on Milliken. His was a relatively young, high-tech company that had not encrusted itself with bureaucracy and bad habits. From the beginning Stata practiced what had not yet been named participative management. He is an unassuming CEO, uninterested in the perks of power. For years he drove an old Olds passed on to him by an aunt to corporate headquarters in Norwood, Massachusetts, and he does not "do" lunch. He does "do" breakfast because it is quick. He has an intense intellectual interest in his job—evidenced by a long relationship with MIT—but he has had a problem with leadership since the beginning.

When Stata and a partner founded Analog Devices in 1965 in a basement in Cambridge, Massachusetts—the cheap digs that seem mandatory for a startup—he and the partner ran the company in an awkward relationship they called "the two-headed monster." Stata did not want to be the chief executive. He regarded that role as the work of a "superclerk." He wanted to focus instead on product development and marketing. When the company went public in 1969 and the partner left, Stata hired a president to run the company. But that did not work because Stata was the major stockholder and driving force. The hired president quit in a year. Stata has run Analog Devices ever since.

Stata divides the story of quality at Analog Devices into three periods. In the first, from 1983 to 1986, the company met TQM without really getting to know it. In the second, from 1986 to 1990, the company hired a vice president of quality but made no fundamental changes. In the third, from 1990, Stata finally committed himself personally to make the change happen.

In the first period—the period when he preached the "flute music" of quality but failed to change the management style—TQM had little impact on the company. Stata explains: "To a large extent this was because neither I nor the other managers understood what this was all about and, more important, what our role in it should be. My attitude was that TQM was for the rest of the organization and not necessarily for me." Arthur M. Schneiderman, at the time a consultant specializing in quality for Bain & Company in Boston, says the Analog people became "more and more sensitized" to quality in this period. "They went to the Crosby college, had a Deming seminar, wrote a manual, but nothing happened. Teams formed, but for other purposes. They took the name TQM for convenience."

To start the second period in 1986, Stata hired Schneiderman as vice president for quality and productivity management. (He has since become a private consultant.) "That was a recognition on my part and others in the organization that in fact we didn't know how to do it and so we had to get somebody in here who was our own quality guru," Stata continues. "And so Art came and we went through a period from 1986 to 1989 with his leadership making some fairly substantial progress in implementing TQM methodology." They established goals and measurement systems, began benchmarking their performance against other companies, improved their internal business processes, put together Quality Improvement Process teams. With new goals and new tools, Analog Devices made remarkable progress. By 1990, the yield of usable silicon wafers for integrated circuits, always a critical factor in semiconductor manufacturing, improved from 20% of the total to 38%, enough to allow the company to defer construction of a new wafer factory for years. On-time deliveries improved from 85% of all deliveries to 97%.

However, even as the company achieved these successes, progress slowed. In 1990, when Stata finally realized he had to demonstrate personally his commitment to quality, a major acquisition and a reorganization, centralizing control over production, diverted management's attention. "The significant point is that we weren't able to pat our heads and rub our stomachs at the same time," Stata says. Analog's quality system "wasn't by any means institutionalized, so that as soon as you glanced in another direction, it did not sustain itself." In the next two years Analog failed to meet some of its quality goals and in some areas its performance slipped (see Chapter 5). That was not the only problem. Stata explains, "We began to hit another wall. How were we going to continue our program with TQM? There was a considerable amount of disarray in the company in terms of 'Well, what does TQM mean?' What dialect of TQM are we going to adopt, because there was a Crosby dialect, and a Deming dialect, and a Juran dialect. There was a lot of dickering and arguing and very little cooperation between the units in terms of standardizing the methodology."

At this point, Stata met Shoji Shiba, a visiting professor at MIT from the University of Tsukuba in Japan, and a Deming prize examiner for the Japanese Union of Scientists and Engineers. What Shiba showed him was the importance of having a structure or organization set up to build up a body of knowledge for companies to learn from each other and to promote a common language and a common set of ideas. JUSE served that function in Japan from the beginning, but the United States had no comparable body (although the criteria for the Baldrige Award are increasingly becoming the standard in America). To make a start in the United States, Stata founded in Cambridge the Center for Quality Management, a nonprofit consortium of businesses and universities where CEOs and other managers can teach and learn together.

With Shiba, Stata learned the power of change agents to transform the culture of a company. Just as Deming and Juran were change agents literally from a different world when they went to Japan—external influences even more powerful than the CEO—so American companies today need external forces. Hewlett-Packard, IBM, and Motorola are playing that role with increasing vigor towards the many companies that supply them, Stata believes, and an organization like the Center for Quality Management can help.

"One of the things I've been learning from Shiba and the Center for Quality Management," Stata continues, "are the skills, and the knowledge, and the role that I have to play in leading the change process. I didn't understand that as well before as I do today." Schneiderman observes that people in Analog Devices were not getting the support they needed. "Ray had been a superb cheerleader, but not a participant," says Schneiderman of his ex-boss. "He supported me but he and the management group were in the stands, not out in the field."

To help Stata get a better feel for his role, Schneiderman took him down to Spartanburg to meet Milliken in October, 1991, and the two found they could learn much from each other: Stata saw the soft side of how to be a more inspirational leader, and Milliken saw the hard side of tools. "I didn't have as deep an appreciation for the symbolic role as I do today," says Stata.

On a trip to Europe in the spring of 1992, Stata heard one of Analog's British managers give a presentation on TQM that so impressed him that on the spur of the moment he jumped up, praised the manager, and announced that for the first time in his life he was going to make an award on the spot. The manager received a check for $2,000. Stata agrees that even a few months earlier he would not have dreamed of making that gesture. "I just wouldn't have recognized that those are the kind of things that establish the mythology and that's the way you can convince the organization that you're really serious. The impact of that gesture was fantastic. The story is running all around the company."

Stata explained yet another step in his evolution as the CEO of a total quality company.

"There is a tendency, particularly in the early stages, to view TQM as extra work. I'm already busy 100% of the time. The real transformation is to view it not as extra work but as an integral part of the way I do my job. There's nothing intellectually or conceptually challenging about learning the tools of TQM, but what makes it difficult is that you have to kill old habits and make some very basic changes in behavior, attitudes, and skills."

For example,

". . . preparing for a meeting now, I spend really hours thinking about the agenda, and thinking about the congruents of how the meeting is going to take place, what the outcomes will be, communicating expectations. I just put a lot more time into thinking about meeting agendas than I used to. Not that I shouldn't have before. I just didn't. Meetings were sort of half-assed, and we were ill-prepared, and we were vague as to the assignments people had as a result of the meetings. All that stuff was very, very loose. We are more precise in providing measurements around the completion of tasks, and the extent to which we insist upon facts rather than opinions in coming to conclusions."

Thus, after nearly a decade, a CEO as extraordinarily thoughtful and open-minded as Stata was still learning. No wonder that most CEOs that Stata meets are telling him, "'Hey, we're doing all this stuff but it isn't getting us where we want to go. What's wrong? How do we make it better?' " He wishes that early on someone had looked him in the eye and said, "Hey, Ray, if you personally don't learn these skills, put them into practice in a way that symbolically communicates to the organization your commitment to it, and get your senior managers to do likewise, all this stuff is going to amount to nothing."[11]

Kidder of Duracell

Without becoming too wrapped up in the language and procedures of TQM, Bob Kidder of Duracell has established himself as a CEO who participates in what the company calls its "XCells." Kidder has survived three big changes in Duracell's ownership. He was there when Duracell was a subsidiary of Kraft Incorporated. He led a leveraged buyout in 1988 financed by Kohlberg Kravis Roberts & Company, which left the company heavily in debt. Then he took the company public in 1991.

When he became CEO in the early 1980s, Duracell typically moved decisions slowly up and down the hierarchy. Kidder wanted to improve quality but says he was frustrated because the company had no mechanism for handling problems that transcended the discrete parts of the organization. After one false start, Duracell did create that mechanism, which works through its XCells teams. Kidder saw that he would have to sit on some teams himself to give the mechanism credibility. At first he encountered the usual resistance. He characterizes the reaction of some people as being in effect, " 'Mr. CEO, you are just realizing what we've known all along and we're working on it. Thanks for your help, but why don't you go back to sleep?' "

Kidder put himself on the corporate XCells council, which picks the priorities for the working teams, and he sat on the working team assigned to improved Duracell's capital forecasts, which he regarded as "dreadful." The company always overestimated its capital spending, he says, took too long to prepare forecasts, had too many people working on them, and the documents that finally emerged were badly written. "I would not pass them on to any literate person," he grumbles, "because they are just impossible to understand or read, and it's only because I know the business reasonably well that I can interpret what these things really mean." Kidder spends about three hours a month sitting on each of the two committees. In addition, he puts in time as a cheerleader supporting "this crusade," making speeches, getting items into company publications, making sure his people understand that the XCells process is an important part of Duracell's culture and strategy.

Kidder did not, however, immerse himself in the kind of total quality training that other CEOs, such as David Kearns of Xerox and Bob Galvin of Motorola, felt necessary. "I don't go to seminars," he says. "I'm very uncomfortable talking about generic expressions, TQM, statistical process, quality control. I happen to be trained well enough to understand that stuff by my engineering background but I'm almost embarrassed when I read some of that generic stuff about quality." This undogmatic approach seems to suit Kidder's style and his company. Some of the frustration of a decade ago has gone. He is more comfortable in the job now because "I have a way of getting something done." It is now easier to take initiatives. The company has a "productive openness."[12]

The Miracle Did Not Last: Clough of Nashua

After struggling more than a decade to make its quality efforts pay off, Nashua Corporation still has not resolved its leadership problems. It is ironic that Nashua should have these troubles because Nashua was held up in the

1980 NBC documentary ''If Japan Can . . . Why Can't We?'' as the example of an American company that could do it right. In 1979, Nashua's chairman, William E. Conway, heard about Deming when a team he had sent to Japan could not get in to see some Ricoh executives because they were busy preparing for a Deming prize examination. ''Who is this Deming?'' Conway asked. One of his vice presidents happened to know Deming, and Conway decided to consult Deming. That was on a Monday. By Thursday Deming was up at Nashua's offices in an old mill building in downtown Nashua, New Hampshire. (It was not long before the demands for Deming's advice were filling up his calendar two years ahead, even as he advanced into his nineties.) Nashua could not control the variations in the thickness of the coating that it laid on paper for copying machines. By showing the company that its technicians were making things worse by adjusting the machinery without sampling the coating properly, and by getting the technicians to use statistical process controls, Deming helped the company save money and improve quality within months. ''It was like a miracle,'' said Conway.[13]

The miracle did not last. Since the company was so successful at coating copying paper, Conway figured it could make copiers too. But designing and manufacturing machinery was new to Nashua's experience. In 1982, Nashua lost $40 million, defaulted on $48 million in loans—and the board ousted Conway. His successor, Charles E. Clough, a Nashua veteran, had to cut costs right away, clean up the books, and get rid of the copying machine business, which he did successfully. He also embraced his predecessor's quality efforts and Deming continued his visits on into 1991, past his 90th birthday.

Clough continues to believe in TQM, but the results are very mixed. Nashua as a whole certainly has not embraced total quality. Clough says that while some divisions have successfully improved their processes, others have not, and all over there is a tendency to backslide. Clough complains that

''Getting people trained so they really understand process and are willing to work on process day in day out, is extraodinarily difficult, just extraordinarily difficult. Unless you reinforce it every single day, my experience is they'll go back to where they were . . . I think it's basically the top management that's the culprit because you know the middle management, particularly in this day and age, middle management is trying to please everybody so they can keep their jobs.''

As much as Clough believes in total quality, he does not convey that belief throughout Nashua. His original mandate to cut costs cast him in a role that still inspires fear, and one of Deming's 14 points is "Drive out fear." Unlike Milliken and others, he does not make discussion of quality a priority item on his agendas. Lloyd S. Nelson, a well-known statistician and Deming disciple who for many years was director of statistical methods (read: quality director) at Nashua, writes that the corporation

"has reached and apparently stalled on a plateau of quality. I believe the level of this plateau is below the best achievable. I further believe that the reason for this is that the culture of the company is still a mixture of the past and what Mr. Clough would like it to be now. . . [He] clearly recognizes the desirability of such a change. To many, his emphasis may appear to be on the usual accounting parameters: profits, gross margins, cycle times, and the like. . . . I believe he feels that processes are what others must focus on, but they have not gotten his message. . ."[14]

Nelson retired in 1992, his deputy left the company, neither of them was replaced, and Nashua's quality office folded.

Robert Geiger runs the masking and duct tape division of Nashua in Troy, New York in isolation from the rest of the corporation. Decentralization enables him to push quality more successfully than other divisions have done, and Clough holds him up as an example for the others. But the tape division has gone ahead in spite of the corporation, rather than with its support. "This is top down stuff," says Geiger. "There is no organized effort in Nashua to carry out Deming."[15] In 1993, Clough decided he had done as much as he could for Nashua and he brought in an outsider, Bill Mitchell of Raychem Corporation, as chief operating officer. Clough planned to retire and make Mitchell, a quality believer, CEO in his place within a matter of months.

A Spiritual Leader: Young of Hewlett-Packard

Hewlett-Packard's John Young and Motorola's Robert Galvin, both now retired as CEOs, seemed to take quality more naturally in stride than others, to know instinctively what to do, and to adapt without great stress. Their own open and receptive characters helped, and so did the corporate cultures of their two companies. They were both quick to see the enormous power of quality and, like Milliken, they keyed their companies' transformations.

John Young believes that neither his own style nor the HP culture, both pretty laid back and tolerant, needed much redirection to adapt. HP is a complicated, high-tech company and nobody at the top, in Young's view, can know that much about what the company is doing. The corporation exists to support the divisions, not to tell them what to do. HP has always been like that, so the HP culture—Young says "culture" is simply a word for what you have been doing anyhow—already contained the right ethos for a quality effort. The head of the company does not make too many decisions, but he does set the tone and direction. "It's more being kind of the spiritual leader," says Young. "You keep talking about it and asking questions and making sure the right criteria get picked."

Young got the whole company's attention at the beginning of the 1980s by setting what now seems a modest goal but was then breathtaking: HP would reduce the rate of defects in its hardware by a factor of 10 before the decade was out. Then he had to show it could be done. He remembers that

> "We spent a lot of time getting some early victories and merchandising quality and getting people to believe that in fact lower defect rates paid off. We finally got some credibility that this works, that it makes a difference, that this wasn't a management game we were playing this week.
>
> "You're trying to win the hearts and minds of people to believe that there's a better way. We looked for the HP mavericks and made sure they had lots of room to go after quality and a safety net if anything went wrong. We did everything we could to ensure that we had wins that we could merchandise. We used the annual general managers' meeting big time. If you budget the most important premium time you have to this (quality), it says a lot about where it sits on your agenda. There's nothing more influential than your peers standing up at a general managers' meeting, getting to tell how they got the job done and getting psychic reward for it."

As the 1980s rolled on and HP became known for its quality successes, Young didn't let up: "One of the challenges is to have a sense of renewal and to keep it fresh and to keep pushing. You tend to run a bit downhill if you don't keep pushing." In his indirect, collegial way, Young did keep pushing, never ordering managers to do this or that, letting them follow their own paths in their own methods, but always expanding the scope of HP's quality effort.[16]

A Lesson in Perfection: Galvin of Motorola

Bob Galvin has served 52 years in the company founded by his father and uncle in 1928 to make a "battery eliminator" that allowed owners of radios to plug right in to the household current. He learned about perfectibility early on. He went to grade school at St. Jerome's in Chicago, where the nuns had high standards. He remembers one in particular, his math teacher, Sister Mary Norbadet, who announced one day that she would not accept any grade less than 100 on a forthcoming test on conversions. "Scared the hell out of me," he says, but his parents supported the teacher and Galvin did score 100. Galvin was at Motorola 40 years before he made perfection the company's quality standard.

Like Young, he set a goal that would make Motorola wake up and stretch itself. Galvin called for a tenfold improvement in quality in five years, which was extended to become a hundred-fold improvement in ten years. "We spent a lot of time moving an institution to a new culture, some of it pedantic or formal or ceremonial and some informal and subtle, Machiavellian," he says. "You use all kinds of techniques." Determined he may be, but Galvin, hale and cherubic at 70, seems an unlikely Machiavelli. Perhaps he meant that contributions to quality came to count in the compensation of executives. "I suppose that moved some percentage of our people," he says. Galvin believes in personal quality improvement—in returning phone calls on time, in being punctual—and showed his personal commitment to quality. When he demolished Motorola's management school and started an extensive new training program, he took the courses. He didn't just tell people to go and find out what customers were thinking. He took a trip each month to question one customer in detail, and wrote up the report when he got back to his office in Schaumburg, Illinois. But in the end, he says, "What really moved everybody over to the side of quality was they finally realized it's right." Yes, that—and Galvin's firm and constant nudging.[17]

On/Off: Hudiburg and Broadhead of FPL

John J. Hudiburg, as chairman of Florida Power & Light, led a drive at the utility that quality professionals cite with reverence as the best case study in the United States of how to do it right. During the 1980s, FPL did indeed make remarkable progress by a whole range of measures, such as numbers of complaints, outages, and injuries. He drove the company to become the first company outside Japan to win the Deming Prize, a process so elaborate and rigorous that it stretches a company to the edge of a breakdown. But even before Hudiburg heard on October 23, 1989 that FPL had won the prize, he was out of a job. FPL's parent, FPL Group, picked a new chairman, James L. Broadhead, from outside the company in January, 1989. Broadhead and Hudiburg were incompatible and Broadhead was unimpressed with the quality effort. Hudiburg decided to retire and did not invite Broadhead to accompany him to the Deming prize ceremony. Broadhead almost immediately dismantled FPL's quality staff and many of the processes, which almost certainly had grown beyond reason. Reflecting now on what happened at FPL, Hudiburg readily admits to some mistakes. The one that undid him as a leader, he says, is that he never made it clear to the board how important TQM had become. The previous utility company chairman, Marshall McDonald, had started FPL's quality campaign, but when he became Group chairman his attention was diverted to the diversified parts of the business. He understood only the early part of the move to quality, when teams were formed, and did not keep track of the evolution. "I reported regularly on our progress to the board, but I didn't tell them how we were getting the result. They took improvement as a given and they didn't realize that TQM was the engine making it all happen. They just appreciated the results. Marshall didn't fully understand what we were doing and the board didn't understand the importance of continuity when it came to choosing the next chairman."[18] A leader cannot ever think he has won the battle for quality; it never ends.

CONCLUSIONS

What distinguishes companies that succeed at TQM from those that do not more than anything else is the behavior of the CEO.

- By action and example, the CEO must personally lead the the quality drive. Cheerleading is important, but is not enough. He must participate.
- The role cannot be delegated to a vice president for quality or other executive.
- The CEO cannot treat quality management as an extra job or burden. It is part of his job.
- The CEO can demonstrate the importance of quality by making it the first item on the agenda of meetings he attends.
- If a CEO has autocratic habits he will have to change fundamentally the way he manages so that he leads by persuasion and example (with a little steel showing).

- The CEO can never relax his efforts to promote quality from the factory floor to the boardroom.
- Instead of focusing on deals and finance, as so many CEOs do, he must focus on customers and the products or services.
- The leader cannot set the right example by hogging the level of pay and perquisites that CEOs seem to think is their due.
- The long-term continuity of leadership, whether it is through family ownership or some other means, is nice if you can arrange it.

3

The People
How Hard It Is

I t is man's nature "to do as little as he safely can" and to spend much of
the day "soldiering." What then can the boss do with people who come
to the plant determined to "work as slowly as they dare while they at the
same time try to make those over them believe that they are working fast?"
These were the views that guided Frederick Winslow Taylor, a mechanical
engineer, when he was asked at the beginning of the century to improve
productivity in a bicycle ball bearing factory. The plant employed 120
"girls" to inspect the tiny ball bearings by putting them in the crevice
between two fingers on the back of their left hands and examining them
under a bright light. With a magnet, the girls removed balls that were dented,
cracked, scratched, or soft. This they did for ten and a half hours a day, and
for half a day on Saturdays. Shocking to tell, the girls did not spend the full
ten and a half hours squinting at minuscule faults on the balls, but would
indulge at times in chatter and other idleness.

Taylor's "scientific management" put a stop to this nonsense. After
"excluding" all the women who had a low "personal coefficient"—that is
to say, after firing those who lacked the perception and quickness to separate
the good from the bad among those wretched balls—Taylor laid out his plan.
"The first step," he wrote, "was to make it impossible for them to slight
their work without being found out. This was accomplished through what is
known as over-inspection." Four of the most trustworthy women were given
batches of balls to inspect that had been checked the day before by the
others, after the foreman had changed the numbers on the batches to exclude
favoritism. The next day, a chief inspector looked at one of the lots checked
by the over-inspectors. On top of all that, every two or three days the
foreman slipped into the system a special batch with a recorded number of
defective balls. Then everyone lived happily ever afterward. (In truth, according to Taylor, the plant did cut the number of inspectors from 120 to 35
"girls," reduced their hours to eight and a half a day, gave them four

10-minute recreation periods a day, raised their pay 80% to 100%, and improved productivity.)[1]

Taylorism, as practiced in the United States, helped create the enormously efficient mass-production system that was the basis of U.S. prosperity until recently. But it was inhuman. By breaking work down to its minimal elements, assigning each element to a worker, and telling that worker precisely how to do that job without flexibility, it denied the worker's intelligence and creativity. By separating so sharply the roles of managers and workers—the one to think and give orders, the other to work and obey—Taylor helped to create a caste system that eventually ate away at the productivity he wanted to achieve.

The factory, and often the office too, became a horrible place to work. The factory was dirty, disputatious, unfriendly. At Milliken, the workers were "mill hands" and their bosses were "lint heads." The worker might see his plant manager once or twice a year, but the manager would be surrounded by other people in suits, and the whole group would pass through the factory as if the blue-collar workers did not exist. I remember years ago talking to a worker at Ford's Louisville Assembly Plant about what it was like there in the 1970s, when the plant turned out trucks that had the lowest quality rating among all U.S.-made Ford vehicles, which was about as low as you could get in the world if you left out the Soviet bloc. He told me the plant was filthy, littered with broken or discarded parts. Workers and foremen shouted at each other; forklift operators deliberately damaged their loads. The worker, Tony Hamilton, nicknamed "Red Dog" because of his beard and hair and his wild ways, said he used to get sick to his stomach as he approached the plant to begin his shift. "I'd sit in the parking lot and think of any excuse I could tell my wife for not working that day," he remembered. Two or three days a week he did skip work.[2] Millions of American workers experienced what Søren Bisgaard describes as "the agony of using your arms and not your brains, of not being valued as a human being."[3]

"STAY WITHIN YOUR LIMITS"

The American manager had his agonies too. As American corporations grew bigger and older they became self-destructive. While the boss might be an egocentric tyrant—the person with the qualifications deemed necessary for a CEO often turned out that way—his executives often became sycophants and careerists. Sheer size led to the creation of large function-based departments within the corporations, and the years turned these departments into bastions to be defended against the rest of the corporation. Donald Petersen, who became the head of Ford, remembers, "You learned real fast to stay inside your limits. When I was head of the truck division, I went to the company product-planning sessions for the first time. You quickly got the message that you shouldn't even dream of saying anything out loud about cars, even though I'd spent virtually my entire career working on product development in the automotive line."[4]

Companies that behaved so churlishly inside their own walls could not be expected to behave any better towards outsiders. Suppliers were kept at arm's length, treated with suspicion and secretiveness, left wondering if they would lose their business the moment a competitor came up with a lower price. As for the customer, he was a chump, someone to be wowed by marketing and then sold whatever the plant decided to produce.

So when American business discovered in the late 1970s that foreign competition had become deadly serious, it had a lot that needed fixing. Instead of using and developing the talents of its employees, the corporation was killing them. The typical American corporation was like a warship unexpectedly caught by enemy fire with its radar not working, its crew untrained in using the new guns, and the bo'sun and the first mate shouting at each other.

"UNINFORMED FADDISM": EARLY QUALITY CIRCLES

When waves of American executives began to visit Japan in the late 1970s, what they noticed most of all was that the factories were clean and disciplined, the neatly-uniformed workers totally focused on their jobs, the unions compliant, and, gee whiz, they had quality circles! Groups of half a dozen or so workers would sit down once a week, sometimes even once a day, to figure out how to do their jobs better. That must be the answer. If we had quality circles, we would be as good as they are.

The idea was not totally new in the United States. Behavioral scientists such as Douglas McGregor had for years been developing theories about participative management. (In opposition to what he called Theory X management, or the Taylor model, which assumes that man is by nature a slacker who must be coerced to work, McGregor offered Theory Y, which assumes that man is a natural worker and that the right rewards and recognition produce his best efforts and fire his imagination and sense of responsibility.)[5] Several American companies dipped into participation in the early 1960s, including General Foods and Procter & Gamble. P&G

established its first self-managed teams—an advanced form of participation the Japanese have yet to adopt—in 1962, and today the majority of P&G's 142 plants worldwide have these teams in various depths.[6] The first quality circles were registered at the Japanese Union of Scientists and Engineers in the same year, 1962. The first quality circles in the United States appear to have been those established in 1974 at Lockheed's Missile and Space Center.

Faced with the need to respond to competition, U.S. business seized on the quality circle in the late 1970s and early 1980s as *the* answer, not realizing that to the Japanese it was only part of the solution. But it certainly was tempting. The quality circle did not cost much, it did not upset the existing corporate structure, the risks were small, and it was something someone else could do. Quality circles proliferated in the United States. By 1982, according to a New York Stock Exchange study, 44% of all corporations with more than 500 employees had them. DEC, Honeywell, IBM, TRW, and Xerox were all heavy users. You had what Edward E. Lawler, III, of the School of Business Administration at the University of Southern California called "uninformed faddism."[7] The fad attracted its retinue of consultants, trainers, and associations. McGregor had foreseen in 1960 what could happen if "enthusiasts" for participation got carried away: "They give the impression that it is a formula that can be applied by any manager regardless of his skill, that virtually no preparation is necessary for its use, and that it can spring full-blown into existence and transform industrial relationships overnight."[8] An incredibly good forecast.

The fad collapsed quickly. At the Lockheed center, it lasted four years. Donald Dewar, who organized them, says some 30 circles did good work for those four years. But a new boss took over in 1978; he announced at a retreat for his managers that he did not like QCs and what did they think? Only one person supported them and the experiment ended. (Lockheed later espoused TQM and turned back to employee involvement under other guises.)[9] At Nashua, an executive remembers, to mention a quality circle soon became as tactful as mentioning rope in the family of a man who had been hanged. Westinghouse got its first quality circle in 1980; by 1981 it had 3,500 of them; by 1982 they were dissolving. For one thing, it turned out that most of Westinghouse's quality problems occurred in the interfaces between one part of the company and another. But the circles were each made up of people in one workplace. They had no authority to dip into other departments. An observer sitting in on a Westinghouse circle meeting in 1981 found it floundering self-consciously in jargon. Its objectives were unclear. The group was trying to "prioritize" its "audibles"—the latter being defined as unexpected interruptions to the day's business, such as telephone calls. When one member grew impatient and suggested a vote on priorities, he was attacked by the others for trying to impose a vote rather than seek a consensus. Chastened, he said, blushing, "Okay, let's consensutize."[10]

A lot was wrong with this early attempt at participation. As Juran points out, when the Japanese introduced quality circles in 1962, Japanese management already had had more than a decade of "massive training" in quality. But when U.S. corporations turned to QCs nearly two decades later, their managers were still almost totally unaware of their roles or responsibilities in a quality context. The Japanese Union of Scientists and Engineers created a focus for QC activity in Japan, supporting industry with training, texts, conferences, and prizes.[11] To this day the United States has no such focal point. Without much support from top management, and with middle management often hostile, the circles could hardly have been expected to make any contribution in this country, much less effect a revolution. Without direction, the circles took up trivial items—the often cited water-cooler and locker-room-paint issues—and then ran out of things to do. Even if they made important suggestions, there was no process in place to handle them if the company as a whole had not embarked on TQM.

Interestingly enough, the Japanese never went overboard on quality circles and neither did they lose faith. From their beginnings in the early 1960s, QCs have continued to grow in Japan. A 1988 survey found a nationwide total of 743,000 circles. JUSE alone had 350,000 circles on its registry in 1992.[12] The steepest growth occurred precisely in the 1980s, just when the United States was losing interest. The Japanese have modest aims for these circles, which were started as a means of training workers in quality techniques.

It is okay to work on small problems in Japan. Toyota addressed that issue after learning that 50% of its warranty losses were caused by 120 big problems, and the other 50% by 4,000 small problems. It assigned the small problems to quality circles and the big ones to engineers.[13] NEC does not mind if its ZD (for Zero Defect) Circles wander a bit, because it considers their most important function to be to help workers improve themselves and understand their jobs rather than improve the process.[14] Honda encourages its New Honda Circles to take up matters that have nothing to do with work, such as hobbies or the problems of older people, with the hope that workers will improve their lives[15] (or perhaps be better prepared for early retirement).

Collecting Dust to Make Mountains

The difference between the corporate cultures in the United States and Japan accounts for some of the difference in the success of the quality circles in the two countries. The Japanese are more patient. As they say, by collecting dust you can make a mountain.[16] The U.S. worker and his boss look for the big, fast payoffs, and are impatient with small, painstaking gains. "In the U.S., workers are not trained or sufficiently educated to handle the problem-solving process as the Japanese [are]," says Lawler.[17] Although membership in such circles is voluntary and their agendas freely chosen—ostensibly, at least—the force of custom and peer pressure kept the Japanese worker in tune with the aims of his company. In the more chaotic U.S. workplace, especially where labor relations were bad, no such harmony existed. Finally, and this affects all participative plans and not quality circles alone, the economic conditions in the two countries clearly differed. Almost throughout the 1960s, 1970s, and 1980s Japan had a thriving, growing economy. Innovation comes easier in growing companies where nobody's job is threatened. By contrast, in the United States the push to participation began in the 1980s, a decade of downsizing and plant closings that ran over into the 1990s.

It is not easy to get a worker or manager to help you run the business if he is worried about getting fired or having his plant shut down. Strikes make it even tougher. Long before Caterpillar broke the UAW's five-month strike in 1992 by offering jobs to outsiders, the company's Employee Satisfaction Program was dismantled. When the workers returned to the plants they wore buttons that read "Employees Stop Participating." When customers visited corporate headquarters in Peoria or the plants, UAW members would demonstrate at the visitors' hotels or in the plants, wearing T-shirts that read, "Unhappy Cats Don't Purr." As far as the union was concerned, participation was dead. "We haven't used the words sabotage or slowdown, but the cumulative effect of checking your brains at the door is the same," says James B. O'Connor, an ex-president of UAW Local 974. "People aren't looking as hard for defects. They just want to put in their years and retire."[18]

By no means did quality circles disappear in the United States, and few would admit that they had failed. Rather, U.S. companies began to see that TQM meant much more than setting up circles of workers on the shop floor. Tom Murrin, who ran the Westinghouse business that had the first circles, says now that "it was a good way to get started and, on balance, a positive phase. As I look back it seems almost trivial, childish. But it had a profound aspect about it. It was the beginning of empowering people."[19] Participation does not have to take the form of the quality circle. After those disappointments in the United States in the early 1980s, participation began to flower in many forms—in work teams, product development teams, self-managed teams, cross-functional teams.

Scoffers might argue that American business has always depended on teamwork. Has not the corporation always valued the team player? Certainly, but the team player in the old sense was someone who did not raise difficult questions, who went along with the boss, who did not rock the boat. The team in the new, quality sense requires a different kind of player. There is nothing soft or fuzzy about the new team spirit. The players must raise the difficult questions, and the boss must listen; together, in a tough but not adversarial way, they must find the best answers they can.

The teamwork that is exploding in business today has a different meaning and a different scope. Big worker-management teams have formed to design whole factories, like the Saturn complex in Tennessee. After the success of the Taurus, Ford adopted the team approach as the way to design cars. Ad hoc teams sprang up to attack crisis problems. Top executives formed teams to direct their companies' strategies. The teams reached out to include customers and suppliers. Some self-managed teams may hire and fire their own members, choose their leader, fix budgets, assign tasks, set schedules and vacations. The "high performance teams" at Corning may make and implement decisions without management approval, and may deal directly with suppliers and customers. Members of these Corning teams spend 15% of their time training and are paid according to the training they have, not seniority or type of job. Most of them have chosen to work four-day weeks.[20]

Channeling the Teams

Bob Kidder finds that the XCells teams make running Duracell a more satisfying task. Following the Juran Institute's usual advice, Duracell at first picked on a few small problems for teams to solve to demonstrate that the new approach worked better in some cases than standard hierarchical decision making. That tactic succeeded. Kidder soon faced the quandary of trying to create some limits and guidelines for the use of teams without heavy-handedly quashing the interest that had welled up within the company. On one hand he saw teams created to deal with problems he deemed too trivial, and on the other hand some employees wanted to look at subjects described as "world hunger projects"—so broad as to be unmanageable. "I don't want to stop the enthusiasm for solving problems," Kidder says, "but if you get too many of these teams going simultaneously you run the risk of getting your organization too fragmented."

To make the team activity coherent, Duracell has a structure of XCells councils. A corporate council helps choose problems for the teams to attack and gets periodic progress reports from them. Though Kidder does not believe Duracell would squash any renegade teams, the structure has helped channel the work of all the teams. The councils try to make sure the targets of the teams are chronic problems rather than one-time episodes, that they are important enough, and that they cannot readily be solved by one person or one department. Unless a problem transcends more than one department, it probably does not justify a team.

Kidder by no means abdicates all power to the teams. When XCells got under way, Duracell had long been debating design changes worldwide. The company sold the familiar copper-and-black batteries all over the world, but slight differences in their appearance and the packaging persisted. Duracell wanted them all to be identical, even though the redesign could be costly. Kidder believed that the debate had gone on long enough, that the facts were in, and that one person could make the decision. So instead of creating a team, he halted the debate in 1992 and ordered the uniform design.

However, in many cases Kidder finds the team approach useful. He thinks the company has changed for the better. "We've always been pretty open and I think most people if you asked them over the years would probably have said this was a good place to work," he says. The big difference is that people now see a way of dealing with chronic problems. Before, "they would get frozen in their tracks by the enormity of the problem, or the fact that it transcended different organizations, or that it had existed for ever, and they just gave up. With this vehicle now they are more likely to say, 'Why don't we get a group of people together and put this on the XCells agenda.' "[21] Duracell people were skeptical of the team approach at first. It had more banners and slogans to it than a real knowledge of how to make teams work. But as the company acquired experience, the Excells idea sank roots even among the skeptical and it was accepted and institutionalized.

The U.S. approach to teams turned out to be more flexible and far-reaching than Japan's. When I mentioned self-managed teams to Junji Noguchi, who presides as head of JUSE over Japan's quality circle system, he asked me to explain the term; evidently it was unfamiliar to him. Edward Lawler agrees that the Japanese are not familiar with self-managed teams; the idea seems anarchic to them. They like things more hierarchical and structured. Lawler believes that "teams are our chance to get a competitive advantage because Japan is not likely to adapt to them."[22]

At Hewlett-Packard, John Young found quality circles to be "a distraction," but the company is moving "very rapidly" towards more use of self-directed teams. HP already has plants with only two levels of hierarchy, if the word can be applied to an almost totally flat organization. The plant has a manager, teams, and that is all. Research by Lawler confirms that "real increases in power sharing are occurring in the Fortune 1000 companies" and the trend is towards self-managed teams. He surveyed the Fortune Industrial 500 and Service 500 lists in 1987 and 1990. (In the 1990 sample, 77% had TQM efforts covering, on average, 41% of their employees.) While the percentage of employees involved in quality circles remained about the same, the percentage serving on other types of participative groups increased considerably. Furthermore, in the 1990 survey, though 73% of the sample companies expected the use of quality circles to stay the same or decrease, 60% said the use of self-managed work teams would increase in the future.[23]

Labor Joins the Teams: Is There a Choice?

Employee involvement puts unions on the spot. If they do not go along, they risk losing jobs, if not the whole business. If they do go along, as they have mostly done, they lose prerogatives and power, which magnifies the effects of declining union membership. The grievances, the job categories, and the work rules that are the stuff of union business are eliminated or drastically reduced. Assuming that workers and bosses really give up their intransigence in the glow of a new collaborative love feast, then the union does have less to get its teeth into. The Communications Workers of America, the United Steel Workers, and the United Auto Workes have been the most cooperative. Indeed, as we have seen, the UAW almost hauled the auto industry along into the new age—in spite of the stupefying insensitivity the auto industry showed at times. In 1982 it did not occur to General Motors that it was tactless to announce a new executive bonus plan just as the union was preparing to ratify a new contract that included givebacks by workers.

The International Association of Machinists does not like participative schemes. The IAM has opposed total quality plans and forbids its members to talk about teamwork directly with their bosses. A 1990 IAM White Paper denounced the team concept as "one of the most dangerous threats faced by working men and women today." It said "the Deming program is actually a top-down, executive-directed, communication, command and control system . . . (that) has very little to do with meaningful worker participation.'' The paper ordered IAM members to let the union handle any discussions about quality and teams, and not to go beyond their contracts.[24] In practice, IAM leaders readily admit that the white paper, while still in force, is honored more in the breach than in the observance. When I asked an IAM member who sat on a team at one of the railroads what the union had to say about it, he replied, ''I don't care what the union thinks.''

When workers and managers serve together on teams it becomes difficult, if not impossible, to avoid matters that normally would be handled by labor-management negotiations. The question is of more than casual interest because the company that lets its team discussions roam unchecked could run afoul of the National Labor Relations Act. The act defines as a union any group that discusses wages or other conditions of employment with management and it bans company unions, that is, unions created or dominated by the company. So a company that created a team which then discussed wages could be in violation of the NLRA. Electromation Incorporated, a non-union company in Indiana, was hauled before the National Labor Relations Board by the Teamsters because it had formed action committees that studied bonuses, absenteeism, smoking policy, and other matters. The NLRB ruled in December, 1992, that Electromation had violated the Act. But the ruling was too narrow to have any application outside the Electromation case.[25] A prudent adviser would urge companies to keep their teams away from wages, hours, and such matters, but in practice they at least skirt these topics, and it is hard to see how they could avoid them.

After the retirement of Don Ephlin and Irving Bluestone, the champions of teamwork, the UAW leadership became merely tolerant of employee involvement. An insurgent group called New Directions tried to reverse the union's policy of working with management, but lost each time it pushed the issue to a vote. At some locations, the UAW-company collaboration has reached extraordinary levels. At Buick City and Saturn the union and the management together designed the plants and then collaborated in running them. At Saturn, which is actually a complex of three plants, the plant managers and the union representatives sit at adjoining desks in the same office. But questions remain about what teamwork will do in the long run to the unions. Will unions become irrelevant? Ephlin suggests they may—if they continue to focus on money and benefits. They should instead play a bigger role in employee involvement and even in corporate management. ''My job was to save GM for the GM worker,'' he says.[26] Philosophically, labor should favor employee involvement. What better way exists today to give labor some control of the means of production?

Fraternizing with the Enemy: Buick City

The saga of how Buick City got to where it is today shows just how hard it can be to achieve teamwork and employee involvement. Buick City is not a city at all; it is a plant in Flint, Michigan, built back in 1910. The "City" was added to give the name a flavor of "Toyota City," one of the sources of the ideas used today by Buick. Flint symbolized the hateful relations between workers and the auto industry. It was there that UAW made its first stand and the workers occupied a Fisher Body plant in 1936, in defiance of court injunctions and the police; they stayed for 44 days until GM recognized the union. When JR Mays came to the plant in 1964 labor relations there were typical of the auto industry.

> "I was one of those guys who liked to come to work, talk to people, have a good time, and collect a paycheck at the end of the week. We were in an adversarial situation and we were comfortable with it. That's all we knew. It was only stressful in the six months leading up to a contract, and then the decision was made that you walked or somebody else did. It wasn't that bad. We had over 60% of the market. Anything you put out the door, somebody would buy it. We didn't worry about quality. If you needed 550 cars at the end of eight hours, whatever it took, we'd give it to you. . . . The plant got a new manager every couple of years. When I was young, if you saw a bunch of white shirts grouped around the guy in the middle, that was the plant manager. You'd see him three times a year and never talk to him. If you did, you'd be called all kinds of names by your buddies for fraternizing with the enemy."

The first efforts to bring management and labor together came in the mid-1970s, after the first oil crisis and the strengthening of Japanese imports. The corporation and the union agreed that it was time to change, and in 1977 they took up the Quality of Work Life (QWL) ideas backed by Bluestone and Ephlin. JR Mays, gray-haired and brush-cut today, still a union member but paid as an "organizational development coordinator," remembers,

> "We all sat down at a big table, superintendents and committee people, and talked about what we could do to improve quality and productivity. Everyone was somewhat leery. We'd been at each other's throats for 70 years and it was tough to ask us to change overnight. Here was a person who could have discharged you last week and now he wants to

sit down at the table and show you what a wonderful person he is. And the elected representative who was supposed to protect you was sitting with him.''

Managers did not much like the meetings either. The workers had too many ideas, some far-reaching and some costly. Little came of the meetings and people just stopped going. ''We went back to our old ways,'' Mays says. The Buicks that came out of Flint had the worst quality scores in all of GM.

Nothing much happened for the next few years, in a formal way. However, a couple of the plant managers who rotated through the Buick plant showed some sensitivity and would actually stop and spend a minute with the workers. Al Christner, president of UAW Local 599 at the plant in the 1970s and a pugnacious veteran of the worst days in the plant's labor relations, did not lose faith after the 1975 QWL experiment and continued to try to drag his members towards a new attitude.

When GM decided early in 1983 to create Buick City as a model of how to build a good car economically in the United States, the plant made a fresh start on teamwork. The company gutted the old plant, leaving nothing but the walls, roof, columns, and 1.8 million square feet of empty space. To design a modern, productive factory for the space, Buick set up a committee of six union representatives and 13 managers. ''We did everything,'' says Russ Cook, the day-shift representative for the UAW, a tall, rangy man with a full beard who always wears a cowboy hat (white in summer, black in winter). He had fought QWL ''kicking and screaming'' but he did not see any alternative now to cooperating, other than being out of work. In this design period, he says, ''we were really active in training, team structure, ergonomics.'' Instead of having pits so that workers could get to the undersides of cars, they arranged the line so the cars would be lifted at those points. Cook went to Europe as a part of a team to look at a GM plant in Zaragoza, automatically-guided vehicles in Turin, and other plants, while others from Buick City went to Japan. Then everybody coming to the plant got 80 hours of training in the new way to work.

Not Even a Dirty Look: The Workers' First View of Quality

Production of the 1986 Buick LeSabre started in September, 1985. ''We had the naïve idea that if you gave everyone 80 hours' training it would be Nirvana in here,'' says Cook. ''That didn't work out.'' Buick City was at the start a disaster, for several reasons, some having nothing to do with the new way. When GM shut down the Fisher Body plant in Flint, workers from

Local 581 there could bump workers with less seniority from Local 599 at Buick City —and 2,200 of them did. Although the Local 599 people never carried out the threats of violence they muttered, the work force was sullen and silent. A manager who spent an hour and a half walking through the plant then reported that he was unable to make eye contact with a single worker. He did not get so much as a dirty look. Many of the managers came from elsewhere and had to get used to each other and a new system. GM still believed it could beat the Japanese by pouring money into automation and it spent generously for Buick City's equipment, but that did not help. The optically-guided robots that installed windshields turned out to be purblind; they smashed the windshields into the frames. The automatically guided vehicles were too under-powered to pull their loads.

The members of the 110 teams that ran the plant were nevertheless eager to produce high quality, so eager that they constantly pulled the cord that lit the red lamp that stopped the line. "We told people to pass on only perfect products," Cook says, "but 2,000 people had 2,000 definitions of quality. Everyone was shutting the line off. We couldn't get the car together." The plant added yellow warning lights so the workers could signal trouble without always stopping the line. The workers did not understand how teams were supposed to function, and the managers gave them little help. The teams kept electing new leaders. Other elements of the new system interfered with both quality and production. Just-in-time delivery of parts proved to be anything but. Trucks missed their schedules, parts arrived too early or too late and they piled up in the aisles and the plant's limited storage space.

During its first three months of production, Buick City produced 10 cars per hour. Normally, production of a new car starts with a "slow build," but this was too slow for too long. The plant has a design capacity of 75 cars per hour. The 1986 and the 1987 LeSabres and Oldsmobile 88s that it did ship were terrible—among other things, the windows came out of their guides in the doors; the plant ranked near the bottom by GM's ratings; and sales slipped. In October 1987 the plant manager came on the in-house TV to announce the layoff of the night shift. "This was a significant emotional event," says JR Mays. "He didn't say the plant would shut down, but a lot of us realized this was the last chance for us or we'd have to uproot our families and hit the road."

What impressed the workers then was that management stuck to its quality strategy. The managers resisted the temptation to throw out just-in-time. Instead, they made it work, by weeding out poor suppliers and improving the scheduling. They made the wayward robots do their job properly, or replaced them with humans. "You had the commitment from leadership,"

Mays states. "They didn't back off anything. If you needed a different wrench or tool, no problems. If I needed to go to Janesville to see how a worker does something I have a problem with, I could go. The line operator sees this happening, gets what he needs, develops ownership, sees the team functioning. We have final car [quality] audits every day and the plant manager takes it."

A Pizza for a Problem Solved: Buick's Prize

That manager, Tim Lee, wears a "plant jacket" or windbreaker with UAW and team symbols on it, and he sits in a windowless plant office, not off in some fancy headquarters. He keeps a model of Pontiac's little two-seat Fiero on his desk "to remind me that the whole team has to work." The sporty little Fiero was to have been a quality car. Deming had been a frequent visitor to the plant in Pontiac, Michigan, and he taught the workers the art of statistical quality control. The plant turned out a well-made car, with excellent "fits and finishes." Statistically, it was under control. Unfortunately, the quality effort for the Fiero did not start where it should have, in the design phase. The designers never made up their minds whether the Fiero should be a jazzy little sports car or a cheap commuter. It inherited the Chevette's inferior steering system, it had a tiny gas tank and a feeble engine, and in the early models the coolant from the radiator up front got so chilled on its way back to the engine amidships that cracks developed in the engine block. Lee was manager of the Fiero plant when GM shut it in 1987.

The teams at Buick City finally started to work well. Lee says the plant has functional teams for each segment in the sequence of steps in assembling a car, as well as productivity and maintenance teams. If a particular problem occurs that no one team can deal with, an ad hoc team springs up. "We have one rule," Lee states. "Anyone who has any input to the problem must be on the team." Teams follow a disciplined five-step approach adapted from NUMMI, the joint GM-Toyota plant in California. The teams meet before or after work or during breaks. When they have given an answer, the results are monitored statistically for seven weeks. Only then is the problem declared solved and the teams get recognition in a very modest way, with the gift of a T-shirt or a pizza dinner.

The cars that were produced late in the 1987 model run improved, and the 1989 and 1990 models were much better. In the 1989 J. D. Power & Associates survey of "initial quality" (based on the number of defects buyers report in the first 90 days of ownership), the Buick LeSabre—the model product at Buick City—ranked second, ahead of all other cars except Nissan's Maxima. In 1990, it came in sixth, still a very good showing. Finally, 15 years after the first encounter with Quality of Work Life teams, Buick City had its teams doing it the right way. JR Mays sums it up, "They forgot to tell us it wasn't going to be easy."[27]

THE FORGOTTEN PLAYER: THE MIDDLE MANAGER

American business may have made the mistake at first of thinking of the blue-collar worker as both the source of its problems and the key to its solutions. At least the worker got some attention, and some worthwhile improvements emerged eventually. But the middle manager was at first the forgotten player. Indeed, Florida Power & Light made the mistake of deliberately excluding middle managers. They were told to stay away from the quality improvement teams for fear of stifling them. Naturally, when supervisors saw that people were working around rather than through them to solve problems in their areas of responsibility they did not like it.[28]

The CEO more typically just neglected to include middle managers. "One of the mistakes we made, and I made it," reported Phil Anschutz, chairman (as well as owner) of the Southern Pacific Railroad, "was I didn't spend enough time preparing middle management. In our company, as in many others, that's really where the rubber meets the road and I think these people in middle management feel somewhat caught between either the labor unions here or the rank and and file and senior management and they are not prepared to deal with the changing environment and the speed with which it's changing."[29]

The 15 unions that the SP deals with would agree with Anschutz. At a contentious meeting of the railroad's labor-management advisory committee, which periodically brings together the union leaders and the company executives, Carl James, the general chairman of the Brotherhood of Locomotive Engineers in Denver, drew what he called a "stuff runs downhill" chart. Since quality professionals are chart freaks, he said, he did not think they would understand him unless he put something on the board. The chart showed the training and information and encouragement all pouring down a funnel from the top of the company towards the workers at the bottom—but before the "stuff" got there it met a fault line at the level of the supervisors and dissipated sideways through the faults. "As a consequence, nothing gets down to the employee," James stated. "We embraced the quality process from the beginning. Our people took the courses. But we've gone from positive enthusiasm to indifference. We're in the game but no one is throwing us the ball." Later in the meeting he added, "When we go back to the real world, no one gives a rat's ass what we're doing here. It's business as usual.''[30] Belatedly, SP did turn to its middle managers with training and attention.

What Were They Smoking in Schaumburg?: Motorola's Management Sends a Signal

To get managers turned around, from instinctive opposition to wholehearted support, is one of the more difficult feats a CEO is called on to perform these days. He cannot be heavy-handed—after all, involvement must spring from within—but he has to lead and apply constant pressure.

Ralph Ponce de Leon, son of a Texas railroad man and grandson of a Basque shepherd, knows how the resentment and the pressure felt at the time. He had spent most of his career at Motorola developing new products, but when the company's quality drive began in 1980 he was working at the government electronics group in Scottsdale, helping to provide communications for deep space probes like *Voyager*. "The first sign that things were changing," he says, "was the appointment of Jack Germain as the corporate director of quality." Germain was a Motorola heavyweight, a corporate vice president and assistant general manager of the communications business, Motorola's largest. The chairman, Bob Galvin, meant by this appointment to signal the importance of the job. Ponce de Leon did not get that signal. "Reading the memo about his appointment, we figured Jack had done something terribly wrong, or was closer to retirement than we had thought. Quality is like KP in the military."*

During this early stage Ponce de Leon was a cynic. "We thought we had all the quality we desired [in the deep space probes]. We absolutely resented the intrusion of headquarters in improving quality. We thought they were smoking funny stuff up there in Schaumburg." When Germain asked him to send his quality people to form a Motorola Corporate Quality Council, Ponce de Leon resisted. "I thought, who is this guy? This failure? I'm damned if I'll spend good money on something so pointless! Jack insisted." Finally, Ponce de Leon allowed one quality manager out of four in four plants to go. The manager reported back that elsewhere the company was getting "meaningful metrics"—that is, measurable good results—and im-

---

* Quality engineers, quality directors, and the like used to have little influence in corporations. The jobs went to junior engineers or to older ones put out to pasture. At GE, engineers fresh out of school typically started in quality assurance. Today, a quality engineer or manager is one of the few professionals who can readily find a new job—if he does not decide to become one of the thousands of consultants who have entered the field.

proving on them. "I told him, OK, but don't commit us to anything dumb."

Ponce de Leon continues: "Then we got the first mandate: Improve quality by a factor of ten. We came unglued. It was too costly. It was impossible. The payback was too small. We met with the leaders of the defense business in Arizona and they agreed that it was impossible. We had meetings to figure out why we shouldn't do it. It would cost more and the customers [i.e., in the government] wouldn't pay for it. A 10% improvement would be bad enough. I don't know what discussions they had up in Schaumburg, but we stonewalled the process. Linsicomb [James L., the executive vice president for defense] was on the fence, but he decided to play along. Anyhow, the pressure from Chicago was irresistible. They said they weren't asking for improvement, 'We are telling you and you had better shape up and do it.' " Having allowed people like Ponce de Leon time to get over the original trauma, Schaumburg now demanded that tenfold improvement.

From Bob Galvin's perspective in Schaumburg, this resistance was troublesome and partly his fault because, like other CEOs, he had not paid enough attention to middle management. Motorola increased its training for managers and Galvin and his top executives put a lot of effort into persuading and encouraging their troops. "You know, you use all kinds of techniques," says Galvin. "We made quality much more evident in the compensation plan. That got their attention. . . . I think ultimately what moved everybody over was that they finally realized it was right. . . . One at a time, dozens at a time, hundreds at a time, said, my God, this is right for the customer, and we'll all be better off if we do what is right for the customer."[31]

The Signal Is Received, with Static

"Very reluctantly we began to measure some significant things in 1982 and 1983 and I decided I had better attend some meetings with Germain to protect ourselves," Ponce de Leon continues. "We still really believed it was foolish, but we began to measure and I have to tell you the improvement was almost instantaneous. This would be like switching to driving on the right in England. You have to do it all at once and people see the results immediately. We in the trenches went from cynics to skeptics. We said, 'Let's experiment a little more before we buy in totally.' We went to the Germain meetings mainly defensively, but we began to refine the process."

Rebellion stirred again when Schaumburg told the government division (and the rest of the company) to spend 1.5% of its payroll on training, and 40% of that on quality. "Again the corporation was telling us to do something, but this time it cost money and we got no relief,'' says Ponce de Leon. He was part of a company-wide group of executives who met periodically to review Motorola's training needs. To respond to the new request, and to meet the challenge of the tremendous changes that were overtaking the company, the group decided that Motorola needed new training in manufacturing and management. Ponce de Leon and the others figured it would cost $2 million to establish the training; they went to Galvin to ask for $100,000 to investigate it some more. He gave them the full $2 million on the spot to establish the Motorola Manufacturing Institute, which later became part of Motorola University.

By now, Ponce de Leon's conversion was pretty well complete. "When I saw the value of quality, saw that we were making progress, and when I began to go to Japan and saw that they were always a step ahead of us, I became an absolute zealot." Today he is the Motorola vice president in charge of relations with suppliers.[32]

On occasion, it takes dramatics, emotions, and even threats to move the stolid middle of the company. The CEO of one Fortune 500 company was talking about quality to a group of several hundred engineers at a plant one night, when an engineer said he agreed that quality was imperative but he did not know how to get the people down on the shop floor to make a better product. The CEO said the question disturbed him because he thought the engineers, not the blue-collar workers, were the bigger part of the problem. He said he would go through the plant in the morning looking for ''butcher books'' to prove his point—and if he did not find any, he would apologize humbly to the engineers. Workers make up butcher books to alert others to design mistakes. The books tell others who may be assigned to the same work stations how to make their product line up, or fit, or work in spite of mistakes in the engineering drawings and specifications. As the CEO made his way through the plant in the morning, the workers kept showing him their butcher books and by noon the plant manager had rushed out a newsletter deploring the plant's quality. Within nine months, the plant's engineers had upgraded and computerized all their drawings so that corrections or changes could be inserted at any time and distributed throughout the business.[33]

Even after they have been converted, managers under duress may abandon the Y-theory participative posture and revert to dominating X-theory habits. Ray Stata says that when Analog Devices was several years into its quality drive he still had some senior managers who were were blocking it. "The way that I ultimately prevailed on certain individuals in the organization was to suggest to them that either they get on board or I was going to get other people to do the job,'' Stata explains. The message must have been convincing because he did not have to fire anyone. He adds, however, that ''when you are going to do a paradigm shift or a revolution in the culture . . . threats are not the answer.'' Threats may get rid of or neutralize the saboteurs and the obstructionists, but they do not lead to the conviction that creates activists.[34]

A BURDEN AND A BOOST FOR SUPPLIERS

If a true quality effort means bringing aboard everybody involved in the process, it cannot stop with employees, managers, and bosses. The effort it has to include the suppliers who provide the parts that make up the bulk of the finished products manufactured by large corporations. The traditional companies' relations with suppliers matched their relations with labor: adversarial, untrusting, and at arm's length, in short, nasty. Companies used their suppliers badly, signing short-term contracts based mainly on price not performance, a destructive policy which most government agencies still follow. Corporations kept many suppliers (5,000 each at Ford and Xerox) and aimed at having several suppliers for every item. The quality of their work was considered secondary to the price, although it was critical to the final product. At Ford, ''the low number would very likely get the contract and we always pitted the current supplier against the bidders.''[35]

If suppliers could improve their quality, the potential savings were enormous. At Xerox, for example, purchased materials contributed 80% of the cost of production in the early 1980s, and 8% of those materials were defective. Just how much potential savings could be achieved became apparent when Xerox told its suppliers to shape up. In one year, from 1982 to 1983, the defect rate dropped from 8% to 3%, and then it continued on down to less than .03% by 1988.[36] These rates of improvement came out of an overhaul of corporate relations with their suppliers. The corporations cut the number of their suppliers sharply, from 5,000 to 350 at Xerox and to 1,700 at Ford. They graded the performance of their suppliers carefully. Xerox divided them into red, yellow, and green categories, and though it continued to buy from the red and yellow, it bought new parts only from the green. Corporations told their suppliers to adopt quality policies, sometimes in a rigorous way, or lose their contracts. Motorola requires suppliers to apply for the Baldrige Award and as of 1992 knew of 175 firms had applied out of a possible 3,000.[37] Each year, Motorola reminds those that have not applied that they should, but obviously is suspending sentence on those that fail to apply and putting them on probation. IBM has asked its suppliers to follow the Baldrige criteria, without formally applying for the award. For those suppliers willing to play along, these companies provide incentives, including training and other help, and long-term exclusive contracts.

In some ways it is easier for a small company than for a big company to move to total quality, simply because it is small. The people know the product, they know each other, they know the customer. On the other hand, the training and the reorganization can be a heavy burden to a small company. Suppliers often answered the demands of their clients with the same rebelliousness showed by middle managers. Motorola was accused of coercion, and Galvin figures that several score suppliers refused to go along with the Baldrige requirement. A. Blanton Godfrey, chairman of the Juran Institute, sees some damage from the demand for suppliers to move rapidly to total quality: "Sometimes this pressure has encouraged cut-throat competition among numerous small companies. Many times the large companies have meant to help by making quality assessments and audits. Although well meaning, many of these activities have been destructive rather than constructive." The burden on suppliers to the auto industry became particularly heavy, since each one of the Big Three had fairly complicated systems for qualifying favored suppliers. Godfrey reported that "some small businesses have shared with me the enormous work load imposed by their three largest customers, the automobile companies, in preparing for the quality audits. Each company's demands are different enough that the small businesses have prepared three sets of quality manuals, briefed their people differently for each visit and wasted hundreds of hours preparing manuals and paperwork for an inspection rather than actually implementing total quality management." But he concluded that overall the effort was useful.[38]

When Honda came to the United States it brought with it the special Japanese view of how to treat suppliers, as well as misgivings about American suppliers. In the first year of auto production at Marysville, Ohio, in 1982, Honda bought a few parts from only a handful of American suppliers. Suppliers in the United States just could not meet the specifications the company expected. Gradually Honda's purchases of U.S. products increased, reaching $2.93 billion from 246 original equipment manufacturers in the fiscal year ending in March, 1993. Tom Griffith, manager of purchasing support and development at the auto assembly plant in Marysville, says Honda has never dropped an American supplier for quality reasons (although it has for other reasons). "As long as they show willing to improve, we'll work with them," says Griffith. "If they are not meeting their targets, we'll send a team to help them rather than end the relationship. We'll put as many as 60 to 80 people working with a supplier to make parts. Several years ago, a supplier was only getting 20% on the first pass [i.e., only 20% of the parts, an incredibly low level, were usable without some fixing] and we sent 12 to 15 people up there to show how we did it. We got them up to 85% in three weeks.'' Honda has one interesting technique for showing suppliers it means business. The contracts say that if they send any bad parts they will have to come to the Honda plant and separate the bad parts from the good ones and remove them. The first time Honda calls to report a shipment of bad parts, the supplier asks, Do you really mean for us to come? Honda does mean it. But on the other hand, Griffith's people spend a lot of time at the suppliers' plants, helping out.[39]

TRAINING: THE MOST IMPORTANT LEVER

Training and education are critical in converting a company to quality. To draw his leery troops into the unknown regions of quality, a leader must give his own strong example of commitment, his patience and persistence, he must use a dash of guile and the occasional bludgeon. But without training, the troops will not know what to do. Galvin believes that "training is the single most important lever" in bringing about change in a company.[40] As a corporate veteran who had a total of about two hours of training (how to use a new phone system) in more than three decades at Time Inc., I am amazed at the amount of training corporations offer today. IBM was famous for insisting that all its managers take 40 hours of training a year, mainly on personnel matters, or human relations, to use the more exalted term in vogue. Today, many corporations have surpassed IBM in the amount of training required. Corning gave *all* its employees an average of 91.5 hours of training focused on quality in 1991.[41] Michael Bennett, president of UAW Local 1853 at GM's Saturn plant, remembers that when he first went to work on GM's line in Flint his foreman said, "Put that there, press this, and then throw it in there." So much for his training. Today at Saturn even an experienced auto assembler cannot touch a car before taking 350 hours of training. Skilled tradespeople must have 700 hours of training—which amounts to four months, full time.[42]

A whole industry has grown up around teaching quality to corporate employees. Crosby College in Florida and the Juran Institute in Connecticut are among the leaders in the field. However, once they are launched on their quality journeys, corporations usually design their own training—which may be an amalgam of Crosby, Juran, Deming, and corporate experience— and they even may create their own schools. Corning and IBM both have Quality Institutes. A much smaller company, Solectron Corporation, a $265-

million-a-year maker of customized circuit boards and winner of the Baldrige Award in 1991, has Solectron University. All employees get 95 hours of training a year, much of it in quality.[43] Motorola's training efforts have grown to a level unimaginable a decade ago. Motorola University has a full-time staff of 110 and a part-time staff of 300. Its training budget of $7 million at the beginning of the decade grew to $60 million by the end of the decade, and that did not include $60 million in salaries paid to Motorolans while they took courses.[44] By 1992, Motorola's spending on training reached $110 million annually. Although Motorola trains its people in many matters, quality is the focus.

In the course of trying to train and educate its work force, corporate America itself received quite an education. Unlike the nation's secondary school system, and its universities for that matter, the corporations proved able to adjust and innovate rapidly to make their training more effective. The first lesson learned was that many workers were too uneducated to be trained. Milliken found most of its workers read below the eighth-grade level. At Motorola, says William Wiggenhorn, the vice president for training and education, "we discovered to our utter astonishment that much of our work force was illiterate. They couldn't read. They couldn't do simple arithmetic like percentages and fractions. At one plant, a supplier changed its packaging, and we discovered in the nick of time that our people were working by the color of the package." Here was a world leader in high technology, and 40% of its employees could not express the number 10 as a percentage of 100! Obviously, corporations had to start with some basic education. You cannot teach the tools of statistical process controls (see Chapter 5) to workers who cannot read or figure a percentage. At Motorola, workers lacking basic skills were given the choice of retraining or being fired if they refused. The company did have to fire 18 long-term employees who refused.[45]

When the quality training began, to put it in the words of Milliken's director of human relations, John Rampey, executives believed "training is something that top management thinks that middle management should do to front-line management."[46] That did not work out. "We made one big mistake in our training," Galvin says, "and that was we failed to train from the top down and very often we trained people at the bottom of the hierarchy of the institution, who came back to their departments ready to do something." But there they encountered bosses who had not had the training and they were just told to do things the old way. Middle managers became the inhibitors.[47] Everybody needed training. Although top executives are quick to grasp quality concepts, their behavior is not likely to change without training. Middle managers need training if they are going to encourage and help their people to work differently. Galvin decided that he personally needed to be as well trained as his Japanese counterparts and he took the quality training. Unless the CEO and his top people understand in detail the concepts that the rest of the company is supposed to use, then they cannot lead the change effectively.

Cascading Through Xerox

The Xerox "cascade" approach to training has become a classic case of how to do it right. David Kearns, the chairman, started the training personally. First the senior management trained. Kearns himself, having already made more than 25 trips to Japan, now visited other companies, attended the Crosby school, and talked to and read the works of Deming and Juran. Then he taught the people who reported to him a six-day, 48-hour course that had already been tested in the company's real-estate group. The course began with a half-day of orientation and then continued with a problem-solving exercises. The course stressed the customer, so that Xerox people would always think of the requirements of the customer, whether external or internal, before taking any action (and if there is no customer, then do not do it). It also stressed the "interactive skills" that are necessary to make teams work; for example, learning not to attack or defend positions.

The training began early in 1984 and began to cascade down through the company. Kearns trained the people who reported to him and they trained the people who reported to them and so it went on down through the company. Since everyone in the company (except at the very top and bottom) both took the training and gave it, they all had a total of 96 hours' training. Not only did the second round reinforce the lesson, but when you teach a subject you learn it better than when you sit in a class as a student. The courses were given in "family groups," that is, all the people from a particular work area or office would train together. When they got back to work they all understood the new doctrine. By the summer of 1984 the cascade was flowing, and by 1985 hundreds of "family groups" were training every month.[48]

Corporations have also learned to give training just in time, that is, when it is going to be needed. Sending people for training before teams and quality improvement processes have started is a mistake, and the lessons are soon forgotten. "Managers think it's great to send people off for training, but there is nothing worse than lecturing to a bunch of people who have been sent by their managers," says Lloyd Nelson, formerly of the Nashua Corporation, who knows what it feels like. "You answer a lot of unasked questions." Nashua sent everybody on its payroll to training over a period of a year and a half, but the training did not take because the people had no immediate use for their new knowledge. Skills learned only in the classroom and not applied fade within a few weeks. But if employees have started work on an improvement or on a team and find they need to know how to take samples or apply statistical process controls, then they are ready for those lectures.[49] L. L. Bean has discovered that if you wait and withhold instruction until it is needed, you create "a thirst for training" and have to hold people back, rather than dragging them to class.[50]

"Do Not Attack or Defend": Facilitators

The quality movement created a special need for training by people who are termed *facilitators*. Essentially, they coach teams. The American manager and worker have no experience with the kind of teamwork required today. They have been to meetings where they are told what to do, or where they make a suggestion or two, and then are told what to do. People come to meetings prepared to defend their positions or attack the positions of others. The classic business meeting is an exercise in one-upmanship, a form of combat civilized on the surface and savage just below. A quality improvement team would disintegrate if it went by the old rules. By definition, the quality team needs the open-minded, unparochial, and creative participation of its members. Without a facilitator to teach the team how to behave, it is likely to get nowhere.

William W. Barnard, a Juran Institute vice president who specializes in training corporate facilitators, defines a facilitator as "a coach, teacher, therapist, ambassador. He's not a member of the team and he sits symbolically against the wall." He is there to achieve consensus, reduce resistance, and manage conflict. The new theory of teamwork says you do not take votes. Rather, you work towards a consensus that everyone can accept. You do not attack or defend. You draw out the ideas of even the most timid member. At the same time, the meeting has to be businesslike, have a purpose and accomplish it, show progress.[51] Without a knowledgeable coach at the meetings, people are not likely to learn how to shed their old behavior or acquire the new behavior. Corporations have adopted many approaches toward quality training, but the use of facilitators seems almost universal.

URGED TO COOPERATE, PAID TO COMPETE: INCENTIVES

Once employees are motivated and trained, what incentives and rewards will work best to reinforce that training? To encourage better performance and productivity, corporations have moved towards greater use of merit pay, CEOs being exempt, of course. But does not merit pay encourage individual contributions rather than team contributions, rewarding the opposite of what we want to achieve today? As *Training* magazine put it in a headline, "When employees are urged to cooperate but paid to compete, you've got a little problem."[52] One of the most difficult and controversial sides of TQM centers on the question of individual recognition. Deming, never one to understate his case, described the merit rating or annual review as "Management by fear. . . . The effect is devastating. It nourishes short-term performance, annihilates long-term planning, builds fear, demolishes teamwork, nourishes rivalry and politics."[53] To neutralize competition in the classroom, Deming himself gave all his students at New York University an "A."

Deming argued that it is impossible to rate people numerically or on a scale, but that is precisely what corporations want to do. IBM, for example, designates the best 10% and the worst 10% of its managers. The best rate promotion and pay increases; the bottom 10% know they must improve or they may be fired. In a company torn up by cutbacks and low morale, that system certainly has the effect of spreading terror. Some companies are modifying their systems. Xerox reduced the categories of performance rankings from five to three, and turned more to coaching than rating. Ford, which frequently discussed its rating system with Deming, tries to de-emphasize individual ratings in favor of team ratings. "Deming would give everybody the same raise for their first ten years with the company or until a real difference opens up between people," says James Paulsen, Ford's director of quality. "We are not yet ready to accept that but we are debating it."[54] Nashua is one of the few companies to have dropped performance appraisals . . . but, says the CEO, Charles Clough, "we meet with the people and review their strengths."[55]

Peter R. Scholtes, a consultant with the Brian Joiner firm in Madison, Wisconsin, which follows Deming's teachings, agrees that not many companies are following Deming's advice. He says only two or three of Joiner's clients have completely dumped performance appraisals and he is not pushing the others. "You can make real progress without getting rid of appraisals and eventually they will get to it," Scholtes says. "As long as people are entrenched in the previous paradigm, not much can be gained by challenging the pivotal symbol of the old system."[56] But it does seem odd to argue against competitive ratings of employees as anti-quality, when the whole purpose of improving quality is to compete better.

The Juran Institute sides with the majority view in business that evaluations remain a valid management tool. John Early, a Juran vice president, says that arguing about appraisals creates a distraction from the main task of improving quality. You will always need some sort of evaluations. Without evaluations, he asks, how do you decide who to promote? Instead of getting rid of evaluations, you should make them serve the purpose of improving quality. That is, include in the evaluations a factor that depends on the employees' contribution to improving quality, as Ford, Motorola, and Xerox have done.[57]

The International Quality Study of four industries in four countries (autos, banking, computers, and health care; in Canada, Germany, Japan, and the United States) found a strong tendency to reduce the importance of individual performance in ratings and raise the importance of team performance. In the auto, banking, and computer industries individual contributions still count for more than team contributions today, but the survey revealed the intention to reverse these priorities. In all three industries, however, profitability is and will remain a more significant factor in rating executives than either individual or team performance. In health care, the survey did not report the importance of individual efforts, but it did show a future leap in the rating of team efforts.[58]

Away with Commissions

Although pay practices tend to go along with appraisal practices, employers seem to be more willing to experiment with pay, both for hourly workers and for management. Companies are moving away from hourly pay rates and commissions (as well as time clocks) to flat salaries, or salaries plus bonuses. The bonus can be based on team efforts as well as individual efforts. Milliken has done away with piecework and instead pays its "associates" (formerly the mill hands) on the basis of the skills they have acquired. Seniority at Milliken also depends on skills, not years. At Saturn, the UAW and management devised a plan that gives the employees a base pay of 80% of the prevailing pay in the auto industry, which is $28,000 a year for assemblers and $32,000 for the skilled trades. Three levels of bonuses can be piled on top of that, one based on quality and productivity, another on Saturn reaching the break-even point, and another on profits (which have not yet been paid). The dollar amounts of the bonuses are the same for the plant manager and the press operator. Some of the Saturn pay is also at risk because 5% is withheld until a worker has completed the 92 hours of training required annually.[59]

At Alcoa, the pay of all employees became partly variable when the company reorganized in 1991, and the more senior the employee, the larger the variable portion of the pay. Half of the variable part is tied to return on equity and the other half to nonfinancial indicators, such as quality, safety, environment, or energy consumption. Each business unit can make its own mix of nonfinancial indicators.[60] Arthur D. Little, the 100-year-old Cambridge consulting firm, has embraced TQM for itself as well as for its clients and has devised an interesting pay scheme for its 12 offices in Europe. To make sure that each office acts as a team, and that the 12 teams help each other to make the whole European operation a success, the variable pay or bonus is divided into three parts. One part of an individual's bonus depends on his own performance, another on the performance of the office, and the third on the overall performance of ADL in Europe.[61]

The commissions sacred to salespeople may not survive TQM. The Saturn dealerships have switched to salaried salespeople and are doing well. James McIngvale, owner of the Gallery Furniture Store and famous as "Mattress Mac" on the TV ads for his store in Dallas, attributes a 40% increase in profits and a 20% increase in sales in 1991 and 1992 to the switch to salaries instead of commissions for his salespeople. He says, "we have refocused the organization to where everybody works for the good of the company and not for the good of themselves, we eliminated turnover, eliminated all the problems that went along with commission sales." Instead of thinking, "How am I gonna ram this furniture down the customer's throat?" the salespeople are patient and low-keyed and they sell more. Instead of fighting each other, now they cooperate. "We have a lot of Hispanics and if an Anglo salesperson greeted a Hispanic customer, husband and wife, that wanted to buy furniture and wanted someone to speak Spanish to them, that was tough," explains McIngvale. "He wasn't going to give that customer up. He stayed with them the whole time even if they didn't buy. About two months after we switched from commission to salary, we had a Hispanic couple come in here. The Anglo salesperson greeted them and wasn't really getting anywhere with them, so he went and got a Hispanic saleslady to help 'em and they spent $45,000. Otherwise, they walk out the door." McIngvale does not rank or rate any of his people. When he got 22 tickets to the 1993 Superbowl, instead of picking his top producers (whom he does not track in any case) to go, he put the names of all 140 employees in a hat and drew winners.[62]

The Champion of Recognition

A boss I had 25 years or so ago once told his assembled staff that when we did a good job, we would not hear from him. We were paid to do a good job and we got our pay check, didn't we? But we would certainly hear from him if we fouled up. Such a tough-guy treatment of employees would be unthinkable to any right-minded TQM employer today. Warm fuzzies abound so much that the TQM workplace sometimes seems to have the atmosphere of a grade-school stage performance where the parents applaud everything, no matter how screechy the violin playing or how many lines get forgotten. Applause has become as important as pay and performance appraisals in reinforcing the kind of behavior that leaders want from their associates. The recognition does not have to be elaborate or expensive; indeed, the low cost is one of its appeals. At Conrail, where workers used to hear only criticism from their bosses, now when they complete a team effort successfully they may get a lunch in the upstairs dining room, or tickets to a Phillies game, or just a thank-you note. Throughout TQM companies you find a proliferation of small prizes—T-shirts, pizzas, plaques, photographs.

The team is the focus of the rewards and recognitions and sometimes team achievements are celebrated with considerable pomp and circumstance. Hewlett-Packard and Motorola, among others, have worldwide team competitions. At Motorola, some 2,000 teams compete on the basis of how well they work as a team, how well they pick their projects, how good their analytical techniques and remedies are, and so forth. From the plant level up, they go through various levels of contests until a few survivors—17 in 1991—meet to make their presentations at a global final for the corporate gold medal. Milliken probably is the champion of recognition. There cannot be a wall left at Milliken that is not covered with plaques, testimonials, thank-you letters, group photographs, slogans, and reports on achievements. Signs in the hallways at Milliken headquarters in Spartanburg say, "Safety belt performance 98%." Milliken security people periodically check whether employees leaving the parking lot have buckled up, and those who have get a coupon entitling them to a free soft drink or something else of similar value. So pervasive is the positive reinforcement at Milliken that another visitor who went through a day's briefing with me asked, "Doesn't this remind you of *1984*?"

Some visitors may find the constant boosting at Milliken corny and a bit oppressive, but there is no doubt that the company finds it useful. "The two things visitors always look at here are our recognition systems and sharing rallies." says Patrick Bowie, the vice president for quality. "Their power is

unbelievable. Our morale scores are the highest ever and absenteeism is at
a record low."[63] The cynic might add: They had better be, or else. "The
critical elements of recognition," said a briefer at Milliken, "is that it be
nonfinancial and frequent." Teams that reach a milestone get a team jacket.
Associates who win the "associate of the month" award get a special
parking slot for that month. The marker for the slot is movable so the
associate picks the reserved place. Roger Milliken and Tom Malone do not
have reserved spots. The levels of recognition at Milliken reach up to the
"sharing rallies" held four times a year where teams get to tell about their
successes (never their failures), the "gazelle award," which is the highest
team prize, and the awards banquet held annually with flags and banners
flying at the company retreat, Calloway Gardens, at Pine Island, Georgia.

Tom Malone becomes pretty enthusiastic himself when he explains the
hoopla at Milliken:

> "You're creating an environment in which it's exciting to make break-
> throughs. But it's even more exciting to be able to share it with others
> and be applauded. This applause, applause, applause comes from your
> peers as well as your leaders. These are key, key things that we learned
> that you have to establish and I know this is controversial with some
> of the consultants, but you have to establish the competition, the score-
> boards have gotta be time and measurement, and you've got to estab-
> lish that you are striving for something bigger than today's game. You
> gotta have championships. You gotta have winners, you've gotta have
> goals, you've gotta have most valuable players, and you've gotta have
> fans in the stands. Those are the four ingredients of what I call creating
> the Super Bowl environment. That's what creates sustained excite-
> ment. If you don't have that stretch goal of the championship, of being
> better than anyone ever dreamed you could be, it's just another day."[64]

CONCLUSIONS

The total quality approach changes fundamentally the way American companies regard and treat their people, moving from policing their performance
to engaging their enthusiasm and talents. Like any major change, this one
has not been easy.

- The first round of employee involvement, the quality circle experiment,
  failed because it assumed that the workers could solve a company's
  problems without leadership or training.

- Subsequent efforts were handicapped by top management's failure at first to include middle managers, who were the most threatened and therefore the most hostile to empowering the people whom they were accustomed to ordering around.
- As the idea of involvement took hold, the team concept adopted many shapes and sizes. There is no one mold. However, the successful team needs to include everyone involved in a process, and that can stretch to people outside the company, the suppliers and customers.
- Unless they are trained in teamwork and quality methods, employees will not know what to do.
- The training needs to start at the top of the company and then cascade down.
- The training needs to be delivered just when it is needed, not before-hand, because employees will forget what they have learned, and not later because employees will get frustrated.
- Management needs to change the incentives, so that pay, bonus, and evaluations contain quality ingredients. Deming and others argue that evaluations to rate employee performance interfere with a company's performance, but most employers cannot figure how else to know whom to promote.
- Employee involvement needs much reinforcement through rewards and recognition. The rewards should be small, even corny, but they should be frequent and widespread.
- Even when the team concept is introduced in the right way, it will be difficult to embed in a company.

4

The Customers
Are You Listening?

"In the middle of the 1980s somebody put a bee in my bonnet that I ought to go out and talk to more customers," Bob Galvin recalls. "I remember my reaction. . . . What does that person mean? I talked to two customers last week. I took a trip for Ford at one time." Like most CEOs, Motorola's chief did not really know the customers, certainly not down at the level of the people who used the products. But Galvin, receptive to his people's ideas, accepted the suggestion. He dreamed up a scheme of spending one day a month with one corporate customer, talking to anyone and everyone there who had a relationship with Motorola, but preferably not vice presidents nor the chief executive.

Galvin got an earful. "We're sitting off in the corner of a cafeteria in the Ford Motor Company talking with the people in the payables department. Not any fancy spot; it's wherever this gang of people normally convenes. They pay us for the computers we shipped them and a fine accountant, no fancy title, can't wait to get at the pile of papers he's got. 'Well,' I said to him, 'Tell me what's on your mind, sir.' This guy comes right out and says, 'Galvin, let me show you something. See all these papers? I've been three weeks trying to reconcile our purchase order to your shipment to our inspection report so I can pay your bill. That doesn't add one penny of value to a Ford car and it's all because you had mistakes in your billings and in your [shipment] ticket that became the basis of our receiving ticket. I've been wasting my time reconciling this situation and if I were in charge of this company, I wouldn't buy any goddamned electronic controls from you because you upset the accounting department too much. Of course, Red Poling wouldn't know that. . .' "

It was the same kind of story wherever Galvin went. The people he saw were very frank, to put it mildly, and after each trip he would write a report of 14 pages or so detailing his findings. Galvin goes on:

"After about the fourth trip, I could have written the fifth, sixth, seventh . . . twelfth. All I had to do was change the name of the product or the name of the person. I discovered we had just about the same problems in every instance regardless of the business. One of the fascinating fundamentals discerned from the experience was that I didn't learn anything. . . I didn't learn anything. . . Now I'll continue the sentence . . . that the [Motorola] account executive hadn't known for two years or nine months or what have you. Nothing. Somebody already knew everything that I learned. But when I came back and wrote this up and sent it out to the relevant people, everybody took each line item and said, 'Oh, Bob, we gotta do something about that.' So now we do what the customer wanted done. Isn't that a shame, because here's the account executive, who's been trying to get it done for two years, nine months, or what have you, and the institution wasn't responding adequately. I advocated that credentialed sales people should have the power of the chief executive officer and that that should become the accepted culture or policy of the organization. We aren't achieving that yet. People are at least paying a lot more attention to salespeople, although they are not acting as if George Fisher [Galvin's successor as CEO] had called and said, 'Fix that and have it by Friday.' "[1]

THE CUSTOMER COMES FIRST

It almost seems too obvious to be worth pointing out that quality must focus on the customer, but it took U.S. business leaders a long time to figure out what that really meant, and some may not have gotten it yet. John Marous, the former chairman of Westinghouse, believes that lack of knowledge of the customer and the inability to understand him and anticipate his needs is, even today, one of the great weaknesses of U.S. business. Visit a company and ask the chairman if he knows on a weekly basis how satisfied his customers are, suggests Marous, and it is doubtful that he will.[2]

At the beginning of the quality campaign in the United States more than a decade ago, it was first seen at some companies, Xerox and Westinghouse, for example, more as an effort to raise productivity. Satisfying the customer was secondary. Then, as the focus shifted from productivity to quality because quality provides a more capacious frame for building competitiveness, companies began looking at customers more carefully, but at first through their own eyes, not the customers'. To judge quality, they used internal measures of their own devising, mainly measures of mistakes, or things gone wrong. When a company got around to deciding what to sell its customers, it would depend on what its own technology had created, what it had available, and what its own managers and engineers thought the customers would like—as IBM customers kept complaining, year after year.

Three decades ago George Moore, the chairman of First National City Bank (now Citicorp), and Tom Watson of IBM commuted together in the New Haven Railroad club car between suburban Greenwich, Connecticut and Grand Central Terminal in New York City. During these hour-long rides, Moore tried unsuccessfully to persuade Watson that his banks could use IBM's forthcoming 360 mainframes and that they should have random access memories (which the 360 lacked at that time). Citicorp finally turned to ITT, which did have random access memory, but the ITT computer never performed well—and IBM didn't learn.[3] Decades later IBM still had the same problem. IBM chairman John Akers proclaimed 1987 to be "The Year of the Customer," but even then IBM did not go much beyond the slogan.

A year later IBM called senior representatives of its biggest customers to an intimate meeting with its top managers and asked them to speak frankly. They did. Again, IBM heard that its clients saw the company as unresponsive, uncooperative, slow—in short, arrogant. "If the product specifications or the price or the support or the timetable isn't to the customer's satisfaction, IBMers have to change it." Akers said, laying down the new law. "We never used to do that. . . . In the past, we never changed a thing. We had one price; we had one date. And that was it."[4] Akers unveiled, early in 1990, a new effort called "Market-Driven Quality" which at least had the priorities right. Now IBM would be studying its customers, not its own navel. But it was getting very late. In 1989 IBM was the most profitable company in the world. For 1992 IBM reported a net loss of $4.97 billion, an all-time record for a corporation. (The record stood for only a few weeks because it was eclipsed by much larger losses at Ford and General Motors. However, these two auto companies' losses were attributable mainly to accounting changes for retiree health benefits. Their *operating* losses were smaller than IBM's.)

Even Xerox, with a better organized approach to quality than IBM's, took its time to get the right focus on the customer. In 1983, Xerox set three priorities for its new Leadership Through Quality campaign: return on assets, market share, and customer satisfaction. The three were supposed to be equal, but they were always listed in that order, with ROA first, and there was no doubt which came first in everybody's minds. In 1987, when the Xerox campaign seemed to stall, David Kearns reversed the order, putting customer satisfaction first and making clear that it was the first among equals. In 1992, Xerox added a fourth priority, employee satisfaction, and put it in the No. 2 position. "Employee satisfaction" does not mean that Xerox wants a company of happy people, but rather a company of healthy discontents who are satisfied because they feel they can improve the company.[5]

"The Same Old Lovable Company": L. L. Bean

Long before TQM appeared, some companies already lived customer satisfaction, none more so than L. L. Bean, the Maine hunting shoe company that came to be loved, if a company can be loved, for its willingness to make the customer happy at almost any cost. The company lives by the Golden Rule written down by Leon Leonwood Bean when he founded the company in 1912: "Sell good merchandise at reasonable profits, treat your customers like human beings, and they'll always come back for more." In fact, the first merchandise L.L. sold was terrible. He shipped 100 pairs of the Maine Hunting Shoe (Beanies capitalize the name) and 90 came back because the leather uppers had come unstitched from the rubber bottoms. L. L. borrowed money, redesigned the shoe, and sent new ones to his angry customers free of charge. These shoes stayed stitched, so L. L. established a reputation not only for selling a good shoe, but also for honesty and for standing behind his product.

Over the years, a kind of folklore grew up around Bean's legendary attention the customer. There was the time, for instance, when an anxious New Yorker called on a Friday evening because he was going on a hunting trip in the morning and his new canoe had not arrived. A Beanie tied a second canoe to the roof of his car and drove the 300-and-some miles from Freeport, Maine, to New York City to get the customer his canoe in time. The company's guarantee was virtually unconditional. A fishing rod would be replaced no matter how much abuse it had suffered. Once, Bean did demur on replacing a roof rack it had sold. The owner had rolled his car over and crushed the rack; he contended that it should have held up under the weight of the car. To make sure that sportsmen hurrying north at strange hours can always get what they need, the Bean store in Freeport stays open 24 hours a day, 365 days a year.

Bean's devotion to the customer was achieved without TQM. It came naturally, as it does to some companies, especially when there is a well-established vision accompanied by a continuity of leadership. So when Bean applied for a Baldrige Award in 1988, its first year, the company came close to winning. The Baldrige examiners said Beans' customer relations were the best they had seen. But the company did not win because it did not have a fully developed quality plan.

Impressed they may have been, but the Baldrige examiners said Bean could do better by its customers. In fact, rushing that canoe overnight to New York may have been heroic, but as quality assurance it was flawed. That was the old way of achieving quality: something goes wrong and you fix it. "Our computers had a lot of 'fix-it' systems to handle returns, to compensate for vendors' poor quality, but the whole system was not designed to make it happen right the first time," says Robert Peixotto, Bean's chief of human resources and quality. When Leon A. Gorman became president after his grandfather's death in 1967, he went through the company systematically upgrading products and services. He also hired a marketing whiz, Bill End, now president of Lands' End [the name is a coincidence]. A lovable little company with sales of $4.75 milllion a year then grew into a lovable big company with sales of nearly $600 million a year. After Bean took a shot at the Baldrige, it started examining itself all over again. "We had high-quality products but not high-quality processes," says Peixotto. "The cultural change from problem solving to prevention is a huge undertaking."

They Can't Say "No"

The trick was to keep all the things that made customers love Bean, but to focus more closely on what they really wanted. It turned out they wanted a wider offering of apparel and they wanted to be able to see the products better in those delightfully folksy catalogues the company produced. With the guidance of a team, which functioned rather loosely without too much stress on formal quality-improvement tools, Bean produced a new style of catalogue with bigger, crisper photos and more informative captions set in larger type. By 1991 Bean had 55 teams working on improvements. They were cross-functional (people from different departments) and cross-level (people of different ranks), and members checked their rank at the door. They looked into the whole panoply of TQM activities, from the systems of rewards and recognition to relationships with vendors, under the guidance of David A. Garvin, a Harvard Business School professor and author of *Managing Quality*.

For the customers who make 9,000,000 toll-free calls a year to Bean, it's pretty much the same old lovable company. The calls come into a vast, pleasantly cluttered hall in the company's Portland offices. Scattered among the scores of booths are displays of Bean gear for the sales reps to check out. Most of the reps are talking unhurriedly on the phone, comfortably installed with personal ergonomic aids, such as foot rests, stand-up desks, and lifts to put the video screens at just the right height. About the only thing a sales rep cannot do over the phone without consulting a superior is say "No." For almost anything else, the rep can make the decision. When a customer calls in with a complaint, the salesperson encourages the client to suggest a fair settlement. The terms of a guarantee are really up to the customer. Sometimes the customers' questions get pretty detailed; then the reps can pass them on to specialists. One of them, Susan Jowett, an unflappable, motherly woman, has taken her children camping so when parents call wanting to know what to take for their small children on a camping trip to Baxter State Park, she knows what they will need. She also knows what flies a fisherman should take to the Rio Grande in the fall. She can talk about shooting tapers (a kind of fly-fishing line) and when a customer wants to find out what to do about an air mattress that leaks, Mrs. Jowett says she recommends foam mattresses; air mattresses almost always leak. A sales rep calls on behalf of a customer in Africa who is looking for a solar heated shower. Bean does not carry them, but Mrs. Jowett finds out who does from a stack of other companies' catalogues at her desk, and the information is relayed to the customer.

Beanies relate to their customers because they are outdoor people themselves. When hiring, says Peixotto, "We look for the outdoorsman in each of us." They are encouraged to borrow equipment for a weekend to test it. All the salaried employees are expected to go out in the wilderness once a year, winter camping, white-water canoeing, or mountain climbing. They know what their customers want because they want the same things. What the customer does not know is that the whole system behind the lovable character was and continues to be improved to eliminate product defects, mistakes in shipments, errors in bills, and delays in deliveries. For example, during the whole period between March 1 and May 27, 1992, the Bean shipping center in Freeport made a total of 50 errors in packaging while shipping 100,000 packages a day. That was 40% better than 1991, which in turn was 40% better than in 1990.[6]

Everybody Is a Customer

If a company as imbued with the tradition of serving the customer as L. L. Bean can learn so much from TQM, think what TQM can do, say, for the auto industry or for banking, businesses that often seem to regard the customer as a pest. Long before Xerox and IBM and the others began struggling with new approaches to dealing with the customer, the Japanese had developed some ways of satisfying the customer that gave them enormous competitive power. They study the customer to a degree bordering on fanaticism. Japanese pencil makers know that Americans prefer a longer point to their pencils than Japanese customers. Japanese automakers know the difference between how Americans and Japanese like their cars to smell. When a Japanese automaker decides to design a new delivery van it sends senior executives out to drive delivery vans for several months. Imagine GM putting a vice president behind the wheel of a delivery van in Detroit or New York, even for a day! When the Takenaka Corporation finishes a building, it does not just collect the certificate of occupancy and pass the building on to the customer. Takenaka comes back in six months to ask the customer how the building is meeting expectations. Then they ask again in one year, in three years, in seven years, and yet again in ten years. Takenaka talks to the users of the buildings as well as the owners or operators. If it is a hospital, do the patients find it quiet enough? If an apartment building, are the housewives happy with the kitchens? Takenaka gets 80% of its contracts without any bidding—which presumably results at least partly from the quality of its work and not entirely from the clubbiness of Japanese construction firms.[7]

Several fundamentally different concepts about the customer underly this kind of performance. When he was consulting for a steel mill in 1950, Kaoru Ishikawa heard one group of workers complain that the steel plate delivered to them had scratches and other defects. Ishikawa asked, why not go to the next work group upstream to find out why the steel plate got damaged? To the workers that sounded at first like consorting with the enemy, as it would in any red-blooded American company. But out of the suggestion arose the whole idea that the customer is not only the final buyer, but, as Ishikawa wrote, "your customer is the next process."[8]

That changes the whole way you look at a company: everybody is a customer and everybody has a customer, and unless you are meeting a customer's needs you are not doing anything worthwhile. The concept is particularly useful in curbing the excesses of corporate staffs. The staff is no longer the lordly ruler of the working divisions. Unless the staff serves the divisions, it is useless. The information systems staff can no longer churn out volumes of data just because the computers are so versatile and the staff is so clever. Unless the data has a customer who needs it, the exercise is pointless.

More important, each employee becomes responsible for quality. If you follow the Honda motto—"Accept no bad parts, make no bad parts, and pass on no bad parts"[9]—you have a good prescription for quality that makes everyone a customer.

THE CUSTOMER SPEAKS OUT

Push versus Pull

Toyota developed the second fundamentally new concept about the customer. It was born when Taichi Ohno, who designed the Toyota production system, observed the U.S. supermarket in the 1940s. He later wrote: "A supermarket is where a customer can get (1) what is needed, (2) at the time needed, (3) in the amount needed." In other words, the customer pulls the groceries through the system. This thought led to a wholly different way of looking at production: "Manufacturers and workplaces can no longer base production on desktop planning alone and then distribute, or *push* their products into the market. It has become a matter of course for customers, or users, each with a different value system, to stand in the front line of the marketplace and, so to speak, *pull* the goods they need, in the amount and at the time they need them."[10]

The Toyota insight led to just-in-time production (see Chapter 5) and to the corollary "market in" concept: you abandon the bad old "market out" approach of letting the engineers and the managers decide what to produce and when; instead, you get the market to tell you what to produce and when, and then you respond, rapidly. To satisfy their customers, companies perform feats that would have been unthinkable a few years ago. In the late 1980s, if you ordered a batch of 18″×18″ carpet tiling from Milliken, you would have to wait 16 weeks for delivery. Today you can get it in one week if you put in a large order. If it is a small order, which Milliken might not even have bothered to fill a few years ago, then it will take four weeks.[11] Solectron, the California manufacturer of printed circuit boards that won the Baldrige Award in 1991, can manufacture and deliver a board to a customer's order in two days, and in a batch as small as one item. Solectron polls all 75 of its clients every week to gauge their satisfaction. The results are reviewed every Thursday morning at 7:30 by CEO Winston Chen and his staff.[12]

The currently favored tool to get the customer to tell you what he wants is called Quality Function Deployment, a phrase that stands as a good example of the quality community's bent for vague and awkward jargon.

QFD (in this case the initials are preferable to the name itself) defines a systematic approach to get the customer to help design the product. First used at the Kobe Shipyards in the early 1970s, it is a powerful and important revision to product innovation. It has to be used in a careful and methodical way. You cannot just let the customer say the window handle in a car should be easy to wind. You have to find out just what that means, in the number of turns, the stiffness of the handle, the reach. You construct carefully a matrix of the characteristics of a product and mesh that with an analysis of the customer's needs and keep turning the data, like a prism, seeking new flashes of insight into what the customer wants. The use of QFD has become common in the auto and electronics industries.[13]

The Bulbous Taurus

To design the Taurus/Sable line of cars that brought Ford back to life in the mid-1980s, Ford turned to the customer for help. Right at the beginning, in 1980, when Ford was thinking of a smaller car than eventually emerged, Red Poling, then head of the company's North American Automotive Operations, persuaded Ford to move the market research staff out of world headquarters and down into NAAO, where the cars were designed. So instead of being a celestial body that cast its mysterious light down through several layers of atmosphere onto the activities of the worker ants, market research became part of the working or, in this case, designing world. Market researchers signed on aboard the Taurus team. They launched an effort to understand the customer far more profound than the cursory process that had gone before when panels of consumers would look at mock-ups or models and pronounce their views. In the case of Taurus, Ford researchers sought out consumers in many parts of the United States. They surveyed 4,500 citizens of Marin County, Californians being considered forerunners of American tastes. Instead of listening to panels just once, the Ford researchers brought them back to drive test cars and then brought them back to again to comment on modifications Ford had made.

At the outset, Ford established hundreds of features of a car that were important to drivers, then went out to "benchmark" the best of these features in cars around the world, and then went back to the panelists to verify what they liked best. To find out whose seats were the most comfortable, Ford had its own engineers, designers, secretaries, of different weights and sizes, drive the 600-mile round trip from Detroit to upstate Michigan and back in a variety of seats taken from five imported cars. (The drivers preferred a firm seat with good back support for long trips.) Ford made hundreds of changes large and small as a result of what the consumers said. For example, they complained that they had difficulty finding the little levers on the floor for moving the front seats, so Ford installed a bar the width of the seat. Because consumers complained that on winding roads they would have to keep switching the sun visor between the front and the side, Ford gave the driver a double visor. The tighter turning radius and the large glove box were checked out with the customer.[14] The radically different Taurus, bulbous on the outside and ergonomic on the inside, was a great success, in spite of having some serious defects when it first appeared in 1985.

Quality has two ingredients, attractive features and freedom from defects. In the case of Taurus, Ford pushed the features side hard but did not pay enough attention to defects at first. Ford corrected the defects belateldy and Taurus became a superb car. Ford spent $700 million to improve the Taurus for 1992, again incorporating hundreds of consumer ideas, and in 1992 Taurus outsold the Honda Accord to become the best-selling model in the United States.

Boeing Company stands preeminent among the world's airplane manufacturers, makes superb aircraft, and has never been through a competitive crisis like the auto industry. Yet Boeing now listens more closely to its customers too. When Boeing began planning the next generation of jets in the mid-1980s, it looked at the gap between its 200-plus seat 767 and its 400-plus seat 747 and thought it could probably fill the gap by stretching the 767. The airlines thought the gap was too big to fill with a stretch 767. They wanted a brand new plane with seating for 300-plus passengers that could evolve into a stretch family of its own. The airlines kept saying, "Boeing, you're not listening."

Eventually Boeing did listen. In 1986 Boeing began developing the 777 by sending dozens of its people around the country to talk to airlines, passengers, pilots, mechanics, and airport managers. From the information they brought back, Boeing developed the specifications for the plane.

At this point in a traditional aircraft development program, the customer airlines would have sat back and waited for four years for the 777 to roll down the runway. This time, the customers became part of the development process. Boeing undertook to develop the aircraft in a wholly new way, using digital rather than paper drawings and involving the customer throughout the process. Many of the 235 design/build teams for the twin-engine wide-body jet included customers. United Airlines, the lead-off customer, kept a permanent representantive at the 777 offices in Renton, Washington. Other airlines often took part in the work. So did pilots and mechanics, who were now seen as customers too. A Japanese mechanic urged and obtained minor changes in the electronics bay to make it easier to work in this tightly packed area—just by moving a light so the mechanic could see better, and putting a latch on the door so it would not keep bumping into him. The cabin got a 6'4" head clearance under the overhead bins and the first kitchens that could be moved around the interior, like passenger seats, to change the aircraft's configuration. Philip Condit, president of the Boeing Company, says the biggest difference between the 777 program and its predecessors at Boeing lies in the customer relations.[15]

A Most Unpleasant Experience

While automobiles and other products improved, their makers were slow to improve the sales and service process that was just as much a part of the customer's experience as the product itself. Indeed, company after company, from IBM to Hewlett-Packard, has discovered to its surprise that what gets the customer really mad is not the performance of the product but the performance of the people.

Nowhere is this more true than in the auto industry. No one who has shopped for a car will be surprised by the results of a Ford survey, which learned that "buying a car was among the most unpleasant consumer experiences in life." The car salesman symbolizes the worst of business practices. Buyers dislike the high-pressure salesmanship, the unresponsiveness, tricks such as splitting husband and wife and working on them separately, and above all they dislike horse-trading to arrive at a price. The people surveyed also found the service side of the dealerships generally expensive, incompetent, uncaring, and out of touch with the owners' schedules. The service stations closed in the afternoon before most people got through work.[16] As the quality movement matured, and the focus shifted from getting rid of defects to satisfying the customer, the attention of the automakers shifted belatedly to that critical point of contact between manufacturers and customer, the dealership. Since the vast majority of dealers are independent franchisees, and since the people in them tend to be viscerally motivated types, it is not easy to make them heed concepts such as "quality function deployment." However, the selling of cars is changing.

For a new experience in buying a car drive up to the Saturn of Madison (Wisconsin) dealership. The circular driveway takes you to a canopied entrance. Inside the bright new showroom you can tell the salesmen by their crisp red golf shirts. There are not many cars in the dealership for sale, only seven or eight. In a market swamped with cars and overcapacity, Saturn sells all the cars it can make. "We could sell two to three times as many cars as we are getting, and that's true nationwide," says Thomas J. Zimbrick, general manager of the Madison dealership. So you will not see any local advertising for the car, although national corporate image advertising continues. The suggested price on the sticker in the window, $9,195 for a basic SL sedan, is the only price. Saturn cannot tell its dealers what the price must be, but it can urge them to have only one price and most of them do. You do not have to haggle. If you bring a trade-in, there is one price for that too: whatever the "Blue Book" says.

Saturn does not play games with its dealers, like forcing them to take unpopular models if they want popular ones. No bad habits have spilled over from GM. Saturn started with a clean slate. If a car has a problem, Saturn fixes it.

When a run of 1,850 cars was contaminated with a bad batch of coolant from Texaco that was eating up the cars' innards, Saturn took the cars back and replaced them without question. (Texaco normally supplies Saturn with coolant concentrate and Saturn adds water and purifiers, but because Saturn's blender was out of action for a few days in May 1991, Texaco blended and shipped a special batch of 59 drums of coolant. In the process Texaco added too much sodium hydroxide, creating a highly caustic mixture. Scratch 1,850 cars. Texaco paid for most of the cost.[17]) Saturn made points with its customers and Texaco made points with Saturn, its customer.

When a supplier, without telling Saturn, changed part of the latch that adjusts the angle of the driver's seat, the teeth on the latch began breaking off. Saturn replaced all the potentially troublesome seats and used the failure as an opportunity to make a positive point. A corporate ad showed an employee flying a replacement seat to an owner in Alaska. Saturn says this really happened. A dealer in Santa Ana, California, invited a score of customers who had been sold bad seats to the regular weekend barbecue he holds once a month at his dealership; while they were enjoying the party, he replaced the seats.

In 1993, Saturn recalled most of its cars to replace a wire between the battery and the alternator that had caused some engine fires. Saturn turned the voluntary recall into what *The New York Times* called a "customer-satisfaction blitz" by offering repairs at home, loaner cars, refreshments, and even entertainment while the dealers performed the repair.[18]

C. Warren Neel, dean of the school of business at the University of Tennessee and a close student of Saturn, finds that these are the kinds of legends that are creating the Saturn culture, much as they did at L. L. Bean.[19]

(Toyota set the pattern when it recalled 9,000 1990 LS 400 models for two minors repairs. It picked up and returned the cars, repaired, washed, and gassed, all free.)

The "Moments of Truth"

Saturn's approach to the customer began with interviews of 5,000 owners of imported cars, the target market, and their thoughts about their sales and service experience. "We had a passion to understand the customers," says Marty Raymond, a manager in sales, service, and marketing. A marketing team identified 35 "moments of truth," as they called them, when the customers' decisions would be formed. The moments of truth begin with the first ad the customer sees, continue with driving by and then pulling into the dealership (hence the circular driveway and the canopy). The salesman is trained to be informative and helpful, rather than pushy and tricky.[20] The concern for the customer continues in this manner through to after-sales service and attention. At the Zimbrick dealership in Madison every buyer gets a call 48 hours after the purchase to see if he is satisfied, and a random-sample mail survey goes out 30 days after the purchase.

Tom Zimbrick says the factory tracks sales information closely so that the output matches demand. Still, the dealers can make adjustments. Through a satellite communications system, he says, "We can change the color of a car up to three days before production. We've never had such flexibility. The Japanese don't have that kind of flexibility." Through the communications system, a dealer can also get diagnoses of car problems and search for parts. If he does not have a needed part, he goes upstream to parts pools in big cities, which can supply parts in half a day. If the pool does not have a part the dealer queries the factory, which guarantees delivery in 48 hours, but usually makes it in 24. The Zimbrick family owns car ten dealerships in the Madison area, including Mercedes, BMW, SAAB, Hyundai, and Buick dealerships. Tom Zimbrick says Saturn's "competence in the field is head and shoulders above the others. From the retail point of view, Saturn is unbelievable. They do so many things right. If there's a problem, they fix it."[21] Customers surveyed by J. D. Power and Associates, which specializes in auto quality surveys, would agree. In the 1992 Customer Satisfaction Index, based on how the dealers handle the customers and cope with initial problems, Saturn ranked ahead of all others except Lexus and Infiniti, both Japanese luxury cars. In the Sales Satisfaction Index, which measures the salesperson, the delivery and the condition of the vehicle, Saturn ranked fourth, behind Lexus, Infiniti, and Cadillac.[22]

FROM SATISFACTION TO JOY

A Speck Worth Removing

What happens if and when you have a thoroughly satisfied customer? If your product and the service that goes with it are both superb, and so are your competitors', then what is left to be improved? Is quality still a competitive weapon or is it just a given? We are still a long way from that level of excellence. Whole industries—construction, publishing, shipbuilding, not to mention government and education—remain almost untainted by any contact with quality concepts. But let us suppose for a moment that TQM has really taken hold in America. What do we do then to win the customer?

A number of auto companies have reached the point where the cars they produce are almost faultless. Buyers report through the J. D. Power surveys that the best Japanese cars (Infiniti, Lexus, and Toyota) have fewer than 100 problems per 100 cars in the first 90 days and buyers of the best American cars (Saturn and Lincoln) have slightly more than 100 problems per 100 cars.[23] Put it another way roughly, the buyer of any of these cars will on average find one thing wrong with his new car. Is it worth making further improvements? If the car being checked at the end of the assembly line has a half-millimeter speck of dirt embedded in the paint—one that I could not see with the naked, untrained eye—is it worth removing? Honda thinks so. It sandpapers and buffs the speck out. Toyota thinks so too. Susumu Uchikawa, a member of the Toyota board of directors who is responsible for production control logistics, says Toyota does not "accept one defect per car" (about what Toyota has now).

> "We don't accept one defect per 10 cars and what we want is no defects per 100 cars. It's not a matter of statistics. We want to make the perfect car. We are not competing with other manufacturers on the number of defects they have. It's just that Toyota would like to perfect its operations. We want to make perfect products and we've never changed that goal."[24]

Richard ("Skip") LeFauve, president of Saturn, elaborates the reasoning behind trying to improve after you have reached the point where the customer will not notice. Saturn's own examinations are tougher than what comes up in the Power surveys. "If the gap on the door (between the door and the post) is supposed to be six mils and it's seven mils, that's a defect. A customer would never bring a car in because of a one mil defect in the door gap." What about the half-millimeter speck of dirt on the paint? "We would catch that too, because if you don't you'll get back to two and three and four and five again. It's a constant focus to get it to less than one."[25] You eliminate a defect that the customer may never notice because it may represent several defects you have not found that will affect the customer. The fact that almost defect-free Saturn has been subject to 8 recalls demonstrates the point.

To keep ahead of the customers' rising expectations, the best companies talk of "surprising" and "delighting" the customer—so much so that these words are becoming cliches. Honda talks of providing "the joy of buying," which goes a step beyond customer satisfaction, as Honda explains it. "Joy" is created by a process beginning when the customer first understands the product, then accepts it and decides to buy it, then is "completely satisfied" with it, and then finally ascends to "the joy of buying" if the products and services exceed his expectations.[26] This means Honda delves deeper into the tastes and wants of the customer, looking for the nuances that will please the owner—the feel, the noise, even the smell of the car. As automakers uncover levels of wants, they find distinctions that complicate the job of the designer and manufacturer.

Honda and Ford have given up the idea of making a world car because meeting the exact requirements in each market leads in different directions. The Honda Accord was the best-selling car in America from 1988 to 1991, but it never did very well in Japan. Americans basically look at a car as transportation. The Japanese get transportation from trains, buses, and subways. The car is a beautiful luxury, like a yacht, that may be used only once or twice a month. Its appearance has to be perfect. Some Japanese even take off their shoes before getting into their cars, as they do when the enter their homes. Tadashi Matsuda, chief engineer of the quality control office of Honda's Saitama factory outside Tokyo, says, "the U.S. and Japanese customers are different. There's a difference in how they sense sound and smell." The Japanese do not like the smell of leather; Americans do. Americans do not like the high-pitched whine of wind and tire noises at high speeds; but those sounds do not matter in Japan, perhaps because the opportunity to drive at a high speed is so rare. Honda works with deodorants (in ways the company prefers not to explain) to create the right new car smell.[27]

The Four-Hour Fix: Quality Service

In the electronics business, quality on both sides of the Pacific has reached a point where there is not much to choose among the products of competing companies, so the companies have to look beyond the product to satisfy the customer and track the results. Yokogawa-Hewlett-Packard has a whole array of devices to check itself and make corrections. First, the customers are surveyed once a year. Second, if any negative comment comes to the company the sales representative files a report, which is analyzed to see who can solve the problem. The team given the problem must make not only a quick fix for that particular problem, but also plan a permanent fix so it does not occur again. (Commercial clients are more likely today to demand not only the correction of a problem, but an explanation of the correction that satisfies them the problem will not recur.) Third, YHP adopted from the U.S. Hewlett-Packard what is known as an escalation program. When a customer reports a problem, HP sends out the service representative to deal with it. If the rep cannot solve it within four hours, a "fix team" is assigned to the problem. And if the fix team cannot solve it within another four hours, then the problem moves up to the product division, which can mobilize its engineers and marketing people anywhere in the world.[28]

David Luther, Corning's senior vice president for quality, summarizes aptly the evolution of his company's attitude towards the customer. His description stands for what many other companies have done or would like to do. First, Corning focused on satisfying the internal customer; since few people at Corning ever dealt directly with external customers, it was useful to consider the next person in any process to be the customer. The exercise was necessary, but delayed by about a year the second step, which was to focus on the product attributes that the external commercial customer said were important. Surveys showed that Corning was meeting these needs, by reducing variations in the products, delivering them on time, and producing error-free invoices, but still the customers were unhappy—because Corning was not fully meeting their rising expectations. So the company took a third step suggested by a concept developed at Texas A&M University which measures the behavior and skills of the Corning people in servicing their customers. This approach requires Corning to find out how the customer views the performance of its people in terms of knowledge, courtesy, responsiveness, empathy, even appearance. (One European customer complained that Corning people were helpful, courteous, and gave good service, but did not dress like the representatives of a world-class company.) The customers' views are not taken in a snapshot, but tracked in a close relationship between company and client. If the third step is taken successfully, then the company has gone beyond simply responding to customer complaints; it now identifies and understands the customer issues before they become a problem, and the customer is "delighted" because the company has gone beyond what was expected.[29]

IBM Doesn't Get It

A company that delivers products and services to customers at a level that David Luther describes as "absolutely seamless and uneventful" probably would be impossible to find today. On the other hand, the businesses, schools, and government agencies that still leave their clients thoroughly dissatisfied are all around us. The meaning of customer satisfaction is only beginning to be appreciated. Even a company like IBM, which has been struggling with quality for more than a decade and which made "market-driven quality" its basic goal at the beginning of 1990, still does not get it.

Certainly IBM has improved. A big client like DuPont, which was one of the companies that urged IBM to pay more attention to its customers back in 1988, says it is better satisfied with the way IBM treats it today. But another major client, big enough to justify the permanent presence of IBM representatives on its premises, still has difficulty dealing with IBM. That company's director of information systems says, "They have been calling on customers a lot more in the last couple of years to assess their satisfaction, but there's almost a superficial feel about it, as if it is what they just learned in class. Very often they are people who have worked only for IBM. They try to relate to the person on the other side of the desk, but they don't feel what the customer is saying, they don't appreciate it, they don't understand that we may have a budget problem. They can't understand why you'd go to a lower cost vendor. They don't get it when you get an IBM machine cheaper from a leasing company, with exactly the same warranties and service as if you bought from IBM." And the employee of a small Midwestern company that lives by IBM hardware and software reports that dealing with IBM is considered one of the nastier chores around the company.

Getting an answer from IBM is never simple. It takes patient phoning around the country to find the person who has the answer. IBM will advertise products that turn out to be no longer available, or not yet available. Confusion abounds.[30] Clearly, it will be a while before the American customer, or consumer, is consistently surprised and delighted.

For all the attention paid to the customer, the quality processes developed so far do not get us any closer to understanding the genius, or knack, or insight, or whatever it is, that leads to breakthrough products. What will it take to create the Walkmen, the CD players, the VCRs, the new medications, the recyclable materials, the avionics, the synthetics, and other truly different creations of the future? How much genius, how much luck, and how much system? QFD and other ways of looking at the customer and the product certainly can contribute incremental improvement to existing products, but they have not yet been linked to breakthroughs to new products.

CONCLUSIONS

The importance of the customer to any company seems so obvious as to be hardly worth mentioning, but it took management a long time to find that out and to figure out what it really meant. What companies have learned includes:

- Always listen to the customer and do not assume that you know what he wants, because you probably do not.
- Since the customer may not be able to articulate what he wants, you have to listen very carefully, and develop fairly sophisticated tools for figuring out his wants.
- Everybody is a customer and everybody has a customer. Anyone who has no customer should probably start looking for a new job. The customer can be internal to the company as well as external. The customer is the next person down the line.
- Rather than *pushing* products *out* to the market, a company should respond quickly to the market, letting the customer *pull* products through *to* the market.
- The performance of the company's people is more likely to upset the customer than the performance of its products.
- The customer sees two kinds of quality in a product: its features and its freedom from defects. The company must provide quality on both levels.
- A quality failure provides a company with a great opportunity to cement relations with the customer if the company goes above and beyond its duty in correcting the failure.
- The customer today may well want proof that not only has the failure been corrected, but the system has been corrected as well so that it will not produce the same failure again.
- As products get better and better, defects may become so minor and rare that the customer may not even notice them. That is no excuse for the company to ignore them. Any level of observable defects may represent a higher level of defects that will not become apparent until later.
- Even companies that worked as hard as IBM and Xerox to define their quality policies took years to get to the point where the customer came before everything else. It is easier to say the customer is always right than to act on it.

5

The Tools

Uses and Misuses

Every organization, it seems, finds its own route to quality. Some go fast and try to do everything at once; others go slow, deploying quality project by project, division by division. Some go by the book, demanding meticulous adherence to a detailed set of procedures; others are loose, allowing individual divisions to follow their own timetables and preferences. L. L. Bean and Nashua Corporation attacked quality from opposite ends of the spectrum of possibilities. Nashua began with the "hard" side of quality, the statistical process controls, and not for years did it go to the "soft" side, the participative-people side, and then with limited success. L. L. Bean, by contrast, was strong on the people side even before it got involved in TQM, and did not work seriously on the hard stuff until several years later.

Two Japanese companies renowned for their excellence, Honda and Toyota, followed different routes for decades. Toyota, the model TQM company, went by the rules—many of which it had itself invented. As much as anyone, Toyota created the "lean" system of manufacturing, developed and used statistical tools, was first with just-in-time manufacturing, and applied the other weapons of total quality. All along, Toyota played close to the Japanese Union of Scientists and Engineers, the godfather of TQM, and won Deming prizes administered by JUSE. Honda, an upstart company compared with Toyota, stayed out of the JUSE orbit and has not applied for the Deming. As one executive describes it, Honda is a flexible, open, free-moving, "amoeba-like" organization. It puts faith in "*waigaya*," a phonetic rendition of what a group of Japanese sound like when they all talk at once. In other words, Honda depends on a lot of free and noisy discussion. Who is to say which approach was better? Toyota probably won more times in the quality ratings game, but Honda was usually so close behind (and in front in some surveys) that a careful buyer could not really choose one car over the other on the basis of quality alone. Toyota and Honda both make superb cars. Honda's nonconforming behavior does not mean that Honda failed to practice quality methods. Certainly, Honda had statistical controls, and quality circles, and employee involvement, but it was all under a loose framework.

But now that Honda has attained maturity (and perhaps also because selling a car has gotten harder), the company is finally embracing quality in a more formal sense. To go along with reorganizations in 1991 and 1992 to decentralize the company, Honda has decided to adopt TQM. Just what TQM will look like at Honda was being worked out when I visited the company in the fall of 1992. Certainly, it will mean deploying quality practices beyond manufacturing, where they have existed all along, to marketing, sales, and support.[1] Honda is becoming a more structured, or bureaucratic, organization. Honda's individualism had its strengths, says Hitochi Kume, a professor of engineering at Tokyo University who occupies the office once occupied by Ishikawa. But as Honda got bigger and older, its relative lack of formalized quality standards and methods became more of a disadvantage.[2]

As they work out their own routes to quality, organizations need to find the right balance in applying the tools. Many companies make the mistake of picking just one tool, says Joseph DeFeo, a Juran Institute vice president. "Then they have to start all over again. I never met a company that went down the right path the first time."[3]

Quality processes can be so successful that it becomes tempting to overdo them. That happened at Florida Power & Light as it prepared for winning the Deming Prize in 1989. James L. Broadhead, who became chairman just before FPL won the prize, soon dismantled much of the apparatus of quality. In explaining his actions in a letter to his employees, he wrote that the mechanics of the quality improvement program had come to overshadow the real goals.[4] C. K. Prahalad, a professor at the business school at the University of Michigan, warns against an overemphasis on mechanics. "Very few companies understand that quality is a state of mind and a process rather than a set of procedures."[5]

MEASURING QUALITY WITH STATISTICS

Bearing in mind these caveats about the use of quality tools, I would like to explore them in this chapter. Since this is neither a textbook nor a how-to book, I will not try to write a manual about their use. I will try to avoid lapsing into the sort of jargon that tells the reader not to fail to "link QPD with QFD (also called BPM)," as a trade journal did recently.* What I would like to do in this chapter is describe some of the uses and misuses of tools and techniques, and the arguments surrounding them. The tools connected with employee involvement have been covered in Chapter 3 and those connected with the customer in Chapter 4. In this chapter I will discuss the process tools and techniques that seem most widespread. They include statistical process controls, benchmarking, just-in-time manufacturing, cycle-time reduction, design for manufacturing, and score-keeping, or measurement of the results. Some of these tools may be pushed by their enthusiasts as stand-alone answers to competitive problems, just as quality circles were once mistakenly seen as the key to Japan's success. The popularity of the various tools comes and goes. Just-in-time manufacturing seems to have lost some of its allure, but benchmarking is in vogue. All of these tools are useful when applied in the right circumstances, but none of them is transcendent.

Tools keep us honest. They save us from doing things in haste and with sloppy data or half-formed thoughts. They make us look at what we do sharply and clearly. They make it difficult for us to give ready-made or habitual responses, or go by "gut reaction." They give us a disciplined and rational way of continuously improving whatever we do.

The tools of quality are sometimes so simple and commonsensical that they hardly seem worth mentioning, except that simplicity and common sense are surprisingly scarce. I remember visiting a GM engine plant ten years ago that had a high rejection rate for connecting rods. The rods came from four suppliers. Until the plant began to improve quality systematically, no one had tried to track the numbers of bad rods to each supplier. When that was done, it turned out that most of the bad rods were made by one supplier. GM fired that supplier and the proportion of usable rods improved immediately and markedly. Just a matter of counting.

Historically and in current practice, modern quality begins with the statistical control chart, developed by Walter Shewhart at AT&T in the 1920s (see Chapter 1). The control chart is the basic building block of quality improvement. A control chart measures the variations in a process by taking samples, be they of the thickness of a coating, the size of a boring, or the number of mistakes in foreign-exchange transactions. Any activity on earth has a natural variation, including death. We know we are going to

---

* QPD = quality policy deployment, QFD = quality function deployment, and BPM = business process management.

die; we do not know when we are going to die, but an insurance company can tell us what percentage of us will die at any given age. We may die anywhere in a wide range of years of special causes, such as an accident or the results of smoking, or, more likely, we may die during a narrower range of years in old age of natural causes, such as a heart attack or pneumonia.

Shewhart and Juran make an important distinction between what they call "random" and "assignable" causes for variation. Deming called them "common" and "special" causes and he was fanatical about distinguishing between the two. To illustrate the difference between them, the assignable (or special) causes are transient and identifiable, such as a flu epidemic, a power outage, or a bad batch of raw materials. Random (or common) causes are a continuing part of the production process; they are the natural variation in the machinery or the system. The assignable causes can be eliminated one by one through quality controls. But the random causes can only be removed or reduced by systematic quality improvement of the process.

Shewhart was the first to say that statistical analysis could be applied to quality improvement. However, he thought it would be economical only to remove the assignable causes; reducing the random causes would be too costly. His successors have showed that both are worth attacking, that the highest quality comes only from reducing both random and assignable causes. Juran's *Quality Control Handbook* (fourth ed., 1988) argues that ideally, only random causes should be present in a process. Then the process is said to be in statistical control, and you can see clearly the process capability and its natural variation. You can then improve the process by reducing the variation.[6]

In thousands of factories today you find control charts at the workers' stations, in the foremen's offices, and in the executive offices. They will usually show a series of points on either side of a line representing the average. Other lines designate upper and lower control limits. The points could represent, for example, variations in a series of measures such as the thickness of sheet metal or the time it takes an operator to answer the telephone. A point outside the limits shows that the process is out of control, as do multiple successive points on one side of the average line, or a series of consecutive points rising or falling. These out-of-control results would have assignable causes. Once the assignable causes have been eliminated, all the points should be inside the control limits but scattered randomly. The process is now statistically under control, and you can begin improving the process and narrowing the band of variation. The less variation you can achieve the better your product, and the lower your costs will be.[7]

Jumping Up and Down on the Scale

Foremen and managers have in the past failed even to understand that any process has a natural variation, much less that there were two kinds of causes. They assumed usually that the worker was at fault, and often took actions that increased rather than reduced variations. Juran cites the case of a watch factory decades ago, when they made mechanical watches. The automatic lathes that produced the tiny shafts for these watches seemed unable to hold the correct tolerances. The factory had to junk 12% of the shafts produced. When an engineer sat down at a lathe for a day to log its output he found that it turned out usable shafts until a workman measured the last shaft out (No. 135 for the day) with a gauge, and found it oversized. "In consequence, the workman changed the machine setting and, with the best intentions, began producing scrap," says Juran. The departmental inspector came around later with his gauge, found the shaft No. 197 undersized, and told the workman to adjust the tool. The lathe then produced good pieces up to shaft No. 392, when the workman took another reading with his gauge and repeated what he had done at No. 135. And so the factory had to scrap 12% of its shafts. For years no one had made the connection from symptom to cause: the workman's gauge was inaccurate. Left on their own, machines can often do better than workers unfamiliar with statistics. Once the problem at the watch factory was understood, the scrap rate dropped from 12% to 2%.[8]

Typically, the use of statistical controls does produce spectacular results at the outset. First, the elimination of special causes results in major improvements. Second, the reduction of the most significant common causes results in more major improvements. At that point most of what Juran calls the "low-hanging fruit" have been picked; further improvements take more work and produce less spectacular results. The initial successes make a point and arouse enthusiasm, but the fruit get harder to pluck the higher they hang. When the Nashua Corp. called in Deming in 1979, Deming discovered that the technicians running a plant that coated copier paper did not understand natural variation. They frequently stopped the machinery to make adjustments to the coating head. But by assuming that *any* variation had to be corrected, they were inadvertently *increasing* the variation. Lloyd Nelson, a statistician and Deming colleague who went to work for Nashua, compares what they were doing to trying to weigh someone who is jumping up and down on the scale. When they stopped meddling with the coating head it turned out to be in pretty good statistical control. Now, with that special cause of variation eliminated, Nashua could go to work on reducing the common causes. By

April, 1980, the coater was saving $800,000 a year in coating, and on top of that Nashua saved $700,000 because it did not have to buy a new coating head to replace the one the company thought was defective.[9]

The initial successes at Nashua did not launch the company on a soaring flight of continuous improvement. Not only was the fruit hanging higher harder to get at, but other obstacles emerged. To this day, 13 years after those initial successes, some Nashua executives remain unconvinced, and the use of statistical controls there is far from universal or consistent.

Statistical controls are not always equally applicable or successful. As Nelson says, a process involving natural products like trees, no two of which are identical, always has special causes. If a process runs at a high speed, and testing samples takes time, then it takes more sophisticated techniques to discover defects in a timely way. Small batches and shorter product lives shorten the time available to improve a process.[10]

THE SEVEN BASIC TOOLS

Control charts are one of the seven basic quality tools that most texts and courses offer for use essentially at the level of quality circles and teams. They are:

1. *Flowchart.* The most widely used tool, the flowchart is simply a step-by-step diagram of a process, with each step in the process marked in its proper place. Useful for understanding and later simplifying a process or eliminating unnecessary steps.
2. *Check sheet.* A tabulation of how many times something happens, such as a day-by-day record of the number of faulty connecting rods delivered. Provides the basic numbers used in other tools.
3. *Pareto diagram.* Named by Juran after an Italian economist, Vilfredo Pareto, the Pareto diagram is a simple way of determining priorities. You translate data from, say, a check sheet, into a bar graph. The cause of the largest number of defects gets the tallest bar and that should be the first priority. As Juran puts it, you separate the "vital few," which need prompt attention, from the "useful many," which can be left until later.
4. *Cause-and-effect diagram.* Also known as a fishbone diagram, after its resemblance to a fish skeleton, or an Ishikawa diagram, after the man who developed it in 1950, the cause and effect diagram is a way of laying out the factors that contribute to a result. The factors (for example workers, equipment, raw materials, work methods) are dia-

grammed along the bones of the fish, all leading along the spine to the fish's head (the result).

5. *Scatter diagram.* To find out the relationship between two factors, say, the number of errors in the billing department and the hours of overtime worked in that department, you make a diagram with the errors on the vertical axis and the hours on the horizontal axis. For each week, you enter a point on the diagram marking the errors and overtime hours worked that week. If the points end up scattered all over the diagram, then there is no correlation between the two. If they cluster along a rising line, then you have demonstrated that the more overtime people work, the more likely they are to make mistakes. Or if the points cluster along a falling line you will have proven, to everyone's surprise, that the more hours people work the fewer errors they make.

6. *Histogram.* A bar chart, the histogram shows dispersion. For example, you could measure the thickness of incoming metal parts, put the measurements in a series of categories, count the number of measurements in each category, and construct a bar chart showing the size of each category. If the measurements all fall into a few categories, creating a few tall bars, you have little dispersion, and if they fall more evenly into many categories, you have high dispersion.

7. *Control chart.* This was explained earlier in this chapter.

In 1990, the Ventana Corporation, a commercial offshoot of the University of Arizona, surveyed 40 companies considered leaders in quality to gauge the popularity and usage of six of the tools (check sheets were not covered). The percentage of the 40 companies reporting frequent use of each of the six the tools was as follows:

Flowcharts	70%
Cause and effect diagrams	67%
Histograms	67%
Pareto diagrams	61%
Control charts	48%
Scatter diagrams	36%[11]

Six of the tools were described in some detail (skipping flow charts) by Kaoru Ishikawa, first in his journal, *Quality Control for the Foreman*, and then in his book, *Guide to Quality Control*, available in English since 1971.[12] A very simple description of the seven tools and others can be found in *The*

Memory Jogger, a handy pocket-size guide put out by GOAL/SPC, a non-profit quality training and research organization in Methuen, Massachusetts.[13] The Juran Institute sells a kit of quality improvement tools with 11 workbooks covering the seven tools and some others in greater detail.[14] Many corporations have produced excellent texts for the use of their employees, notably AT&T's *Statistical Quality Control Handbook*, a detailed guide to control charts written for Western Electric employees in 1956 and now available to the public.[15]

Rather than belabor the reader with descriptions of yet more statistical tools, I will assume that I have at least sketched them enough to indicate their nature and uses. Statistical tools are relatively simple, but if you wonder why America may be having trouble improving quality, look into Ishikawa's book and imagine an American college graduate, to say nothing of a high school graduate, trying to take it in. Getting workers and managers to use the tools consistently is also tough. Charles Clough, the head of Nashua, which has been keeping charts since 1979, says that to make sure people use them day after day is "just extraordinarily difficult." He complains,

"Even after you have supposedly done quite a good job of training the people and you've shown them the benefits and they've seen the benefits, once it starts running fairly well, you know, people will go back to where they were. You'll have people working on control charts and they're running the control charts and they're paying off beautifully and then all of a sudden you go into the operation and you find they're not doing the control charts anymore. I think they feel, well, we don't need it anymore. So it's an attention to detail that the management, I guess, just doesn't seem to find natural. Now the workers, I still believe, understand and will do these things and are happy to do them and they can see the benefit, but the management . . ."[16]

Like a lot else connected with quality, statistical controls may be simple, but they are not easy.

Five Times Why

These statistical tools are the building blocks of quality. They are for everyone to use. Ishikawa's work was intended to help foremen and their workers learn together how to improve quality. Several common-sense procedures are widely used along with these and other tools. Taichi Ohno instructed Toyota people to "ask why five times" to get to the root cause.

You must not be satisfied with knowing that the machine stopped because
the fuse blew. *Why* did the fuse blow? Because the bearing was overloaded.
Why was the bearing overloaded? Because it was not lubricated. *Why* was it
not lubricated? Because the lubrication pump was not working properly?
Why not? Because the shaft was worn. *Why* was the shaft worn? Because
there was no strainer and scraps of metal got in. After all those *whys*, you
have reached the root cause, and now you know how to stop the problem
from recurring.[17]

The five whys can be applied in the most unlikely place. Take the matter
of the erosion of the Lincoln and Jefferson Memorials in Washington. Why
is the marble sugaring, as if it were being rubbed by sandpaper? Because it
is washed so frequently. Instead of just deciding to wash less often, the
National Capital Parks Service asked a second question: Why do we wash so
often? For one thing, because the birds leave so many droppings. Why are
there so many birds in the memorials? Because the sparrows and swallows
gather there to eat all the spiders. Why are there so many spiders? Because
the spiders like to eat midges. Why are there so many midges? Because the
lights, which are turned on at dusk when they are swarming, attract them. So
you turn the lights on one hour later and get fewer midges, fewer spiders,
fewer sparrows and swallows, fewer droppings, fewer washings, less erosion. Now about those starlings and pigeons . . .[18] In both the case of the
birds in the monuments and that of the blown fuse, as it happens, the root
cause was revealed with five whys. Obviously, the number of whys does not
have to stop at five, but should go on until the root cause is revealed.

Another basic common-sense approach is embodied in Deming's Plan-
Do-Check-Act Cycle, or, as he prefers to call it these days, the Plan-Do-
Check-Study Cycle. You identify an opportunity for improvement and *Plan*
a process for achieving it, then you *Do* on a small scale to carry out the plan,
then you *Check* or *Study* the results to see what you can learn, then you *Act*
on what you have learned and repeat the cycle.[19]

Juran, more oriented to larger management theory, writes of the "un-
varying sequence of events" through which companies break out of old
levels of performance to reach new standards. The breakthrough starts with
a change in attitude and goes on to a Pareto analysis to separate the "vital
few" which can really make a difference from the "trivial many." You then
create an organization for the breakthrough, with a steering arm to run it and
a diagnostic arm to provide the data. Data in hand, you try to achieve first
a cultural breakthrough to deal with the inevitable resistance, and then you
go for the breakthrough in performance, which is the purpose of the whole

exercise. Finally, to keep things running at the new level, you establish controls.[20]

JUST-IN-TIME: A PILLAR OF THE SYSTEM

On a recent trip to Japan I found that whenever I raised the subject of just-in-time inventories, the adjective "controversial" soon followed. In the country where just-in-time began to evolve more than 40 years ago, it is still not fully accepted. In the United States just-in-time enjoyed a wave of popularity in the 1980s, since replaced by a more sober appraisal of its virtues and troubles. Taiichi Ohno describes JIT as one of the two pillars of the Toyota production system, the other being "automation with a human touch, or autonomation." He introduced it in 1949 in the Toyota machine shop he managed at the time; as he rose in the company, eventually becoming executive vice president before retiring, he pushed it wider. But it was not until 1962 that Toyota adopted JIT company-wide, and it took 20 years in total before the process became embedded in the company.[21]

JIT is critical to the lean production system developed by Toyota because it is a powerful weapon for reducing waste as well as improving quality. By delivering parts or supplies in small batches on a daily or even hourly basis, you can attack many levels of waste. You reduce the waste of bulky inventories. When companies went to JIT in the early 1980s, they found they could make huge reductions in inventories. GM, which was certainly no exemplar of lean production then or even a decade later, reported in 1984 it had cut its inventories by 17%, or $1.7 billion, in three years.[22] The manager of the Hewlett-Packard plant in Greeley, Colorado, told me in 1984 that when the plant went to JIT that year, work in progress dropped from 20 days to one day and stocks dropped from a 50-day to a two-week supply. Since factories no longer have all that work in progress and inventory hanging around, the factories themselves can be reduced in size by around 30%.[23]

As for quality, in the favorite cliche of JIT enthusiasts, when you lower the water in the pond, all the rocks stick out—in other words, you no longer have several feet of inventory to conceal the rocks of defective parts. If defective parts come from a supplier you find out right away and you make the correction, before the supplier runs on for days making the same defects. Since parts go right into the production line, the likelihood of them being damaged in storage or while being moved around the plant is less. Since tools as well as supplies have to be ready just in time, JIT forces manufacturers to cut the time it takes to retool. It has become routine to hear that the time it takes to change a die has been cut from several hours, even a day or two, to a few minutes. The advantages of JIT are multiple.

The risks too are considerable. JIT cannot be superimposed on a production system that otherwise remains unchanged. If it is not part of a transformation to total quality, the result will be chaos, as has often happened. Unless the whole process is redesigned to move smoothly from supplier to customer it is too vulnerable. Poor quality in one step of the process shuts the factory. JIT removes the safety cushions provided by those large, sloppy inventories, which, of course, is one of the reasons for having JIT. Any interruption in supplies can shut a plant down within hours, or even minutes. In the early days of JIT, that Hewlett-Packard plant in Greeley shut down 156 times in one month.

Just Shifting Inventories: Degrees of JIT

JIT may also involve a degree of hypocrisy or deception. The manufacturer may cut *his* inventory, but the supplier merely delivers just-in-time products out of the same old inventory. *The Machine That Changed The World,* the superb study of the auto industry that came out of MIT, confirms that JIT in the auto industry, at least in the United States, was something of a fiction. By 1988, 10% of the industry's suppliers were making their deliveries hourly or daily, which represented a considerable change in delivery schedules over five years. Japan has gone much further, with a combined 83% of deliveries daily or hourly. But U.S. suppliers had hardly speeded their schedule of tool changes at all. Sixty percent changed their tools less than once a week in 1983; 55% did in 1988. Without frequent, quick tool changes you cannot produce for JIT deliveries. So the inventory had simply shifted from assembler to supplier. That defeated the purpose of JIT, because the suppliers were not cutting their costs or improving their quality through JIT.[24]

Ten years after those initial efforts at Greeley, Hewlett-Packard still is not of one mind about JIT. Craig Walter, corporate quality director until recently, says it has been institutionalized but not in a rigid kind of way demanding daily deliveries. He says,

> "What just-in-time does for you is if you shrink the inventory you expose the problem, and then, having exposed the problem, you raise the level of the inventory again and fix the problem. Having fixed the problem, you lower the inventory again until you expose another problem and so on."[25]

But John Young, the Hewlett-Packard chairman through 1992, seems to have found JIT less appealing:

"I think almost any of these techniques are suspect. They become a means to an end. God, if you reduce your inventory, all of our problems would be solved. It's just not the case. There are kind of technique-of-the-month clubs that need to be seen in a large agenda of a menu of techniques that can be applied for continuous improvement and they need to be evaluated and sorted out and fit to the circumstances involved."[26]

The Hewlett-Packard division in Corvallis, Oregon, which makes calculators and the very successful palmtop PC, the 95LX, uses JIT selectively. Bulky packaging material produced nearby in Oregon is at times delivered twice a day. That makes sense. But it would make no sense at all to have daily deliveries of miniature parts like integrated circuits made in Japan. The plant tries to keep its inventories of ICs to no more than a three-weeks' supply. William C. Martin, manufacturing manager at Corvallis, says he could increase the frequency of deliveries from Japan and cut inventories but that would increase freight and customs costs. "JIT was very popular a few years ago," he continues, "but some people overlooked making the right trade-offs between costs and storage. The concept of JIT, the minimum inventory, makes sense. It keeps clutter out of the way." Another Corvallis manager, Kent Stockwell, head of the quality department, says, "JIT was oversold. QFD (quality function deployment) was oversold. Good ideas are often oversold and then the world settles down to reality."[27]

Reality in Japan is a little different, partly because of geography. Toyota continues to use JIT as one of the two pillars of its production system, valuing it highly for its ability to reveal the rocks, but others complain that Japan's growing traffic congestion and pollution may force some revisions. In some ways America is more suited to JIT than Japan. Auto supplier plants are spread out all over Ohio and Michigan, for instance, and connected by excellent, open highways to the assembly plants. By contrast, Japan's highways are dreadful and the streets in and around Tokyo, Nagoya, and Toyota City are packed. Yoshio Kondo, a respected consultant and Kyoto University professor, says that deliveries on three- or four-hour schedules in Toyota City have drawn complaints which may lead to a reduction in the use of JIT there. Katsumi Yoshimoto of Yokagawa-Hewlett-Packard believes that the auto companies will have to review their JIT practices. He says the trucks stack up around the plants early in the morning trying to beat the traffic and make their deliveries on time. NEC practices JIT at some plants but finds it very "controversial." Honda is rethinking JIT for its Sayama plant in the outskirts of Tokyo, not to drop it but to find a delivery system that will have less impact on the residential area that surrounds the plant. Hitochi Kume of the University of Tokyo worries about the traffic problems and some of the sham that exists in Japan as in the United States. "Often you will find that when Toyota has no inventory, the supplier does," he says. "Somewhere there usually is an inventory."[28]

BENCHMARKING: STEALING SHAMELESSLY

If just-in-time production peaked in popularity in the 1980s, benchmarking is having its day in the sun in the 1990s, judging by the volume of seminars, conferences, and the activities of consultants and trade associations. But benchmarking is at least as old as JIT. You could argue that it began with industrial espionage, when businesses began collecting information about their competitors. But there is a difference. Industrial espionage is sneaky and seeks proprietary information. The intelligence-gatherer tries to find out the enemy's marketing plans without the enemy knowing what he is doing. The benchmarker is open and aboveboard, often consorting with the enemy—and he is not after proprietary information, or should not be. Rather, the benchmarker is looking for the best business practices and product features anywhere he can find them, and is brazen about copying them. "We steal shamelessly," is the open confession of the benchmarker.

Benchmarking is a focused, systematic way of improving quality by finding out how others do something better than you do, and then applying what you learn to your own company. Sending senior executives breezing through other companies that they have heard have a good quality thing going is not benchmarking; it is just industrial tourism. Benchmarking means getting very specific, first by understanding thoroughly the process in your own company that needs improving, then finding out which half-dozen companies are particularly good at that process, and then sending the people who are responsible for your process out to visit the others that you have targeted.

The first recorded instance of benchmarking, it could be argued, lies at the origin of just-in-time manufacturing. Taiichi Ohno recalls in *Toyota Production System* that the Japanese became fascinated with the American supermarket in the postwar years; and when he toured the United States in 1956 he was more impressed with the supermarkets than with the Big

Three automakers that he visited. By then, Toyota was already adapting to the supermarket concept of putting the shopper in control of the process, pulling items through the store, on demand, on time (as explained in Chapter 4).[29]

Xerox probably gets credit for being the first and most assiduous American benchmarker. When Xerox woke up in the late 1970s to find Ricoh and other Japanese manufacturers of copiers chewing up its market (see Chapter 1), it had the novel idea of sending a team over to Japan to find out how they were doing it. When you learn that somebody else is doing the same thing as you are, but at half the cost and in half the time, and selling profitably at a price below your manufacturing cost, then it becomes difficult to say it cannot be done or that you are doing your best. Before the quality movement came along to disrupt their lives, American managers looked inward. They were the best, so what could they learn from others? Benchmarking opened their eyes.

"Well, maybe you could learn from studying competitors, but companies in other industries certainly cannot teach you anything." Xerox proved that this was wrong too. When Xerox was thinking of redesigning its warehouses in the early 1980s, Robert C. Camp, its director of benchmarking, read a trade journal article on how L. L. Bean's warehouse worked and thought Xerox could learn from Bean, even if Bean was in a totally different business. A business process is a business process, whatever the industry. Besides, companies that are not competitors are more likely to be forthcoming. Xerox sent a team up to Maine and learned some things that helped it design better warehouses without going high tech. Bean's warehouse workers could "pick and pack" items three times faster than Xerox's because, for one thing, Bean's goods were stored according to velocity not category. The items that sold the most were closest to the desk where the pickers got their order sheets. Xerox felt that it got so much out of benchmarking that when it announced in 1983 the goal of achieving "leadership through quality," it made benchmarking one of the three components of that effort, the others being employee involvement and the quality process itself. Bob Camp became something of a celebrity in this arcane field, and wrote a text on the subject.[30]

Just Count the Cars

Ford furnished another celebrated example in the early 1980s when it used benchmarking extensively to create the Taurus and Sable line of cars (see Chapter 4). Having established through extensive interviewing the 400 features of a car that are most important to a customer, Ford went out and systematically looked for the best of those features in other cars and copied or improved on them. In the first model year, Ford felt that it had succeeded for 320 of those 400 features, and it added more successes later. When Ford gave the Taurus line a $700-million facelift for the 1992 model it repeated the benchmarking process. It reached across to the other side of Detroit to copy Pontiac's idea of putting three basic stereo controls up by the steering wheel so that the driver does not have to fiddle around in the dark below the dashboard to change station or volume.[31]

Juran recalls with some amusement what happened when Ford decided that the 600 people in Accounts Payable could not be doing the job right because Ford's suppliers were screaming for their money. (Remember in Chapter 4 the Ford accountant complaining to Bob Galvin about Motorola's billing mistakes!) After cutting the staff from 600 to 450 by computerizing functions previously done by hand, Ford looked outside for help and benchmarked against its Japanese partner, Mazda. When Mazda replied that it had six people in Accounts Payable, Ford could not believe it had 75 people for every one that Mazda had doing the same thing. Mazda must have misunderstood the question and Ford asked again. The answer came back, "Yes, it really is six." So Ford decided to study the Mazda system in detail and was amazed by what it found. Basically, Mazda had an invoiceless system, which eliminated one entire stream of documents. The Ford accountants spent most of their time trying to reconcile different kinds of documents. But Mazda understood that every car that went out of the plant had one windshield. It never shipped a car with two windshields or with no windshield. So Mazda counted the number of cars shipped and multiplied the number by the cost of a windshield. Since there was only one supplier of windshields, Mazda just wrote out one check for the total cost of all the windshields and sent it off. Well, it was not quite that simple, but that basically is how it worked.[32] At last count, Ford had cut its accounts payable department to 200 people and was planning further reductions.

Many other large corporations, AT&T, Digital Equipment, Du Pont, Eastman Kodak, and IBM, for example, have benchmarking departments that perform hundreds of studies. Milliken benchmarks safety with Du Pont, innovation with 3M, teams with Goodyear and Procter & Gamble, customer satisfaction with AT&T and IBM, education with IBM, goals with Motorola, and, of course, it benchmarks how to benchmark with Xerox.

In the late 1980s, the practice became contagious. The Baldrige Award heightened interest because each year the criteria for the award raise the emphasis on benchmarking. The Ernst & Young-American Quality Foundation study of quality practices found in 1991 that of 580 major organizations in four industries—autos, banks, computers, and hospitals—31% regularly benchmarked and only 7% never did.[33]

Like any other tool, benchmarking can be overdone. Bob Camp tells what happened when Xerox decided to follow up a suspicion that it was spending too much on processing orders for small items, like toner and typewriters, shipped to retailers. So it put together a steering committee of five vice presidents and a full-time benchmarking team of five other people. They studied their own process and visited six other companies. Their conclusion, after 18 months, was alarming. Xerox was spending $80 to $95 processing each order, compared with $25 to $35 at the others. Since the result was so damning, the team had to hire consultants to confirm their findings before Xerox management would accept them. But by then it did not matter anyhow. Xerox had quit making typewriters and reorganized the departments involved.[34]

The Xerox experience explains why Yotaro Kobayashi, chairman of Fuji Xerox, finds that ''benchmarking is not as easy as it sounds because you are always looking at a moving target.'' The first time Fuji Xerox benchmarked in the 1970s, it compared products it was planning to introduce in two years with current Ricoh products. ''That didn't do us any good,'' says Kobayashi. Furthermore a senior consultant upbraided Fuji Xerox for setting its sights too low because he did not consider Ricoh the best in Japan. Benchmark against the best, he said, or be a loser.[35] Benchmarking can have the effect of merely bringing you level with your competitor—a year or two after he moved on ahead.

The Westinghouse Productivity and Quality Center, which advises outside clients as well as corporate divisions on matters such as benchmarking, tries to avoid the error of excess by making projects short and simple when possible. Carl Arendt, communications manager for the center, says the enthusiasts, who are trying to make a profession out of benchmarking, are too inclined to make a full, formal study every time. Sometimes a few phone calls will raise the necessary information. ''We have seldom found the need for long, drawn-out studies,'' says Arendt. ''We prefer continuous improvement in small steps.'' If the rate of calls received by the Center for help on benchmarking projects is any help in fixing the time when benchmarking became really popular, then it happened in mid-1991.[36] Like other tools, benchmarking can be extremely useful if not overdone, if you do not spend too much time worrying whether to use the nine-step AT&T method or the ten-step Xerox method, and if it is part of a larger effort to improve.

DESIGN: SPEED AND SIMPLICITY

"Gliders Instead of Airplanes": Designing at Boeing

When the first giant Boeing 747s rolled out of the factory in Everett, Washington, in 1969 they sat on the runways by the factory with blocks of concrete hanging from where their engines should have been. The Pratt & Whitney engines were late. The director of the 747 program complained he was making "gliders instead of airplanes." After the engines did start arriving, the 747's problems were far from solved. Although the plane was safe to fly, its engines kept overheating, wearing out too fast, and using too much fuel. Twenty years later, in 1989, when the new 747-400 version started to fly passengers, Boeing had to assign 300 engineers to get rid of bugs in the plane. For two decades, Boeing kept engineers busy on the 747 doing what should have been done right in the first place. The 747 is a fine and safe plane to fly, but it was full of costly design mistakes that have occupied engineers for years.

To design the twin-engine 777, the next generation wide-bodied jet, Boeing was determined to avoid the mistakes of past aircraft projects. It took the risk of designing the plane in a radically new way. Boeing people are not the radical sort, but they know that their style of design and development, successful as it has been in the past, must change if the company is to remain competitive.

The new way depends on a combination of high technology and behavioral change. The high technology is based on a cluster of eight IBM mainframes plus software developed in France, which enable engineers to design the entire plane digitally. For the first time at Boeing designers are not using blueprints. This highly advanced form of computer-aided design (known as Computer Aided Three-Dimensional Interactive Application, or CATIA to its friends), is meant to get rid of the bugs before the plane is built. Its three-dimensional pictures show what fits and what does not fit, which means that Boeing does not have to build mock-ups. It shows whether or not a mechanic can get at a part to repair it. It makes available to any engineer the changes made by all the other engineers, as they make them.

On the human side, Boeing has organized the design effort in a new way. Design is too important to be left to the designers. The 235 "design/build" teams assigned the different pieces of the plane include people who have never had anything to do with design before: manufacturing engineers, plant representatives, marketing and finance people, representatives of the mechanics who will maintain the 777, representatives of the big Japanese companies that will build significant parts of the plane, and (as related in Chapter 4) some of the customers—the airlines. The whole idea is to iron out problems now, and not after manufacturing has started. If the designers call on the manufacturing engineers to do something that cannot be done, Boeing does not have to wait until the tools have been made to find that out. Deming's plan-do-check-act cycle is applied continually so that each piece is checked by all the players as it evolves. Boeing wants to have a service-ready plane when it delivers the 777 to the airlines and not spend years fixing things.[37]

Robust Design

The design of products and services is a whole separate subject, beyond the scope of this book, but good design is intimately connected with quality. First, you cannot make good products if they are not well designed to begin with. Second, design responds very well to the application of quality methods. Design is the subject of much esoteric and interesting (when comprehensible) theorizing. When a Japanese engineer named Genichi Taguchi visited Bell Labs for the first time in 1980, the eminent scientists and engineers there thought at first that it was his poor English that made him hard to understand, until they discovered that the Japanese had just as much trouble following them. But they did see that his ideas worked. He had a way of dealing with many variables in a product so that he could find the best combination with a handful of experiments, rather than the hundreds or even thousands of combinations theoretically possible when one deals with more than a handful of variables. He also had an intriguing concept for improving quality called "robust design." If you have a quality problem with a ceramic product because you cannot control the temperature of the oven finely enough to suit the clay you are using, you have two ways of solving the problem. The usual quality approach would be to get the oven's temperature under control. Taguchi offers a different approach: forget the oven and find a clay that is not so sensitive to temperature variations. That would be called "robust design." Taguchi's approach is controversial because statisticians say there are simpler and more sophisticated ways of coping with variables and because robust design, in a sense, goes against our faith in continuous improvement. Giving up on the oven is a defeat that we just do not accept.[38]

The broader design principles grasped most eagerly by TQM companies are speed and simplicity. The simpler the design, the easier it is to make and the less likely it is to fail. The faster you design it, the more likely you are to please your customer and take your market share. *In Revolutionizing Product Development*, Steven Wheelwright and Kim Clark, both professors at the Harvard Business School, list some of the rules for designing for manufacturability: minimize the number of parts, and reduce the numbers of adjustments, fasteners, jigs, and fixtures. A snap-on clip beats a screw. The result can be electrifying, they say. When NCR replaced an electronic cash register with a new model, the application of these principles reduced assembly time by 75%, the number of parts by 85%, the number of suppliers by 65%, and eliminated altogether the need for tools for assembly.[39]

The speed of design—for that matter, speed in all things to meet the customers' requirements—has become critical to quality and competitiveness, especially in high tech industries. Speed does not mean haste. Rather, it means reducing or eliminating all the wasted time and effort in a traditional development process where each department works in its own silo, isolated from the others. In the standard cliche of the quality movement, engineers tossed their designs over the transom and let the manufacturing engineers figure out what do next. As often as not, the manufacturing engineers would toss the designs back as unworkable, and so the designs would fly back and forth betweeen two warring departments. Now, with a team approach and the practice of concurrent engineering, designers and manufacturers work together. As the design of the product emerges, the team also designs the manufacturing process and the tools. Add advanced technology aids for design and the whole process becomes both faster and better. "It's a lot slower when you work on paper and you make more mistakes," says Bill Martin at Hewlett-Packard's Corvallis plant. "Checking for fit is electronic now. Without that, you would spend six to eight weeks tooling and modeling. The more you have to go back and fix, the more you open Pandora's box. Now, once you pick a configuration, you can move remarkably fast to manufacturing." All the while, you push to fit more functions into fewer parts into less space. "You have to break design rules," says Martin. If you go by industry standards on the spacing of components in an integrated circuit, you would never get where you want to go, so you keep enhancing the performance of the ICs and keep pushing the suppliers.[40] Since half its orders come for products that are less than two years old, Hewlett-Packard cannot let research and development dawdle along.

How much have all these efforts speeded the process of creating new products? Quite a lot, but it is hard to tell how much exactly. When does a cycle begin? When does it end? Hewlett-Packard figures that its cycle for wholly new products has come down from about five years to something like two to three years. (Derivatives or spin-offs of existing products, of course, come to market faster.) Hewlett-Packard tried for a while to track its cycle by using the concept of "break-even time," the time elapsed between the date of conception of a product and the date when the company got its money back.

John Young explains,

"We like to cut that in half. It's a great conceptual fuel for everybody to have, but it's an awkward metric because it's just too complicated and it's so retrospective in its view. I can't tell when I have reached to breakeven time until it's done. The nice part is, it tells everybody what you are doing. How do I do engineering faster? How do I design for manufacturability? How do I make sure I use quality function deployment or other kinds of tools to characterize real customer needs so that I've got a winner? If you look at HP's overall product line in the last decade, our product life has exactly cut in half."[41]

Whether or not this cycle is precisely measurable, the idea of getting to market faster drives corporate R&D efforts today.

MEASURING QUALITY

Making Accounting Accountable

Quality people like to have measures, lots of them. They put out a deluge of numbers. "If it moves, we measure it," says a briefer at Milliken. "We are passionate about it. If there's no score, you're just scrimmaging, practicing." A stroll around Milliken reveals a company obsessed with knowing how many mistakes accounts payable has made, what proportion of invoices were paid on time, what proportion of deliveries were made on time, and on and on. The numbers and graphs are posted in corridors and offices and by the stairs and elevators. At the First National Bank of Chicago, the commercial banking division uses some 500 measures that are checked weekly. The retailing part of the bank uses 150 measures, reviewed monthly. How long are customers standing in line at the bank on average? (The goal is to get 98% or more out of the bank within five minutes.) What is the average processing time for incoming Federal Reserve Bank transactions? (The goal is five minutes.) How many errors has the bank made on lockbox transactions? (The goal is not more than one in 10,000 transactions.)[42]

Business lives by numbers; numbers are its language and numbers rate its performance. Over the years, accounting rules have evolved that everybody in finance understands and that give a detailed portrait of a company. But the accounting portrait is distorted, and it distorts the actions of business leaders. H. Thomas Johnson, a professor of quality management at Portland (Oregon) State University, argues in *Relevance Regained* that accounting, as it evolved in what he calls the Dark Ages of American Business (1950-1980) and is still practiced, prevents executives from managing companies effectively and encourages damaging habits. The business schools have sanctified the bad habits and, of course, as more financial officers and lawyers rose to the top of companies those bad habits became even more embedded.[43]

Standard accounting, with its emphasis on costs and short-term results, pushes managers to consider training as a cost rather than a way of satisfying customers. It encourages them to buy from the lowest-cost vendor, because it measures cost but not quality. A purchasing manager might win a bonus for buying the cheapest materials available, whereas the manufacturing manager who has to work with the same materials may lose his bonus because he could not reach production quotas on account of their poor quality. Ray Stata, the chairman of Analog Devices, complains that his accounting people used to waste the time of division managers arguing with each other about who should absorb certain costs, when the corporation as a whole was going to have to absorb them anyhow, which was all that really mattered. He describes how managers would alter shipments toward the end of the month, replacing scheduled small shipments with unscheduled big shipments so as to goose the numbers. The monthly figures looked better, but the small customers whose shipments were late certainly were not happy.[44]

Obviously, traditional accounting cannot be cast aside. A company has to know where it stands, and ultimately the success of a company's quality effort and everything else it does is ratified by its profitability. But new measures can certainly round out the picture and create new incentives to encourage managers to do the right thing to satisfy customers. Measurements serve TQM as a tool in four important ways:

1. To describe where you are.
2. To set "stretch" goals or otherwise describe where you need to be.
3. To figure out what to do first.
4. To measure progress or keep score of the results.

John Marous, the former Westinghouse CEO, described the transition from the old to the new way of thinking about standards:

"We had a culture that said 'Design it 95% right.' I remember a man telling me that a long time ago. Anything more than that and you're putting too much cost into it and you're losing profit. We had a '95%' mind-set. Well, the Japanese proved that that was wrong and then all of a sudden, we said 'hey, maybe we need something like 99.9%.' Then we said to ourselves, 'what's a 99.9% world like?' "[45]

In some ways, we already do a lot better than 99.9%. In 1991, out of a total of 6,800,000 commercial airline flights in the United States, four planes crashed. That performance yields a success ratio of 99.9999%. Had our airlines completed only 99.9% of their flights without accident, we would have had 6,800 crashes in 1991, which would have wiped out most of the commercial air fleet as well as the public's interest in flying. The human body does well too. If the heart operated 99.9% of the time, it would stop beating for eight hours and 45 minutes a year. But it usually goes on working, decade after decade, without a murmur—or even with one. So we already have examples of performance much superior to 99.9%. Of course, the failure of a heart or of an aircraft is life threatening, so their quality has to be extraordinary; but if it is possible for them, why not extend the same standards to other human activities?

That is just what many companies did by setting themselves goals that at first seemed unattainable. That got people to thinking about really changing the way they worked, and once the goals were attained they became the launching point for another huge improvement. Hewlett-Packard set a goal of improving its quality by 10 times in the 1980s. Milliken declared a 10–4 target, meaning a tenfold improvement in four years. IBM announced it would improve tenfold by 1991 and then, even though it did not achieve that goal, kept driving for a second tenfold improvement by 1993.

Six Sigma: Motorola's Standard

At the beginning of the 1980s corporations measured their quality in percentages, or the number of defects per hundred parts. Xerox typically had a 92% quality level, or eight defects per 100 products or processes. By the end of the decade, performance had improved so much that the companies in the vanguard of quality needed a new scale, so they began counting their defects in "parts per million." Xerox got down to a defect level of 300 parts per million, which can also be stated as a quality level of 99.97%. That represented a huge improvement over the 92% level at the beginning of the 1980s, which would translate into 80,000 defects per million parts.

Motorola set the most ambitious goals of all. In 1981, it decided to reduce defects by nine tenths in five years. But through benchmarking Motorola realized that rate of improvement was not fast enough, so it set the new goals of improving tenfold again by 1989, and yet again by 1991. Then Motorola announced what became the most famous quality goal in the United States—Six Sigma by 1992. Statisticians use the Greek letter sigma (σ) as a symbol to denote standard deviation. The higher the sigma number, the lower the rate of defects. By setting a goal of Six Sigma, Motorola said that whatever it did, whether it was making pagers or writing invoices, the rate of defects would not exceed 3.4 per million. By way of comparison, the average large corporation operates today in the vicinity of Four Sigma, or 3,000 defects per million. When your doctor scribbles a prescription or your waiter tots up the bill, they tend to do a bit worse than Four Sigma, which means that about 10,000 out of a million prescriptions or restaurant bills are wrong. In giving tax advice over the phone the IRS is off the sigma chart, with more than 100,000 mistakes per million pieces of advice. As we have already seen, the airlines do very well on safety (better than Six Sigma) but as for baggage handling, they are only a trifle better than Four Sigma.[46]

Motorola failed to reach the Six Sigma target by 1992. Some units did reach it; some units were even better. But the company as a whole got to 150 parts per million, somewhere between Five Sigma and Six Sigma. Never mind; Motorola came close, and without that aggressive goal it might have not have come so close. Motorola still wants to improve tenfold every two years, into the 21st Century. That would put Motorola up to the level of one defect per billion parts.[47] Why would Motorola be so fanatical as to want a defect rate as low as one in a billion? Who would notice? As electronic systems get more complicated, one part per billion does become a significant defect rate. By the end of the decade, semiconductors will contain as many as one billion transistors each.

As the defect rates fall into the range of only a few hundred per million parts, corporations run into a peculiar problem. Sampling is no longer practical when the rate of failure is less than 0.1% of 1%, that is, below 1,000 problems per million. IBM's Steve Schwartz explains that the screen used before to sample and study errors no longer works. You might have asked a sample of 25 branches out of a total of 200 outlets to return defective products to the company to be counted and analyzed. But at the lower failure rate you may find that none of the 25 outlets turn up a single defective product. Now you have to change the system and collect products from all the branches, which is more complicated.[48] Eventually corporations will have to invent defects or simulate them on the computer in order to have something to study.

Measuring the Wrong Things

All the measurements in the world will not help if they are the wrong measurements, and many companies found that indeed they were measuring the wrong things. They were elaborating on the internally developed old measures, rather than using measures that focused on the customer. Critics say Motorola's Six Sigma is too much of an elaborate internal measure, and does not mean much to the customer. As they understand these measures better, corporations are finding new ones or changing the old ones, looking more outward. The business units at IBM are now judged by seven measurements. Four of the measurements are traditional financial or business measurements: revenue growth, profit growth, return on assets, and free cash flow, but the other three are new: customer satisfaction, employee morale, and quality improvement. At Conrail, CEO Jim Hagen found that the company was keeping a mass of statistics and most of them were "awful." The Conrail people measured the wrong things. For instance, they counted the number of cars per train, and thought that the longer the trains were, the better they were doing. So if a train looked as if it was going to be too short, they would cancel it and add the cars to another train—much as airlines sometimes discover "mechanical problems" with underbooked planes and shift the passengers to another flight. By the internal measures, the long trains were saving money. But when Conrail looked outwards and asked the customer what he thought, it turned out that reliability mattered very much. Long term, it was not cost effective to cancel short trains. Conrail now sends its trains off on schedule, whether they are short or long.[49]

Analog Devices' chairman, Ray Stata, has long been unhappy with the accounting measurements that he felt distorted a company's activities and goals. When Analog Devices set out its five-year plan for 1987–1992, it asked each of its divisions to meet four standard types of business goals, such as a 15% return on capital and a 20% to 25% growth in sales. But it added three goals based on what customers said was most important to them: on-time deliveries to improve from 85% to 99.8%; outgoing defects to drop from 500 parts per million to less than 10 ppm; and the time for filling orders to shrink from ten weeks to less than three weeks. In addition, Analog Devices added four other goals that would track improvements in internal performance: reducing manufacturing cycle time from 15 weeks to four to five weeks; reducing the level of process defects from 5,000 ppm to less than 10 ppm; improving the yield of usable silicon wafers from 20% to more than 50%, and cutting the time to market for new products from 36 months to six months.

What happened to some of the new measures at Analog Devices shows just how tricky it can be to try to set new kinds of goals for a company, admirable as they may seem at first. For instance, the goal of reducing lead time on orders to three weeks was scrapped. It turned out that what the customer really wanted was not necessarily speed but an assured delivery date. Some customers wanted delivery within days, others, especially the military, did not need delivery for a year or more. So the significant measure here was not the three weeks, it was consistently meeting the date set by the customer. Analog Devices therefore established a new measure, the percentage of "customer request dates" matched—which was 44.6% in 1992. Analog had trouble meeting delivery dates because it ran out of capacity in some product lines.

The goal of reducing time-to-market for new products from 36 months to six months also made trouble. The engineers, it seems, "consciously or unconsciously" turned away from riskier new products and stuck to derivatives of old products. In other words, they feared that they would not meet the new six-month deadline if they took on a major product development. Analog scrapped that goal too. The goal of reducing outgoing defects from 500 ppm to less than 10 ppm surprisingly upset many long-standing customers. If Analog had to redesign the product to eliminate its defects, the customer often had to go to the expense of getting the product "requalified" (that is, tested and approved by Underwriters Laboratories or some such organization) before it could be used. It turned out that many customers preferred the defects to the expense. So Analog left many of the old products alone, with their defects, and concentrated on defect-free new products.

Curiously, although Stata has fought hard for the new measures and they have become important to the company, his annual reports are still set in the old accounting format. In 1989 Stata came very close to including performance data along with the usual financial data in the annual report. But he pulled the addition at the last minute. One reason, which turned out to be well justified, was that the measures were not yet tested and mature. Analog management also felt that although its stockholders, customers, and employees might understand the new metrics, Wall Street would be deeply suspicious and regard them as a ruse to conceal problems. Stata was disappointed not to become the first CEO to use this kind of metric in an annual report, but it was just as well he did not. The management of Analog became absorbed in other matters—a reorganization, an acquisition, and a weak market; and quality improvement got put on the back burner in 1990. "The fact that we weren't able to pat our head and rub our stomach at the same time indicated the fragility of the quality system," Stata says. "It wasn't by any means institutionalized, so as soon as you glance in another direction, it doesn't sustain itself." Art Schneiderman, the company's former quality director, now regards this diversion of efforts as an "immense mistake," because when you lose momentum you start sliding back. Had the annual report been publishing performance figures, it would have shown a decline. For instance, on-time deliveries, instead of improving from 96% in 1990 to 99.8% in 1992 as targeted, fell to 92.7%. The manufacturing cycle time, instead of being cut to four to five weeks in 1992, increased to more than 10 weeks.[50]

You Get What You Ask For

As its quality policies matured, Corning also refined its measurements. Like many companies, at first it measured too many things and the wrong things. The standard measures that Corning required at first were hours of training per person, numbers of teams, participation on teams, and numbers of suggestions received. Although these numbers might indicate the degree of involvement in quality efforts in the company, they had little to do with satisfying the customer. They came to be regarded as an irrelevant nuisance by plant managers and some refused to submit them. In January 1990 Corning introduced a new set of "key result indicators." Once a quarter, each of Corning's 54 units has to report the results of five key indicators related to customer satisfaction, employee satisfaction, and the improvement of processes, such as on-time deliveries. They are not the same indicators for each unit, but each has to report on five measures. Corning wants to get the number down to three indicators per business unit.[51]

The Baldrige Quality Award itself, in a sense, has turned out to be a significant tool for measuring and improving quality. Many companies, including IBM and Corning, use the Baldrige criteria internally to track their quality efforts, using their own examiners and judges. The criteria for the prize cover the essential elements of good quality, and the scoring, on the basis of a possible maximum of 1,000 points, provides a good reading on how a company is doing. IBM ranks its best performers on four levels. A score of 876 points or better rates a chairman's award, which no group has won yet, although the Rochester division, winner of the real Baldrige, came close. A gold plaque goes to those with 751 to 875 points (which in Baldrige competition would probably be enough to win the award), a silver plaque to those scoring 626 to 750 points (enough to qualify as a finalist in the Baldrige), and a bronze for 501 to 625 points (which is not great by Baldrige standards, but better than most U.S. companies could do). In the first three years of the award (to the spring of 1993), of 380 units and sites at IBM, 44 had won the bronze awards, 20 the silver, and four the gold.[52]

At Conrail, which is newer at the game, employees make their own evaluations with a simplified Baldrige form, and score themselves fairly consistently around 350 points. A Conrail executive allows this level of scoring is "the pits . . . but it shows how far we need to go." The widespread internal use of the Baldrige criteria can be gauged by the fact that although only 106 companies actually applied for the award in 1991, the National Institute of Standards and Technology, which administers the award, received requests for 240,000 handbooks describing the criteria.[53]

The measures used by a company are crucial not only because they describe the company's condition but also because they determine the company's priorities. People will deliver what they are asked to deliver, as defined by the measures a company uses. Sometimes what seem like the most commendable measures will have unexpected results, so they have to be chosen with great care and then tested.

Like the other tools of quality, measures should be applied judiciously, without becoming an end in themselves. Used on their own, the tools may be useless, if not harmful. They need to mesh into an overall quality strategy.

CONCLUSIONS

From the experience of U.S. companies since 1980, it seems clear there are many ways of applying the tools of quality. Just-in-time manufacturing may suit one situation, but not another. Statistical process controls will likely work better with a repetitive manufacturing process than with a free-flowing creative process. However, certain points stand out fairly consistently:

- Tools should be used to exterminate the root causes of a problem, not merely to fix the problem itself. You want to stop that mistake from happening again.
- The elimination of variation lies at the heart of the use of the tools of quality. Variation means defects.
- Like other pieces of total quality, the tools are relatively simple and

commonsensical, but they are not easy to apply because they upset the way we are used to doing thing.

- A large part of the American workforce is too uneducated to use the new TQM tools, even if they are simple.
- Some tools, especially just-in-time manufacturing and benchmarking, seem so powerful that it becomes tempting to use them on their own, isolated from total quality management as a whole process. That is not a good idea.
- The use of quality tools can backfire if they are applied with too much zeal and become an end in themselves rather than the means to achieve a quality product.
- Measurements are an essential tool because they create a rational basis for action, they set up the goals to be achieved, and they record the progress towards the goals. Without measures, you do not know what to do, where to go, or whether you have arrived. Measurements keep you honest.
- Tools should not be applied piecemeal, but should fit an overall quality strategy.

Part Two

6

The Automakers

Almost There

Japan discovered a better way to make a car; as a result, the U.S. automotive industry will never be the same again. The most powerful industry in the most powerful economy in the world had to discard the system that had made it so successful in the past and recreate itself. What emerged was a fundamentally different industry, one that was smaller, humbler, and made cars that are much, much better. The quality of the cars made in America in the 1990s is markedly superior to what it was in the 1970s, before the full force of competition struck Detroit. For example, using the Detroit style of counting "things gone wrong" as a measure of quality, as the 1980s started Detroit produced cars with 300 to 400 TGW per 100 cars, but by the close of the decade the average had shrunk to close to 100. The J. D. Power "initial quality study" of 1992, based on queries to buyers three months after they purchased their new cars, found that American cars on average had 136 problems per 100 cars, compared to an average of 105 problems per 100 Japanese cars. Both have been improving for years, but American cars have been getting better faster. (European cars, on average, lag a bit behind American cars and had more problems in 1992 than in 1991.) The best of the American cars, Saturn, had a count of 109, compared to Honda's 105 and Infiniti's 70, the best of all. Mercedes scored below average; the Power survey organization does not give the scores of below average performers.[1]

In 1993, *Consumer Reports*, which has never been particularly partial to American cars (or at least, its readers have not been so), changed its method of scoring the quality of cars because improvements in the cars had made the old method obsolete. In the 1980s, said the magazine, "the average trouble rate of American-made models dropped by two thirds, approaching the reliability of Japanese models at the start of the decade. Meanwhile, Japanese automakers improved their products' reliability by one third." The difference between "average" and "better than average" had become insignificant, so *Consumer Reports* stopped using those terms and instead just assigned percentages to the symbols it uses to indicate the reliability of the different components of the different models. For example, the highest rating meant that 2% or fewer owners reported problems with that particular component.[2]

There is no question that American cars are now much better than they were, but it seems a miracle that the industry has survived the effort. Indeed, Ford came to the brink of disaster once in the early 1980s, and Chrysler looked like a goner twice, in 1979 and again in the early 1990s. And after struggling for more than a decade to get it right, General Motors found itself in the early 1990s in more trouble than it had ever been before. Anyone who has the illusion that quality is easy should look at the history of the auto business since 1979. The specific steps the Big Three had to take to make better cars may not have been so difficult in themselves, but changing the organizations so that they *could* take those steps turned out to be appallingly difficult. The whole concept of a corporation created at GM by Alfred P. Sloan, Jr., and confirmed by decades of successful car-making had to be thrown out and replaced. Naturally, resistance within the company was enormous.

THE 1980S: GM'S BIG MISTAKE

The auto industry wasted much of its efforts to reform in the 1980s by twisting and turning to find some way out of its crisis other than doing what it had to do. It tried to get government protection from foreign competition and did get a reprieve in the form of quotas. The restraints on Japanese imports helped boost the profits of the Big Three in the mid-1980s, but at the cost of raising the price the American consumer had to pay for all cars— which also gave the Japanese manufacturers additional profits to finance the construction of transplant factories in the United States. The Big Three sought shelter and help in diversification. General Motors acquired Electronic Data Systems and Hughes Aircraft, Ford bought a savings bank, and Chrysler bought four car rental agencies (all money losers), as well as an aerospace company and a defense electronics firm. They made what *Fortune* described as ''frivolous'' investments in small European luxury-car manufacturers, GM in Lotus and SAAB, Chrysler in Lamborghini and Maserati, and Ford in Aston Martin and Jaguar.

GM made a major mistake which the others were lucky enough, if you can call it that, not to be able to afford. During the 1980s, GM spent a total of $77 billion on new plants and equipment and, to quote *Fortune* again, "investing that much money sensibly is almost impossible."[3] GM made an enormous bet that automation would solve its quality and productivity problems, but of course it did not, because the problem was in management and not in the factory. For a lot less money, GM could have acquired Toyota and Honda had they been for sale.

To be fair to the U.S. auto industry, it had to carry extra burdens that made the reform more difficult than it might have been. Back when the Japanese industry was creating its "lean" manufacturing system, markets were growing and the Japanese companies had plenty of work for everyone. This growth absorbed workers who otherwise would have been made superfluous by productivity improvements. But when Detroit tried in the 1980s to do what Japan had done the auto markets turned erratic, and after some boom years in the 1984–1986 period, sales went into a fast slide.

Therefore just when the U.S. auto companies were trying to enlist the enthusiasm and trust of their employees they were dismissing tens of thousands of them and, at least at GM, shutting many plants. Domestic sales of cars and trucks dropped from 17.6 million in 1988 to 13.9 million in 1991, lower even than in 1979, by 9%. At the same time production capacity grew, from 15.3 million cars and trucks in 1989 to 16.4 million in 1992. All that overcapacity drained both the capital and the enthusiasm of the auto companies. Of course, the Japanese also confronted a worldwide overcapacity for making cars, but their loss in sales was less dramatic. Indeed, in the United States, while Big Three sales fell between 1989 and 1991, Japanese sales increased; the transplants were operating at 81% of capacity in 1992, a lot better than Chrysler's 47% and GM's 67%, but not as good as Ford's 82% (for its car factories only).[4]

You can drum up sympathy for the auto industry on other grounds. Japan could keep its costs down then because its workers were paid less, but that is no longer so, and in any case a sharp rise in the value of the yen wiped out much of the cost advantages that the Japanese might have had. The U.S. auto industry pleads for sympathy on the grounds of much higher medical insurance and pension costs, and somewhat higher capital costs; these burdens are, or were, in the case of capital, indeed heavier for American companies. The Economic Strategy Institute in Washington concluded in a study of the auto industry in 1992 that "after 40 years of losing market share, the U.S. automotive industry has become a world-class competitor on a current operating basis." That restrictive phrase "on a current operating basis" is a big one because it assumes that the plants are running at full capacity and it excludes retiree, pension, and health care costs.[5] If you include them, as of course you must in real life, then the competitiveness of the U.S. industry rests on very thin margins today.

A CLONED INDUSTRY: THE BIG THREE

None of these diversions and excuses altered the fact that the Big Three had to transform themselves to stay in business. The locomotive pulling them through the transformation is total quality management. The story of the industry's efforts to change—and to resist change—has been in the press almost daily for many years and has been told in a number of books, notably *The Machine That Changed The World* by James Womack and other members of the MIT International Motor Vehicle Program, *Managing On The Edge* by Richard Tanner Pascale, and *Rude Awakening* by Maryann Keller; the last book takes the GM drama up through 1989, after which the story became even more dramatic.[6] I will not try to retell here the whole tumultuous epic of the auto industry since 1979 as so much of it is familiar to my readers, but I will attempt to relate some of those events to the themes of this book.

When the crisis broke in 1979, the Big Three were much alike, or at least followed the same paths. Though it is true that GM resembled a federation because of the powerful divisions in the company whereas Ford was more centrally controlled, in other respects they were similar. They were dominated by financial people, and the "real" car people—the engineers and manufacturing specialists—played second fiddle. Over the years, the Big Three bred powerful functional empires that had more interest in protecting their own prerogatives than in making good cars—a familiar malady in large organizations, made worse in this case because these auto companies were so big and had been so successful for so long. They kept peace with labor by agreeing to demands that made them very generous, though not congenial, employers. GM had 44.4% of the North American car and truck retail market and the other two pretty much followed its lead, in models and pricing. It was a cloned industry.

But the Big Three did not react to the crisis at all like clones. Each reacted according to its resources, prejudices, and preferences. Eventually though, by the early 1990s, the different paths they followed had led them all to the same conclusion: that the way to compete lay in caring carefully for the customer, in teamwork, in collaborating with labor, in simplifying and speeding design, and in continuously improving every part of the business—all the basic tenets of total quality management.

FORD

As related in Chapter 1, Ford had the luck to get a good start early on because its chairman, Philip Caldwell, recognized the importance of employee involvement and believed, at least officially, that quality was Job 1. Because of the happy coincidence that Don Ephlin of the UAW and Pete Pestillo of Ford worked well together, the company made a healthy beginning in employee involvement. Top management and labor were enlisted in the cause relatively easily. What Ford had to fight hardest to overcome in the beginning was its notorious "chimney" structure, which had turned the company into a battleground of warring functions. James Bakken, a former Ford vice president of corporate quality, describes the state of mind that existed in Ford's middle and senior management in the 1960s and 1970s:

"We had a highly functional structure, with each function doing the best for itself. The fact that a function was an internal supplier to other activities never entered people's minds. We didn't have teams. Engineering would withhold information from manufacturing until the due date even if the material was ready earlier so that they wouldn't be expected to deliver early the next year. The head of engineering might decide to stop overtime and he'd get accolades for succeeding in cutting costs dramatically. But the plans and the products would be late, and manufacturing management careers were affected for the failure to meet the sacrosanct Job 1 date. People responded in a manner that made their function stand out regardless of the impact on the company."[7]

A plant engineer at Ford told Richard Pascale: "The games we played were amazing. We'd sabotage the other's projects. We'd freeze the other side out of discussion, swear, blow up, ignore people, or simply not show up at meetings." The product revealed these games. When Ford tried make a world car out of the European-designed Escort with the same parts all over the world, each region redesigned the car; in the end, only six of the Escort's 5,000 parts were the same in Europe as in the United States—and one of those was the radiator cap.[8]

To break the chimneys, a daunting task, Stuart Frey, vice president of engineering, established a blue-ribbon committee in 1980 that began by trying to de-layer and down-size the engineering department in order to cut costs. But the committee, confined as it was to the engineering department, made no progress; so it expanded its membership to include representatives of design, manufacturing, and truck operations. Now it was a cross-functional group. It did not accomplish much in its first two years, other than recommending that engineering be pruned from five to three layers of management and that the jobs of 200 middle managers be eliminated. Nevertheless the heads of two warring departments, engineering and design, met every Thursday evening for two years to try to establish a base for cooperating. Their effort so impressed other executives at Ford that by 1985 more than 100 chimney-breaking groups were at work, bringing together arch-enemies who swore and threw temper tantrums at first, but gradually learned to work together.[9]

Tremendous Trifles: The Taurus

Team Taurus legitimized the team approach at Ford. The Taurus project began in 1980 at a time when gasoline prices were high and predicted to go higher, so Ford started with the idea of making a small four-cylinder car. Then the price of gas went down instead of up, and Ford paused to reconsider. By this time Ford had assembled the multi-function Team Taurus, so the recommendation it made came not only from designers, who would have been the only people involved up to that point in a traditional project, but also from representatives of engineering, manufacturing, marketing, and finance (once the most powerful of the empires at Ford). Since Ford was making a $3-billion bet-the-company investment in Taurus, it was just as well to have solid backing from everyone who would be responsible for making the car a success.

The team made other bold decisions that top management backed. If Ford had followed the usual me-too pattern, it would have imitated the Chevy Citation, but priced slightly lower. Instead Team Taurus decided to emulate the Audi, but to come in about $4,000 below the price of the Audi. Upscaling meant that Taurus would be about $800 more expensive than the LTD, the car it replaced—another break with usual practice. Normally the new model would come in at the same price as its predecessor, or lower. Instead of copying all the boxy designs of the times, the Taurus team chose to go with the ovoid shape. The new car was stacked with features developed through much probing of customers and benchmarking the 400 ''best-in-class'' features of other cars around the world (see Chapter 5).[10] The ''tremendous trifles,'' as they were described by the late Lewis Veraldi, head of the Taurus project, were developed painstakingly. They included the double sun visors on the driver's side and the gimballed cup holder. ''We made sure that even the common things were done uncommonly well,'' Veraldi said.[11]

But here Team Taurus slipped up. To create a really successful product, you need not only to find out just what features the customer wants and give them to him, but also to give him a product free of defects. You design quality into the car.

Team Taurus did not pay enough attention to the second part of the challenge: it did not apply quality processes with enough rigor. When Taurus came out in 1985, it had problems. The exhaust system gave off a strong rotten-egg smell, the engine tended to stall and surge, the steering would stiffen up, and the car suffered electrical failures. After first extolling the car, *Consumer Reports* took it off its recommended list.[12] But even Lexus had two minor recalls at the beginning. As L. L. Bean had shown at the beginning of the century, you can take failures at the start and turn them to your advantage if you treat the customer right. Whereas GM continued through the 1980s to stiff-arm customers who complained, Ford took care of them and the early troubles of Taurus faded. It became an enormously successful car, outstanding for its quality and advanced design. Ford's earnings soared, surpassed GM's earning for three straight years (1986 to 1988), and peaked at $5.3 billion in 1988. The two Taurus assembly plants in Atlanta and Chicago became more efficient than any GM or Chrysler plant in the United States or any of the Japanese transplant assembly factories. Only one Ford car assembly plant, the one making the Tempo and Topaz models in Kansas City, is more productive.[13] In 1992, with a freshened-up model, Taurus won the ultimate prize; it became the best-selling car in the United States, passing the Honda Accord with a little help from what marketing people call "aggressive pricing."

Dedicated and Collocated

Team Taurus became the model that broke down Ford's functional organization. Subsequent Mustang, Continental, Thunderbird, and Escort models were all born of the team approach. The Taurus team was "dedicated" but not "collocated", that is, its members worked full time on the car but they were not physically located in the same place. All new Ford models will be produced by dedicated and collocated teams. Their members represent marketing, manufacturing, engineering, finance and, in some cases, dealers. One troublesome vestige of the old system remains. Team members still have two bosses, their boss at the home unit and their team boss. Both in theory determine the team member's pay and progress, but that works against the team concept; the team performance should determine pay. Deming tried for years to argue Ford out of individual ratings tied to pay increases, but while the company has made major changes in its appraisal system it has not eliminated individual ratings. How else would you identify and encourage high potential people?[14]

In the plants, the teams have clearly taken root. Michael Oblak, a burly, enthusiastic man with a big mustache, gold necklaces, jeans, and a grey sweatshirt with "Bad Boyz" written across the chest in pink, is clearly a union guy. He is plant chairman for UAW Local 900 at the Wayne (Michigan) Stamping Plant. He is as proud of the plant as if he were the plant manager. Back in 1989, "we were given an open hand to assess what we needed to do to change what needed changing."

Members of the union went to Japan and visited Fremont, California, where GM and Toyota have their successful joint operation, the New United Motor Manufacturing Inc. or NUMMI. They read "damned near every team contract" they could find and "were not impressed" because the contracts put the team leader above everybody else. They wanted to make it easy for team members to change the leader, and to have a sense that they had a say in how the plant was run. When the teams started up it was so easy to change leaders that some teams dumped their leaders 20 minutes after electing them. But Oblak told them, "This is our opportunity to show Ford we're not just a bunch of ignorant workers." They did settle down after a while and began to vote more seriously.

The union ran most of the meetings that trained workers and answered their questions. They found out what would make workers feel better about their jobs, and what had to be removed so that people would not "grind their teeth" when they came to work. It turned out that one important improvement was reducing job classifications, from 30 to just one, "body stamping technician." This meant that all the members of a team had to learn everybody else's job. "They were all scared when they came here," says Oblak, "but rotation couldn't be as bad as doing the same thing day in day out." Some teams rotate jobs daily, some weekly. All the plant's 1,320 workers belong to teams. The teams schedule vacations and personal days off and are strict about attendance. Absenteeism at the plant runs to 2% to 3%, which Oblak thinks is the best in the industry. Each team has a pool person who can fill in for members who are absent, or can be loaned to another team if his own does not need him. The skilled-trades people kept their specialties but are allowed to help each other out.

Teams can call supplier plants to complain or bring their workers in to show them why it is important, for example, not to ship steel with burrs. When workers report a quality problem it goes on a schedule specifying the number of days that problem may remain unsolved. If the problem remains open beyond the allotted time, Oblak takes it to the assistant plant manager.[15]

A little more than halfway through what Ford people describe as a 20-year journey to quality, the culture you find at the Wayne stamping plant is taking root in the company. Ford's CEOs have pointed steadily in the right direction. From Philip Caldwell, chairman in the late 1970s and early 1980s, through Donald Petersen to Harold Poling, the leadership provided continuity of purpose without the autocratic, egocentric behavior that has often characterized the bosses in Detroit. Petersen, in particular, played well in the role of encouraging employee involvement, and he allowed a lot of good impulses to rise up through the company.

The results are striking. In addition to Taurus, Ford has had other extremely successful models, the small Ranger truck, the jeep-like Explorer, and the Lincoln Town Car, all either highly rated for quality or highly successful in the market, or both. Ford's share of the North American car and truck market climbed from a low of 18.8% in 1981 to a peak of 23.8% in 1989, while GM's share fell resoundingly from 42.4% to 33.3% in the same period.[16] While GM tried to trim its overcapacity, Ford strained to produce enough cars. Ford's quality efforts were not always successful, of course. The 1989 Thunderbird/Cougar had some serious problems at the start, and the quality ratings of the Lincoln Town Car slipped when the Wixom plant in Michigan was pushed to raise output to meet demand in 1988. Output did climb by 30%, but the defect rate went up 75%.[17]

When car sales began to slide in 1989, Ford could not escape the consequences of the recession combined with a worldwide overcapacity for building cars. It lost $2.3 billion in 1991 and $502 million in 1992—$7.4 billion if you include accounting changes in its pension plan and other one-time accounting charges. However, because of the improvements in quality and productivity, Ford was in a far stronger position to face the setbacks than GM, far stronger than it would have been without undertaking the long journey. The productivity and quality of Ford's plants rank with the best in the world today.

CHRYSLER

When Chrysler chairman Lee Iacocca introduced the new line of K-cars in 1980, he boasted that they were "already the most talked about cars in the history of the business—a household word before a single one hits the dealers' showrooms."[18] But what people said about the K-cars, those boxy Dodge Aries and Plymouth Reliants, was not what Iacocca hoped. They were consistently rated below average in quality. Iacocca said that if people mistook the K-cars for Mercedes "we can live with that." Not many people made that mistake. If Chrysler survived the 1980s, after surviving the crisis of 1979, it was sustained if anything by the bombast and salesmanship of Lee Iacocca, brash and flamboyant long after his cars ceased to be, and his ability to get a federal loan guarantee. Iacocca went on television to advertise the quality of Chrysler's cars, but the surveys showed their quality was not competitive. Actually, in the beginning, in 1980, Chrysler *did* have the best quality among the Big Three, but over the next five years, while Chrysler's quality improved somewhat, Ford and GM made better progress, according to unpublished data from the Maritz (formerly Rogers) Survey, leaving Chrysler in third place.[19]

By the mid-1980s Chrysler had little to keep it going except for its TV star, Lee Iacocca. At least it could not make the mistake GM made and try to spend its way out of trouble. It enjoyed what the auto industry analyst Maryann Keller describes as "timely poverty."[20] And it did produce one very successful line of vehicles in the minivan, a comfortable family vehicle which for a time completely dominated its market. By 1984 Chrysler had 75% of the minivan market, and even when others produced their versions Chrysler held on to the biggest piece of it. But Chrysler was not a company where total quality could take root nor where productivity could make real gains. Other than cutting costs, marketing vigorously, and maneuvering financially with devices like the rebate, the company hardly changed at all. It was still dominated by strong functional divisions working in run-down, out-of-the-way offices, far from the splendor of the Ford and GM offices. Like his former boss, Henry Ford II, Iacocca ruled imperially and mercurially. He would sweep into designers' offices and, to their dismay, tell them to add some wire wheels and vinyl long after they had gone out of fashion.

Hanging On

By 1989 old Chrysler hands began to think "here we go again." With no really new models since the K-cars, Chrysler's already small share of the auto market was slipping and the company could not live forever off its minivans. The acquisition of American Motors in 1987 with its old, inefficient factories and poor quality was still a liability. The Jeep line of sports-utility vehicles that Chrysler had acquired with AMC had yet to come into vogue. In June 1989 Chrysler's top management met at the Bloomfield Hills Country club and outlined a whole new approach to the car business.[21] By this time Iacocca's reign was coming to an end and although he hung on for another three and a half years, much of the power in the company shifted to President Robert A. Lutz.

Iacocca acquiesced in what happened next, rather than leading it. Chrysler's actions paralleled remarkably what Ford had already done, but Chrysler moved more rapidly and surely, perhaps because it had the example of others to draw on, and also because it had the pressure of $6.8 billion in debts to roll over in 1992. Chrysler replaced the function-based organization of the company with teams, cut out overhead, benchmarked products and processes extensively, thinned the ranks of suppliers, and started training dealers how to be nice to the customer.

The first car the new Chrysler rolled out was the Viper, shown as a concept in 1989 but not manufactured until the end of 1991. At a price of $50,000, this flashy little two-seater was not supposed to get Chrysler's market share up, but it was supposed to create a stir and bring people into Chrysler's showrooms, and it did. Just as important, the Viper project served as a laboratory for Chrysler to learn the new way of making cars. The car was developed in 36 months, rather than the four and a half years normal at Chrysler, by a team of only 75 engineers working in one large room where they could clear up problems and make decisions on the spot. The team practiced the technique of simultaneous engineering, so that design and manufacturing engineers, market specialists, and representatives of the suppliers worked together all along, rather than sequentially. They could see and solve problems early on. Suppliers provided more than 90% of the parts for the Viper, rather than the usual 70%.

"Last Hope": A Team Car Flies

When Chrysler moved on to its next project, the so-called LH car—immediately nicknamed "Last Hope," of course—the team approach took hold. The LH was Chrysler's first basically new car for the masses since the K-car of a decade before. It was meant to re-establish Chrysler in the large, lucrative market for mid-sized cars. The LH team benchmarked extensively against upscale cars like the Acura Legend, the BMW, and the Nissan Maxima. The team cut the number of suppliers from the 600 to 800 Chrysler usually used to 170 and brought them in at the start to work closely with the engineers. Some of them took up residence at Chrysler for three years. The LH cars that emerged in 1992, the Chrysler Concorde, the Dodge Intrepid, and the Eagle Vision, had something missing at Chrysler for a long time— style and excitement. The so-called "cab-forward" look with the windshield ending somewhere over the front wheels achieved a styling success, and both the quality and the performance impressed the buffs and buyers. Although dealers begged for cars in the fall of 1992 and the company gasped for cash, Chrysler ramped up production slowly to get it right. The first 4,000 cars did have a problem, a faulty washer in the steering gear; and like Lexus at its outset, Chrysler tried to turn a mistake into an advantage by changing the washers quickly and without quibbling. With its new approach to the LH, Chrysler had reduced its cost of a developing a new car from $2 billion to around $1.5 billion and cut the time it took to three and a half years.

Chrysler totally adopted the team approach. Two thirds of the company's 6,000 engineers formed into teams to develop a whole series of new vehicles—four cars, a Jeep, a minivan, and a truck. Chrysler pulled them together into the new $900-million Technical Center north of Detroit. When Iacocca finally retired at the end of 1992, he was not replaced by Lutz. (Perhaps the Chrysler board could not face dealing with another hot-tempered chairman). Instead they picked Robert Eaton, who had run GM's highly successful operation in Europe. In the three years following that meeting at the Bloomfield Hills Country Club, Chrysler knocked $3 billion off its costs and improved the productivity of its plants by 18%, putting them far ahead of GM and within reach of the plants at Ford and the Japanese transplants. *Consumer Reports* recommended the LH family of cars for their quality and was happy to report that Chrysler "finally has some truly competitive models to sell." Chrysler was saved, again.[22]

GENERAL MOTORS

When we turn to General Motors, the strange, if not tragic, element in the story is that the company saw and even tested most of what it needed to do within its own walls and failed to learn the lessons or get the message. NUMMI, the joint GM-Toyota venture, proved how effective Toyota's production system and teams could be with GM's UAW workers. GM in Europe showed how profitable and productive a lean, nimble manufacturing system could be. Buick City demonstrated (after considerable difficulties) that with teamwork an old factory could be turned around. Saturn proved that you could take GM managers and workers and create a wholly new company based on the best of what is known about new production systems and participation. Saturn produced a world-class car.

All these things happened inside GM, and still the company did not get it. How could a company full of bright engineers and able managers fail for more than a decade to respond to what was happening not only all around it, but inside it too? Perhaps it cannot respond. Perhaps an organization as large and old as GM, successful for so many years, simply cannot function competitively today. That is a possibility.

But rather than dismissing the GM experience, perhaps it is more useful to look at what prevented GM from learning for so long. Like Ford, GM was divided into empires, only more so. Ford at least was something of a family, almost in the literal sense since for most of its history members of the Ford family ran it, but GM was a conglomerate of separate units. GM had been created out of separate companies, and even though that happened back in the 1920s, their old loyalties remained. Fisher Body built the bodies and answered to the president. General Motors Assembly Division put the cars together and answered to the president. The five car divisions believed they were responsible for their own cars—even though the same basic car bodies ran throughout GM—and answered to the president. To put an end to this wasteful vertical organization, GM's leadership announced a major reorganization in 1984. Fisher and GMAC would be broken up and handed over to two basic car divisions: one for Buick, Oldsmobile, and Cadillac, and known as BOC, and the other for Chevrolet, Pontiac, and GM of Canada, known as CPC. The rank and file at GM seethed at what was happening to their old organizations, and management's famous inability to communicate with virtually everybody made it even harder to sell the reorganization.[23]

A Figure of Ridicule: Roger Smith

Roger Smith, the chairman of GM from 1981 to 1990, was not the man to transform GM, if indeed anyone could. He came eventually to symbolize GM's impotence, a figure of ridicule more than an object of criticism. Smith talked the language of quality and productivity, even made Saturn his own baby, but he did not "walk the talk," as Roger Milliken would say. William Scherkenbach, who served both the Ford and GM quality efforts in a senior capacity, describes Petersen of Ford as truly committed whereas Smith's attitude was one of "benign neglect."[24] By his actions, Smith showed his conviction that it was investments in new plants and technology that would lead GM to new successes. His was a classic mistake, made on a massive scale. Buying the most automated tools and imposing them on the existing GM framework, was worse than useless.

While GM was making this mistake, its executives were visiting NUMMI in Fremont, California, where they could clearly see that excellent cars could be built economically by reorganizing the production system, even if you automated on a relatively modest scale. But somehow the GM people could not communicate what was staring them in the face. Ross Perot joined the

GM board full of respect when GM bought his company, Electronic Data Systems, but soon was saying things to Smith in his direct way that no one inside GM would have dared say: that he was autocratic, that he intimidated people, that he had little tolerance or interest in what others had to say, and that he ran over people who disagreed with him.[25] Smith was not the kind of leader who could inspire a gush of creative activity.

The GM-10 Series: A Midsize Flop

GM's critical condition became evident when the company decided it was time to begin developing a new mid-sized car to compete in the lucrative market where Taurus, the Honda Accord, and finally Chrysler's new LH cars have done so well. GM made the decision to start work on what was called at first the GM-10 in 1981, just after Ford started the Taurus program. GM allocated $7 billion to the project—remember that Ford invested $3 billion in the Taurus and Chrysler $1.5 billion in the LH cars—and assigned Robert Dorn, the chief engineer at Pontiac, to run it. But unlike the Taurus project and others that followed later at Ford, Dorn's had no dedicated team and little authority. He worked out of the Chevrolet division, but had no power over the division's engineers. To get a concept approved, he had to consult all four divisions that were going to use the car (Buick, Chevrolet, Oldsmobile, and Pontiac). Then, to get a design, he had to request one from the GM Styling Center. To get the specifications for the car, he had to go to Fisher Body and the other component makers. He was a coordinator, not a team leader, and the groups he was trying to coordinate became even more difficult to deal with after the 1984 reorganization of GM. The program fell behind schedule and Dorn quit. A successor came in and became equally frustrated. The first GM-10, a two-door Buick Regal, got to the market in 1988, two years late, and the more frequently requested four-door version did not come out until 1990.[26] The other members of the family, the Chevrolet Lumina, the Pontiac Grand Prix, and the Olds Cutlass Supreme, came out in 1989.

While the Ford and Chrysler mid-size cars had great appeal, the GM-10 cars, with the exception of the Buick Regal, just did not catch on. GM had not really listened to the customers. The competing cars had air bags because that is what people demanded, but GM did not put them in the GM-10 cars at first. GM did not simplify design or improve manufacturability enough. After all the effort and pain of producing a new car, GM found it had lost an enormous chunk of its share in the bread-and-butter market for mid-sized cars. Between 1985 and 1992, GM's share of the mid-sized market fell from

59% to 34% (while Ford's grew from 21% to 31%).[27] Moreover, some of the plants building the GM-10 were hopelessly unproductive, in spite of (or perhaps because of) all that investment in plants and equipment. The Doraville, Georgia, plant requires twice as much labor to assemble a Cutlass Supreme as Ford's Atlanta plant needs to put together a comparable Taurus or Sable. Overall, GM's auto assembly plants require nearly 50% more labor than Ford's.[28]

The Group of 99: Saturn Rising

GM just could not seem to get it right ... and yet ... there were those exceptions. In 1990, much to the surprise of the quality fraternity, Cadillac won the Baldrige Award. After years of decline, Cadillac started heading in the right direction in 1985 by switching from the old sequential process for designing a car—from styling engineer to product engineer to manufacturing engineer to suppliers—to simultaneous engineering. Teams from all the relevant areas work on the design from the beginning. With Robert Dorn, the refugee from the the GM-10 program, serving as chief engineer, and with coaching from Deming, Cadillac saturated its operations with teams—teams for vehicles, for vehicle systems, and for components. Cadillac proved to the skeptics that it had earned the Baldrige when it produced the 1991 Seville, moving *Car and Driver* to say that America finally had a car that could go up against Mercedes and BMW.[29]

GM also produced the Saturn, one of the most interesting and advanced experiments anywhere in the new way of developing, manufacturing, and selling a car. Like the Japanese transplants, Saturn had the advantage of starting fresh in a "green field" in Spring Hill, Tennessee, far from Detroit and GM headquarters. Saturn does not use the GM logo, the GM credit card, GM rebates, or "Mr. Goodwrench." Saturn is a separate corporation. Everything about Saturn is new—the plants, the technology, the suppliers, the design, the materials, the work force, the people system, the management, and the car itself. There is a lot of risk in all that newness.

The Saturn difference is evident as soon as you arrive at the complex in Spring Hill. The main avenue is not named after some GM Pooh-bah or Tennessee politician, but after Don Ephlin, the UAW vice president who stuck his neck out to help design the new people system at Saturn. The buildings are democratic; the one that contains the office has the same grey siding outside as the factory buildings, and inside the furniture is standard all over. The UAW plant chairmen share offices with the plant managers; Saturn has three plants on the site: one for engines, one for assembly, and one for body systems, which makes the steel and plastic panels for the car. Whatever happens to Saturn, labor will share fully in the responsibility for the outcome. The UAW has been involved in Saturn almost since the beginning. GM's technical center did a couple of years' work on the concept of a small car to match the Japanese, beginning in 1982, but once the idea was approved, in 1984, the development of the plant was turned over to a so-called Group of 99, consisting of 55 union representatives, mostly line workers, and 44 management people. The Group of 99 broke up into seven teams that spent months traveling to find out how the human side of factory work was evolving. They visited 60 GM sites and 85 other companies, including Hewlett-Packard, Procter & Gamble, Cummins Engine, and General Foods.

"We started off with a 'nice' stage," recalls one of the Group of 99. "Then we went to the stormy stage. We had quite a bit of conflict over issues like seniority, job security, cost of living allowance, and risk–reward systems. These were tough issues. We had pretty seasoned people with an average of 15 to 18 years' experience and the gutty issues really got to people's backgrounds. They would storm out saying, 'I'm not going to put up with this any more.' But they came back and we got to feeling good about what we were doing."[30]

Getting Comfortable at Saturn

It turned out that the seven teams all came to much the same conclusions and the Group of 99 made, appropriately, 99 recommendations that formed the basis for the way Saturn is structured. Instead of a labor contract, management and the UAW signed a "memorandum of agreement" which governs the corporation. At the top is the Strategic Action Council, which runs the business. Both Saturn's president, Richard ("Skip") LeFauve, and Mike Bennett, the UAW president, sit on the Council. Next comes the Manufacturing Action Council, then business unit teams, then teams for modules of work units, and finally the actual working teams on the floor. Labor sits on all these groups. All Saturn employees belong to teams, which consist of 6 to 15 members.

The teams have 30 defined responsibilities or functions, including making their own budgets, dealing with scrap, scheduling, hiring, fixing vacations. They can deal directly with suppliers. When they need to hire someone, they fly the prospects in to Spring Hill with their families for interviews. They can make the hiring decisions, within certain guidelines about matters such as minority hiring. Saturn has brought in GM workers from 136 plants in 34 states. They obviously take their new role seriously. When Robert Stempel, then chairman of GM, visited Saturn in the fall of 1991 he found a slowdown in progress and the workers wearing black-and-orange armbands: they were protesting what they saw as a threat to the quality of Saturn cars in a production speed-up that management had planned.[31]

Decision-making at Saturn is aggressively consensual. You cannot reach a decision unless all the parties involved agree. At the same time, you cannot block a decision unless you can offer an alternative, but you are not supposed to block a decision if you are 70% comfortable with it. In practice, Saturn has had trouble reaching decisions and making them happen at the right level. At first, says LeFauve, the Strategic Action Council made too many decisions that should have been made lower down in the organization, but as the Saturn people got comfortable in their roles, the decisions moved down. Critics have said that Saturn gets bogged down in too much consensus-seeking, but LeFauve believes he can act when it is necessary. In 1992, when Saturn was dealing with the recall of the new coupes because it turned out to be easy to pop open the trunk, the decision had to be handled quickly, over a weekend, before the Strategic Action Council could meet. LeFauve made the decision to recall on the spot. He was challenged at the next SAC meeting, but got an agreement approving what he had done as a policy for the future.

Since Saturn is partly an experiment, LeFauve & Co. test the limits to see how far they can go. The policy on just-in-time inventories was "to see how lean we could get," and it turned out that in some areas Saturn was too lean to operate smoothly. The assembly plant started with one hour's worth of engines in the pipeline from the engine plant but that proved to be too tight, so the inventory was raised to an hour and a half. Saturn constantly adjusts inventory levels. Although the complex at Spring Hill is highly integrated, 60% of the components still come from the outside; to get them to the plant on time Saturn has leased a fleet of Ryder trucks, painted white and emblazoned with the red Saturn logo, to pick up parts all over the country and bring them to Tennessee.[32]

Can Production Meet Demand?

I have already described Saturn's exceptional dealership system (Chapter 4) and its unusual training and compensation plan (Chapter 5). Saturn has achieved breakthroughs in quality, especially on the service side, that no other American automaker can yet match. The results could be seen in 1992 when J. D. Power surveys ranked Saturn third for customer satisfaction (measuring service as well as the car itself), fourth in sales satisfaction (for the way the customer is handled in the showroom), and sixth in initial quality (a measure of the number of defects discovered in the first 90 days). The Power surveys may not be the ultimate in scientific accuracy, but they do parallel what the auto companies themselves learn. Only Lexus and Infiniti, both expensive luxury cars from Japan, scored better than Saturn in all three surveys.[33] For a small cheap car to have scored so well, ahead of BMW, Cadillac, Lincoln, Mercedes, and other nameplates, is extraordinary.

In spite of all these achievements, the Saturn concept remains controversial because the big question remains unanswered at this writing: Will it be able to make a profit, or enough profit to make the venture worthwhile? Did GM in its spendthrift days saddle Saturn with such a huge capital investment, $5 billion, that it can never make money? And now that Saturn is a success on the market, can production meet demand? Original plans called eventually for two production lines with a capacity to make more than 500,000 cars a year. But GM's cash shortage has postponed the second plant indefinitely. With the addition of a third crew—with each crew working 10-hour days, four days a week—the one existing Saturn plant has raised its output to 320,000 cars a year. Both LeFauve and Bennett argue that at this level Saturn is profitable—in the Saturn setting the senior union people get to see the same numbers that senior management sees.

Observers of the auto industry have split their forecasts for Saturn. James Womack, the author of MIT study, and James Harbour, the consultant who produces studies of auto productivity, believe Saturn has no hope of succeeding financially. David Cole, who heads the Office for the Study of Automotive Transportation at the University of Michigan, says Saturn is productive and could prove quite profitable.

A Passionate Basque Bites the Bullet

What about the parent? Can GM, after all the mistakes it has made, after wasting all those billions on near useless automation in the 1990s, find the right way now? The future of America's biggest corporation is linked intimately to its ability to transform itself into a total quality company. Quality is not the only thing that GM needs—the market, the economy, the competition, exchange rates will all have a lot to do with the company's future, as will its finances and the new models its designers are producing. However, unless GM adopts TQM in the broadest sense—meaning not only the quality of its vehicles, but also of its design, its customer relations, its dealerships, its labor relations, its manufacturing—then GM may not survive, or so it seems late in 1993 as this book goes to press.

When Robert Stempel, that homely, honest engineer, succeeded Roger Smith as chairman of GM in 1990, he believed in the teachings of the quality gurus. But he never called on the company to make the effort to change. He was too steeped in the old ways of GM to make the break that had to happen. He plodded along, and the company's losses mounted alarmingly, from $2 billion in 1990 to $4.5 billion in 1991. Stempel did undertake a massive downsizing, announcing that 21 plants would be closed and 75,000 workers laid off or retired early. But he did not move fast enough; nor did he undertake the necessary reorganization of what would be left of GM.

The GM board of directors, like other boards, rebelled against management in 1992 and installed John F. Smith, Jr. first as president and then as chief executive, replacing Stempel. As head of GM's international operations, Jack Smith had shown that he knew what needed to be done. He turned the European operation into a lean machine. When GM decided as a matter of policy in 1989 to start benchmarking (a decade later than Xerox and nearly a decade later than Ford), Smith took the decision seriously and started benchmarking in Europe. As a result, GM found it could build plants much more cheaply in Europe than it had thought possible. But in North America, GM only paid lip service to benchmarking. Under Smith, GM's operations in Europe became extremely profitable while the mother company sickened.

In Detroit, Smith moved substantively and symbolically to make basic changes at GM. He tore up the disastrous organization plan of 1984 and put a new North American auto operations headquarters into a small building in Warren, Michigan, well away from the GM corporate offices in Detroit. He slashed the corporate staff from 13,000 to 2,000 people and closed the executive dining room, where GM vice presidents had isolated themselves with their coteries from the rest of the world. GM's losses in 1992 set a new corporate world record of $23.5 billion, but most of that amount was an accounting charge for future health benefits for retirees, and the company showed a modest profit from auto operations in the fourth quarter.

Smith shook up GM with the appointment of a passionate Basque, José Ignacio López de Arriortúa, as vice president for purchasing, a position he had held under Smith in Europe. In the few months he spent in Detroit before heading back to Europe to help save Volkswagen (pursued by allegations that too many of GM's proprietary secrets had accompanied him), López terrorized GM's vast and sluggish supply train, most of which is inside the company, as GM buys 70% of its parts from its own subsidiaries. López, who distributed to his staff a diet for "feeding the warrior spirit," wielded short-term and long-term weapons against the suppliers. Short-term, he simply told them to cut prices faster than the 2% or 3% a year provided for in the existing contracts, and if he thought it necessary he revoked these contracts even if they covered the oncoming model year. Long-term he offered, indeed insisted on, large-scale assistance from GM teams to help suppliers improve productivity and cut prices. The idea had an unmanageable name, Purchase Input Concept Optimization With Suppliers, which fortunately was shortened to "Picos." In Spanish, "pico" means pick-axe, among other things. Whether a blitz campaign by GM's purchasing staff, people who themselves were not well trained in quality processes, could turn around an army of suppliers seemed questionable.[34]

After López' sensational departure, GM set about repairing its relations with suppliers while continuing to run PICOS workshops by the thousands to encourage them to perform better. GM told the suppliers it wanted to established long-term relationships, that it did not focus on price only, but also took quality and service into account, and that it would respect the suppliers' proprietary secrets, which had not been respected during López' reign. It offered suppliers world-wide contracts for the life of the product.[35] Although GM reported improvements among its suppliers, the introduction of some of the 1994 models was marred by supplier failures. GM had moved much closer to where Ford and Chrysler had already arrived but was still struggling.

THE SUPPLIERS

Since the battle for quality began in 1980, the auto industry has had an impact on its suppliers as great as the impact of competition on the auto industry itself. The auto companies, as customers, have hauled the suppliers through their own transformation. Supplying Detroit is a huge business. Sales of auto parts amount to $100 billion a year and companies dedicated to the auto industry employ 600,000 people.[36] Examining just one of these suppliers, the steel industry, you can see the influence of the automakers. The steel industry had become, if it is possible, even more encumbered by hubris than the auto industry because of its size and success during and after World War II. Big Steel simply dropped small clients when business was good, told its customers what prices to pay, ignored new technologies such as the basic oxygen furnace and continuous casting, and developed a venomous relationship with labor (while handing out extravagant pay and benefits).

Many pressures came to bear on the steel industry to force it to change: with the new technologies the Japanese and German steel makers overtook the U.S. industry in productivity in the early 1980s, the rust belt recession of 1982 and 1983 undercut the demand for steel, the new mini-mills competed vigorously with the big, old integrated mills on price and quality, aluminum and plastic stole whole markets from steel, and some clients like the beverage can industry started to insist on better quality. However, it was the demands of the auto industry that most shook up the steel makers.

Ford's former vice president for quality, James Bakken, recalls that U.S. steel industry standards allowed a 16% variation in the thickness of sheet steel. Anything within that range was okay to ship. "No wonder we had problems producing quality stampings," says Bakken, adding that the service provided by the steel companies, as measured by their performance on deliveries, was "pathetic." With their plants running at only 62% of capacity, the U.S. mills were still late 20% to 25% of the time. In 1980, the auto companies rejected about 8% of the steel they received for critical parts from domestic suppliers.

Gerald S. Hartman, a fourth-generation Bethlehem Steel employee and the first in his family to go to college, was chief metallurgical engineer at Bethlehem with responsibility for quality when the auto companies began making the new demands. Hartman, who is now a consultant to the steel industry, had watched employment at Bethlehem Steel drop from 105,000 to 60,000 when he left in 1984 and on down to 22,000 active employees and 67,000 pensioned retirees. For ten years, says Hartman, he tried without success to get Bethlehem to pay attention to quality. Based on what he had learned from Juran about the cost of poor quality, he figured that Bethlehem's quantifiable poor-quality cost was 13% of sales, or $850 million. That included scrap and rework, shipping emergencies, selling flat rolled steel rejected by customers at a discount, product liability, and other claims. He estimated that Bethlehem lost an additional 6% of sales for nonquantifiable reasons related to quality, such as late deliveries and loss of business.

Educating Bethlehem

What started the change at Bethlehem was Ford. "When our biggest automotive customer said shape up, we paid attention," Hartman remembers. Ford could see that its European sources provided steel with only a 3.5% reject rate. In Japan the rate was only 1.5%. Ford first encouraged the steel companies to attend its courses in statistical process controls and then insisted that they attend. Bethlehem itself adopted the structured Juran plan as its approach to quality. The results came rapidly, says Bakken. Within two years, the reject rate of U.S.-made steel at Ford was down to 1.5%, a

Japanese level, and late deliveries dropped from 20% to 2%. Some mills, he said, did not have a late delivery for three years.

The standards were stricter too. Before, if Ford found defects in a 50,000-pound coil of rolled steel (enough to make 5,000 to 10,000 parts of cars), it would throw out the defective metal plus another 300 feet of the coil and keep the rest. But now, if any part of the coil is defective, Ford will throw out the whole 50,000-pound coil.

Most important, Ford changed its approach to buying steel. Instead of splitting an order for 1,000 tons of steel for car hoods among three companies, it gives the whole order to one company and encourages a long-term arrangement—so long as the supplier keeps up its side of the deal. Ford selects one steel company to become a partner for each component.

The steel industry was notorious for living from day to day, but in the early 1980s for the first time Bethlehem Steel had a five-year plan. By 1986, Bethlehem got the reject rate for its steel down to 1.5%, and by late 1987 to 1%, better than Japan. At the beginning of the decade, it took 10.3 man-hours to produce a ton of steel in the United States, slower than in Japan or Germany. By the end of the decade, American steelmakers could produce a ton of steel with 5.3 man-hours of work, slightly less than in Japan or Germany. By 1992, productivity had reached 4.8 man-hours and the industry was shooting for three man-hours per ton. Some companies were there already. U.S. Steel, one of the Neanderthals, had come to life again as USX and produced a ton of steel with 2.7 man-hours in its huge Gary Works in Indiana.[37]

Statistical process control, process teams, cooperation with labor and customer, and the other tools of TQM certainly helped save the steel industry. However, so did modernization. Whereas heavy investment in modernization proved to be almost a handicap to the auto industry, the $27 billion the steel industry spent on new equipment was pivotal simply because Big Steel had fallen so far behind the rest of the world in technology. In addition, through most of the 1980s, American steel producers were protected from dumping by foreign companies through "voluntary" quotas. The steel industry perhaps does not give as clear-cut an example of the redeeming nature of total quality as does the auto industry, but it still yields an important example.[38]

THE BATTLE IS NEVER OVER

Now that the U.S. auto industry produces cars so much better than it did in 1980, is it close to establishing parity with the Japanese industry? It is certainly much closer to being competitive (with the help of a higher yen). Is there any significant quality difference remaining; and if not, is that battle over? No. Just as quality improvement is continuous, the battle is never over. A snapshot of comparative performance at any given movement misses an essential—the dynamics in the picture. Japan may have let up on the pressure, because its own market has become saturated and because fewer opportunities are visible elsewhere. But they will continue to improve. Remember that Toyota, still the leader in auto productivity and quality, claims it will not stop improving until it makes the perfect car—even though reality may be telling Toyota that the ultimate car would be too expensive. Even if defects become rare enough not to matter—and we are close to that point if we have not already reached it—automakers find other ways of differentiating the quality of their products. Abraham Maslow's theory of the "hierarchy of needs" argues that once people's basic needs have been satisfied they then develop a higher level of needs.[39] David Cole of the University of Michigan sees five ways for the auto companies to satisfy those higher needs in the future and differentiate their cars:

1. Executing quickly, whether in developing a new model or filling an order.
2. Selling and servicing cars better, which Saturn succeeds in doing but which other American car companies need to improve more.
3. Offering new technologies, such as airbags and antilock brakes. The technologies have to be those which the customers, not the engineers, want.
4. Behaving as good corporate citizens, which really does begin to matter to the buyer.
5. Exploring a factor the Japanese call *kansei* and which we might call appeal. It is whatever makes the owner feel his car is just right.[40]

Kenichi Yamamoto, president of the Mazda Motor Corporation, attempted in a speech at the University of Michigan to explain *kansei*. "There is something general about the tactile, sensual and therefore psychological relationship between people and their physical environment," he said. "People have learned to associate certain sensations and certain emotions as part of their overall feeling of well-being." Mazda uses its test circuit to analyze a model's *kansei* appeal. As the car rolls around the track and sensors report the measurable conditions of the car, the driver simultaneously talks about his sensations. "As to be expected, it was confirmed that the vibration of the floor panel and seat has a lot do with the feeling of solidity," Yamamoto said. "More interesting, however, we also found that the linear relation between the yaw or roll motions and steering operation was affecting the driver's feeling of solidity to a considerable extent.'' Shapes, colors, noises, vibrations, the consistency of response, all relate to *kansei*.[41]

Over the last ten years or so, Ford has shifted the focus for gauging quality from Things Gone Wrong (TGW) to Things Gone Right (TGR). As cars get better and the number of TGWs goes down, rival models move to more of an equal footing. The absence of defects becomes the basic requisite of quality, the kind of quality a manufacturer needs to achieve acceptance. To gain a competitive advantage, you have to move on from basic quality to feature quality or excitement quality. One way to achieve that kind of quality, says Thomas Gorcyca of customer quality research at Ford, is to surprise the buyer by executing some feature particularly well. For example, for a large car to have good fuel economy would be an unexpected bonus. The other kind of TGR is a feature that itself is unexpected, such as automatic headlights on a lower-priced car. Aluminum wheels are a TGR. So are automatic window locks, integrated child seats, intermittent rear wipers, storage compartments of any kind, a mirror in the glove compartment, remote power controls for the outside rear-view mirrors, and a device to stop you from locking the car when the key is still in the ignition. They are mostly little things. Making air bags standard for both driver and passenger in an economy car, as Chrysler plans to do on the Neon, is a big feature. Of course, once people get used to a new TGR, the absence of it becomes a TGW. When Ford put the cup holders in the Taurus they were a TGR, but if you failed to put them in a car today, you would get a TGW.

To uncover possible TGWs, Ford puts more of an effort into talking to customers. Instead of sending just marketing people out to interview the public, the company now sends planners and engineers out too so they can probe for the meaning behind the often inarticulate opinions of America's drivers.[42] They will keep doing it until none of us can find a TGW and we are all saturated with TGRs, and then the auto companies will have to find some other way to surprise us.

CONCLUSIONS

The auto industry probably gives the clearest, certainly the most important, examples of what works today and what does not work.

- All of the Big Three started off on more or less the same footing, took different paths to get out of the crisis, but then all ended up doing essentially the same thing. They have found no substitute for TQM.
- The industry's past success and resulting size made it that much more

difficult to transform the auto companies when the time came to do it.
- The Big Three found they could accomplish little until they tackled entrenched management empires.
- Dedicated and collocated teams produced better cars faster and cheaper than the old fractured system.
- The Big Three have finally proven they can produce good cars as efficiently and as well as the Japanese, but they are still handicapped by higher costs of medical care and pensions.
- Quality may be enduring, but it is not static.

7

The Pacesetters
So Much Left to Do

Motorola states its vision for the year 2000 baldly: to "become the world's premier company."[1] Exactly how you could know if you were premier, or second best, or even among the top ten in the whole world is hard to tell, but let us not quibble. If there were a way of scoring to find the best companies in the world, Motorola would very likely be up there. Motorola unarguably keeps getting better at what it does, and that is already very good. But sometimes Motorola still slips badly.

John Young, until recently CEO of Hewlett-Packard, has a case in point. Young is a very nice man; in fact, you might say that he suffers from the "terminal niceness" that Richard Pascale believes afflicts HP people and prevents them from making hard decisions.[2] But Young is not so nice on the subject of Motorola. In the summer of 1992—five years after Motorola won the Baldrige award—Young, still the CEO at that point, said that "the honest truth is that their semiconductor activities still need enormous improvement." What got Young riled up was Motorola's failures with a new microprocessor, the 68040, which in 1990 was to have been the newest in the 68000 series that power many manufacturers' workstations. In May 1989, HP acquired Apollo Computer Inc. of Chelmsford, Massachusetts, with its $500-million workstation business, also based on the 68000 series. The idea was that together HP and Apollo would leap ahead of Sun Microsystems and Digital Equipment Corporation to become the market leader in workstations. But that plan depended on Motorola delivering the 68040 in the first half of 1990 in good working order. Since computer power increases by about 70% a year, creating new products rapidly and on time is vital. Slip up by a year and you have lost a whole generation of products.

Robert Weinberger, marketing manager for HP's workstation systems group, remembers visiting customers with an early 68040 in his pocket and telling them that the new workstation would be ready in six months. The trouble was that "that went on for a year and a half." Weinberger believes

Motorola had been overly optimistic about bringing a complex new chip onto the market. The 68040 would have given HP a RISC (reduced instruction set computing) capability to make the new workstations perform faster. Motorola's software simulators did not catch the initial defects in the chip, so they showed up when the chip was in production and in use. Each time a customer discovered a defect, Motorola had to redesign and remanufacture the chip. Especially tormenting to HP, the delays came in chunks of one or two months each, so that the new chip stayed just out of reach. In the end, HP put out its series 400 workstations with the earlier 68030 Motorola chip, and prepared to upgrade the machines when the new chip was ready. Jack Browne, director of marketing at Motorola's 68000 division, agrees with Weinberger's account. He says,

"We tried to do a little too much. If we had designed a chip to be 10% slower we probably wouldn't have been in trouble. Each fix took six weeks, but actually we were usually doing two fixes at the same time, so the fixes came out every three weeks. It was the most stressful program I have ever been on. We try to give our customers everything we can on the leading edge of technology and sometimes we fall over the edge. The 040 was just over the edge."

A Lost Chance

The 18-month delay in perfecting the 68040 hurt HP badly. "It was an enormous cost to our company to have that product delayed," says Young. "It was the linchpin for the merger of Apollo and HP's computer platforms, so the whole acquisition was thrown off track and that had a lot of repercussions." When the 68040 finally came through in 1991, says Weinberger, it was excellent but too late. A whole product life cycle had gone by; HP had lost the chance to displace Sun Microsystems as the No. 1 provider of workstations.

Motorola sold 500,000 of the chips in 1992, but it could have sold many more. HP switched from using 80% Motorola chips in its workstations in 1990 to 80% of its own chips in 1991. Motorola went on to develop the 68060 chip, three times more powerful than the 68040, which already had 1.2 million transistors. But long before then Motorola conceded the HP market. "We won't get a shot at their business with the 060," says Browne.[3]

I tell the story of the 68040 not to expose the holes in Motorola's quality effort, but to show how much even the best companies have left to do. As Young says,

"I don't think anybody ought to have the expectation that even practicing a lot of these process-based (quality) things is going to prevent you from making bad decisions about a business strategy or having things go wrong."

In this chapter I would like to review the performance of four of the very best and earliest entrants in the quality movement, Hewlett-Packard, Milliken, Motorola, and Xerox. They, along with Ford, were the pacesetters. Much of what they did has already been reported in earlier chapters, but it seems worthwhile to take another look at their performance to see what they did right, what they did wrong, and most of all, how much they have left to do. A striking thing about quality is that even when the best do their best for years, they still have much left to do. I have included a fifth company in this group, Intel, because it is something of a maverick. Intel has achieved superb quality as well as superb business results, but without formally embracing TQM. In fact, Intel specifically decided not to change its culture, but it does most of the things it would do if it had adopted TQM.

HP, Milliken, Motorola, and Xerox all shared essentially the same experiences and circumstances. They all had continuous, firm leadership dedicated to improving quality. They set almost impossibly high goals and then carefully measured their progress. They put an enormous effort into training their people in the specific tools of quality and also more generally in the cultural changes that had to happen. They pushed power downwards and made teams rather than individuals their driving force. They all listened carefully and learned from the great quality experts—Crosby, Deming, Juran, Feigenbaum, and others—but they did not adopt any one approach whole hog. Each developed its own version of TQM. What happened to these companies deserves to be described by that overused phrase, "a cultural transformation," with the possible exceptions of Hewlett-Packard and Intel, which already had cultures that went a long way toward being what was needed.

HEWLETT-PACKARD

Hewlett-Packard people talk reverently of "the HP Way." It consists of five basic values which, with some modifications in wording, have guided the behavior of HP people since 1957. They are:

- We have trust and respect for individuals.
- We focus on a high level of achievement and contribution.
- We conduct our business with uncompromising integrity.

- We achieve our common objectives through teamwork.
- We encourage flexibility and innovation.[4]

These values, laid down four decades ago, fit right into the TQM philosophy. When the company called in 1980 for a tenfold improvement in hardware quality in a decade, the environment for achieving that goal already existed. But the HP Way also had some weaknesses. The very lack of a top-down style of management meant that TQM drifted through the company, but it was not driven through as it was at Motorola and Milliken. That "terminal niceness" prevents the company from making tough decisions.[5] While all of the company's divisions (about 60, but the count keeps changing) understood clearly that they had to improve quality ten times in a decade, their attitudes and approaches varied from an enthusiastic embrace of TQM to what one manager describes as "malicious compliance." Newer divisions, like the plants in Corvallis, Oregon and Greeley, Colorado tended to be fanatics, whereas older ones, like the test and measurement business in Palo Alto, California, did pretty much what they pleased. The headquarters quality staff was unable to lay down a clear set of guidelines or requirements, so the paths chosen by HP's divisions to achieve the 10× improvement were varied and the results mixed.[6]

With its receptive culture, with its stretch goals, with its supportive leadership HP overall has done extremely well, as a business and as a quality company. The company's sales, profits, and stock market performance, somewhat sluggish in the 1980s, picked up markedly in the 1990s when other computer companies were hurting. HP became fast and smart at issuing successful new products, such as the DeskJet and LaserJet printers, the new 700 series RISC-based workstations, and the 95LX palmtop PC.

A Notable Success

Specifically in the field of quality, HP became much admired for some of its achievements. Even though just-in-time manufacturing was not adopted throughout the company, others came to learn from HP about JIT because the results were formidable where it was well applied. The MIT Commission on Industrial Productivity found in 1989 that HP's "notable success" with just-in-time manufacturing included the following results at the plants that practiced it:

- Inventory reduced by 60% to 80%.
- Floor space reduced by 30% to 50%.

- Lead time reduced by more than 50%.
- Labor costs reduced by 30% to 50%.[7]

At those levels of improvement you can get nearly two factories for the price of one old one.

Other practitioners of total quality look to HP as the benchmark for a technique known as *hoshin kanri* or *hoshin* planning. In Japanese the words *hoshin* and *kanri* mean something like "shining metal" and "pointing direction" and the idea is that *hoshin* planning will get the whole company moving in the right direction. "Strategic quality planning," to use the more generic name, is one of those quality exercises which can become exceedingly complex in description and in practice can get lost in its own processes. To put it in the simplest terms, *hoshin* planning is a means of pointing all of a company's energies at achieving a few priority breakthroughs. *Hoshin* planning has a methodology for translating these priorities into specific actions and goals all the way through the company, for divisions, groups, and individuals. *Hoshin* planning tries to get rid of the usual alienation felt in the lower echelons when orders descend on them from the executive offices. People up and down the company get to define their own roles in the plan, and indeed help shape it.

When it got into trouble back in the 1970s, Yokagawa Hewlett-Packard used *hoshin* planning to guide the organization towards total quality. Then in 1985, when it became evident that HP was probably not going to reach John Young's goal of a tenfold improvement in quality by 1990, the parent company asked its Japanese joint venture what it should do. YHP suggested that *hoshin* planning was the missing element in HP's quality brew.[8]

For all HP's success with *hoshin* planning, John Young personally is not all that sold on it; this is one of those contradictions that makes HP such an interesting company. Young says he "doesn't assign any big activity to it." He says back in the early 1980s, "before we discovered the word *hoshin*, I always had my list of ten things we needed to work on this year. Frankly, I don't think it makes a whole hell of a lot of difference how you signal to the organization what's important. What matters is that you do it." He enlarges on his skepticism by saying of hoshin planning, "Bureaucratic is one word for it but data-driven is another word for it." But in the end he does agree that "it's a rigorous planning tool to assure that you do get results," and he says that at the operating level it is a useful tool for making sure that the right things get done.[9]

One of HP's *hoshin* goals in 1992 and 1993 was to improve its order fulfillment, generally regarded in the company as a mess. When a customer orders a system from HP, the pieces may come from many places. Monitors may come from Japan, keyboards from Singapore, workstations from Massachusetts, printers from Oregon, and so forth. The order gets scattered organizationally as well as geographically because it is handled piecemeal by many parts of the company, from sales to manufacturing to shipping. Systems may be assembled and tested at an HP site or at the customer's offices. Through lack of good process and coordination every order, on average, has one mistake in it; often this consists of shipping the wrong cables to connect the components. To put it another way, as did the company's former quality director, Craig Walter, the defect base on order fulfillments is 100%. The client does not necessarily see the mistake, but HP has to waste resources fixing it. Young says that just as poor quality equipment diverts test engineers into working as repairmen, so bad business processes, like order fulfillment, make managers spend time repairing business processes. At this writing, HP has taken the first step of applying quality processes to order fulfillment by describing carefully the existing procedures.

Software is Hard, Too

HP was also slow to realize that it had to make a major improvement in the quality of its software. The company's original goal of achieving a tenfold improvement in quality by 1990 applied only to hardware. But the top management soon realized that the quality of software was also a real problem, so in 1986 it added the goal of reducing errors in software tenfold. As mentioned in the Introduction, a sampling of the errors in HP's software research and development in 1990 came up with a total cost of failure of $400 million for that year, or two thirds of the company's earnings.

The campaign to improve software quality has not gone well. It is inherently more difficult to apply TQM to software than to hardware because writing software is treated like an art. Software springs from the minds of free spirits encouraged to work and think in unorthodox manners, unhampered by rules and formalities, or so goes the mythology. As we will see in the next chapter, IBM thinks it does have a handle on how to systematize writing software. But HP is still struggling and each division still has its own approach. The divisions that have applied TQM to software are getting better results.

When Lewis Platt, head of the company's computer systems organization, succeeded Young as CEO at the end of 1992—and Richard LeVitt, a quality professional since 1987, succeeded Craig Walter as director of quality—improving the quality of both software and order fulfillment remained priorities. Platt delivered a message strongly backing the company's quality efforts and also expressing concern that in the eyes of some customers HP's quality might have slipped. It was the complaints of customers in Europe a couple of year earlier that made HP aware that it needed to improve its order fulfillment. Platt also added a new priority: that every division has to make a profit in 1993. Even though the objective of any business is to make money, setting the timer at one year can conflict with a fundamental tenet of TQM, which is that you ship nothing until you are sure you have it right. Pressure to produce quick profits can make managers cut corners, and that has been happening anyhow in some divisions of HP in the absence of clear directives from the top. However, in HP's case the company's "niceness" had allowed some units to run at a loss for years. Platt aimed his remarks specifically at these units. One of them, the maker of personal computers, achieved a big turnaround in 1993.

Like the others leading the long march to quality, Hewlett-Packard has much left to do. At the end of the ten years it had given itself to improve hardware quality tenfold, it fell short. The hardware was only (!) eight times better than in 1980. HP is hard on itself. Under an in-house audit it calls the Quality Maturity System, the company set a goal of reaching a score of 3.5 on a scale of 5 by 1994. That would put it at a level of a Baldrige Award winner. In mid-1992, the company rated itself around 2.2.[10] That harsh self-evaluation may goad HP to do better than it has, and the record of what it has accomplished is good. For example, during the 1980s, HP reduced the cash tied up in inventory by $620 million and cut its warranty costs by a cumulative $800 million. Productivity increased 15% annually in the last half of the decade.[11] The disk memory division in Boise cut the mean interval between failures of its magnetic disk drives to once every 70,000 hours, or once every eight years, and then in a second push to improve it further reduced the failure rate to once every 300,000 hours, which means a customer rarely sees a failure. Total quality, says Young, "has transformed how we approach our work."[12]

MILLIKEN

In contrast to Hewlett-Packard, Milliken & Co. is a privately owned and tight-lipped organization. It has been generous in taking time with others to explain its success in total quality, but has presented it mostly as a very tidy process. Milliken is not the sort of place that displays its dirty laundry.

Milliken does not reveal its sales, market shares, or much of anything else about its business. *Forbes* magazine and one Wall Street analyst estimate that Milliken's sales for 1992 were $2.4 billion, which would make it the biggest company in a $70-billion-a-year industry. Milliken is widely regarded as a leader in the textile industry in almost any category you might mention; quality, technology, investment, and political activism. ''The Milliken Corporation [*sic*] has been a front runner in research on performance fabrics,'' according to the MIT Commission on Industrial Productivity. ''Milliken channels about 2% of sales into R&D, developing both product and process innovations and backing it up with a strong patent acquisition policy.''

Being privately owned, Milliken is not under pressure to pay out fat dividends, and it invests 96% to 98% of its cash flow back into its own business. Although textile manufacturers are notoriously impatient and like to see their investments pay off in less than a year, Milliken accepts a three-year payoff period. The MIT report, issued in 1989, said that while Milliken controlled 3% to 5% of the U.S. textile market, it accounted for 10% to 15% of its capital expenditure—a good formula for growing success.[13] In politics, Roger Milliken, a conservative, has led the industry's protectionist fights against the growth of imports and even broke with the industry association when the latter supported NAFTA, the free-trade agreement with Mexico and Canada.

After Milliken became one of the first companies to win the Baldrige Award, its landscaped, arbored headquarters in Spartanburg, South Carolina, and its spic-and-span plants around the South became a focus for seekers after quality wisdom. Exactly how well Milliken performed is hard to tell, given the secrecy under which the company is able to operate. The warts do not show. As near as the many visitors to Spartanburg can tell, Milliken did it all and did most of it right, beginning with Roger Milliken himself. His own transformation led the transformation of the company (see Chapter 2). While the original Hewlett-Packard culture had the kind of freedom that fits the TQM philosophy, Milliken was a top-down organization. Roger Milliken and Tom Malone, the president, have led the democratization of the company by their own example. The top executives have no private offices, no private dining room, no reserved parking places. A former plant manager recalls a revealing visit by Malone to his plant. Malone noted that the white-collar people—the ''lintheads'' in old company parlance—had a fancy office building apart from the plant itself. He asked the plant manager to get an estimate of what it would cost to demolish the office building and put the office staff inside the plant in glass enclosures where everyone could see who they were and what they did. The cost came to several hundred thousand dollars and Malone approved right away. "I can't describe what that did for the plant in improving morale and making management accessible," says the plant manager.[14]

Milliken even succeeded in establishing a functioning suggestion program, something that has eluded American companies. Milliken started by not calling it a suggestion program. In America, employee suggestion programs are regarded, usually with justification, as one of those futile hypocrisies like Secretaries' Day. Nevertheless most companies make at least a gesture at having one. In Japan, by contrast, suggestions swarm out of the offices and factories by the tens of thousands, like people emerging from the Tokyo subways at rush hour.

When Milliken developed its employee-involvement approach it assigned the new teams the role of finding solutions and charged individuals with the task of finding the problems that needed solving. At first "associates" were asked to report problems on an Error Cause Removal form. Nothing happened. Then Milliken tried a new ECR form, asking associates to report on what they thought other people were doing wrong. Again, nothing happened, understandably. Then Milliken renamed the whole plan the Opportunity For Improvement (OFI) process. Now that the program was cast in a positive light, with the implication that you might be ratting on your co-worker removed, the company was swamped with ideas. But that success resulted in a third failure. Milliken was unprepared for the huge response and could not process all the suggestions. To take care of that problem Milliken adopted the 24–72 rule. A manager who receives an OFI must acknowledge it within 24 hours and must come up with an action plan in 72 hours, if the problem has not already been solved. Managers are also urged to respond positively to the suggestions if they possibly can. Under the new rules, the number of OFIs per employee has blossomed from 4.5 in 1987, to 19 in 1989, to 59 in 1992. The suggestion rates at some plants puts them in the same league as the sedulous Japanese. But the variations are large. Some plants get 150 suggestions per associate a year, some only 10.

Piecework Does Not Pay

Milliken does not pay for successful suggestions. The basis for its elaborate reward system for contributions to quality or productivity through team or individual efforts (see Chapter 3) is not money but recognition. Photos, plaques, pins, jackets, letters, prizes, rallies, banquets are fine, but cash is not. Milliken could probably carpet the Pentagon with photos of Roger

Milliken and Tom Malone taken with proud associates. The company believes that recognition rather than money is critical to maintaining the level of enthusiasm that Milliken seems to have achieved.

But Milliken did have to change its pay system. Piecework pay was the tradition in the textile industry, but that conflicted with the use of teamwork and *andon.**

How can you expect an associate to stop the line because of a quality problem if the action cuts his pay? Milliken eliminated 30 levels of wages and replaced them with just three, based on skill levels and not on seniority as in the past. Milliken salespeople went from commission-based pay to salaries.

For an old-fashioned, hierarchical company Milliken was unusually successful in moving towards the team style of working. Roger Milliken and Tom Malone cooked up an approach that combined firm and involved leadership with an unaccustomed independence down the line. The company's four divisions were granted considerable autonomy in devising their specific approaches to quality; but at the same time TQM began, as it should, with top management. With Malone himself leading the way, Milliken's executives took training first and then let it spread throughout the organization. The same happened with teams. Management formed the first "corrective action teams" and then started drawing the office support staff and the production workers into a variety of teams. It was not easy. Workers accustomed to the old "mill hand" days and lacking education (a majority of the work force reads below the eighth-grade level) needed a lot of coaching, training, and remedial education to be able to operate in teams. At first, the plants sometimes went downhill before they started to climb to higher productivity and quality. Eventually, the team concept caught fast and today 18 of Milliken's 47 plants are run essentially by self-managed teams. Except in some very large plants, the teams have no supervisors other than the plant manager.

Since it is governed so much by fickle fashion, you might think the textile industry would be flexible, adaptable, fast on its feet. On the contrary, it was among the most sluggish. It took 66 weeks for a collection of threads to become a garment and reach the customer: 23 weeks in the textile and fiber stage, 24 weeks with the apparel industry, and 19 weeks drifting through the retail industry. Only during a fraction of that time was value added to the product; 55 of those 66 weeks the threads spent waiting in inventory.[15] Factories designed for long production runs of a single item were not flex-

---

* *Andon* is the Japanese word for the board with green, yellow, and red lights that show if a worker has slowed or stopped the line.

ible. They operated on the old "market-out" theory rather than the new "market-in" theory. In other words, they sold what it was convenient to produce rather than what the market demanded. A many-layered distribution system also dragged out the response time.

"Quick Response"

In 1981, when Milliken was becoming aware of quality, it was a slow company, though not as slow as some. Its average lead time for filling an order was 42 days. And orders were delivered late 25% of the time. Its Magnolia plant, built in 1963, was designed to run 15,000-yard batches of fabric. Milliken became one of the first to try to cut the cycle time by joining with a retailer, Wal-Mart, and an apparel manufacturer, Seminole Manufacturing of Columbus, Mississippi, in a plan called "quick response" developed by a New York consultant, Kurt Salmon Associates.[16] The plan combined a whole lot of devices, new technology, bar coding, more frequent ordering, electronic reordering, up and down the chain. Now retailers could order small batches in response to what they were currently selling, rather than what they might be selling a year hence. Milliken, which has adopted the quick-response idea for all its operations, had cut its lead time to 18 days by 1991 and aims at reducing it to seven days. Some plants could deliver in less than seven days by 1993. Deliveries are 99.6% on time and the goal is 99.8%. The refitted Magnolia plant can run batches of fabric as small as 500 yards, one-thirtieth of the minimum run in the original design.

When the government first offered the Baldrige Award in 1988, Milliken applied and got what its chairman describes as "the most important thrust we've had in ten years" on the road to quality. Milliken did not win that year, but the Baldrige examiners, as they are required to, provided the company with a feedback report describing their findings. They said Milliken did not have goals that stretched the company enough. They also said not enough people in the company understood statistical process controls and other tools.

Milliken set about fixing these defects. Management did not believe it could apply Six Sigma to its continuous process manufacturing or to its administrative processes, but it could set a goal for reducing defects. Therefore, Milliken adopted the 10–4 goal, that is, a ten-fold reduction in defects of all kinds—in the plants and in the offices—in four years, which meant by the end of 1993.[17] A Milliken manager admits that in the early 1980s the statistical-control charts in the plants were largely for show; when the visitors left, the charts were tucked away. But after getting the Baldrige examiners' comments, Milliken put the whole company through a new round of training on statistical-process controls and the other tools.

In 1989 Milliken applied again for the Baldrige, "worked like hell," in Roger Milliken's words, and won. Again the examiners rendered their comments. This time they said Milliken was not paying enough attention to its internal customers—for example, the weaving plant was not listening to the dyeing plant—and the secretaries, or "administrative associates," had not been drawn in to the teams and the whole quality process as much as they should be. Roger Milliken sums up the experience: "Applying for the Baldrige and getting that feedback is of incredible value to a company."[18]

The textile industry has no public quality monitor like *Consumer Reports* or the Power surveys in the auto industry and since Milliken is private it keeps its numbers secret. However, Milliken does commission its own annual surveys of quality and performance in five categories of the things that matter most to its customers. Milliken does not publish these results either but it claims that in the five-year period ending in 1992 it ranked first in the industry in all five categories.[19]

MOTOROLA

When describing Motorola's exemplary role in the quality movement today, it is useful to remember that a couple of decades ago Motorola was producing television sets that had 20 times as many defects as sets subsequently produced by the Japanese in the same plant by the same work force (see Chapter 1). Since those times—the times that caused Art Sundry to say "our quality stinks"—Motorola has taken to quality as intelligently and thoroughly as any company in the United States. Bob Galvin, who started the company along the quality road and headed the effort through most of the 1980s (see Chapter 2), reached the eminence of a business statesman largely because of what he accomplished in quality. His successor, George Fisher, continued to involve himself as much as Galvin did to improve quality. (When Fisher left unexpectedly in 1993 to take over the Eastman Kodak Company, Gary Tooker succeeded him as CEO and Christopher Galvin, Bob's son, became president. Both executives had grown into their jobs during Motorola's quality revolution.) The company has taken all the important steps towards embedding continuous quality improvement in all it does, from making pagers to practicing corporate law. Motorola has bound together training, rewards, teamwork, and technology, shortening the cycle time, talking to customers, pushing the suppliers, and the other elements of TQM to reach goals set in the stratosphere.

The company has succeeded well in spite of some lapses such as the late arrival of the 68040 chip mentioned earlier in this chapter. Considering the scale of the transformation it had to make, and how much resistance Galvin and the other leaders encountered at first from people like Ralph Ponce de Leon (see Chapter 3), Motorola has moved with extraordinary deftness.

Motorola's push for quality succeeded because its commitment was so unambiguous. When Bob Galvin was chairman, not only did he put quality at the top of the agenda of every meeting, but once that item of the agenda had been covered he would often leave the meeting. Motorola enforced its commitment most emphatically. Back in 1980 the executive group was measured for bonuses mostly on the basis of profits. Company profits counted for 60% of the bonus, quality for 5%. By 1989, 70% of the bonus depended on quality, cycle-time improvements, and contributions to participative management. That left only 30% to be doled out on the basis of traditional measures like profits and market share. Furthermore, without an *annual* reduction of 68% in defects and 50% in cycle time there is no bonus.[20]

The one serious mistake Galvin and others acknowledge is that they started the training for quality at the bottom of the company. Not only were many workers unable to understand statistical-process controls and other techniques without first taking some remedial education, but if they were trained and the people above them were not, then they returned to a totally unreceptive workplace. "We wasted $7 million trying to train from the bottom up," writes William Wiggenhorn, Motorola's director of training and education. "By 1984 we realized we had started at the wrong end. In 1985–86, we put the top 2,000 people through 17 days of classroom training."[21] Galvin overhauled Motorola's training schools. He says, "Like Mao Tse-tung, in effect, I destroyed the system to rebuild the system." He had shut down the existing executive training program at Tucson in 1983 and established new institutions which evolved eventually into "Motorola University." Galvin himself went back to school. Motorola requires every employee to take 40 hours of training a year and the company spent $110 million on instruction in 1992, not including the salaries and travel expenses of the trainees. Galvin believes that training pays for itself rapidly by many multiples.[22] Motorola ran three return-on-investment studies of the value of training in the 1980s and found out that every $1 invested in training quickly paid about $30. In one case, Motorola tracked a group of salespeople who had taken quality training against a control group. Within nine months the performance of the salespeople with training had returned $30 more than people in the control group for every dollar invested in training.[23]

Motorola is a high-tech company that dominates the markets for portable communications equipment, mainly cellular phones, pagers, and two-way radios, and it is a major player in other advanced electronics such as integrated circuits. Motorola competes in markets that shift rapidly into new technologies; therefore its approach to quality stresses automation and speed more than that of other companies. When it comes to working with wires only one or two mils thick, robots are better than humans. Motorola must be, as *The Wall Street Journal* called it, "a nimble giant."[24]

Shortening the cycle time for developing and manufacturing new products was not part of Motorola's quality program at the beginning in 1980. Industrial engineers took the classic approach to cycle time: they used a stopwatch. But that method only kept a record of how long it took to do something; it did not tell whether that something was worth doing in the first place. Paul Noakes, director of Motorola's external quality programs, says that in the bad old days the manufacturing cycle of 56 days consisted of one and a half days of value-added time; all the rest was spent in queues—in the office, waiting for factory time, in inventory. As for documentation, Motorola worked on the same principle as the federal government: as long as you have enough documents, you are okay.

As a result of those visits Galvin made to see customers, Motorola added a faster cycle time to its priorities in 1987. (Given a second chance, Motorola would have done that in 1980.) Now, instead of using a stopwatch, Motorola engineers concentrate on simplifying the process, on reducing all those useless stretches of downtime, of cutting out paperwork. It used to take as many as 15 signatures to make an engineering change; now one or two will do. They trust people rather than trying to control them. Shorter cycles have yielded a "tremendous success" in cutting costs, increasing productivity, and getting market share, says Noakes. Now when Motorola receives an order for two-way radios it no longer take 56 days to ship that order. Motorola promises to deliver within two to five days depending on the model and accompanies that promise with a two-year warranty, no questions asked. Motorola had no share at all of the low end of the market for two-way radios in 1987. The Japanese and Koreans had all of it. But with its new fast deliveries and warranties Motorola took more than 50% of the U.S. market in two years.[25]

In the late 1980s, Operation Bandit became Motorola's best-known and most publicized experiment in speed and automation. Operation Bandit—the name signified the team's willingness to cast aside the "not invented here" attitude and borrow ideas from anywhere—created a totally automated factory to produce Motorola's Bravo pagers at the customer's command. Orders flowed directly from the customer through an IBM mainframe to the computer-integrated manufacturing system in Boynton Beach, Florida.

The pocket-sized Bravo may seem to be a simple device but it has many variable features: size, color, battery life, the frequency, the code, the number of messages it can store, the manner of displaying the message, the manner of alerting the wearer (one or more buzzes or a vibration), the ability to delete or preserve messages. The customer could pick any combination of features in any lot size, down to a lot of one, and put his order directly into the system—and the 27 robots on the Bandit line could produce the pager within minutes of receiving the order. The plant required no setup time because the robots were programmed to handle any order. In a highly competitive business where a sale might depend on a feature like an illuminated display, the ability to customize all those features rapidly became vital.

Creating Bandit in the space of 18 months built up so much pressure that some of the original members of the team had to leave for more tranquil lines of work before the project was completed. Many problems had to be solved during those 18 months, as you might expect. The software failed significantly at times. The suppliers, even though they had been selected from among many candidates, had difficulties meeting Bandit's demands. Motorola was still handling suppliers ineptly, issuing poorly written specifications, and emphasizing price rather than value. The very speed of the new process created a quality problem. When it was discovered that the pagers were drifting off their assigned frequencies, it turned out that they were being tuned while the solder was still warm; as it cooled the frequency drifted. And the engineers who designed the plant became a problem themselves once production started, because they wanted to keep tinkering with their creation while Motorola wanted to push production.

By 1987 Bandit was in production, turning out custom-built pagers within minutes of an order's receipt. With Bandit's help, Motorola today dominates the market for pagers and succeeded in selling more than a million of them to the Nippon Telegraph & Telephone Corporation. Bandit also served its second mission of proving out the technology of a fully automated batch-of-one, zero-setup-time line. It proved the value of a self-contained plant with all the manufacturing located not just in one factory but in one room.

In 1991, Motorola converted Bandit to Speedy to manufacture a new line of pagers. Motorola used more than 70% of the automated equipment from the old plant in the new. But it did step back a bit from total automation. Workers now perform some operations manually, such as tuning the receivers. The new plant has the same flexibility and speed as Bandit. "We can build lot sizes of one or lot sizes of 100,000," says Russell Strobel, resource manager in the Paging Products Group. "It doesn't matter to us."[26]

Accelerated Stress

The extreme competitiveness in Motorola's markets demands speed in developing new products as well as in manufacturing them. The Pan American Cellular Phone Division used to spend five to ten years developing a new product. It has cut development time down to six months to a year. Instead of spending two to five years working up new features for an existing product the division creates them in a few months. That kind of speed enabled Motorola to go to market in 1991 with the first cellular phone weighing less than half a pound, a considerable feat considering that the first mobile phones weighed 27 pounds.[27] The 7.5-ounce cellular phone introduced in 1991 was followed in 1992 by the 5.9-ounce UltraLite model.

To develop these new products faster Motorola has to test them faster, but the test also has to simulate a longer lifetime, since the products are now more reliable. At the lab in Arlington Heights, Illinois where they put new cellular phones through "accelerated life tests," Motorola technicians shake the equipment, heat it, cool it, drop it, close a simulated door on the cords, stretch the cords, open and shut the phone's flipper thousands of times. The lab has a thermal-shock chamber that goes from hot to cold in two seconds, revealing poor soldering and weak plastic parts. It has a dust chamber supplied with five grades of genuine Arizona dust, obtained from GM for $40 a pound. It has a "highly accelerated stress test" that raises the temperature to 100°F, the humidity to 100%, and then tries to force humidity under pressure into the equipment. With this test, a new cellular phone can suffer through many years of living in a mere week.[28]

Wiggenhorn divides the company's experience with quality into three periods. In the first, in the early 1980s, Motorola tried to *meet* customers' expectations. Then it moved on to try to *exceed* customers' expectations. In the current phase, Motorola is trying in an organized way to *anticipate* customers' needs.[29] Efforts like Operation Bandit and the Arlington Heights test lab certainly address the first two requirements. The third requirement, anticipating the needs of the customer, demands a different kind of effort, more of an intellectual exercise at the top of the company. Bob Galvin's father Paul, who founded the company in 1928, had a sure instinct for anticipating the market. Years ago Bob Galvin established an intelligence department to uncover who was going to do what next in the company's markets. Motorola people turned up at conferences and trade shows that its competitors would not bother with. Over the years, Motorola's anticipations were pretty good. The company missed the transistor revolution at first, but pulled out of consumer electronics at the right time and led the competition in pagers, cellular phones, and mobile phones.

At Galvin's urging, Motorola wants to systematize its forecasting through what he calls an "anticipations registry." As he explains it, when executives look into the future, anticipating a new market or a new management technique or a new technology, these anticipations will be written down, recorded, and collated. At the same time, Motorola's intelligence-gatherers would be finding out and recording what other companies were anticipating. Galvin explains,

> "We would take this data and learn how to compare. If we discovered that three or five of our competitors are anticipating substantially more and better than we are and making commitments—and that would be quite measurable—then we would know that if they are getting more points now they are going to get more gold medals in the Olympics of business. The future of quality to me is the future of quality leadership, as determined by the ability to anticipate and commit, which you can measure against the other person's registry."[30]

In the here and now, Motorola is doing extremely well. Its improvements in productivity run to about 12% annually, three times better than the average for U.S. manufacturing. The company expects to double its output in five years without adding any employees. The field failure rate of its semiconductors amounts to two parts per billion; in other words, a customer rarely if ever will encounter a bad chip. The mean time between failures of the pagers it ships to NTT in Japan runs to 150 years.[31]

XEROX

Just as happy families are alike, successful TQM companies are much alike too. To give a detailed description of the Xerox quality campaign might seem superfluous after the discussion of a somewhat similar company, Motorola, especially since the driving force behind Xerox's efforts, David Kearns, the former chairman, has written his own intimate account of how his company did it.[32] However, several points may be worth mentioning.

Xerox may be a model of how to move to total quality, but that does not mean that the move was quick or easy, or that the company avoided misadventures along the way. Even though Xerox was mortally threatened by Japanese competition, it still took years to get its managers to change the way they think and act. Xerox became aware of the Japanese challenge in 1979, developed what it called its "Leadership Through Quality" approach in 1983, yet even in the late 1980s large pockets of resistance or obstruction persisted.

In 1985 Xerox released its new 4045 printer only to have it flop on the market because the software failed to perform as expected. People who developed the printer knew of its weakness but failed to speak up, a capital offense among quality professionals. The next year Xerox introduced more second-rate products. "By late 1986 doubts had really become widespread about our progress with Leadership Through Quality . . . it was evident that not only hadn't we met all [our] goals; we were not even on a trajectory where we would meet them anytime soon."[33] In 1987 when Xerox held a review of its international operations, the executives in charge of Rank Xerox tried to keep quality off the agenda; when they failed, they put the subject last on the agenda hoping there would not be time to take it up. But Paul Allaire, then the new president of Xerox and now the chairman in Kearns' place, switched the agenda in the middle of the day, making quality the first item after lunch.

In spite of the resistance, TQM thinking was becoming embedded at Xerox. Xerox was the originator of benchmarking and maybe carried it to extremes (see Chapter 5). Xerox did not make Motorola's mistake of starting the training at the bottom of the company. When Xerox's 25 top executives secluded themselves at the company's training center in Leesburg, Virginia to hammer out a quality policy and plan, they devised the idea of "cascade" training (Chapter 3). The training began with Kearns himself teaching the team of executives around him, who in turn taught their teams, and so on down through the company. The teaching teams not only learned quality methods during the course but worked together on a problem.[34] The cascade approach avoided the mistake that Motorola made by sending trained workers back to bosses who had no training and who were still resistant to the quality approach. The Xerox people instead trained in their work families with their bosses, who got a double dose because after being trainees they became trainers.

A List of "Warts"

By 1988 Xerox's effort began to pay off with a flood of new products: copiers, printers, plotters, scanners, and even a portable reading machine for the blind. They had been developed with quality built in from the design stage. The "50" Series copiers were better than anything that Xerox had produced before.

At the beginning of 1989, Xerox geared up to go after the Baldrige Award in its second year, and that gave "leadership through quality" a fresh impetus. Xerox approached the Baldrige as if it were a major business initiative. A full-time staff of 20, mostly line managers rather than quality boffins, worked stressful hours for most of the year under the vice president for quality, James Sierk, and spent $800,000.

Xerox assigned a senior executive to oversee the preparation of the application in each of the seven categories of the the Baldrige. Kearns and Allaire themselves took charge of the work in the first category, leadership. As the preparations went forward, Sierk and his crew developed a list of "warts," things that needed fixing, which eventually numbered 513 warts. A wart could be anything from poor housekeeping to the need for more statistical-process controls to the fact that executive bonuses were not tied to quality. Xerox, or at least its Business Products and Systems division, which is the biggest part of the company, won the Baldrige in 1988 along with Milliken. The list of warts plus the feedback comments from the Baldrige examiners gave Xerox a whole new list of quality objectives—and another push to keep improving. The examiners said that Xerox needed more management by fact, in contrast with management by hunch or intuition, and needed more emphasis on continuous improvement.[35]

Xerox offers about as spectacular an example of the benefits of total quality as you can find. Xerox came back from the near-dead to being best in the field. By any standard—market share, quality, productivity, profitability, stock market performance—the company has done extremely well. Buyers Laboratory Incorporated, an independent and consumer-oriented testing company, gave Xerox copiers poor ratings up until 1987, but after that Buyers began to recognize Xerox's achievements. Buyers named the whole 50 series of copiers the most outstanding for 1990 and named other copiers for individual awards. Buyers says that most copier manufacturers have reached parity on price, features, and performance. However, Xerox stands above the others in three respects. Xerox machines are more productive (i.e., they print more sheets per minute than comparable machines made by other companies). Xerox has better manuals, controls, and "language," at least for American users. With its three-year warrantees and customer satisfaction guarantees, Xerox has a marketing advantage. Buyers Laboratory says the big Xerox machines are most clearly superior. In the mid- and low-range of copiers, Xerox is not so good.[36] Even Wall Street, the home of short-term thinking, recognizes the benefits of Xerox's long struggle to improve quality. Here is what Prudential Securities had to say at the end of 1992:

> We continue to believe that Xerox has the strongest product line in the industry, with more significant new products introduced over the last 18 months than in the rest of the industry combined. We see Xerox continuing to take market share from the Japanese at the low end of the copier market and from Kodak at the high end. We believe that Xerox is able to obtain share gains as a result of its emerging low-cost manufacturing position, the highest quality products in the industry, and its strategy to expand distribution in the low end, which frees up the direct sales force to focus on higher-volume, higher-margin equipment.[37]

INTEL

In the brotherhood of quality, Intel is a misfit. It produces such superb microprocessors and other computer equipment so efficiently that in 1992 Intel became the largest manufacturer of semiconductors in the world, putting an American company in that position for the first time in nearly a decade. To achieve that eminence, Intel follows many of the best quality practices, but it refuses to call what it does "total quality management" or anything like that, and it avoids getting wrapped up in processes or procedures. Intel likes action and results.

Craig Barrett, the handsome, athletic chief operating officer and heir apparent to cofounder and CEO Andy Grove, explains Intel's reasoning:

> "We bounced around the whole quality process issue and concluded that we didn't want to set up something which was external to the values that the corporation already had. We tried to fold in the concept of continuous improvement underneath the banners that we already had flying. We decided that we should really focus on improving our performance according to those values that we already had rather than going out and adopting or inventing or borrowing a new set of values and starting over again. As you wandered through the 1980s, my impression was that many companies and many consultants walked around and said, 'What you really must do is throw away the old and usher in the new,' and to us that was a message that said, 'Well, everything you've done in the past is corrupt and what you need to do is adopt this new set of principles and move forward.' We rejected that

and said, 'We like the principles we have. We just need to do a better job with them and that's going to be our quality program.' ''[38]

Intel's six guiding principles were actually not a bad foundation for good quality habits. Three of them were adopted in the decade following the founding of Intel in 1968. They said that Intel should be a results-oriented, risk-taking, disciplined company. The second set of three values, added in the 1980s, pertain more directly to quality. They are:

- Customer orientation: Partnerships with customers and suppliers are essential to our mutual success.
- Quality: Our business requires continuous improvement in the quality of our products and services.
- Great place to work: Our people are our fundamental strength, and we are a team.[39]

Being young and laid back in California, the sort of place where men do not bother to wear coats and ties and call everyone by their first name, Intel had not accumulated a lot of cultural baggage that would slow change. Intel executives have never been distracted by perks. Parking at its headquarters in Santa Clara and at other sites is on a first-come, first-served basis, and the offices there are no more than partitioned cubicles, even Andy Grove's and Craig Barrett's. But Intel is not a place where people can relax; it is a highly disciplined company where ideas are tested rigorously, sometimes brutally, in the close combat of meetings. Intel grew so fast and was so successful that it started to go out of control early on. Late in the 1970s, Grove discovered that its administrative costs were rising faster than any other indicator. Intel's business processes had become cumbersome and bureaucratic. It took 12 pieces of paper and 95 administrative steps to order a $2.79 mechanical pencil. Intel used some small, precious items, such as the gold that went into its microprocessors, and was handling procurement of all items as if they were small and precious.[40] Intel applied some process-simplification techniques at the time, primitive by current standards, to reduce costs.

A Cavalier Attitude

But Intel resisted taking some of the formal steps that are usually part of going to total quality management. It did not study the cost of quality, for example. "Every time we think about doing one of those studies we usually conclude that, 'Yes, it's obvious there is waste and redundancy in the system,' " Barrett explains. "So finally we have shied away from doing any of those detailed calculations and say that we recognize that we waste some engineering resources because of poor planning, we recognize that we waste manufacturing resources because yields aren't what they could be, therefore it's obvious that we ought to work to improve and we're going to do that." In the integrated-circuit business, the yield of chips from silicon wafers is a critical cost and quality factor. "This was an obvious opportunity to improve and we didn't bother to debate it and we didn't bother to try to quantify it," says Barrett. "It was obvious so we said 'Let's go after it.' " Through the application of statistical process controls and other tools, Intel has improved the yield of usable silicon from around 50% early in the 1980s to 90% or close to it, depending on the product, early in the 1990s.

In 1990 and again in 1991 Intel, or to be precise, its Embedded Controller and Memory Group, applied for the Baldrige Award and failed to win both times. It was probably the company's cavalier attitude towards the formalities of quality management that cost it the prize. "We were not as structured as the Baldrige process would have liked us to have been" Barrett allows. "The process they would like us to have might in fact slow us down considerably and our industry places an immense value on time-to-market and cycle time . . . if you look at some of the detailed planning methodology that is espoused by certain Baldrige criteria, it would suggest that you'd almost get into a gridlock in terms of planning."

He cited a case in point. One morning in the fall of 1992 a client introduced a new PC priced at $2,900 at the opening of business at 8:30. By around 11:30 the company had to drop the price by $300 to match what the competition was offering. Barrett continues, "Structured planning methodologies are wonderful, but if you can give me a structured planning methodology that would allow you to anticipate and respond with a 10% price reduction between 8:30 and 11:30 on the morning of a major product introduction. . . . You don't have time to go out and collect customer feedback. Sometimes there are instances where you do it by the seat of your pants." The total quality fan would retort that structured quality planning might not help make a decision in a crisis but it could avoid the crisis.

The Ultimate Weapon

The difference between the Intel approach to quality and the more formal approach of the other companies discussed in this chapter may be more in form than in substance. You can find every TQM practice somewhere in

Intel, and many of them are well deployed in parts of the company. Intel practices concurrent engineering by bringing customers, suppliers, and manufacturing engineers into the design process. It uses teams, but in an informal and unsupervised way. And Intel people have always spoken their minds and taken the initiative. When the Embedded Controller and Memory Group (which no longer exists) applied for the Baldrige, it reported in its application that it had more than 650 teams and that 95% of its decision were team based. The company spent 5% of its payroll on training in 1990.[41] The company uses quality function deployment (see Chapter 5) to develop new products. Its "vendor of choice" program surveys the company's top 90 customers once a month to ask them their opinion on Intel's product quality, service, delivery, pricing, technical support, and so forth. According to Barrett, failure to deliver a product exactly when the customer specifies is the most frequent complaint.

Intel excels at getting to market fast with new products. "Ultimately, speed is the only weapon we have," says Andy Grove.[42] The earlier versions of its famous microprocessors, the 286, 386, 486, and then the Pentium (which would have been the 586 if Intel had continued the serial names) were introduced at four-year intervals. Intel plans to develop the 686 (Hexium?) and succeeding chips at two-year intervals. The Pentium arrived, slightly delayed, early in 1993 and the 686 is due at the end of 1994. To maintain that frequency of introductions, Intel keeps three development teams going simultaneously. At the same time, Intel upgraded the existing chips so as to keep them ahead of competitors' chips. Intel got a lot of extra mileage out of the 486 by "doubling its clock," which means that the microprocessor could operate twice as fast in the same piece of hardware. In fact, the 486 was selling so well in 1992 that Intel did not mind if the Pentium introduction slipped into 1993.

Each generation of chips is several times more complex than its predecessor. The Pentium has 3.2 million transistors, compared with 1.3 million in the 486, and operates at a speed of 112 million instructions per second, whereas the 486 with the clock doubled operates at "only" 54 MIPS.[43] "In the chip-making business the important parameter is the defects per square centimeter in the manufacturing process," says Barrett. "Each defect has a potential to make a good transistor a bad one. As you get more and more transistors on bigger and bigger chips, to get the same yield in the manufacturing process the number of defects per square centimeter that you play with has to go down. We've been able to drive the defects down faster than the chip size goes up."

Customers expect new chips to be at least as reliable as the old ones, and they are. Intel and the other chip manufacturers have reached a point in quality where the reliability of the chips is no longer an issue. It is a given. Intel shipped 20 million chips in 1992 and expects to ship 30 million or more in 1993. Very few get sent back. Intel's internal failure rate is around 100 parts per million, but most of the faulty chips are caught before they are shipped. When problems occur in the field, and they amount to a handful a year, the customer likely has attempted some difficult and unexpected application that Intel did not foresee.

How much does Intel's success come from its brilliant innovation and sense of the market—and how much of that depends on one individual, Andy Grove? How well would Intel do without Grove and in a more stable market? These are questions raised by Richard Pascale in *Managing on The Edge*.[44] Intel's cavalier attitude toward process, toward what might be considered the bureaucracy of quality, may be regretted when Barrett takes over from Grove.

CONCLUSIONS

The stories of Hewlett-Packard, Intel, Milliken, Motorola, and Xerox (and Ford in the previous chapter) carry a clarion message for any organization attempting to travel along the TQM journey. They share these characteristics:

- Leaders who are committed to quality and stick to that commitment in spite of crises and distractions. Continuity over a long period is important, whether that is achieved because one person remains in the job for many years or because the successor is like-minded.
- Intensive training, starting at the top and continuing permanently throughout the company.
- The extensive use of teams which bring together people from different divisions and disciplines, not in amiable harmony but in a very tough-minded search for solutions.
- Use of the whole family of quality tools, rather than a reliance on one or two to provide easier answers.
- A genuine and lasting effort to find out what the customer thinks.
- The vision to set stretch goals and the attention to detail to measure the progress toward those goals.
- The integration of specific quality goals with a company's basic strategic goals.

- High speed in developing new products and services, but holding off marketing them until they are virtually defect free.
- A willingness to transform the way they work.
- The realization that good as they already are, they still have a way to go.

8

The Fumblers
When The Fires Went Out

If the reader has any doubt, at this point, that total quality management is extremely hard to do well—or if it is done well, to sustain—or if it is done well in one part of an organization, to spread that success to the rest of the organization—then read these cautionary tales. Some of the best companies in the United States have been trying for quality for years without succeeding—or, having succeeded, have then let slip what they had accomplished. Five or ten or even more years after starting, some fine companies still do not have it right.

The surveys cited in the introduction to this book indicate that even though the adherents to total quality are growing and probably will keep growing, more of them that try it are dissatisfied than satisfied. Those that do succeed find it hard to keep improving. And the longer they are at it, the harder it is to sustain enthusiasm, as Tony Kobayashi learned at Fuji Xerox, years after winning the Deming Prize. Sometimes a company will stumble on rocks that have nothing to do with total quality: a change in the economy, a shift in technology, and in the ensuing panic the company reverts to its old ways. Or a change in leadership may be what sets a company off in a different direction. The very act of succeeding in a total-quality effort may signal a change in course as the enthusiasts slump in exhaustion and the unconvinced get their chance to lash back.

We have already seen how much difficulty General Motors has had over more than a decade in attempting to become a total-quality company. I could have picked many other examples for this chapter. I have chosen four companies all of which are well known, in one way or another, for their quality. IBM has stood for excellence through most of this century, but has fumbled its total-quality efforts as well as several other undertakings. Nashua Corporation became in 1979 Deming's first major convert in corporate America, and was held up in the 1980 NBC documentary "If Japan Can . . . Why Can't We" as a model of how to become competitive, but it has never come close to fulfilling the potential of total quality. Florida Power & Light Company reached the pinnacle of quality as the first company outside Japan to win the Deming Prize, and then relapsed. Caterpillar Incorporated's bright yellow machines symbolize muscular dependablity around the world, yet Caterpillar has fumbled its efforts to become better, especially in handling labor. What happened to these companies is perhaps even more instructive than what happened to the most successful.

IBM

IBM had the misfortune, or good fortune, depending on how and when you look at it, to have much in common with General Motors. Both were so profitable and dominant at the beginning of the 1980s that they did not feel the chill threat of competition that woke up lesser companies. Both were huge, arrogant, inward looking, bureaucratic. They had lost touch with their customers. Their quality was slipping, but they hardly noticed. After all, GM made record profits in 1984 and IBM had its best year ever in 1985. The leaders of both companies during most of the 1980s paid lip service to the idea of quality, but never really demonstrated commitment to it. IBM and GM each had within them pockets of exceptional excellence that could have showed them the way, but they chose not to pay attention to these until it was almost too late. Both of them made gestures towards adopting total quality as early as the late 1970s, but it took a decade for them to understand truly what needed to be done. One difference between the two giant companies: GM's management philosophy was outdated, but IBM had had the right philosophy all along. The Watsons, father and son, who built and ran the company for a total of six decades, believed in excellence in everything the company did. Thomas J. Watson, Jr. summarizes the precepts that his father followed in these terms:

- Give full consideration to the individual employee.
- Spend a lot of time making customers happy.
- Go the last mile to do a thing right.[1]

Those sentences could stand today as the right vision for a company seeking excellence. In the late 1970s, IBM still gave full consideration to the employee—too much, some said. The 40 hours a year that IBM managers had to spend in training focused on handling personnel, and how well a manager dealt with personnel matters was critical to his career. The company still virtually guaranteed lifetime employment. It was almost impossible to get fired. IBMers still tried "to do a thing right," but they did not do it right the first time. Instead, like others, they maintained an expensive service army in the field correcting the mistakes that came out of the development laboratories and the factories. And the customers were not happy. Banks complained about the performance of IBM's mainframes (see Chapter 1) and industrial customers were finding defects in the products. IBM's own research on other companies showed that their competitiveness was improving rapidly.

IBM's business changed in the late 1970s and early 1980s to a degree that obscured and intensified some of its problems. IBM shifted from a lease-based business to a sale-based business while the whole computer industry was beginning to move from specialty sales to commodity sales. Enormous increases in the power of computer chips brought the PC to prominence and pushed the mainframe to the background. Thus three of the elements of IBM's success—mainframes, leasing, and specialty products—lost their preeminence. Customers saw less reason to pay the large premiums IBM charged them for the privilege of dealing with such a fine company. As IBM turned leases into complex sales deals with multiple allowances and discounts, the company developed "a horrendous error rate," in the words of one who saw it happen, in the bills it sent its customers; this was particularly embarrassing for a corporation built on processing data. The error rate in the billing was about 7%, which was typical for U.S. companies then both on the production lines and in the offices.

Upset Customers

The shift to a commodity market required excellence in mass producing small-ticket items, and that exposed some weaknesses. The same IBM plant at Raleigh, North Carolina that had been turning out 15,000 to 20,000 display terminals a year in the mid-1970s had to whip out 200,000 or 300,000 of them a year at the end of the same decade. At the lower production rate, the plant's 5% defect level was not too noticeable and indeed was somewhat better than that of U.S. industry as a whole. But as sales increased the sheer numbers of defects became too obvious. "When you are shipping 200,000 boxes and having the same defect percentage, that's a lot of boxes that are bad and a lot of customers that get upset," says Stephen Schwartz, senior vice president for quality (now retired). "If one customer installs a lot of displays at one time, you are really going to get them mad."

Many of these terminals were used by bank tellers dealing with the public, so a failure would be obvious not only to the bank but to the bank's customers waiting impatiently in line.[2]

IBM's first exposure to modern quality, as contrasted with the old excellence of the Watsons, came about in the late 1970s because of the friendship between Phil Crosby and Paul Rizzo, a senior executive (who was called back to IBM in its crisis at the end of 1992). They played golf at the same club in Greenwich, Connecticut, and just after Crosby left ITT, where he had been director of quality, Rizzo asked him to speak to IBM's management (see Chapter 1). Crosby also visited IBM sites, including Raleigh, to talk about his cost-of-quality ideas. The Raleigh plant became IBM's pilot for trying modern quality, and it achieved some good results quickly. IBMers who listened to Crosby came back charged up with the promise of his message. However, they complained that Crosby had not given them the tools they needed to apply that enthusiasm.

After listening to the theories of Crosby and other quality consultants, IBM designed its own training courses and set up a Quality Institute which eventually settled in Thornwood, New York. In the early 1980s, IBM also appointed its first vice president for quality, another signal that management regarded quality as important. One chronicler of IBM's attitudes noted that the company devoted 3% of its 1979 annual report to quality, raising the quality content from year to year until it reached 17.5% in 1985—after which it dropped sharply.[3]

By the mid-1980s IBM, it appeared, had declared a victory in the battle for quality even though the culture of quality had not penetrated the company and the leadership had not made quality its cause. Quality was something extra that managers did with flip charts, slides, and slogans. It had not become part of their real jobs. Profits hit a record high in 1985 and worldwide IBM employment peaked at 407,000 in 1986.

However, the matter of quality refused to go away. The new chairman, John Akers, did something unprecedented in the fall of 1986: he invited major customers to take part in IBM's annual strategic planning conference at Purchase, New York, a sacrosanct event normally limited to a score of the company's top people. As Schwartz recalls, "In a fact-filled, hard-hitting way [the customers] told us that our priorities had gotten screwed up, that we were putting IBM needs ahead of customer needs. They had always felt that they came first and that is why so many of them were doing business with us, and somehow we had strayed from that path. When six of your very closest customers look you in the eye and say, 'You know, you've lost your way,' that's a wet towel across the chops.'' IBM's success, particularly with the 360 family of computers introduced 20 years earlier, had gradually shifted the company's focus toward technology and away from the customer. The customers said that IBM was more enamored with technology than with solving their problems. Now it was time to turn back.

Akers declared 1987 to be the Year of the Customer, which one hopes was a misnomer. If 1987 was the year of the customer, what were all the other years supposed to be? In fact, 1987 turned out to be not the year of the customer but the year when IBM began to attack its enormous overhead costs. What really worried Akers and his executives was not quality but productivity. The route they chose to better productivity was not total quality management, but cutting back facilities, programs, and people. This was the beginning of what in IBM-speak is called ''management-initiated attrition,'' or MIA. Generous early retirement offers started an exodus from the company that was voluntary at first but later became partly involuntary. The emphasis on efficiency, not quality, situated IBM's thinking in 1987 about where the auto companies' and others' had been at the end of the 1970s. If you continued to name IBM's years, somewhat in the Chinese fashion, 1988 would be ''The Year of Reorganization.'' At the beginning of the year, Akers announced the restructuring of IBM into largely autonomous lines of business in the United States. Quality took a back seat again as managers got used to their new situations, and reconstructed the informal ties that pull an organization together. They also wondered about their own careers, trying to balance their future prospects at IBM with the uncertainties of early retirement. The company had by now let 20,000 employees go, and moved 21,000 others out to sales and programming.[4]

Market Driven

Round Three (the reader can be forgiven for losing count at this point, or for thinking that this seems more like Round Six or Seven) of IBM's transformation came in 1989, with Akers's declaration at the beginning of the year that IBM was now to be ''market driven.'' Four principles lay behind being market driven:

- Make the customer the final arbiter.
- Understand our markets.
- Commit to leadership in markets we choose to serve.
- Deliver excellence in execution across our enterprise.

All of these principles were to fit into IBM's enduring constitution:

- The pursuit of excellence.
- The best customer service in the world.
- Respect for the individual.[5]

Notice that Akers reordered the original Watson constitution, putting excellence first in place of the respect for the individual ["employee" in the original]. Those who were working on quality at IBM at this time report that Akers still did not have total quality at the top of his list. Perhaps he was too preoccupied with restructuring, inflated costs, rapidly changing markets, declining market share, and . . . well, IBM certainly had enough problems to distract the most dedicated CEO.

Akers stated at the beginning of 1989 that IBM was the most profitable company in the world. As the year wore on it became clear that even this statement was not necessarily going to remain true. Earnings declined 35% on sales of $62.7 billion in 1989. The company took a charge of $2.4 billion to cover the costs of cutting facilities and people.[6] IBM paid out another $2.4 billion in warranty costs, mostly attributable to defects.[7] IBM's quality was still not good. At the end of the year the rate of defects on all its operations were running at about 6,000 defects per million parts—or Four Sigma, to make a comparison with Motorola's goal of Six Sigma, which represents 3.4 defective parts per million.

Even before all these bad numbers came out, IBM had started to prepare another round in its quality campaign. In the spring, summer, and fall of 1989, an IBM task force worked to devise an approach to quality that they hoped would be not merely another program but a new way of doing business. Going by the book, they went out to benchmark IBM against companies whose success in quality was recognized. They were embarrassed or amused, depending on their temperament, to discover that some of those companies, including Motorola, had themselves benchmarked IBM when they set out on the quality journey early in the 1980s. The strategic planning conference of top IBM executives drafted the new plan at the fall meeting in 1989. It was rolled out under the banner of "market-driven quality" at the annual meeting of the 500 senior managers in January, 1990.

The casual observer might be forgiven for wondering what the difference was between 1990's plan and 1989's. Stephen Schwartz believes that IBM finallly did embrace total quality management this time and try to bring it into the mainstream. The 1989 plan had focused on the customer and marketing plans, but the new plan demanded TQM in all parts of the business.

Like others, IBM gave itself stretch goals: a tenfold improvement in quality by 1991, a hundredfold improvement by 1993, and Six Sigma by 1994. Akers declared that IBM should focus on this commitment: "We want every IBM product and service, every contact with our company, to be perfect in the eyes of our customers." He recognized that "we've had some major problems."[8] Akers made better quality IBM's primary objective and said that market-driven quality was the first item to be discussed when senior executives visited IBM offices and plants. At least you can say IBM's interest in quality had intensified.

A Burst of Cheers: Silverlake

Something nice finally happened to IBM late in 1990. On October 10, the top 20 or so executives at IBM were locked up in their strategic planning conference when a call came in for Akers from Larry Osterwise, the curly-haired, exuberant general manager of the IBM plant at Rochester, Minnesota which manufactures midrange computers and hard disk drives. *Nobody* interrupts the strategic planning conference. But Osterwise insisted. Akers did not come to the telephone, but he did receive a note. When Akers read it he said, "Hot damn!" Akers passed the note to Steve Schwartz, the current speaker. When Schwartz read the note out loud the assembled executives burst into cheers. Rochester had won the Malcolm Baldrige Award.[9]

Rochester was something of a backwater in IBM, geographically and otherwise. But it had advantages that other units did not have. Because people like living in Rochester (*Money* magazine named it the best place in the United States to live in 1993), the work force was more stable than at some other IBM locations, and it was a good work force. Because the facility combined research labs and a manufacturing plant, the two parties in the development of a new product could work side by side.

In the early 1980s, Rochester was in deep trouble. With a fine disregard for the customer, IBM had produced five lines of midsized computers, none compatible with any of the others. IBM launched an effort in 1982, code-named Fort Knox, to create a new computer that would be compatible with all of the other five. It was IBM's general custom to scatter parts of projects around the world in the name of efficiency, "re-missioning" available people to a new task when they finished the old one. Rochester was one of the many labs assigned to Fort Knox. But by 1985 it became clear that Fort Knox was just too complicated. It would never work. It was abandoned. IBM's existing midsized computers were coming to the end of their lives.

To fill the hole that suddenly opened, IBM assigned Rochester to hurry to develop and manufacture a new mid-size computer in half the normal time, that is, by 1988. The lab got a new director, Tom Furey, a programmer who had become a manager of programmers and something of a visionary in technology. Steve Schwartz, who supervised Rochester as head of applications business systems, appointed Furey with the hope that he would find new ways to get the job done in two to three years. Larry Osterwise was already head of the manufacturing facility at Rochester. On a visit to Rochester in the fall of 1985, Steve Schwartz found a group of seven engineers working feverishly in the basement on a project code-named Silverlake (after a lagoon in Rochester) which seemed to have the answer. Schwartz told them that if they could produce a prototype by January 1986 he would take it to headquarters in Armonk. They worked through Thanksgiving, Christmas, and New Year's and met the deadline.

The usual way of doing things would never bring a new computer to market in time. The new director, Tom Furey, began by asking a lot of questions about the lab's customers and the lab as a business, things the scientists and technicians at Rochester did not normally bother about. They were researchers; let the marketing and sales people worry about the business. With remarkably little interference or even attention from IBM headquarters in Armonk the coequal heads of the operations at Rochester, Furey in the lab and Osterwise in the plant, put together an approach to develop Silverlake. Since the project had to break time barriers, they created parallel rather than sequential processes, and insisted on getting things right the first time by eliminating defects during design rather than after manufacturing had begun. In fact, Silverlake had most of the characteristics of TQM, including a vision, cross-functional teams, empowerment, partnerships with outsiders, and a good understanding of customer requirements. At a company historically as secretive as IBM, bringing in suppliers, distributors, and customers to study and comment on your plans would have been suicide for a manager only a few years before.[10]

Silverlake did come through on time and Rochester started manufacturing what was now known as the AS/400 in 1988. IBM sold 25,000 units (in six models priced from $15,000 to $1 million) in four months, making it IBM's most successful introduction ever. So well had the whole program gone that Rochester applied for the Baldrige Award in 1989. Rochester did not win. But the required feedback that IBM got from the examiners proved invaluable. One problem was unavoidable: the AS/400 did not have enough of a track record to prove that the operation was improving continuously.

But the Rochester people could and did act on some of the other comments: that they were not benchmarking effectively, that they were not giving enough support to their cross-functional teams, that they needed mandatory and directed training, and most interesting of all, that management should show more commitment to quality. Osterwise later admitted that "I wasn't as committed as I should have been" and he set about improving communications and getting people more empowered and excited. The workers at Rochester were so disappointed at the outcome of the Baldrige application that they considered not trying again, but Osterwise was convinced that they had learned much in losing and could learn some more. He persuaded them to apply in 1990. They did and they won.

Schwartz was so impressed with the power of the Baldrige process that he created a whole internal Baldrige process, with annual reviews and plaques for the top scorers throughout IBM (see Chapter 5). "An extraordinary thing happened when we took on the Baldrige," Osterwise stated. "It gave us a unifying vision. Now we could get the whole company moving in the direction of market-driven and customer-driven quality."[11]

An Artsy Tradition: Software at Santa Teresa

Moving on to run IBM's Santa Teresa, California software lab, Furey went even further by instituting not an annual but a quarterly Baldrige assessment there. Santa Teresa employs about 1,500 people developing software for IBM. The software fraternity has proved irritatingly impervious to quality processes. Victor Tang, an electrical engineer, linguist, and software developer who followed Furey from Rochester to Santa Teresa, says, "programmers have traditionally been very artsy . . . trying to get quality from a community of artists is really a major challenge." Engineers are accustomed to disciplined thinking, but programmers view their craft as fundamentally a creative process, thus not susceptible to TQM. Software failure rates remained high during the 1980s. When Furey got to Santa Teresa in 1989 and started running Baldrige appraisals, the scores at first were around 300—a miserable showing on a scale of 1,000. By contrast, Rochester had won the Baldrige with a world-class score of about 800. As Furey and the others started bending the lab towards total quality, the scores in the quarterly appraisals rose in time to 650, enough to win IBM's internal silver medal.[12]

The quality of software normally is expressed in terms of errors per thousand or per million lines of software instructions written. But the Santa Teresa scientists decided this was a meaningless measure in terms of customer satisfaction. What was the customer supposed to do if you told him his software had seven errors per million lines? (For that matter, what is the buyer of an automobile supposed to make of the information that his car, judging by the averages, has two defective parts among about 5,000?) Tang points out that a major client, Fuji Bank, does not care how many errors per million lines IBM gives them or, for that matter, how many million lines of instructions IBM writes. IBM equipment executed 18 million transactions a day for Fuji and ran 24 hours a day, seven days a week, for four years without crashing. But what the Fuji people mention every time they talk to IBM is the crash of 1988, when the system did go down.

To change its quality measure to something meaningful to the customer, Santa Teresa set a goal of no more than ten defects in the product it ships, a defect being whatever a customer says is a defect. Normally software defects are detected when the product is received and the customer starts using it. To reduce those unpleasant surprises to the minimum, Santa Teresa brings the customers in at the development stage. Victor Tang refers to them as "co-developers." They examine and discuss what IBM is doing, test the software, and run their own programs on IBM's software and hardware. When a defect is discovered, either in the lab or in the field, Santa Teresa not only corrects it but looks back through the production process to see how that defect came about, so that the process itself can be corrected.

The process of writing software exists mostly in the minds of an idiosyncratic brotherhood but the people at Santa Teresa believe they are creating systematic methods, based on the total-quality approach, with the Baldrige criteria as a template. At first the programmers resisted the idea that total quality management applied to them, but as they worked on teams, and as they saw more clearly how their work tied into chains of functions, they warmed to it. The lab created councils of people from different areas to discuss critical topics together in a setting removed from their departments. In a gesture towards the working style of programmers, Furey encouraged something like teenagers' clubhouses, called "knowledge mining centers," where they can meet informally, eat popcorn, sip soft drinks, and work on pieces of code projected on the ceiling. By means of a computer connected to the projector, they can rewrite code together on the spot and see the results projected immediately. Santa Teresa has 14 of these knowledge mining centers. Furey reports that the same lab workers who in 1991 were complaining about how difficult it would be to achieve the tenfold quality improvement demanded by the corporation by 1992 were telling him how they were going to get the 100× improvement. Old hands at the lab were excited, some even canceling plans to take retirement.[13]

Good in Parts: Reorganization

The enthusiasm did not spread through IBM, however. Just as GM's Saturn and Cadillac divisions excelled without lifting the rest of the corporation to their levels, so Rochester, Santa Teresa and other parts of IBM that endorsed market-driven quality succeeded dramatically but without pulling the rest of IBM along. IBM did not achieve its ten-fold improvement in 1991. In fact, IBM's problems piled up so fast that the goal could well have been forgotten by most IBMers. In 1991, for the first time in its history, IBM lost money and sales shrank for the first time in more than four decades. IBM's problems were becoming overwhelming: loss of market share, still too much reliance on mainframes, more competitors and more agile competitors, a sales force that still did not understand how IBM's position had changed, and on and on. When Chairman John Akers decided on a new plan at the end of 1991, it was not another quality initiative but a reorganization of the corporation into 13 separate business units; these were supposed to develop the spirit to survive on their own.

IBM continued downhill in 1992. To reduce the company's still excessive overheads the cuts in sites, functions, and jobs started in 1986 deepened and became more threatening. Retirement was no longer necessarily a voluntary act. People leaving the company reported abysmal morale. In *Fortune's* annual survey of the most admired corporations in America, IBM, ranked first in 1985 and 1986, had dropped two thirds of the way down the list to 206th by the beginning of 1993. IBM's losses soared to nearly $5 billion in 1992 and its shares, once almost of heirloom value, dropped to less than one third of their 1987 price. Finally, at the beginning of 1993, the board of directors revolted and replaced Akers with Louis V. Gerstner, Jr., the head of RJR Nabisco. Although Gerstner made a point of not announcing grand visions on quality or other matters, he did make appointments that could strengthen IBM's market-driven quality. He brought in Gerald M. Czarnecki, a TQM fanatic who was CEO of Bank of America–Hawaii, as the senior vice president for human relations and administration. Larry Osterwise, who had managed the Rochester site when it won the Baldrige Award, now reported to Czarnecki as director for quality.

In all the panic and turmoil, quality had not figured large. In his reactions to the crisis, Akers had shown that the quality culture he had presented to the company in various guises had not taken root. While other companies chose quality as their weapon to fight their crises, IBM reverted to other, older weapons—reorganize, cut, and harangue. IBM did not reach its quality goal of a tenfold improvement by the end of 1991. Even at the end of 1992, the company's overall improvement stood at only seven times the 1989 level. The chance of becoming 100 times better by the end of 1993 looked very slim. Yet within the company there were large variations. Marketing and services had been able to improve only two-or threefold, but in some areas of software and technology the improvement by the end of 1992 was on target at 32×.

In spite of all it has been through, IBM still has enormous strengths—in the superb quality of much of its hardware and some software; in the long-term reliability of some of its systems; in the performance of some of its divisions, such as the ones that make personal computers and midrange computers; and, most of all, in an extraordinarily talented if demoralized group of employees. Like GM, IBM has enough good examples of its own to lead the way out of its troubles.

NASHUA

Today, if you wanted to find an example of total quality or Demingism at its best you would not pick Nashua Corporation, as did the NBC documentary in 1980 and many books and articles written since then. After its initial successes, Nashua had many bad years. In current dollars, its revenue was about the same at the end of the decade as at the beginning and its net income was about the same too, that is, close to nothing. (Literally hundreds of acquisitions and sales and radical shifts in the market have muddied the record.) In earlier chapters we have seen how statistical process controls never really permeated the company, how quality circles failed and team-work succeeded only partially, and the leadership did not create the kind of driving commitment to be found at, say, Milliken or Motorola.

Nashua's early success evaporated quickly when then chief executive William Conway, thinking that its understanding of quality methods had given the company the secret to success in whatever it did, decided to manufacture copying machines. Expertise in coating paper did not translate into expertise in making the machines that used the paper. Nashua lost $40 million in 1982 and Conway lost his job.

Nashua never did find statistical process controls all that helpful in im-proving the making of coated papers. When Deming got the technicians to stop constantly adjusting the equipment, the variation in the process was reduced, but improving much beyond that level proved difficult. Paper has a lot of natural variation. The raw material, trees, is not in anyone's con-trol.[14] SPC proved more applicable to Nashua computer products, particularly the manufacture of disks. However, when the technology of disks advanced from iron-oxide coating to thin-film coating, Nashua's disk plant at Merrimac lost most of its business. Management at the new thin-film plant that Nashua acquired in Santa Clara, California, at first strenuously resisted the quality approach. Nashua's computer products business lost $23 million in 1991.

Ironically, the most profitable horse in Nashua's stable, the mail-order photo-finishing business that operates under the names of Scot, York, and Truprint in Canada, the United States and Britain, respectively, shows the least interest in total quality. The photo business headquarters in Parkersburg, West Virginia rarely invites any quality specialist from New Hampshire to visit. The business made an operating profit of $19.5 million in 1991, just enough to overcome to poor performance of the other three divisions and give the corporation overall a slight operating profit for the year. Nashua's 1991 annual report boasted that in the photo-finishing business "inspectors check every print on every roll as part of the production process"—a heresy in quality doctrine. As nearly a generation of quality gurus has kept insisting, you do not inspect in quality, you build it in. But Nashua's photo-finishing group inspected 30 million rolls in 1991.[15]

A Good Showing for the Next Quarter

Lloyd Nelson, a Deming disciple and friend who served as director of statistical methods and an officer at Nashua for a decade, retired in 1992. Since he was 70 years old, nothing unusual attaches to his retirement. However Charles Clough, the chairman, did not replace him. Nor did he replace Nelson's assistant, who left the company at the same time. Nashua no longer has a quality department, but Lloyd Nelson remains a consultant to the company. Nelson did not rush off to make a fortune giving seminars on quality as have other consultants, even those with the most tenuous claims to expertise. A tall, stooped statistician, Nelson is happier writing technical articles and software programs and reviewing technical books. He has, however, ruminated with dry humor on what happened at Nashua (see also Chapters 2 and 3). Nelson says that Nashua stalled at a level of quality below what could be achieved. He writes:

I believe the reason for this is that the culture of the company is still a mixture of the past and what Mr. Clough would like it to be now. However, changing the culture of any well-established company is

very difficult. Mr. Clough clearly recognizes the desirability of such
change. He continues to try to convince others that such change is
essential. To many, his emphasis may appear to be on the usual accounting parameters: profits, gross margins, cycle times, and the like.
Note that because he interfaces with the financial community, he must
deal with outcomes. I believe he feels that processes are what others
must focus on (as indeed they must). But others have not gotten the
message that he wants them to do this. In addition, there is the classic
resistance to change . . .

The usual structure of a quarterly review involves outcomes. On the
face of it, this is most reasonable. After all, an operations review has
always been a get-together to report on "how we're doing." Notice
that "how we're doing" translates to "how we've done." It is a rare
event when someone puts a control chart on the table. There are few
efforts to discuss the basic idea that process improvement results in
lower costs and in greater profits.

Nelson states that Clough wants his people to understand that process
improvement is *the* goal, but he "may underestimate how difficult it is for
them to carry it out." Nelson explains:

They need technical help, of course; but perhaps what is even more
important, they need to know that upper management wants them to
think and work this way. Too many people think that Mr. Clough wants
only a good showing for the next financial report. They try their darnd-
est to give him this—time and again by shipping everything they can
this month even if it means borrowing from next month. They postpone
routine maintenance to save its cost. When such actions become *rou-
tinely* acceptable, as I like to think they are not at Nashua Corporation,
where is the quality philosophy? It is not a quality philosophy; it is a
quality façade.

Nelson then goes on to make a more general point:

More companies (I suspect) have a quality façade than have a quality
philosophy. Unfortunately this gives quality a bad name. How easy it
is to imagine a company CEO looking for examples and, seeing all the
quality façades around, saying, "Well that sloganeering is not worth
our attention. Obviously, it's not effective." He would, of course, be
right.[16]

James Brian Quinn, a member of Nashua's board and professor of management at the Amos Tuck School of Business Administration, says Clough believes in TQM, presses hard to get it, but lacks the charisma to put a glitter on it as Galvin can at Motorola. He thinks Nashua's quality shows up well in the high-tech, lost-cost market for disks and diskettes, and once the Santa Clara plant had more or less forcibly been converted to TQM, it began to pay off in thin-film technology too.[17]

Down with the Charts: The Tape Division

Clough's belief that each division can best determine its own approach to quality and other matters admits much variety within Nashua, from the Santa Clara operation, which did not greet TQM happpily, to Merrimac, which became thoroughly "qualitized" (while its outmoded technology reduced its business to almost nothing). The losses at Santa Clara exceeded Nashua's tolerance limit, and a team of the corporation's senior executives spent much of 1992 in California turning the division around. But the $60-million-a-year tape division in Troy, New York, is almost eccentric in its independence from Nashua. The manager, Robert Geiger, is an original. Tall, slim, long-haired, mustached, dressed in work clothes, he looks more like one of his craftsmen than the boss. But then he went to Antioch, that free-floating Ohio college, in the unrestrained 1960s and he studied sociology rather than business, which he did not like. He did, however, like making things, and that led him to factory management and eventually to turning around troubled factories. After he had rescued a couple of plants for other employers, Nashua invited him to Troy to fix its money-losing tape division, which makes duct tape and masking tape.

Geiger says he is a quality enthusiast but, having studied sociology, he has an approach that stresses the human side rather than the methodology. He downplays the formalities of quality. "We don't do quality circles," he says, "We have no slogans and we are real careful about teams. We don't have permanent management teams. When we have a problem a team can fix, we form a team, and we break it up when the problem is solved. I just ask some people to get together to solve a problem." At any one time, the division is not likely to have more than two active "A-teams," as they are called.

When he first came to the plant in 1988, he took down the control charts, because the plant was charting everything without really understanding what should be charted. Says Geiger, "They'd be tracking variations in a coating system that were the result of causes several steps back. They should have been charting processes further up the line to determine special causes and common causes.'' To get a useful chart, you need to understand the process. The people at Troy had learned to make charts, but they had not learned how to understand the process. Geiger suspended chart-making until the process was understood; then he began to allow a limited number of key charts. ''There's a lot of crap in quality,'' says Geiger. ''The charts are covered up except when Deming comes around.'' What he meant was that plants will not pay much attention to charts until they have an interested visitor, and then they will put the charts on prominent display—after massaging the readings to reduce variations to a level that is less than embarrassing.

Geiger explains his approach in these terms:

> ''I get along with people on the floor. I want to fix problems. I am intrigued when I talk to people on the floor who want to do it right, but the bureaucrats interfered. I don't like SPC. But I like making things. I like manufacturing. Taking off your necktie and talking to people is the key. Then someone will tell you, 'They haven't fixed the main bearing on this machine for three years.' You fix it. You want to establish trust. You start thinking about things. Think about inventory; it's not an asset; think of all that money tied up. It's a liability. People are the asset. I began thinking about process and I began thinking about values. Juran and Deming focused on methodology, not people. They say if you can't measure something, you can't improve it. I say you can. At some point, I became very good at turn-around management. I always ask the guys' names and I introduce myself. That's my rigid methodology. How do you get people to want to do a good job? You've got all that baggage of mistrust.''

To get that trust, he shares information. He is willing to tell anyone his salary ($150,000 a year) and he does not believe in bonuses. ''I think you should be paid what you are worth and get no personal bonuses,'' he affirms. He has shared some of his Nashua bonuses with his staff.

He said he found no organized, top-down effort at Nashua to do quality. He also found a decentralized organization with six layers of management between the chairman and the factory floor (since reduced to four). ''The decentralization of Nashua made it possible for me to do what I wanted to do in this division,'' Geiger says. He has isolated his division from the corporation, to the point of not allowing the corporate newsletter on the premises. ''I didn't want interference, and I didn't want our successes to be seen because as soon as you are successful you get detractors," he explains. Some of the middle managers balked at his approach, and he fired them. Geiger believes a couple of his superiors would not have minded seeing him go too.[18] Clough is proud of the way Geiger has turned around the tape division, and he encourages visitors and his own executives to see what has happened at Troy. The tape division started to make a profit in a depressed market after Geiger had been there about 18 months.

After trying for more than a decade, Nashua still has a hodgepodge of uneven quality efforts. Process improvement has taken hold in some manufacturing operations, but not in others. The best news is that the Santa Clara division, which was losing customers because of its poor quality, did turn around. Nashua's top management spent much of 1992 convincing the computer disk operation to convert to quality. They were successful, the products have improved, and the results should show in 1993. A booming market for its products helped too. Nashua's offices and business systems have partly adopted quality, sales and marketing hardly at all. The leadership of the company has not taken the kind of unequivocal stand that Galvin or Milliken took. Clough remains torn between the traditional demands on a CEO to give a good performance by normal accounting standards and the desire to follow the total quality route. He is frustrated by the tendency of units that have gone far in quality to backslide, and of those that have not, to resist. Crises in Nashua's affairs keep distracting his attention. From the heart, he says, "I tell you anyone who thinks it's simple, just doesn't understand or hasn't worked with it."[19] He has announced he will retire in 1994.

FLORIDA POWER & LIGHT

In the late 1980s, some of the leaders of the quality movement regarded Florida Power & Light Company as one of the best examples of what they were trying to accomplish, perhaps *the* best in the United States. In 1989, FPL became the first company outside Japan to win the Deming Prize, which exposes candidates to a rigorous, nerve-wracking preparation and testing. The utility's headquarters in Miami became something of a shrine for those who wanted to learn how "to do the right thing right the first time," as FPL put it in its copious quality literature.[20] But in the early 1990s, FPL had very little to say about its quality efforts and turned visitors away. Most of its large quality staff had dispersed to other businesses—which were glad to have them, and to pay them considerably more than the tight-fisted utility. John Hudiburg, the CEO who led the quality campaign, had retired angry.

What happened to FPL's quality improvement program, as it was called? It still exists, but in muted form. A new management of quality agnostics had taken over. At the same time, some of the excesses of zeal and bureaucracy committed during the drive to win the Deming Prize created a backlash inside the company. Perhaps the whole thing had been a bit exaggerated in the first place. Few of the visitors noticed that as FPL achieved enormous improvements in its performance during the 1980s, so did other utilities in Florida, without fanfare or prizes.

FPL had heard about and even experienced a touch of quality management way back in the 1970s. When it started the design and construction of its St. Lucie 2 nuclear power station in 1977, FPL was determined to avoid the horrendous costs and delays that other utilities had experienced. It established quality standards up front, brought contractors' work in-house, trained workers, and established some interdepartmental teams. The results were excellent. When St. Lucie 2 was completed in 1984 it had been built, tested, and licensed three and a half years faster than the average nuclear station, and the final cost hit the original estimate of $1.4 billion on the button—(and that was far less money than the cost of most nuclear plants— see Chapter 1).[21]

Well before the completion of St. Lucie 2, its evident success prompted Marshall McDonald, then head of the utility, to investigate total quality ideas and practice. In 1981, FPL set up the first ten pilot teams, carefully organized so that they would be bound to succeed. Savings achieved by the early teams on diverse problems, from reducing billing errors to speeding the refueling of nuclear stations, began to appear as early as 1982. Kent Sterett, who will reappear in the next chapter working for the Southern Pacific railroad, helped to get FPL started and became head of its quality-improvement department. He recalls going around to some of the equipment yards to persuade them to try total quality. One crusty old superintendent at the Central Yard said to him, "I don't know if you guys know what you're talking about, but I'm going to make it work. Just don't get in my way."

A first wave of teams that followed the pilots proved disappointing because the members lacked training and direction. But the company trained them and the results improved. These were not quality circles vaguely searching for something useful to talk about, but focused teams pointed from above at selected problems. Regardless of their assignment, they had to follow what came to be regarded by some employees as an overly rigid seven-step process. Managers visited Japan to see Kansai Electric Power Company; listened to Crosby, Deming, and Juran; and used Juran's model rather more than the others to develop its own approach to quality.

An Act of God

FPL declared its vision ("to become the best managed electric utility"—not quite as grand as Motorola's "to become the world's premier company") in 1984, and in 1985 formally adopted its quality improvement program. The company renamed its executive committee the Quality Council, and the budgeting committee became the Policy Deployment Committee. It adopted strategic quality planning or *hoshin* planning, an idea that FPL picked up from Kansai Electric, to link individual and unit actions to corporate goals and thus focus the whole corporation on certain significant goals. Policy deployment, as FPL called it, replaced management by objectives, a standard tool which sets numerical goals for managers and holds them responsible for getting there.

FPL moved rapidly from being a second-rate utility to being one of the best. The teams paid off in many ways. Outages had been too frequent, too long, and on the rise in the western division. A Pareto analysis showed that lightning was the chief culprit; mid-Florida is the most lightning-struck part of the United States. FPL managers had always thought of lightning as an act of God that they could do nothing about. But when engineers and maintenance people got together for the first time in teams, they realized that their equipment could actually withstand a direct hit if only it were properly grounded and constructed. FPL made the necessary modifications, and the number of power outages began to fall rapidly after 1986. Other indicators of FPL's performance also showed dramatic improvement. The rate of consumer complaints dropped by two thirds between 1984 and 1989, as did the rate of injuries to employees. FPL had become a first-rate utility.[22]

In 1984 FPL had begun using counselors from JUSE, the Japanese Union of Scientists and Engineers, which supervises the Deming Prize, to guide its improvements. John Hudiburg, who had succeeded McDonald as CEO of the utility and become a quality fanatic, informed JUSE that his company wanted to seek the Deming in 1989. In Japan you do not brashly apply for the prize. You work with JUSE counselors, sometimes for years, and when they say you are ready then you may apply. Four Japanese university professors, well known in the quality field, became counselors and together with six FPL executives formed a steering committee. The group included Tetsuichi Asaka, one of the originals in the quality movement in Japan, and Noriaki Kano, who has become one of the new leaders. After satisfying themselves that FPL was serious about quality (unlike a number of American companies that had wasted their time in the past), the Japanese entered into a deep four-year involvement with FPL.

Serious preparation for the prize application began early in 1988. Ask anyone who was involved, says Sterett, and "they'll say it was a real bitch." In his book *Winning With Quality*, Hudiburg describes an atmosphere that seems to have grown more and more hellish as the dates for the examination in Tokyo and the dreaded audits in Florida approached. The company submitted a 1,000-page description of its quality improvement program and prepared mountains of data to back it up, retrievable in seconds. When a visiting JUSE auditor asks a question, the answer has to come within three minutes to get full credit. The company cafeteria found itself serving more food on weekends than on weekdays as Hudiburg, Wayne Brunetti, the executive vice president supervising the effort, and Sterett scheduled reviews on Saturdays.

"The company resembled a giant ant colony with each person carrying about his or her own cargo" of files stacked inside milk crates, Hudiburg wrote. "The roof fell in," he says, when a U.S. attorney called in May 1989 to inform FPL that his office was investigating drug trafficking at Turkey Point, one of FPL's nuclear stations. In the panic that followed, Hudiburg thought of withdrawing the prize application, but after a couple of sleepless nights he decided to go ahead. (Only one of the people arrested on the drug charges turned out to be an FPL employee, and he worked outside the plant.) The FPL teams, rehearsed and prepared to exhaustion, passed the examinations in Tokyo, then the audits in Florida, and at 3:30 A.M. on October 23, 1989, Tokyo called to say that FPL had won. Congratulations poured in, along with cold water. The callous press flicked the news aside with the report that FPL had spent $1.5 million to win some prize nobody ever heard of.[23] (Only slightly more impressed, the Florida Public Service Commission knocked 25% off a request from FPL to charge $2,450,022 in 1989 expenses to the Deming quest. The commission attributed that much of the effort to public relations rather than real quality improvement.[24])

A New Course: Away from Quality

Even before FPL won the prize, the utility was charting a new course. As already outlined in Chapter 2, the utility's parent, The FPL Group, hired an outsider from GTE, James L. Broadhead, to be CEO; in that position he was Hudiburg's boss. As the two got to know each other, they did not like what they saw. The meetings were "strained," Hudiburg writes, and one of the few things they agreed on was their incompatibility. Hudiburg retired and then went to Tokyo accept the prize without Broadhead.

That Broadhead saw different priorities for the company soon became evident. (He also had other preoccupations in extracting the Group from unhappy ventures into insurance, real estate, and cable television. He had to write off $752 million for these acquisitions, principally the Colonial Penn insurance group, in 1990.) He saw the quality improvement program as more of a problem than a solution. In a memo to his "dear fellow employees" on May 15, 1990, Broadhead said that in meetings with 20 small groups of randomly chosen employees he had found that the quality program was the subject of greatest interest. "The vast majority of the employees with whom I spoke expressed the belief that the mechanics of the QI process have been overemphasized," he wrote. "They felt that we place too great an emphasis on indicators, charts, graphs, reports, and meetings in which documents are presented and indicators reviewed.... I was most troubled, however, by the frequently stated opinion that preoccupation with process has resulted in our losing sight of one of the major tenets of quality improvement, namely, respect for employees.... Employees often expressed the view that they now have the commitment, training, and tools necessary to achieve continuing quality improvement and that management should trust them to use these tools as they and their supervisors feel are appropriate, without constant checking from above."

A second memo followed a month later dismantling much of the bureaucracy Hudiburg, Sterett, and others had created. Broadhead abolished the quality improvement department and several related units. He eliminated a whole series of structured reviews and visits. He told all units of the utility to review their indicators and teams and get rid of the ones that did not make substantial contributions "for the purpose of streamlining and simplifying our quality process." He canceled the quotas his predecessor had established for teams, suggestions, and other activities as being "inconsistent with respect for people." He made the seven-step quality improvement process voluntary rather than mandatory, and he required that FPL's training program be more balanced rather than focused overwhelmingly on quality.[25]

Former employees who worked in the quality area say that Broadhead got his views of the quality program by interviewing its opponents. They say that at the senior level some of these opponents had migrated to the Group staff, where they were closer to Broadhead. But these ex-employees agree that some scaling back was due; the staff and the procedures did need to be simplified and reduced. In fact, the headquarters quality staff of 25 had already been cut. Broadhead chopped it down to four people and got rid of most of the other quality specialists in the company, in a general and overdue reduction in staffing at FPL. A score of former FPL quality staffers ended up running the quality processes at other corporations, where they could command salaries of $100,000 or so—about double what they were getting at the regulated public utility.

The Japanese Did Not Catch On

The big question now arises: what happened to FPL's quality after the the fall of Hudiburg? The company does not talk about it any more. We know that the utility did exceptionally well after Hurricane Andrew scored a direct hit on FPL's service area on August 24, 1992, leaving 1.4 million FPL customers without power. Within five weeks, just over a month, all the customers who still had buildings or facilities capable of receiving power were connected up again. Floridians, including the Public Service Commission, thought FPL made a remarkable comeback from Hurricane Andrew. However, on the matter of the quality of its daily service the company's performance is harder to gauge, since it no longer releases a mass of data on how it is doing. Joseph Jenkins, director of the commission's electric and gas division, believes that FPL is reluctant to give the commission comparative data on outages because it would compare unfavorably with other Florida utilities. (Recall that until 1989 FPL was proud to show how well it was doing in reducing outages.)

Jenkins says the commission gets far more calls about outages at FPL than about outages at all the other Florida utilities. "I don't know what their problem is," he says, adding, "My feeling about their quality program is that they made a big effort to impress the Japanese, but there's not much substance behind that. They reduced complaints by telling the public to complain directly to them rather than to the PSC, but the Japanese didn't catch on to that." (The published complaint figures are taken from the PSC's log, not from calls directed to the utility itself. A former FPL executive says the Japanese examiners *were* aware of both the internal and external complaints. What impressed them was the steep slope of improvement on the charts—but they did not realize how awful the complaint level at FPL has been to start with.) Had the Japanese examiners compared FPL with other Florida utilities, Jenkins suggests, they might have thought differently about making the award to FPL.[26] The Florida Public Service Commission adopted a quality-of-service reporting rule in 1989 and is beginning to receive comparative data from its utilities.

From the numbers that are available it would seem that FPL's quality reached a plateau in 1989 and has stayed there since, with some slippage here and there. The PSC does collect data on consumer complaints and on safety variances in electric installations. Consumer complaints against FPL dwindled from a level of about 2,000 a year in the early 1980s to about 800 a year in 1989 and in the following two years. But then complaints jumped 41% from 811 in 1991 to 1,145 in 1992. The obvious excuse of Hurricane Andrew does not hold up because complaints increased before the storm but were at a low for the year in the month after the storm. In terms of complaints per thousand customers, both the raw total and the number considered "justified" by the PSC after investigation, FPL had the highest rate among Florida's utilities. By contrast, the state's second biggest utility, Florida Power Corporation, continued to show a reduced flow of complaints in 1992. FPC received half the complaints and one quarter the justified complaints per thousand customers that FPL got.[27]

The Public Service Commission also keeps a record of safety variances on the work the utilities do. The commission looks at a whole series of features like the proper spacing between power lines and telephone lines, the "riser guards" that protect lines going up and down poles, and so forth, and comes up with a quarterly number of variances it finds for each inspection point. The commission found the rate of variances rising slowly between 1987 and 1990 at FPL, dropping in 1991, and rising sharply in the first half of 1992. At Florida Power Corporation, the rate was consistently well below FPL's, but also took a fairly steep jump in the first half of 1992.[28] Commission officials suggest that the increase in variances can be explained by FPL's attempts to cut costs by replacing some experienced union workers with less experienced contract workers.

Assuming you think it was wrong for FPL to back away from its quality program, what went wrong? In the view of a number of veterans, Hudiburg made his biggest mistake by not keeping the FPL utility and Group boards (they are almost identical and meet on the same days) well clued in on the progress of the quality efforts. Hudiburg agrees that this was a mistake (see Chapter 2). The chairman of the board, Marshall McDonald, had started quality at FPL but had lost touch with it once he moved to the holding group and concentrated on the diversified businesses. Hudiburg told the board how well the utility was doing, but did not explain the whys and wherefores. "They took improvement as a given and they didn't realize that TQM was the engine making it all happen," he says. "They just appreciated the results."[29] So when the board came to choosing a new chairman, the quality factor did not enter into the choice. Then you had the classic case of the new boss wanting to make a mark of his own. Besides, Broadhead now had other pressing problems to deal with in the money-losing diversified companies.

Was it a mistake for FPL to go after the Deming prize? Quite possibly the intense effort to win, while a spur to the company, detracted attention from its business goals. Certainly the effort helped pile on the reports, procedures, and bureaucracy that later became onerous to many in the company. By the time Broadhead came along, the company probably just needed a bit of a rest from the frenetic applications of quality processes—and meanwhile many of the processes had become embedded in the company and remain there today.

Is TQM finished at FPL? Blanton Godfrey, the chairman of the Juran Institute, discovered that for some who stayed on at FPL, "quality improvement has become a way of life." He fell into conversation with a team from an FPL fossil-fuel plant that had performed a fairly sophisticated quality analysis which had resulted in a reduction in downtime at the plant caused by pump failures. As a prize the team members (with their spouses) won a two-week trip to Japan—which, of course, they spent talking about their work at the International Council of Quality Control Circles. When Godfrey expressed his surprise that the team had gone to Japan in view of reports of a fall in interest in total quality at FPL, the team leader replied: "No one here could kill quality improvement. Now that we know how to solve problems that have been bothering us for years, why would we stop just because some manager doesn't support it?"[30]

CATERPILLAR

Caterpillar tells us a brief, cautionary tale about what happens when you try to marry quality improvement with awful labor relations and cannot make up your mind whether machines or men matter the most. Like Boeing or, in other times, GM and IBM, Caterpillar Incorporated has been a world leader for decades. It made money for 50 consecutive years, profited its investors handsomely, and dominated its markets. Unlike the auto companies, it never got into trouble because of its lack of quality. Caterpillar makes fine, durable earth-moving, mining, and construction equipment. As *Fortune* put it, "Cat could push, crush, or roll over just about anything that got in its way" like one of its huge yellow D10 tractors, "standing 15 feet tall and weighing in at 73 tons." The company felt that its "competitors were too weak to be taken seriously. Customers were willing to pay fat premiums for Caterpillar quality and service."[31]

Caterpillar still makes about half of the world's heavy equipment. And it is still very good. But as we have seen, what used to be good is no longer good enough. The recession in the early 1980s, combined with the rise of a strong Japanese rival, Komatsu Ltd., gave Caterpillar a new view of the world. The company saw that both its productivity and its quality had to improve. Unfortunately Cat did not focus its efforts to improve them under a single overarching theme or organization. It did not see the two as part of the same thing. Productivity came under the company's six-year, $2-billion Plant With a Future program for renovation of its plants. PWAF, pronounced "pee-waf," was completed in 1993. But quality came under the Employee Satisfaction Process, or ESP, started in 1986, which drew Caterpillar's unionized blue-collar work force into the planning and execution of process improvement.

Under PWAF, Caterpillar made the change from classic mass production, with its big inventories, long product runs, and slow retooling, to fast, flexible, lean manufacturing. At Caterpillar's KK plant in East Peoria, which makes 120 kinds of transmissions, long rows of old machines were replaced by flexible cellular systems. On the old line, the transmission casings for each model would pass in batches through a whole series of tools, each with an operator, and each requiring anywhere from four hours to two days to retool for the next model. The aisles would get cluttered with batches of casings awaiting their turn. The new work cells are programmed to handle any of the 120 models of transmission casings coming down the line. They can pick out the tools they need and go to work within seconds under the supervision of one worker for two clusters of machines. The time it took to build a transmission has dropped from three months to 15 days.[32]

Winning the Workers, or Trying To

To get the Employee Satisfaction Process going, Caterpillar and the UAW had to overcome years of hostility and prejudice. Between 1955 and 1982, Caterpillar suffered eight strikes, the eighth lasting 205 days. However in the mid-1980s, as the idea of employee involvement gathered strength, Caterpillar decided, like the auto companies, that it was time for new attitudes. Gradually the company won over its work force, at first extremely suspicious. Workers helped plan the layout of the modernized plants, became instructors and facilitators, and shed much of their hostility to management. Caterpillar held up its factory in Aurora, Illinois, as a model of quality and planned to nominate it for the Baldrige Award.[33]

ESP and PWAF overlapped, of course. The employee teams helped boost productivity and cut costs in the new plants. However, Caterpillar saw the two programs as different animals. Caterpillar executives were more comfortable with the "hard" idea of modernizing machinery (PWAF) than with the "soft" idea of using people to improve quality and productivity (much as GM the people were) through ESP. PWAF got the visibility. The champion of PWAF, Pierre Guerindon, a brilliant Frenchman who had become an advocate of flexible manufacturing while working for Caterpillar in Europe, became an executive vice president.

Donald Fites, a tall, rangy engineer with years of overseas experience with Caterpillar, became CEO in 1990 with new priorities. First he carried out a reorganization, dividing the company into business units and pushing his engineers, marketing people, and even accountants out of headquarters and into the factories where they would work more closely with the manufacturing people. Second, he wanted to change the ground rules of the company's relationship with its extremely well-paid workers. In particular he wanted to end pattern bargaining, which the UAW uses to get the same concessions from one company as it has negotiated with another. With sales off all over the world in 1991 and a loss of $404 million for the year staring him in the face, Fites, a determined man with a prominent jaw, became more stubborn than usual. The UAW, down from 40,500 members at Caterpillar in 1979 to 17,000 in 1990, felt equally stubborn.

When it came to a strike, Fites proved to be the tougher. After the workers had been out for five months through the winter of 1991–92, Fites announced that he was ready to hire permanent replacements. The economy was down, and even at the $7-an-hour second-tier wage offered by Caterpillar (compared with the $17.56-an-hour first-tier wage) the applications poured in. The UAW capitulated and the workers returned on the basis of Cat's final offer.

Losing the Workers, For Now

It looked like a victory for Caterpillar management, but if we consider the long-term effects, both sides look like losers. Employee involvement, or ESP, died during the strike. The UAW immediately ceased participating in ESP; and workers who had been coaxed gradually to accept the idea of cooperating with management went back to the old mind-set that "you cannot trust them." James B. O'Connor, ex-president of UAW Local 974, says, "We feel a sense of betrayal. Initially we were supicious of ESP, to say the least. But over six years people really embraced it. They were bringing their best ideas to the company. Caterpillar threw all that away. . . . We check our brains at the plant gate. We don't take initiatives, just do what the foreman says. People want to do a good job, but they don't feel good about going to work." [34] After the workers went back, the UAW organized a campaign to embarrass and harass Caterpillar. Pickets appeared at trade shows and at hotels where Caterpillar visitors stayed. Workers showed up wearing buttons saying, "Employees Stop Participating" (see Chapter 3). Inside the plants, the UAW instructed workers to do just what they were told—nothing more, nothing less.

At first, the company maintained that ESP was still alive and functioning, but soon the company too acknowledged it was dead. Just how much it cost Caterpillar to break the strike became apparent when the manager of Building Center H, one of the model plants at Aurora, Charles Elwyn, sent a hand-written memo to all his employees. After congratulating them on a good safety performance, he turned to the matter of quality:

Defects per tractor are going the wrong way. Before the lock-out last November, we had reduced defects per unit down to about (3). In April this year, we averaged about (5) defects per tractor. In the last several months, the average has risen to about (7) defects per tractor. . . . As our defects go up in "H," defects found by our dealers at pre-delivery and by our customers during the early hours of operation also go up. And, as defects go up, customer satisfaction goes down. . . . We had our worst month ever in terms of production. We missed our build targets by a total of (71) tractors. That's the poorest performance in this plant's history. . . . A personal word of caution to anyone who might be glad we've just had the worst months ever: if the in-plant strategy is responsible for hurting our production, perhaps if we can cause hurt bad enough and long enough, we'll be successful at putting this company out of business. If you're at all proud of that, you deserve to be without a job. . . . We're hurting our business. Our percentage of the available sales has declined in some markets. The best managers in the world can't get the job done without your help.[35]

Elwyn's letter was written in the spirit of the pre-strike days, when management and labor could talk frankly to each other. In the new confrontational mood, of course, the UAW grabbed the letter and passed it on to the media as proof of. . . . proof of what? That Caterpillar was losing the battle? That quality was slipping? That productivity was off? Obviously, no one was winning. In the poison that fills the relationship between the two sides, it is hard to see employee participation resuming. And without the workers' contribution, it is hard to see quality at Caterpillar improving.

The quality efforts at Caterpillar, FPL, IBM, and Nashua cannot be called failures. These four companies, and others that have struggled with quality, are certainly better off for the attempt. They just have not come close to realizing the full promise of what they set out to do.

CONCLUSIONS

Many mistakes in applying quality can be overcome or corrected. A poor start in training or in team efforts can be set aside and replaced with fresh efforts incorporating the lessons learned. But some mistakes or problems will cripple or doom any attempt at converting a company to TQM.

- As has been made clear before, a true commitment by the top leaders is the essential ingredient. The commitment must be durable, single-minded, and solidly based on actions as well as words. The leader cannot, like Akers, change priorities from year to year. He cannot, like Clough, ask for quality but leave quality out of the essential indicators of performance.
- The leader needs the support of everyone in the company, from the board to the blue collar worker. If he does not educate the board about the contribution of total quality to a company's success he may find himself, like Hudiburg, succeeded by a CEO who wants to turn policy on a new course. If he alienates the blue-collar workers, as did Fites, he will pay an enormous price for whatever gains he hopes to achieve by taking on labor head to head.
- In a company demoralized by layoffs and early retirement, like IBM, or rent by the hostility arising out of a bitter strike, the chances of sustaining a quality effort are slim.
- Once the commitment is made to quality, leaders must not be shaken from the course by business crises. Leaders should use total quality to solve the crisis, not the crisis as an excuse to suspend quality.
- For all that has been said, management can still overdo it. Too much zeal, too much bureaucracy, too many charts and indicators, too many buzzwords, are likely to have a backlash.
- Islands of quality can flourish in a company that is floundering, and they may serve as a good example for the rest of the company, but they may also survive only as long as the division or plant manager responsible remains in the job.

9

The Railroaders
All Aboard for Quality

No industry stands more in need of total quality, nor would seem more likely to resist it, than the railroads. The railroads pioneered in the 19th century and they lived their glory days before World War II. The meeting of the Central Pacific and the Union Pacific at Promontory, Utah—a feat comparable to, say, the first transcontinental jet flight—occurred in 1869. Hollywood stars raced from coast to coast by train in as little as 56 hours and 55 minutes—but that was in 1934. The rails carried 70% of the nation's freight—but that was at the end of World War II.

By the 1980s, all that was past history. With the help of the interstate highway system, long-haul trucks offered fast, reliable service. The rails offered neither. The tracks were in such disrepair that derailments became a serious drag on profits and a serious worry to customers who transported hazardous chemicals by rail. Nearly one locomotive in five was unavailable at any given time because it had broken down or was already in the shop being overhauled. Freight cars were so decrepit that even the coal companies rejected a proportion of them when they were sent to fetch a load. The Interstate Commerce Commission wrapped the railroads tight in regulations and complex set rates. As many as 16 mostly bloody-minded unions acted as if they wanted to strangle the companies even though, paradoxically, railroadmen love their work and are proud of their railroads.

Long after brakemen and firemen became superfluous on modern long-haul freights, labor contracts obliged the railroads to carry crews of four, five, and even six when two would do, and to pay them a day's work for every 100 miles covered, a rate based on how far a train could travel in eight hours—in the 19th century. The term "feather-bedding" fitted the railroads well. Once diesels had replaced the steam engines, which had to be stoked, the fireman could spend his working day lying on a feather bed. Worst of all was the railroad management itself, a collection of militaristic, hierarchical, turf-conscious petty disciplinarians who thought they had learned all there was to learn about railroading decades ago. They ran the railroads to suit themselves and measured their performance by their own standards, not the customers'.

The railroad equipment was terrible, but what came out of the offices was even worse. When Conrail looked at a batch of bills it had sent out recently, it found that 14% contained errors. And when Southern Pacific asked its freight customers if they were satisfied with the accuracy of their bills, less than half said they were.[1]

Even though the railroads appeared determined to commit suicide, they did retain certain advantages over trucks—and even gained some new ones. Freight trains are inherently more economical than trucks. A single train can move 280 trailers double-stacked with two or three locomotives and a crew of two, unions permitting. The same load shipped by road requires 280 drivers and 280 cabs. A truck might get six miles to a gallon of diesel fuel, but a train can move that same truckload 60 miles on just one gallon. Trucks travel on congested highways; trains on underused tracks. Environmentalists love trains.

Railroads may not seem to demand much technology, but in fact railway technology has taken large strides. The engineer no longer needs to lean out of his cab when he hits a curve to look back along his train for smoke or sparks coming from a wheel. Automatic sensors along the tracks can spot a hotbox and relay an alarm to a central control room, which radios the engineer to stop. Much like automobiles, but with no fanfare, the locomotives produced by General Electric and General Motors improved vastly in performance and reliability in the 1980s. Locomotives need an oil change and new filters, just like cars, but instead of coming in every 20 days for servicing, as they once did, they can now run for as long as six months before they need attention. Locomotives introduced in the 1980s work harder, covering 20,000 miles a month instead of 8,000 or 9,000 like the ones they replace. With 4,000 horsepower they are nearly twice as powerful as the older locomotives.[2] They haul bigger, lighter cars. The new locomotives have computerized sensors which diagnose and record their performance in "real time," as technical sophisticates say, just as they do with jet aircraft.

Congress handed the railroads their opportunity in 1980 by passing the Staggers Rail Act, freeing them from most regulation. But the railroads continued to decline while the truck companies took more and more of their business. Between 1970 and 1989 railroad freight revenues stagnated at a steady $25 billion a year approximately, then moving up to about $28 billion in the early 1990s. Truck revenues, to the extent they can be known, roared by, starting at about $50 billion in 1970 and reaching $175 billion in 1989. Surveys of customers consistently rated the railroads inferior to trucks in convenience and service.[3]

The railroads finally heard the alarm ringing in the mid-1980s. By then some were close to bankrupt and it was almost too late for them. But once awake they moved remarkably fast to improve their services and reassert their competitiveness. By the early 1990s, a Wall Street analyst could say that the "railroad renaissance" had begun.[4] The seven largest American railroads, Burlington Northern, Conrail, CSX, Norfolk Southern, Santa Fe, Southern Pacific, and Union Pacific, are transforming themselves, as the behaviorists say, and the basis for that transformation, unlikely as it sounds in the context of railroads, is total quality.

UNION PACIFIC

While the Staggers Rail Act made the railroad renaissance possible, its beginning could be tied to the arrival of an outsider, Mike Walsh, to take over the Union Pacific in 1986. He did not carry any of the baggage of an old railroad man. In fact, his background could hardly have been more foreign to the railroads. A running back at Stanford and one of the first White House Fellows, Walsh chose to become a public defender in San Diego when he graduated from Yale Law School. In California he also served as a U.S. attorney and helped to found the government watchdog organization Common Cause. When finally at the age of 37 he decided to experience corporate life he joined Cummins Engine in Indiana. That was in 1980. There he moved like a shooting star. Six years later, Drew Lewis, CEO of the Union Pacific Corporation, asked him to run the railroad. Walsh is open and direct; he has a sense of humor and plays popular music in his office. As if all this were not enough of a shock to the old hands at UP, Walsh informed them that henceforth their No. 1 objective would be to serve the customer—a novel idea to most of them.[5]

With the help of Armand Feigenbaum, the one-time general manager of quality at GE and now the president of General Systems Corporation, a consulting company, Walsh led his company through what is becoming a fairly classic quality process.

First came the analysis: UP's cost of poor quality added up to 26% of total revenue in 1987; customers were especially unhappy about errors in their bills; derailments were costing $84 million a year. Then came the planning phase, which set ambitious goals in every area of the railroad's activities from dealing with customers on the telephone to fixing or replacing locomotives to making trains arrive on time. In a third phase, beginning in 1990, UP started involving workers in quality-improvement teams.

In five years, UP rose from being one of the worst U.S. railroads to being one of the best. Dick Davidson, who succeeded Walsh as chief executive when Walsh moved on to run Tenneco, finds three achievements especially important. First, by 1992, 93% of the railway's locomotives were normally available, compared with 86% in 1987. Each percentage point of improvement freed up 25 $1.5-million locomotives. Second, UP cut the costs of derailments from $84 million in 1987 to $42 million in 1992. Third, personal injuries dropped 25%.

Other improvements were just as striking. UP started putting computers in the cabs of its yard locomotives and connected them with a customer-service center in St. Louis so that conductors can respond to last-minute requests or correct errors quickly. To improve productivity, the company began buying out employees or putting them on reserve at reduced pay, and it negotiated agreements cutting the size of train crews down to two. Productivity climbed from 8.3 ton-miles per employee in 1986 to 13.9 in 1992. The cost of poor quality dropped by half, from $1 billion to $500 million a year, and net income nearly doubled, from $385 million in 1986 to $662 in 1992.[6]

CONRAIL

Much the same story could be told of Conrail after James Hagen returned from CSX to become chairman in 1989 (see Chapter 2). Consolidated Rail Corporation was formed on April Fool's Day 1976 out of six bankrupt Eastern railroads, and for the first five years of its life the government owned it. The government unloaded this unpromising enterprise onto public ownership in 1981. It took years more for Conrail to shake off the classic railroad maladies of rigid hierarchies, departments working for internal goals in isolation from one another, and poor service for the customer. "You couldn't find a better example of what not to be," says John T. Bielan, Conrail's vice president for continuous quality improvement.[7] As mentioned in Chapter 2, Hagen began with an unusual ploy, waiting for his executives to ask him to initiate a quality effort rather than telling them he was going to do it. They knew that he had become a believer at CSX, but he feared that in a militaristic organization if the boss said, "We are going to do quality," the rest of the organization would merely go through the motions.

To shake off the old culture, Hagen also changed the format of the Monday-morning meetings of the Operating Committee. He found these meetings were "useless" because when he was there with the other top people in the company, "I could have said the sun's going to come up in the West tomorrow and I don't think anybody would have disagreed. I never heard anybody disagree really with anyone else." So he withdrew from the meetings, taking the most senior officers with him, and told the remaining executives to go to work on key questions like defining service, providing service, and controlling costs. They were to report the results at lunch on Mondays. "They get in there and they argue and they really work at it, and it's a good open process," says Hagen.

To give Conrail's managers the information they needed to really understand the organization, he decided to share vital data such as profit-and-loss estimates with about 70 people, instead of keeping it closely guarded among the top three officers. The Conrail lawyers had fits about the potential for leaks that might result in insider trading, but Hagen just made all 70 insiders.[8] Conrail began to understand teamwork and trust.

Hagen and a strategic management team created just before his arrival drew up a five-year plan with a measured approach to quality. They sent delegations to look at Xerox, Motorola, and other exemplary companies. Conrail acquired a vice president for quality improvement, a quality council, and departmental quality councils which started sponsoring standing quality-improvement teams and temporary process-improvement teams. In 1991, Conrail started its own courses, beginning with a two-day awareness course on the fundamentals of TQM. The course is voluntary, and the company suggests that employees do not train until they know they will use what they learn, but within a year 12,000 employees, nearly half the total, had been through the course. Other courses on specific quality skills and teamwork were added. A survey of employees in 1992 revealed that they thought management did not communicate well with them—a basic requirement of total quality—so management staged a blitz of 100 "town hall" meetings among officers and employees at 50 locations, patterned after a similar device Walsh had used at Union Pacific. The meetings were both testy and productive. It was the first time many of the workers had ever laid eyes on a company officer.[9]

Seamless Service by Truck and Train

Improvements came rapidly. Take the matter of "trains held for power" (which means the locomotive has broken down). Conrail used to have some macho idea that unless a large number of HFPs showed up every day the locomotives were not being worked hard enough, as if they were football players and had to be muddied and bloodied to show they had really played. The fact that an HFP also meant customers were not getting their freight on time did not matter then. But now it does. After analyzing the causes of breakdowns, Conrail reduced the number of daily HFPs from as many as 25 or 30 on some days in 1991 to seven on one fine day in October 1992.

False alarms from the automatic hotbox detectors spaced out every 20 miles along the lines were a nuisance. Whether the alarm was true or false, the train had to stop and wait while the conductor walked the length of the train checking for a hotbox. In the past, Conrail would simply have fixed the detector giving the false reading. But now, with quality tools such as Pareto charts, a team traced the false alarms to a particular type of detector—and all the detectors of that type were replaced. Conrail negotiated with the unions to cut its crews from three or four per train to two. And the trains started reaching their destinations when the schedules said they should.[10]

The brightest element in Conrail's outlook, says David LeVan, senior vice president for operations, is growing cooperation with the very truckers who caused the railroads so much grief. The economics favor the railroads on long hauls; meanwhile the truck companies face a real problem: today's truck drivers are no longer willing to stay away from home for days or even weeks at a time. The turnover among drivers for the long-distance truck companies exceeds 100% a year. So the truckers and the railroads are becoming allies. Truck companies pick up the freight from the customer at one end and deliver it to a railroad yard: the freight then moves by train; trucks from the same company pick it up at the other end and deliver it to its destination. The drivers can get to sleep in their own beds every night and, with double stacking, the savings to the customer can be spectacular. The customer gets on-time delivery at a better price. Since he deals only with the truck company, he experiences what Hagen calls "seamless service."

At first Conrail did not want to join the "intermodal" movement, partly because tunnels through the hills of Pennsylvania, Conrail's home state, needed a lot of work to accommodate double-stacked cars. In 1992 Conrail began hauling containers for J. B. Hunt, the Arkansas trucking company, between New York and Chicago. Agreements with other trucking companies followed. Conrail also began raising the clearance of bridges and tunnels in Pennsylvania in an $80-million effort shared with the state. Anthony Hatch, a PaineWebber analyst, predicts that Conrail will "spearhead the coming railroad renaissance"[11]—which, as we have seen here, is already under way.

SOUTHERN PACIFIC

Last among the seven major railroads in the eyes of its customers and in its financial performance, the Southern Pacific railroad had more reasons than most to miss the renaissance. From 1983 to 1987, the SP lived in limbo, waiting for the Interstate Commerce Commission make up its mind about its bungled application to merge with the Santa Fe. By the time the ICC delivered a final "No" in 1987, the trust that controlled the line had let maintenance and capital spending slip for five years. Then SP went through a merger and a management reorganization. Philip Anschutz, a billionaire entrepreneur in Denver, had bought the Denver Rio Grande Western railroad in 1984. Now he added the much larger SP to his holdings with a leveraged buyout in 1988 and became the only living railroad tycoon in the United States. The managements of the two proud old railroads did not merge happily, and they were further riled when Anschutz began hiring outsiders, including a contingent of executives from American President Companies who were promptly named "the boat people." Others came in from CSX, Eastern Air Lines, and UP.

Philip Anschutz is an extremely successful oil, gas, and land operator, a considerate, helpful boss, an art collector of some distinction, a devoted family man, modest about his wealth and achievements to the point of almost disappearing in Denver; but he had never before managed a large organization, and it showed. The Rio Grande people thought they had taken over and the SP people thought *they* had taken over; the operating stiffs kept getting contradictory orders; the "boat people" thought *they* were going to save the company. The confusion made a bad railroad worse. SP's own surveys of customers show it consistently running last among its competitors in the West, especially when compared to trucks. Whether the question touched its inability to resolve clients' problems, the speed and punctuality of its trains, service on its telephones, the condition of its equipment, the accuracy or timeliness of its bills, SP usually ran last compared to the Santa Fe, the Burlington Northern, UP, and trucks.[12] Its locomotives, many of them long overdue for overhauls because maintenance had slipped during the years in limbo, functioned for a mean time of 44 days between failures, compared to 79 days for the best companies.[13] The railroad lost money too, $66 million in 1989, $35 million in 1990, and $78 million in 1991. Only by selling off chunks of the vast real-estate holdings that history had bequeathed to the railroad was Anschutz able to satisfy the banks. And, as indicated in the Introduction to this book, SP's safety record gave its customers nightmares—especially the shippers of hazardous chemicals.

Houston Shows How to Run a Railroad

Southern Pacific's recovery began in a manner that the Juran Institute particularly recommends: with a pilot or demonstration project that can take a piece of a company widely known for its poor quality and improve it rapidly and conspicuously for the rest of the company to see and use as a model. SP did not deliberately create a pilot project, but it was handed one by the Houston Switching District, a major hub for SP serving the chemical industry. Houston handles trains on the main route from Chicago south and then on west through Texas, New Mexico, and Arizona to Los Angeles. The operation was notorious for sending cars in the wrong direction, losing cars, missing pick-ups at the chemical plants, and minor accidents in the yards. The problems were chronic and historic.

The district's superintendent, Douglas Wills, and SP's vice president for marketing chemicals, Edward Kammerer, decided soon after Anschutz acquired the line to try to bring sanity to their district. Their approach was simple. They asked the conductors and switchmen—people used to having arbitrary orders barked at them by yardmasters—to form teams and work out switching plans that they could live with. They did and the plans worked. The unions were happy because the district had to hire extra crews. The company was happy because the plan saved overtime. Customers were happy because they could depend on SP's deliveries and pick-ups. The workers were happy because calm and order replaced yelling and chaos, and they knew in advance whether they would get home for dinner. As an unexpected bonus, which often comes with quality efforts, the rate of "incidents" (minor derailments and accidents) in the yards dropped from three or four a week to almost none. With less pressure, people made fewer mistakes.[14]

Anschutz had read about successful quality efforts in the business magazines and had listened to his customers urging him to adopt total quality at SP. But when he heard a presentation by the Houston team members about what they had done on their own, he became convinced that *this* was the right way to run a railroad. Still, he hesitated because of the fear that a quality effort would be costly. His senior management group argued against it, saying that SP needed lower costs and more customers, not another fancy program. He delayed for about six months, in spite of the urgency of doing something to save the railroad; but he finally became convinced, as he says, "that those companies that need the quality process the most are those that can least afford it."[15] (Orthodox doctrine says, of course, that quality is free. That is, the savings from improved performance quickly cancel the expenses of training and other preparations to start the process. But for a company close to bankruptcy, even those expenses may seem an extravagance.) The rival Union Pacific was already achieving major improvements and savings through its quality drive.

Fast Start, Fast Track

Once he decided to move, Anschutz launched in 1990 one of the most daring, some might say foolhardy, quality campaigns in America. SP set out simply to do everything at the same time, right away. Anschutz kicked off "a fast-track quality program" which he admits his friends told him "was fraught with risk and could end in a bit of a disaster."[16] On top of the usual difficulties of turning a whole corporation to the TQM way, SP had to overcome its managerial confusion, stubborn resistance from some of the top operating executives, the decrepitude of its equipment, and opposition from its 14 contentious unions. During the first three months of the blitz at the end of 1990, Anschutz and his staff took the company's top executives to visit such companies as Milliken and Xerox, drafted the SP's first mission statement, as well as one-year objectives and five-year strategies, outlined the framework of an improvement process, and hired an executive vice president for quality, W. Kent Sterett, and a quality staff of 14.

Like SP, Sterett was on something of a fast track himself after working 18 years at Florida Power & Light. He directed the quality improvement department at FPL during its sometimes frantic efforts to win the Deming Prize and left when the new chairman dismantled the quality staff (see Chapter 8). He zipped through Union Pacific and then Anschutz recruited him. Now in his mid-40s, Sterett has a missionary zeal about quality, and with his big voice and 6'4" frame he can project that zeal some distance.

The second three-month phase of SP's push began in January 1991 with the annual management meeting in San Francisco, which was dominated by the unveiling of the quality plan. SP wrote more plans for training, for working with labor and with suppliers, for managing the quality process, and for keeping employees informed. The company registered the first 165 quality teams, started monthly reviews of its progress, and set up the measuring system for judging that progress. The measurement consists of 114 "key performance indicators" on the road to 1993, by which time Southern Pacific Lines intended to be no less than a world-class railroad.

In the first three months of 1991, the SP management fanned out all over the system to participate in "town hall" meetings with the troops, explaining the quality plan and listening to their gripes and comments. But Anschutz added a leveling touch that was absent in the UP and Conrail town halls. After the morning meetings, he expected the executives to put on blue jeans and spend the afternoon working on the railroad. They could not drive a locomotive, because that requires certification, but they could do a lot of other jobs. One executive spent a frustrating afternoon trying to acquire a "frog" (a device placed at the intersection of two tracks) and could not do it because the required forms were missing, he could not find the people who would know where they were, and so forth. The chairman himself spent at least one afternoon driving spikes. Anschutz, who is in his mid-fifties, is a sturdy, adventurous fellow who takes his children on bicycle camping trips and ran with the bulls in Pamplona in 1992, but driving spikes requires a whole higher order of muscles. He needed help to get his jacket off when he returned to the office. The workers on the railroad may have regarded the behavior of their bosses with some bemusement, but the managers certainly learned a lot from the experience. "We saw that nothing worked," says one participant. (Since then, at the request of the workers, SP has modified its approach. Instead of picking up a sledge hammer, the executive now spends the time listening to what the blue collar people have to say.)

During the second quarter of 1991, the planning continued and SP launched surveys of employees and customers. Team leaders were trained, and so were instructors to train more team leaders. By now SP had 311 of its own quality-improvement teams and began forming teams with suppliers. That fall Anschutz felt confident enough to tell the 1991 Juran Impro conference in Atlanta that total quality was working at SP and "working well." SP's director of quality and reliability engineering, Robert J. Scanlon, told the same conference that quality at a high speed kept everyone focused, just as a driver keeps his eyes on the road when he is speeding. "Speed is exciting," he said, and "we're having fun!" Of course, it is also easier to crack up when you are speeding.[17]

The Meetingest Bunch: Labor Relations

For another view of the process, listen to labor. Southern Pacific set up a top-level labor–management advisory committee of the general chairmen of the 14 unions and the senior people in management. They meet quarterly, intermixed around a table, to speak frankly and thrash out their problems; or perhaps it is for labor to lay out its problems and thrash management. The meeting I attended in Denver in July, 1992 (see Chapter 3), was not positive. To put labor's harsh words in perspective you have to consider that the meeting occurred a few days after a one-day strike or shut-out, depending on which side you view it from, and you have to remember that these union leaders are fast losing their members. Like other railroads, SP has made huge cuts in its work force. It employs 19,000 people, down from 30,000 in 1985.

Labor's chief complaint was that SP does not really back up its rhetoric. Carl James, general chairman of the Brotherhood of Locomotive Engineers in Denver, said, "We took training, charged out full of piss and vinegar, and then nothing happened. This is the meetingest bunch of people I ever met. We have very successful meetings and then nothing happens. . . . You came to us, we opened our arms, and then nothing happened." Other union officials talked of quality teams disbanding because they had nothing to do, or nothing came of what they did do. The big question labor asked was whether management itself had bought the plan.

That was a good question. As Anschutz admits, his worst mistake was not to focus earlier on converting middle management, which he finally did in 1992. Up until then when the workers returned, "qualitized," from training, they bumped into managers who had *not* been "qualitized." Even after Anschutz focused on management some of the senior people remained less than enthusiastic. William Holtman, the crusty old head of the Rio Grande & Denver who became vice chairman and operations chief of the combined railroads, supported quality officially—but unofficially, other executives talked of knocking him over the head to get him aboard. He retired at 70 at the end of 1992 and was replaced as head of operations by the 47-year-old Glenn Michael, recruited from CSX. Another long-time executive, Mike Mohan, a sympathetic but passive supporter of the quality efforts, resigned in September 1993. He was not replaced. To be CEO, Anschutz brought in Edward L. Moyers, a cost-cutting efficiency expert who had turned the Illinois Central railroad around. He quickly lopped 3,000 more people off SP's payroll, reducing the total to 19,000. His appointment could have signaled a turn toward cost-cutting rather than TQM to help the railroad.

Some of the union people are positive, speak of a growing sense of trust, find that some of the teams are productive, and think that the railroad is attacking real problems. Considering the history of labor–railway relations, it is noteworthy that labor even attends these meetings and returns for more. Even the International Association of Machinists shows up, although as a policy the union opposes participative management (see Chapter 3). Under new leadership, the IAM units that deal with Southern Pacific have split with the international and started to cooperate. IAM officials are even teaching quality courses.

At the contentious meetings between management and labor, management adopts a calm, conciliatory attitude. Mary Powell, the SP's "facilitator'' for the meetings and the only woman in attendance much of the time, remains courteous and unruffled. Having been a caseworker in Harlem and a labor negotiator for the city of New York she does not find the atmosphere in Denver (or in San Francisco, where the council also meets), particularly raucous.

Southern Pacific certainly has something to show for its all-out assault on poor quality. All those decrepit, failure-prone locomotives are being overhauled or replaced at a faster pace at a single facility, the Burnham Shops in Denver. SP shut down its huge, uneconomic old shop in Sacramento and moved all the major overhauls to the old Denver Rio Grande Burnham Shop after spending $15 million to turn it into a compact just-in-time facility. The Sacramento facility had a mile-long line and covered 600,000 square feet, while Burnham is only 600 feet long and covers only 148,000 square feet. Sacramento took 30 to 45 days to overhaul a locomotive; Denver takes five to seven days. Denver gets JIT deliveries twice a day from its major supplier, GM's EMD locomotive division. Working three shifts seven days a week, Burnham can overhaul 300 locomotives a year; at that rate SP will actually catch up with its overdue repair work some time in 1995.[18]

Old-timers on the railroad used to say, "If I didn't have to answer the phone, I could get my work done." A client calling in to find out what happened to a missing freight car might likely connect with a clerk at the local depot who had no idea where the damned car was and no way of tracing it through the system. Now railroaders are taught that answering the phone *is* their work. Instead of talking to an isolated clerk, customers can call SP's customer-service center in Denver, where clerks and professionals (for the more complicated calls) can call up on a computer screen the current status of any car in the system and tell the customer how it is doing. SP computers monitor how quickly the customer-service representatives answer the phone and how many calls are abandoned because the caller hangs up before getting an answer. The goal is to answer calls within 10 seconds and to keep abandoned calls down to 2% or less. If the abandoned calls get up to 5% you are likely to have some unhappy customers on your hands, says Dennis Jacobson, a recruit from Union Pacific who is managing director for SP's customer service. At 11 A.M. one day in 1992 when I visited the center, the computer showed one abandoned call so far that day, and an average answering time of one second (the operators wear headsets so they do not have to pick up a receiver). Like many telephone-based operations today, the SP customer-service center listens to its operators from time to time to see how they greet the callers, whether they use their names, and whether they ask the customer if they need anything else before before hanging up.[19]

How is SP doing? Those 114 Key Performance Indicators (KPIs) that Sterett established are the critical gauge for the railroad. The results are very mixed. Here are some examples:

KPI	1991 Actual	1992 Goal	Benchmark
Reliability of scheduled service	70.7%	90%	94%
Customer satisfaction on the accuracy of bills	46.8%	55%	none
Mean time between locomotive failures	48 days	52.5 days	79 days[20]

The benchmark numbers represented the best in the industry, a goal to be achieved and then, SP hoped, surpassed. By the end of 1992, SP had reached its goal on reducing locomotive failures, but with big monthly variations. It had not achieved its goals for reliability of service and customer satisfaction with the bills, although in both respects it had improved. By several other indicators, particularly tonnage, carloadings, and revenue, SP did well in 1992. However, customers still compared SP unfavorably with the other railroads on the KPIs and by one critical measure, the cost of poor quality, SP was far behind the other railroads and U.S. industry as a whole. The cost of noncomformance, as SP calls it, amounted to an astronomical 45.5% of revenue in 1992.[21] (This was an estimate of the measurable costs of poor quality plus the unmeasurable costs such as sales foregone because trains are running late. The number has been coming down slowly. In the narrower sense of measurable losses directly related to poor quality, such as derailments, SP's cost dropped from 24% at the beginning of 1992 to about 21% of revenue at the end of the year.)

Too Much, Too Soon

What do you hear if you listen to the customers? That depends on which customer you talk to. Nabisco seems delighted with an intermodal agreement it has with a partnership between SP's trains and Schneider International's trucks. Schneider's orange trucks pick up products from five Nabisco plants, deliver them to an SP yard, pick them up at the other end of the run, and deliver them to the customer. Nabisco deals only with Schneider. William G. Ditoro, director of national inventory for Nabisco, calls it a seamless transportation system that works so well that Nabisco takes it for granted. "We have no transportation problems," he says. Shipments usually take a day longer by train, but cost $200 to $500 less per trailer or container than if they go by road.[22]

Other shippers have decidedly different views. Big users of the railroads keep careful records of the comparative performance of the competing lines and know who delivers on time regularly, who makes the most mistakes in billing, and who has the most accidents. Two large shippers, United Parcel Service, which is most concerned with on-time arrivals, and Olin Chemicals, which is most concerned with safety because it ships hazardous chemicals, rank SP at or near the bottom of the railroads and say they have not seen much improvement. A UPS transportation manager rates the nine major railroads it uses every month and SP is usually eighth or ninth. (Union Pacific and the Santa Fe are usually at the top.) SP's efforts to provide reliable service on the important I-5 corridor from Los Angeles north to San Francisco and on up to Portland have not made anyone at United Parcel smile yet.

Olin Chemicals is understandably edgy about the safety of using Southern Pacific. On July 14, 1991 SP dumped a car containing weed and tree killer belonging to Amvac Chemical Corporation into the Sacramento River, wiping out all the fish in the river and the vegetation in or beside it for nearly 50 miles, to Shasta Lake. Two weeks later SP spilled hydrazine (a corrosive and inflammable chemical) belonging to Olin in an underpass beneath Route 101 in Sea Cliff. The highway, California's main North–South route, was closed in both directions for five days. John Badger, Olin's director for transportation and distribution services, recognizes that SP is making an effort to improve quality, but as of the spring of 1993, he said, he had not seen the fruits of it. He said SP still has not cured all the troubles in the Houston switching district, which is a critical hub for chemical transport, and he is unimpressed with SP's efforts to reduce derailments. "We've removed a lot of business from the line," Badger says. The bills coming in from Union Pacific and Conrail are far more likely to be accurate than SP's bills.[23]

Clearly Southern Pacific tried to do too much too fast. It did not come close to being a world-class railroad within the time frame it set, or even one of the better railroads. Did it do the right things? Not altogether. One prominent consultant in the field who is familiar with SP describes its quality plan as "a paper tiger" that has no chance of succeeding. But did SP have a choice? Certainly; if it had more time, if had not been going through an organizational crisis, and if it had not carried such a dead weight of tradition, it might have sought quality in a more measured fashion, step by step.

However, Anschutz and his executives did not feel they had that time. They believed their railroad could not survive more than another couple of years. As of the end of 1992 SP was still losing money, but less than before; the operating losses for 1992 were reduced to $25 million. To shore up its finances, Southern Pacific went public in 1993 and also plans to continue selling off chunks of real estate to make up for operating losses. The prospectus for SP's stock offering said that "the company must improve substantially the reliability and ontime performance of its rail operations, which have generally lagged behind those of its competitors."[24] Total quality exists at SP more on paper than in practice. The real estate will not last forever, and the railroad will have to carry its own freight.

CONCLUSIONS

The railroads show us a case where a whole industry beset by very serious problems has chosen total quality to save it and is achieving mostly good results. What does that tell us?

- Old industries encrusted with bad practices and truculent unions can use total quality.
- Although the unions might appear to be the chief obstacle for the railroads, management is the hardest to deal with.
- Even for companies whose problems are as bad as the ones the railroads had, total quality yields big benefits quickly; at least it did at Union Pacific and Conrail.
- At Southern Pacific, which has several more layers of problems than the others, total quality is helping, although it is not clear yet if SP can provide first-class service.
- Given the situation the railroads faced in the 1980s, did they have any other choice if they wanted to become competitive?

10

The Services
When Scrap Walks Out the Door

To set aside a special chapter about quality in service companies may seem odd since they have already appeared in this book mingled with manufacturing companies. We have already met L. L. Bean, Florida Power & Light, and the railroads, among others. Even in the case of manufacturing companies, the service they provide—rather than the products they sell—is often the most troublesome to consumers. The principles and the methods of total quality are the same, whether you are dealing with a product or a service.

Yet circumstantial evidence indicates that service companies have more trouble getting their hands around total quality management than manufacturers do. The Baldrige Award judges may choose two winners among manufacturing companies and two among service companies every year. However, in the first five years of the award (1988–1992), 182 manufacturing companies applied and ten, the maximum possible, won the award, while 69 service companies applied and only three won. They were Federal Express (in 1990) and AT&T Universal Card Services and The Ritz-Carlton Hotel Company (both in 1992). Even in the category of small business, for companies with not more than 500 full-time employees, there were more applicants and winners, 148 and four respectively, than in the service category.[1]

Are there special reasons for the discrepancy, which is all the greater in that the United States today has primarily a service economy? Service companies may be biased against the methods of TQM because they do not have the history of measuring their activities, other than profits and losses, that manufacturing has. Possibly poor quality is harder to see and measure in a service company than in manufacturing. If the transmission in a new car breaks down you have an undeniable quality failure on your hands, but if the client walks out of a bank in disgust because a teller was rude or incompetent, this service failure may or may not be recorded. The Thing Gone

Wrong may be perceived by nobody but the unsatisfied customer. Or perhaps the service companies have been slow to realize the value of good quality because they did not face the same kind of mortal foreign competition that woke up the manufacturers at the end of the 1970s. Service companies are more likely to operate within a national or even local market which foreign companies cannot enter. Some of the blame for the discrepancy may lie within the Baldrige Award itself; perhaps its design made it easier for manufacturers than for service companies to win. Whatever the reasons, service companies were slower than manufacturers to catch on to the importance of continuous improvement. (The Baldrige organization has since made its criteria more friendly to service companies—after all, if the Baldrige organization did not improve continuously, who would?)

Some of our services are excellent, if not superb. Telephone service in the United States, always a world leader, today is better than ever, with satellite links, optical-fiber cables, digital communications—and, of course, direct dialing to almost anywhere in the world. The car you rent from one of the large agencies is almost without exception clean, new, well maintained, and delivered efficiently. But rotten service is easy enough to find too—in auto repairs, home repairs, some of the hotel chains, and increasingly in the airlines. Banks and insurance companies are little loved by their customers. Quality of service at one location is highly variable too. The bright, helpful teller and the surly, unskilled teller may work side by side.

The nature of service is changing, perhaps not as fundamentally as manufacturing, but significantly. Some years ago my wife kept a small account in a bank in London; every time she added a miniscule deposit to this account, she received a personal thank-you note from the bank manager, along with a comment on the weather or some other pleasantry. That kind of service, a mixture of servility and attention, is obviously gone for ever, except for the very, very rich depositors, and will not be missed much. But the kind of service I received at Citibank in New York years ago, when the branch manager knew my name and credit rating and could fix a loan for me over the telephone, definitely is missed. In many service industries, the old style fell victim to growth—in the volume of checks flowing through the banks, in the numbers of investors in mutual funds, in the number of air passengers, and so on. The old systems would have been swamped by the sheer volume, and in fact were for a while. The back rooms of the banks and brokerage houses nearly drowned in the 1960s, after piling massive computer power on top of swollen bureaucracies where responsibility for anything was lost in long chains of small sequential acts for customer services. A transfer of funds abroad, for example, would be handled in several different places, one for data entry, another for check encoding, and so forth. Errors could not be traced; responsibility could not be fixed.

In the 1970s the back rooms of major banks were brought under control. Citibank led the way by reorganizing and simplifying work so that one person or one unit handled all the steps in a transaction through a workstation. Errors could be cleared up quickly; responsibility was unambiguous. For a while, financial services might have led what became the total quality movement. But the banks did not stay in the lead. They failed to keep progressing; they failed to make the essential link with the customer. They continued to rely on marketing gimmicks, "free gifts," and advertising to draw in customers, as if they were peddling garment remnants or remaindered books at a close-out sale, rather than trying to provide solid quality to their longterm customers. Computers took over the grunt work of banking, which was perhaps just as well since the large banks seemed unable to hire anyone on the frontline who could tell a cashier's check from a get-well card, at least not at the low pay they were offering to tellers. Computers may not smile and say "thank you," but at least they save the customer from contact with a snappish teller.

The Value of Speedy Service

A good relationship and understanding of the customer is important for any business, and especially so for services. If you manufacture cars or shoes you build up an inventory, and if one customer turns down a car or a pair of shoes, the inventory will still be there the next day when another customer comes along. But if a plane takes off with an empty seat or if a hotel room stays unoccupied all night, they do not remain in inventory; it is lost forever. Customers who defect from a bank or a credit card company represent an appalling loss. "Service companies have their own kind of scrap heap: customers who will not come back," said a *Harvard Business Review* article in 1990.[2] The cost of a defection may be harder to see than the cost of discarded bad parts, but it is there. The article estimated that a service company can boost its profits 100% by retaining 5% more of its customers. For example, a credit card company may spend $51 to acquire a new customer. In the first year, the profit on that customer is a modest $30. But the profit increases year by year, reaching $55 in the fifth year. The authors of the article found in a study of 100 service companies in two dozen industries that sales per account continue to increase over the years, into the 19th year of a relationship in the case of one company. Profits grow because customers spend more with a given company the longer they deal with it, because they are willing to pay a premium for its good services and because they promote it by word of mouth. The loyal customer saves the company the expense of replacing him.

What the customer wants today is not the old servility with a smile. In fact, today's customer can sometimes do without the smile altogether if he can deal with an automatic teller that works faster and is more conveniently located than the human teller, with or without smile. For whatever reasons— perhaps it is the prevalence of working couples, or perhaps just the enormous choice of things to do and things to buy that offer themselves to an American today—more Americans always feel rushed today than in the past. The success of automatic tellers, one-hour film processing, fast mail-order houses, and express home-delivery services (beginning with Domino's Pizza), shows how much we value speed and convenience today.[3] For many kinds of services, for meeting the many routine needs of life—getting cash, renting a car, buying a ticket—speed and convenience are what count the most.

BANKING

If you consider that a decade ago customers of The First National Bank of Chicago would stand in line for as long as 45 minutes for the privilege of getting at their own money, then you can see how much opportunity banks had for improving service and building some customer loyalty. First Chicago, the oldest bank in the United States operating under its original charter, found out in the early 1980s that its customers "were indifferent to financial institutions, brand loyalty was low, images were fuzzy, and willingness to recommend a particular bank was almost nonexistent."[4] A later survey revealed the employees of First Chicago would steer friends to other banks and would not even use the bank themselves were it not for free checking and point-free mortgages for employees. (As a veteran and near-paranoid former customer of a large New York City bank, I empathize with the people in Chicago.)

Although customers hardly noticed at the time, some big city banks were among the first service companies to start moving towards total quality. Irving Trust Company hired William J. Latzko as its first quality-control officer in 1970. He applied standard statistical methods to a problem that particularly vexed management: the high proportion of checks rejected by the bank's automatic check processors. The rejected checks had to be cleared by hand. Latzko, now a consultant, learned that the machines were rejecting 7.5% of the checks (something management had not figured out), and he found out why: certain check manufacturers were not imprinting the magnetic characters properly on the checks, and some encoding machines were unreliable. Latzko cut the reject rate to 2%, which was a huge improvement since the banks had come to depend on automatic document processing to manage the vast increase in the flow of paper.[5]

In the late 1970s, Continental Illinois Bank took up quality and some of the other Chicago banks followed. The CEOs of several of the banks formed a roundtable where they discussed their quality efforts. Continental Illinois dropped out in 1984 when rumors of impending losses started a run on the bank by its foreign depositors. The federal government averted a greater disaster with a $4.5 billion bailout. In the process of downsizing by half, Continental Illinois threw out its quality efforts along with the quality staff. First Chicago, however, had realized that total quality management could make a whole lot of difference—it could get rid of that fuzzy image, reduce costs, possibly justify charging premium fees, and if that poor guy with a "bad back" who had been standing in line for 45 minutes could instead whisk through in one minute or two, then he would be more likely to remain a client, to recommend the bank, and to use the bank for other financial services. Like any industrial company, First Chicago carried a huge cost of poor quality. When the bank handles a corporate money transfer correctly, the transaction costs less than $10. But correcting a bungled transaction costs nearly $500 on average—and a lot of transactions got bungled.

It was the corporate and institutional side of First Chicago, not the retail arm, that first turned to quality. Banks had started to change dramatically in the early 1980s as they were deregulated. Forced to be more competitive, they learned that the people they should be concerned with were the clients, not the regulators in Washington. First Chicago went through its own upheaval in 1980 when the board revolted against a dictatorial CEO, Robert Abboud, and replaced him with Barry Sullivan, a more genial, collaborative banker from Chase Manhattan. The bank needed a thorough overhaul, as Sullivan discovered when the bank's planned conversion to a new computerized system for reconciling corporate accounts came on line six months late and even so was full of bugs. For a while First Chicago was quite unable to reconcile its corporate customers' accounts. It would be hard to imagine a more embarrassing failure for a bank. Sullivan hired Lawrence Russell—a brilliant free spirit, a most unbankerly fellow, a former McKinsey consultant—and asked him to make sure that this kind of thing could never happen again. Thus, almost accidentally, First Chicago launched itself on the road to quality.

"We stumbled into TQM long before anyone else in the service industries,'' says Aleta Holub, First Chicago's manager of quality assurance for corporate business. ''We saw the power of employee involvement based on teams, recognition, and measurement. We incorporated the thinking of Juran, Deming and Winter Park [i.e., Crosby] and we stole shamelessly. We tried to make a home brew out of what we learned and twelve years later we are still doing it. We are not world class at this point. But we are still very enthusiastic and striving for it.''[6]

Russell got the bank pointed in the right direction by insisting on the use of measures of the things the customers thought were important (not the things the bankers thought should be measured) and by getting employees involved in solving problems. The working stiffs at the bank had known all along how to solve the problems of reconciling corporate accounts, but could only watch as management made the wrong decisions. Russell, with Sullivan's backing, insisted that no one would take the reforms seriously unless they were tied into the reward system. Under Abboud, only making the budget had mattered at First Chicago. Now the senior management team's bonus depends partly on the quality and customer-satisfaction numbers, and that incentive has rippled all the way down through the bank to the check encoders. Their accuracy ties into their performance appraisals.

Waiting in the Lobby

The key to First Chicago's quality process is unusual. Every Thursday the bank's senior people get together for a performance meeting to hear how well the corporate side of the bank is meeting its quality goals. Every product line at the bank has from ten to 75 quality charts, depending on the complexity of the product and the number of sites where it is sold, and the total adds up to something more than 500 measures. Each measure has a minimum acceptable level and a goal, and these are revised upward from time to time. For example, when the measuring started in 1981, the bank set a goal of not more than one error per 6,000 lockbox transactions. (To speed collections for their customers, banks set up special postal boxes to receive remittances, and collect the money themselves, sometimes several times a day.) In 1982, the bank was not meeting the goal, but coming close some weeks. By 1989, the goal had been raised to not more than one error per 10,000 lockbox transactions, and by 1993 First Chicago consistently reached that goal. The numbers are broken down by type of error—Did the payment get credited to the wrong party?—and by location—how many errors did the office in Charlotte, North Carolina make? The lockbox operation is also gauged by other standards. How quickly are funds made available to the client? That should be done within one day. How quickly is the bank responding to phone inquiries from clients? Ninety percent should have their answer within an hour.

At the Thursday meetings, one unit after another reports its latest performance figures, over speakerphones or in the flesh. The meetings are low-keyed and numbers-oriented—but at one session in 1992 applause greeted the news that one unit had achieved the goal of issuing letters of credit within 24 hours (compared with the industry standard of three days). And when investment securities services reported that four of its 25 indicators were running below the minimum acceptable level, considerable explanation followed. Customers can attend these meetings, and so can suppliers, although they risk getting an earful about their products. The public and the press can attend too, if they make a reservation in advance. The bank hangs out its quality laundry in plain view.[7]

First Chicago's Community Banking Group, the name the bank gives the retail operation, did not join the quality movement until 1987. That was three years after Citicorp moved into the Chicago area by buying a failing savings-and-loan association with 44 branches. Now First Chicago realized that competition had come to banking. Because of the arcane banking laws of the state of Illinois, First Chicago could deliver retail banking services in only three locations in the city until 1984, when it was allowed to have five locations; these have since grown to 74. It was in the vast main lobby of the bank headquarters, almost the size of a football field, that customers were waiting in line up to 45 minutes, using the time to fill their minds with negative thoughts about the bank.

The retail side of the bank understandably moved first to get rid of those lines; they had to disappear, whatever it took. Technology helped a lot. New IBM terminals told the tellers all they needed to know about the customers facing them, including verification of their signature. New automatic cash machines produced the exact amount of money keyed into them, saving about 30 seconds over the time it takes a teller to select the right bills and count them twice. An infrared sensor judged the current waiting time and displayed the wait where both the tellers' supervisors and the customers could see it.

The attitude of the bank's employees had to be overhauled too. It was in 1987, the year when quality started on the retail side, that a survey of employees revealed that a "frightening number" of them would not bank at First Chicago if they were not employees. (The bank will not say exactly how many.) In 1988, when First Chicago successfully advertised a new equity credit line in the regional editions of *Business Week* and *Fortune*, fully half the callers to the special number in the ad got only a busy signal. It turned out that the manager of the new enterprise had limited the number of incoming lines for that number to two. Why? Because he feared that a lot of calls responding to the ads would interfere with his work—whatever he imagined that to be.

To improve their performance, tellers got better pay and more recognition and rewards for good work. The supervisors' role expanded from taking care only of what happened behind the tellers' counter (balancing the books, for example) to looking out front too. They were asked to "cruise" the lines to see if customers needed help before they got to the tellers. On busy days (Mondays and Tuesdays; paydays—the 15th and 30th of each month—and Social Security days—the 4th and 5th) the supervisors keep cash boxes ready and start moving into empty tellers' slots when the wait gets up to four minutes. The bank expanded its lobby hours to 56 a week, including some hours on Sundays. Within months in 1988 the lines had been cut to a fraction of what they had been, and by 1989 95% of the customers were getting to the teller within five minutes. By 1992 the customers waited an average of two minutes and 12 seconds, and 98% got out of there in five minutes. Waiting time is one of 150 quality measures the retail bank regularly tracks. Linda Cooper, who runs the retail bank's quality effort, is co-author of an article describing First Chicago's line-shortening that concludes: "Institutions that steal consumers' precious resource of time—whether they be banks, supermarkets, department stores, restaurants, or even the post office—are committing competitive suicide."[8]

BANC ONE

Banc One Corporation of Columbus, Ohio has surprised competitors for years with its boldness and innovation. It was one of the first to install automated tellers and bank cards. From a regional Ohio bank it grew rapidly through acquisitions into the nation's eighth largest, and one of its most consistently profitable. It became an important player in Arizona, Louisiana, and Texas, while expanding in Ohio and other Midwestern states. John B. McCoy, the third-generation head of the bank, led its expansion; he started to use quality as a unifying force in 1986 as he drew the acquisitions together, according to Charles A. Aubrey, who was then vice president for quality at the new bank. A few months before a merger became final, Banc One would start a Juran-based process at the new bank, training its people, setting up a quality council. Banc One's financial managers would also get there early, setting up an accounting system and budget that would mesh with the parent. As one participant saw it, they had sort of a good-cop/bad-cop routine. Banc One's financial staff would beat the people at the new bank down and the quality staff would build them up again.

To minimize risks during the rocky years that banking passed through, McCoy left a lot of autonomy to the acquired banks. The portfolios remained small and scattered, so that no one unit was betting the bank. To be consistent about decentralization, McCoy had let each acquired bank make up its own mind about quality. The corporate quality department could help but it could not enforce. Out of 85 units, says Aubrey, half a dozen had no quality plan and a dozen had one but did not pay much attention to it. The rest adopted quality, perhaps one third of them with real enthusiasm.

So that its front-line employees would treat the people who came into the bank as valued customers rather than pests, Banc One changed its hiring criteria, its job descriptions, and its training, says Aubrey. In hiring, the bank looked for people with a friendly disposition who liked to help others and who had sales skills. Job descriptions and training used to focus on getting to work on time, handling money, and balancing the books. Now they focus mainly on the people skills. Employees go through a course called "first impressions" which teaches them to smile, use the customer's name, say "please" and "thank you," and finish up by asking if the customer needs anything else. "First impressions" was based on surveys to find out what was important to the customers. It is curious that when First Chicago surveyed its customers, they did not care much about smiles and pleasantries. They wanted speed and accuracy. Perhaps that is the difference between a big city like Chicago and the rest of America. To reinforce the new behavior required of its employees, Banc One ties appraisals and pay to being nice to the customers, and "shops" every teller and loan officer two or three times a month. Bank customers can get a free account by agreeing to "shop" the employees.

Banc One tried without success for some years to link its quality performance data with its financial data on return on assets, equity, and investment. Although the research could not establish that link, it did establish a close connection between customer satisfaction and customer retention. Among those who pronounced themselves plain satisfied, 55% would still be using the bank a year later, but of those who were *very* satisfied, 85% would still be there in a year. As we have seen earlier in this chapter, defections are to services what scrap is to manufacturing.[9]

Quality Means Retention

Banc One Wisconsin, a 14-bank subsidiary based in Milwaukee that merged with the Columbus bank in 1988, embraced quality right away and soon became one of the system's showcases. The retention rates at the different units of the bank in Wisconsin run from 85% to 90% a year and have all gone up a couple of percentage points. The bank's goal is now 93%, which may be the theoretical maximum, since 7% of the population moves at least as far as the next county every year. Fred Cullen, chairman of Banc One Wisconsin, named the three essentials of successful banking: acquisition, consolidation, and retention, of which retention is the most powerful. It costs money to acquire a customer, but you begin to make money when you sell him a product. If you consolidate and sell that customer three or four products, you make more money. If you then lose the customer after a couple of years, you have wasted an awful lot of time, energy, and money. Says Cullen,

> "When we talk about quality, we talk about it in terms of retention strategies. How do we make it easy for our customers to do business with us? If they have a problem, how do we make it easy for them to tell us about it and how do we make it easy for ourselves to solve the problem?"

Banc One is developing a model to show the net present value of a customer who is acquired, sold two or three services, and retained for ten years. Cullen elaborates:

> "If we know that we are going to have $5,000 of profit on this relationship over ten years, and if we make an error on your statement in the second month of our relationship, we're going to go to great lengths to make you happy."

Banc One Wisconsin learned through surveys that what keeps its customers coming is short lines, fast and courteous resolution of problems, accurate and timely statements, and convenience. The bank has targeted each of those goals. For example, to make the statements faster and more accurate, Banc One changed its software, automated some functions, and talked to the Postal Service about speeding deliveries. To make banking more convenient, it developed a five-year plan to relocate automated tellers and branches and added evening, Saturday morning, and even Sunday hours in the branches where they seemed necessary. It uses the same hiring criteria and training course as its parent.

Banc One is developing a wholly unbankerly responsiveness to clients. In 1988 it started issuing indirect auto loans (loans made through an auto dealer rather than directly to the auto buyer) and has captured 50% of the market share for that business in the Milwaukee area, with a $400 million portfolio. What the customers, in this case the auto dealers, wanted was a fast turn-around to nail down a sale. So Banc One guarantees approval within two hours or they lop a quarter point off the next loan that comes in. The bank acquired technology and software to make the process largely automatic and installed fax machines in the dealers' offices to get the paperwork through fast. Since many people want to buy cars on weekends, the bank opens its car-loan service at 7 A.M. on Saturdays. Banc One is now looking for ways of getting the loan approvals back within five minutes.[10]

INSURANCE: ALLSTATE

The firestorm that swept through the hillsides in Oakland, California on October 20, 1991 killed 25 people and destroyed more than 3,000 dwellings; it also triggered another conflagration in the months that followed as the victims confronted their insurance companies. So many of the victims complained that the insurance companies were dragging their feet, underpaying, and making arbitrary and inconsistent decisions that state insurance commissioner John Garamendi held a public meeting with 500 angry victims and then launched an investigation of the insurance companies.

As it happened, one of the victims of the fire was Robert E. Cole, a professor at the business school at the University of California at Berkeley and one of the country's top experts on Japan and quality. He has seen the inside of Japanese auto factories as a blue-collar worker. In a letter to Garamendi about his insurer, State Farm Insurance Cos., he wrote, "To be sure, the Oakland fire was unprecedented in many respects but the level of incompetence displayed seems well beyond what might be expected."

Cole wrote that State Farm's "policy of rotating large numbers of adjusters for short periods is a recipe for quality disasters. It is the same reason that GM can't compete with Toyota. The policy of linear handoffs of the baton leads to a lot of dropped batons." He says he had five adjusters in the four months after the fire, which worked out to 3.4 weeks per adjuster. He says, "Typically it takes an adjuster a week or so just to get into a file and as the file got thicker and thicker, it took longer and longer. The last two never did master my case. Indeed, sometimes it was easier for me to send them another copy of a letter than it was for them to find it in the file. The loss of organizational memory inherent with such rapidly rotating personnel is incredible. Predictably, it results in an extraordinary combination of omissions, overlap, repetitive demands, and errors.''

The adjusters did their best, Cole acknowledged, but their skills and training varied enormously. The work of the less skilled ''had to be redone (tons of rework, to use the language of the quality discipline.)'' Gross errors got into the estimates and could not be budged: for example, the cost of replacing Cole's entire roof kept showing up as $475. Cole said the insurance company made rules on the run, changed them arbitrarily and never did clearly explain all the steps in the insurance process. One adjuster told Cole he could charge for the rental furniture in his temporary home, the next said he could not, and a third agreed with the first.[11] (In the end, and after considerable agitation by Cole, State Farm settled on a sum to replace his house which he agrees was fair.)

The Trouble with Experts

The insurance companies clearly share with the banks several characteristics apart from the obvious one that they both provide financial services. Like the banks, the insurance companies do not have a very good public image. Like the banks, they are limited in the weapons they can use to compete. If they try to compete on the basis of price, they have an advantage only as long as it takes the competition to match the price. If they try to compete on the basis of new products, the advantage lasts only until competitors imitate the product, which can be a matter of days or even hours. In a regulated industry such as insurance it may be difficult to introduce new products; in any case, new financial services are easy to imitate. That leaves only one enduring way to compete—by offering better personal service, which also yields a cost advantage over companies that do not practice TQM.

Allstate Insurance Company decided in August 1988 at a meeting of senior executives and directors that the company had to make a major change in how it operated, and it created a search team to recommend what that change should be. Customers and employees had been telling the company that its quality was not the best—as the ads were saying it was. It did not take the search team long to decide that total quality should become Allstate's basic business strategy. Up until then, says Thomas Clarkson, Allstate's vice president for corporate quality, the company's efforts to please the customers had been mostly sloganeering. Beginning in March

1989 Allstate adopted total quality, first in the property and casualty business, which is 80% of the total business, and then by the end of that year in the life and corporate insurance businesses. The board of directors made quality the first item on its agenda at every meeting and constituted itself as the quality steering committee. All of the company's 54,000 employees got at least 20 hours of training. Allstate benchmarked against two early entries in the quality race in the insurance industry, Paul Revere and USAA. (Since then, many other insurance companies have adopted total quality or have begun thinking about it). "What we are learning most about is the customer," says Clarkson. "That's the most important. First you have to recognize the importance of the customers, then talk about them, and then finally think like them. We've made literally thousands of changes. It's a different company to what it was four years ago. The results are beginning to show with the customers."

Allstate's quality process is much like what you would find in many other companies. However, it does have one unusual feature. Lev Landa, a large, bearded Russian émigré with a Boris Godunov voice, brought with him when he came to the United States in 1976 an interesting theory about education and training that he had developed in Russia. As a doctoral student and postdoctoral researcher in psychology and later as director of an educational psychology laboratory at the USSR Academy of Pedagogical Sciences, he determined that experts have difficulty teaching others what they do because they do not fully understand it themselves. Experts are aware of only about 30% of their own mental processes, says Landa, and the rest are unconscious and intuitive, learned through experience. Consequently insurance companies, to take one example, find that it takes too long to train claims representatives and that when they finish the training the new reps perform poorly. The expert claims rep cannot tell the trainee how he reaches a decision because he himself does not know all of his own decision-making processes.

Landa bridges the gap by making a detailed analysis of all the steps the expert takes so that the process can be described. Then he constructs an algorithm, or decision tree, to lead the non-expert through the process that the expert would follow, only partly consciously. With the help of an algorithm, the non-expert arrives at a complicated decision through a series of simple decisions that are laid out for him in an either/or fashion. During the 1980s Landa worked with a score of organizations, mostly American businesses, to teach them what he calls "Landamatics." Their training time was reduced to a fraction of what it had been. The graduates worked from the start faster and with greater accuracy than people trained the old way. In a sense, they became instant experts.

Allstate invited Landa to run a pilot program for its data-entry centers, which were producing too many mistakes. Even after three months' training, the operators could not do satisfactory work. As usual, Landa found the manuals they used confusing and incomplete. He picked one apparently simple operation, filling in addresses, to make into an algorithm. It turned out to be fairly complex because there were no written rules for dealing with abbreviations, names with prefixes like "De," "Mac," or "Van" in them, the differences between Canadian and American addresses, and so forth—on through to the end of a six-foot algorithm. With a new manual and algorithm, operators worked faster and made fewer errors.

The experiment impressed Allstate favorably enough so that Landa was asked to introduce his methods to all the departments. Landa pointed out it would take him between 100 and 150 years to write algorithms for all the processes at Allstate, so instead of doing it himself he created an eight-week course to teach the Allstate people how to do it. Allstate now has eleven Landa-trained experts working full time looking at processes throughout the company, from the basic functions of insurance such as claims processing and underwriting to the more general functions such as human resources and marketing. Whereas Landa thinks of his algorithms chiefly as a way of turning a novice into an expert quickly, Allstate finds his techniques more useful as a way of picking a process apart and simplifying it. Allstate is using it as a way of taking the flaws out of the process, in which case the training problem disappears. "Landamatics is not central to our quality process," says Clarkson, "but we believe it gives us the ability to integrate our efforts and allow us to use it as rocket fuel for the rest of the plan. It is a critical tool, like flowcharting."[12]

AIRLINES: MIDWEST EXPRESS

A discussion of the quality of the airlines should begin with the acknowledgement that on the question of safety, which matters more than all else in flying, the airlines perform superbly well. That said, the personal service offered by the airlines is dreadful. In a survey of airline passengers in 1991, *Consumer Reports* found that its readers had more complaints about airlines than about auto insurers, hotel chains, or even auto repair shops.[13] It is curious that the antiquated railroads should have made customer service the key to their response to the challenge of deregulation whereas the jet-propelled airlines, in the chaos that followed deregulation, did everything *but* serve the customer well. The major airlines have tried every gimmick they could think of, a jungle of cut rates, frequent-flier bonuses, two-for-one tickets, tie-ins with hotels and car-rental services, everything but treating their passengers like valued customers. On the contrary, they reduce the number of attendants in the cabin, cut the flow of fresh air (to save fuel), shave a quarter inch off the little space remaining between seats, and take another olive out of that wilted salad. As *Consumer Reports* points out, the government sets minimum space standards for the transportation of dogs and cats by air but not for humans. In the hub-and-spoke system, the airlines created the ultimate in convenience—for themselves, not for the passengers. The hub-and-spoke system makes maximum use of aircraft and airports, but it sends passengers off on long roundabout journeys interrupted by totally unwanted stops in airports crowded with other unfortunates who want to be somewhere else.

The airline scene is not altogether bleak. American Airlines has long maintained quality measures such as the speed of baggage handling and the length of time customers stand in line, and reemphasized them in the early 1990s in spite of its horrendous losses. Caterair International Corporation, the successor company to Marriott's airline-food business, is turning towards TQM in what is admittedly a difficult business—feeding people in the sky. The caterers have to prepare breakfast, lunch, and dinner for a dozen airlines, try to keep the food fresh if the flight is delayed, or make a quick switch from breakfast to lunch if the flight is badly delayed, all without holding up the flight any further.

The most striking thing about quality and the airlines is that three smaller airlines which have found a particular way of serving their customers are also the only ones that have been profitable. Southwest Airlines has created a loyal following with its bare-bones but efficient, convenient service. Southwest has no reserved seats and serves only peanuts and drinks (cookies on long flights), but it has won aviation's "triple crown"—for best on-time performance, fewest complaints, fewest lost bags in a given month—eight times. No other airline has ever won it.[14] Southwest, which flies mostly in Texas, turns around 80% of its 1,300 daily flights in 15 minutes, one third of the time it take most airlines.

Alaska Airlines and Midwest Express created their niches by giving their passengers good service. Alaska spends twice as much as the average airline on meals and has a good on-time record. In *Consumer Reports'* 1991 survey of fliers' preferences, Alaska ranked first and Southwest fourth (after Delta and America West). In the Airline Quality Ratings survey for 1991 and 1992 put out by the National Institute for Aviation Research at Wichita State University, Southwest ranked second both years (after American) among nine airlines. The survey did not rate Alaska.[15]

Midwest Express is too small to figure in most of the national surveys, although travel publications rate it highly. It operates out of Milwaukee, flying regional routes and a limited number of flights to both coasts, Washington, D.C., and Florida. It focuses on the business traveler. As soon as you sink into one of its large leather-covered seats you realize that this is a different airline. When Midwest Express buys a DC-9-10 it removes the 80 to 90 seats normally squeezed into the cabin and replaces them with 60 seats. Midwest Express's 16 aircraft have only two seats abreast on either side of the aisle and all the seats are of the type normally found only in business or first class. When the flight attendants serve a meal, they set out linen, silver, and china on your tray. The meals are good. Midwest Express buys them from the same caterers that all the other airlines use, mainly from Skychef, but spends about $12 per meal, three times the airline average. These amenities add 25% to the costs of operating per passenger mile but Midwest Express compensates by appealing strongly to the business traveler with its service and scheduling, so it sells relatively more seats at full price than other airlines and fewer seats at discounts. Midwest Express also shaves costs by operating out of Milwaukee, which is cheaper than other hubs, and by getting the most out of an efficient, participative work force of 1,200.

Midwest Express, founded in 1984, has made a profit every year since its second year of operations, a remarkable record considering how much money the airlines have lost in the years since and how many of the small airlines founded since deregulation soon disappeared. In 1991, Midwest Express, Southwest Airlines, and Alaska Airlines — the three niche players who have a particular formula to please the passenger — were the only major carriers to make a profit. In 1992, Midwest Express and Southwest were the only profitable ones, Alaska having dropped out during a cost squeeze.*

Tim Hoeksema, the chairman and founder of Midwest Express, first learned about total quality as a pilot for the Kimberly-Clark corporate fleet and then as president of its KC Aviation subsidiary. Kimberly-Clark began introducing quality processes in its mills in the early 1980s. When the airline

* In contrast to the major carriers, many commuter lines were doing just fine. Mesa Airlines Inc. of Farmington, New Mexico, the largest of the commuters, ranked among the fastest-growing and most profitable service companies in the United States in 1992.

started up it borrowed a Kimberly-Clark quality manager to help set it on the right path. Says Hoeksema,

"I think all of us involved in starting the airline nine years ago had a dedication to doing things right, had a customer orientation. We tried to listen to the customers. We felt good about people and had a respect for people. We worked together as a team and had respect for our employees. We had some of the right fundamental ingredients, and whether we knew Pareto charts and fishbone charts, all that stuff, really didn't make any difference. We wanted to provide a good quality product to the marketplace and we tried to listen to people at the point of customer contact."

Midwest Express had difficulty teaching the use of quality tools to its employees. "The terminology and jargon in our first booklet put people off," says Daniel Sweeney, director of passenger services. On the second try, the airline used narrative descriptions and cartoons; it found them more effective than jargon-laden brochures. So the tools were introduced, gently. But the airline remained the opposite of, say, Florida Power & Light, by going easy on methodology. Hoeksema says that managers would be better served spending less time "getting involved in all the jargon, all the lingo" and more time "walking around, talking to their employees, getting teams together, and saying, 'If I was the passenger, how would I like to be treated?' To me," he adds, "it's not rocket science, it's just very practical common-sense stuff."

The "practical stuff" at Midwest Express includes a lot of customer contact, customer surveys, and teamwork. The airline tracks on-time performance, baggage handling, waiting time at ticket counters, waiting time on hold on the telephones. Flight attendants have forms to note down any problems they encounter in flight, complaints about the food, excessive leftovers. If the problem is serious, they phone the caterers when the plane lands. Midwest Express surveys its passengers once every six months.

Hoeksema sees employee participation growing as part of the airlines' quality effort. Midwest already relies heavily on teams. An on-time service team meets every week, bringing together the director of flight operations with representatives of airport operations, customer services, maintenance, marketing, reservations, and scheduling to track and categorize delays. Like other airlines, Midwest Express practices what is known as "cockpit resource management," a nice example of jargon for collectors of such things. The idea is that if the captain and first officer (pilot and copilot) are more of a team, less the commander and the subordinate, if the copilot speaks up more, then the flight crew is less likely to make mistakes than if the captain remains omnipotent. Midwest Express goes one step further by training the flight and cabin crews together to practice emergency procedures. Other airlines train them separately.

Hoeksema does not see Midwest Express becoming a large airline—he has purposely restrained growth so that newly hired people can be attuned to the company's culture—and he does not think the Midwest Express formula offers a profitable solution for the big airlines. But he does think the major airlines see that they have to do a better job, and they have improved their on-time performance and reduced the number of complaints in the last few years. Like the banks and the insurance companies, only through better service can the airline stand out competitively.[16]

TELEPHONES: AT&T

As the birthplace of modern quality, AT&T has a lot to live up to. AT&T in the 1980s was an excellent company, but it was not getting the full measure of the advantages of total quality (see Chapter 1). By the time Walter Shewhart formulated his thoughts on statistical process control in 1925, AT&T had developed over the previous 50 years many ideas that are basic to total quality today: quality is a core value; customer satisfaction drives quality; excellence requires that the designer be tied to the manufacturer; inspection after the fact is inadequate; and appraisal of quality must be founded on data. AT&T subsequently furnished superb telephone services, manufactured extraordinarily reliable equipment, and produced world-shaking research at its Bell Labs. However, AT&T lagged behind others in pushing its quality philosophy to its logical extension. As one AT&T executive put it in 1987,

> "What AT&T didn't do well in the next 50 years was to take steps to assure that quality became everybody's job. In its zeal to put quality on a scientific, disciplined basis, quality became [sic] the job of some people—even many—but not all people. That is the traditional view of quality: quality experts are responsible. The modern view . . . is that everyone is responsible for quality."[17]

Like other large, successful, technologically advanced companies, AT&T focused its quality efforts on the things technology can do best. And since AT&T was so good at what it did, it assumed that it knew best how to judge quality, and it was often right. It believed its quality was the best, which was probably true. However, like the others, it let its quality slips show in unsuspected areas, such as bookkeeping and accounting—in the business systems more than in the product lines. Then came the distraction of divestiture in 1984, which totally absorbed the attention and energies of management. AT&T had to change quickly from a regulated monopolistic business to a free enterprise beset by competitors.

Marketing, financial planning, managing a competitive business, managing cultural change consumed the attention of AT&T's top people. Then (as mentioned in Chapter 1) when the late James Olson, chairman of AT&T, presided over a quality forum the AT&T people who attended realized that the company was not doing total quality. The quality policy that Olson subsequently wrote did not get much beyond the slogan-and-banner stage. But when Robert Allen became chairman (after Olson's unexpected death) he did initiate an aggressive total quality movement. This was not an emergency measure, as it was at the auto companies and at some of the other early starters. Since AT&T is a decentralized company, Allen did not decree policies and requirements. Corporate headquarters did not tell the business units and divisions how to run their teams. However, Allen did expect the units to empower their people. He expected them to work with suppliers and, of course, to satisfy the customer. He set an aggressive goal of a 20% improvement every year. The corporate quality department made itself available to help those who wanted help, and recommended a seven-step Process Quality Management and Improvement methodology. The department also created an internal Baldrige Award clone as a standard for units to judge their performance and find their weaknesses. The level of corporate-wide interest in total quality (as well as the independence permitted by decentralization) can be judged by the fact that 32 out of a total of AT&T's 50 business units and divisions participated in the internal Baldrige in 1992, when AT&T achieved the feat of winning two real Baldrige Awards. Nearly all units were expected to participate in the internal Baldrige competition in 1993.[18]

The Ultimate Threat

If any American company was predisposed to favor total quality, AT&T would seem to be the one. After all, it had all that experience and background. But even at AT&T introducing TQM was not easy. (Is it ever?) Consider that the company had been through the turmoil of divestiture plus downsizing plus reorganization. AT&T people were angry, bitter, and demoralized. A quality manager who dealt with one group that served internal clients, the comptroller's office, has said that the atmosphere in that office "could be described as one of considerable churn. Frequent and major reorganizations of AT&T, significant consolidations of financial operating centers and methods/systems management staffs, and the lack of common financial language and practices created considerable frustration." The "customers" (i.e., other parts of AT&T) of the comptroller's service "were voicing their dissatisfaction with their top management, who in turn were communicating the need to 'fix it.' These customers' complaints were coming in more and more forceful language and were based on many failures (e.g., employee paychecks misdirected to the wrong location, lack of common courtesy on the 'hot lines,' late or inaccurate data on key reports, etc.)" Allen gave the company's business units the power to negotiate contracts with the divisions that served them, such as the comptroller's office, with the ultimate threat that the business units were authorized to contract for the same service outside AT&T if they were not satisfied with the internal supplier.[19] After running a pilot project as a test and establishing a quality council, the comptroller's office created teams for most of its processes and within a year could see some clear results: faster turnaround for reimbursements to employees, more user-friendly forms, and elimination of superfluous reports.

Another AT&T manager describes the difficulty of introducing total quality into the organization that administers the support for the company's 5ESS switches. The switches themselves, which are the basic workhorses of a telephone system, are excellent, but in 1989 customers were unhappy with the software support provided by an AT&T organization called 5ODA. Fixes took too long, too many errors cropped up, and the support cost too much. The unit carried 700 unresolved customer problems on its book. Realizing that the crash quality-improvement plan selected by the organization would cause trauma, the leaders of the quality push took some unusual steps. They decided to start in secrecy so that the process could not be shot down in its infancy. They identified the stake-holders, power centers, and influence brokers in the organization whose jobs would be dislocated, and negotiated with them to bring them aboard. The first quality efforts, following a Juran scenario, were applied in an area where they would be most welcomed and the chances of rapid success most likely. When the plan went public, management was ready to fight the inevitable rumor mill— particularly about possible job cuts—with facts and counter-rumors. Troublemakers in powerful positions surfaced, as expected, and they were quickly identified and either persuaded or ordered to fall in line.

"Culturally, it was a rocky road," according to Brian Churm, the quality manager involved. "There were times when it appeared the organization had crossed the line into culture shock." The lessons he drew from the experience included the following:

- It is going to be more complex than you think.
- Troublemakers can destroy you, or at least (as happened in this case) slow the process and reduce the benefits.
- Teamwork is fine, but sometimes leaders must be "heroic" and wade in, especially if you are in a hurry.
- And finally, outsiders cannot be the initiators of change because they will be rejected by people within the culture.

In spite of these cultural crises, the effort succeeded. Within a year the 5ESS switch unit had reduced its backlog of unsolved problems on the books from 700 to 200.[20]

The Center of the Universe

AT&T is certainly not winning all its competitive battles. One of the "baby" Bells, Ameritech, picked a competitor for a $1-billion order for switching equipment. The Federal Aviation Administration turned to a competitor for a $1.7-billion communications system for air trafffic controllers. Several major failures struck AT&T's long distance system, notably an outage at a switching center in New York City in September 1991 that shut down much of Wall Street and the air-traffic-control system in the East. Most of the time, even on "big" days, AT&T's telephone system works superbly well. On an average day, AT&T handles 140,000,000 long-distance calls; all but some 1,400 get through on the first try. On its biggest day ever, June 1, 1992, at the height of the air-fare wars, AT&T's clients placed 177,400,000 calls and all but 2,078 got through to the system—although if they were calling an airline the number may well have been busy.[21]

AT&T's 50 business units and divisions are still at various stages on the quality ladder, but the fact that two of them won Baldrige Awards in 1992 would seem good evidence that the company is headed in the right direction. The winners were the Universal Card Services unit, which issues credit cards, and the Transmission Systems Business Unit, which develops and manufacturers voice, data, and video transmission equipment. The card service is an entirely new AT&T business built from the ground up on a

Baldrige Award template. The AT&T board approved the new business in 1988, the year the company designed its new approach to quality.

Universal Card's enormous success at the outset led to its one major quality failure, if a surfeit of success can be called a failure. AT&T launched its advertising campaign for the Universal Card on the Academy Awards television show broadcast on March 26, 1990, and set up a staff of 35 to handle an expected 10,000 telephone calls to the "800" number given out with the commercials. Instead of 10,000, 250,000 people called to sign up. The marketing staff had wildly underestimated the appeal of the offer.

The commercials worked because of the appeal of the AT&T brand name, which people trusted (and which could have been stained had AT&T mishandled the new card). The ads also worked because AT&T offered the card free for life in the first year and announced a variable interest rate pegged to the prime rate.

Universal Card recovered from the initial fumble by flying extra staff from all over the country to the headquarters in Jacksonville, Florida within 24 hours to cover the telephones. From then on, the card succeeded extraordinarily well. Within 78 days it signed up its millionth client. In two years it had 10,000,000 customers, making it the second-largest card company in the industry, after Citicorp.

Universal Card's near-fanatical focus leaps out of an engraving in the lobby in Jacksonville: "The customer is the center of our universe." The company follows its performance with 110 measures that are updated daily and posted for employees to see. For example: How fast is UCS processing telephone applications for cards? The answer: in three days, compared to ten days for the nearest competitor. Employees are authorized to raise a customer's credit limit, to look into complaints, and to issue extra cards. Guided by total quality from the start, AT&T created a new company and a new product, delivered in a new way, and succeeded phenomenally.[22]

CONCLUSIONS

* The principles of total quality are just as applicable to services as they are to manufacturing.
* The benefits of providing excellence in services are perhaps greater than the benefits of excellence in manufacturing.
* Curiously, automation seems to be as critical to achieving excellence in services as it is for manufacturing.

- Speed is absolutely vital to the quality of many services.
- Inherently there is no greater difficulty in applying total quality to services than in applying it to manufacturing, but the services have been slow to come around, perhaps because the competition was not so pressing, perhaps because the earliest measures and methods of TQM were adapted for manufacturing, perhaps because historically the services have not measured what they did or studied their own processes as have manufacturers.

11

The Professions
They Need It Too

The idea that their work can be improved systematically with outside help does not sit well with doctors, lawyers, teachers, and other professionals. They do not like to be measured or compared to others or held to standards other than their own. People in almost every line of work, when first approached with the suggestion that they might benefit from total quality management, react by saying it cannot be applied to them. The instinctive rejection of quality is particularly strong among professionals:

- *The Professor*: How dare you suggest that I regard students as customers? They're lucky to be in my class.
- *The Doctor*: The patients have been been waiting for three hours in the admissions lounge? Well, we're very busy here.
- *The Lawyer*: You think three years is too long to spend on pretrial discovery? This is a complicated case, you know, and we've got a long way to go with interrogatories, depositions, and affidavits, *inter alia* and *ad infinitum*.

The very term "professional" resounds with high standards. The doctor or lawyer answers to requirements beyond the grasp of the lowly layman. Teachers' integrity depends on their independence from authority, their answering to no one but their own consciences. Medicine is a science, it is true, but it is also an art. How can you systematically improve an art? Do you propose to stand between the lawyer and the client, or the teacher and the student, and govern or monitor this sacred relationship with performance standards?

The professions certainly do create special problems for quality management. They are harder to measure. The processes of surgery or litigation are extremely complex and subtle. How can you reduce the variations in such processes? Professionals are harder to fit into a system. A college dean cannot tell the faculty that TQM is the way we do business from now on, as a corporate CEO can tell his executives. Professionals do not take to authority. Wholehearted involvement underlies any successful quality process, but in business at least you can prod firmly. Just try that with a professor or a doctor and see how far you get! You have to wait for them to want to come aboard.

If you look at the professionals not as individuals working on their own, but as part of a system and of a culture, then you see that TQM can indeed improve their performance and can certainly upgrade the system within which they perform. Medicine is not a skill practiced just by individual doctors on their patients. It is a vast system involving nurses, administrators, orderlies, housekeepers, pharmacies, insurers, government, and all the specialists waiting in line for referrals. Doctors sit at the apex of this system, more or less oblivious to the processes that may be delivering the wrong drug to the patient or losing a lab report needed right now. They may be as much a victim of the system as the patients. The teacher presides over the classroom, ostensibly in charge but in fact dangling in a web made of budget constraints, inefficient administration, legal requirements, and the social burdens imposed on education. Even if he wants to, the lawyer may not be able to find a prompt, sensible, and economic solution to the client's problem. The lawyer performs willingly within a slow, costly, inefficient system frustrating even to the plaintiff with the clearest and most justifiable case.

If the essence of excellence is service to the customer, then medicine, education, and the law are barely even pointed in the right direction. (I will not even bother to discuss my own profession of journalism, or publishing, or infotainment, or whatever it has become. It could be argued that it is pointed entirely in the wrong direction.) The patient, the student, and the client are on the periphery of the processes meant to serve them. Unlike the buyer of a car or an airplane ticket, the customer of the professions may lack the knowledge even to know whether he is being well served, and in any case may have no choice but to accept the service. How does a layman know if he really needs brain surgery? How does he know if he really needs a credit shelter trust? Slowly, however, these professions are being demystified, exposed, judged, and compared. Hospitals are responding widely to the demand for better quality, schools and colleges considerably less, and law firms hardly at all.

MEDICINE

Many doctors will argue that you cannot apply industrial measures of variation to their work. Heart surgery is not like stamping auto-body panels. However, the variations in medicine—the differences in costs and success rates from one hospital to another, the differences in the prevalence of some operations from one place to another—are precisely what alerted the health industry to the need and opportunity for applying TQM to medicine. "By the late 1970s, a maturing line of investigation in health services research was bearing a message no one was happy to hear—namely, that almost anywhere one looks in health care, variability of patterns in clinical practice is rampant," wrote the authors of *Curing Health Care*, Donald M. Berwick, a Boston pediatrician who was then head of quality for the Harvard Community Health Plan, and A. Blanton Godfrey, chairman and CEO of the Juran Institute. The variations are not slight. They are enormous. One example: In one county in Maine, 70% of the women had had a hysterectomy by the time they were 70, while in a nearby county only 20% had had the operation by the same age. On the reasonable assumption that the women in one county in Maine are pretty much like the women in another, medically speaking, then the doctors in one county or the other, or both, were making a lot of bad decisions. Statistically speaking, the system was utterly out of control. If these and other similar numbers are correct, Berwick and Godfrey concluded, "then the health dollar is not only inflating, it is being spent largely in some colossal game of dice."[1]

In the 1980s, the data produced on variability in medicine grew into a deluge. The federal Health Care Finance Administration began to publish comparable "outcome" figures for Medicare patients treated in 6,000 U.S. hospitals. A small research and consulting industry grew up around the data, massaging the numbers to show health insurers where their dollars could best be spent and to show hospitals how they were doing. Lexecon Health Service, which began comparing outcome data and cost data in 1984, found that survival rates for coronary-bypass surgery varied by a factor of ten from one hospital to another. Moreover, when the patient survived the operation the cost was frequently half the cost of a comparable operation which ended in the patient's death. The average charge for a successful bypass operation was $23,000. Patients who survived but with complications incurred a charge of $33,000, and patients who died ran up a bill of $56,000. Lexecon found that high quality helped both market share and profitability. For example high quality in surgical urology, mainly prostatectomies, yielded a high market share and an average profit of $112 per patient, while relatively low-quality institutions had a low market share and an average loss of $500. In different lines of surgery the results were similar, although the findings are not so clear for nonsurgical patients.[2] Other studies pointed to big differences in the rates of Cesareans performed, the costs of heart-valve replacements and the costs of normal childbirths, and the overwhelming percentage of hospital bills that contained errors.

Such high levels of variations in medical care cry out for statistical process controls and the application of the tools of total quality. Errors by doctors and nurses, adverse drug reactions, errors in medication, and hundreds of other indicators need to be tracked and analyzed. In principle, physicians should by their training be sympathetic to statistical analysis. In practice they may not be, however. They accumulate subjective wisdom on what works and does not work. "Many physicians have a deep distrust of clinical measurement projects initiated by management," writes Brent C. James, director of the Institute for Health Care Delivery Research at Intermountain Health Care Incorporated, a nonprofit chain of 24 hospitals based in Salt Lake City. "That distrust has a well-established basis in experience. For several decades healthcare quality assurance programs have used inspection to identify—then punish—'bad' practitioners."[3]

Surprisingly Obvious Answers

A meeting of some 100 physicians, health-care administrators, and quality specialists in Boston in September 1987 launched an experiment unique in the quality field. With funding from the John A. Hartford Foundation, 21 hospitals undertook demonstration projects to test the feasibility of applying total quality management to health-care organizations. The projects would be limited in scope and completed within eight months, therefore obviously no major transformations could happen, but perhaps the medical world would be awakened to the potential of total quality. Donald Berwick and Blanton Godfrey, two of the principals in the National Demonstration Project (NPD), as it was named, describe it in *Curing Health Care*. They write that only "a few of the project teams actually ventured into clinical terrain" where they would directly encounter physicians—and instead "stayed on the comfortable fringes, working on problems in medical organizations that more directly resembled quality problems in other industries."[4] The projects were simple, direct, and often produced what the authors called "aha's!"— surprisingly obvious reasons for problems that no one had bothered to figure out before. By using standard quality tools such as brainstorming, flow charts, and Pareto diagrams they found some simple answers to what had been baffling problems. Here is what some of the pilot projects did:

- Children's Hospital in Boston learned that the the ambulances sent to fetch critically ill children were inordinately slow because 95% of the time the ambulances did not even leave the hospital until at least 35 minutes after the call came in. It turned out that the ambulances needed authorization from a physician to leave, but no specific physician had been assigned that responsibility, so each time a call came in someone with an M.D. had to be found to release the ambulance.

- At Butterworth Hospital in Grand Rapids, Michigan a team discovered that to save pennies the purchasing department was replacing the original 9-volt batteries in the oxygen analyzers with shorter-lived 8.4-volt batteries. As a result, when patients came in for their tests, they would find that the machines they needed were down with dead batteries.
- Evanston Hospital in Illinois discovered that delays in day surgery, assumed to have been caused by a shortage of staff, in fact resulted because the records for the day's first patients regularly arrived late, leading to a cascade of delays through the day. Once the hospital required those records to be in place the day before, the delays virtually disappeared.

Other hospitals found out why Medicare was rejecting so many claims, why it took so long to answer the phones, and why emergency-room files did not get back to the patient's home medical center. These relatively simple but extremely vexing failures were reduced or eliminated fairly quickly, and about half the institutions in the demonstration project went on to develop full-fledged TQM efforts.

The NDP itself evolved by stages with further funding from the Hartford Foundation into an organization that provides education in health quality, runs a national forum on the subject, sponsors further demonstrations, disseminates information, and presides over a network of health networks. The whole enterprise comes under the Institute for Healthcare Improvement, whose president is Don Berwick.

A Tension for Change in San Diego

The original NDP had the desired effect of galvanizing others. Rear Admiral Robert B. Halder, former head of San Diego Naval Hospital, the Navy's largest, recalls being "mesmerized" when Berwick and others from the project talked to the annual conference of naval hospitals and clinics in October, 1989. "About three hours into the presentation the lights went on," says Halder. "I could see how to apply it. Back in San Diego I could feel a tension that demanded change."

The San Diego hospital had moved the year before to a brand new $350-million facility with new data systems to help its 4,500 employees. But it had the same old inefficiencies that Halder recalled from the time he had trained at San Diego nearly two decades before, "things like lost lab reports, missing X-rays, long waits for pharmaceuticals." By all standards San Diego was an excellent hospital, Halder states, but "I could see the frustration in the medical staff over the length of time it took for admissions or discharges. The nurses, patients, administrators were frustrated and it's hard to be upset in Southern California."

While other doctors and administrators who attended the conference waited for word from Navy headquarters, Halder decided to "proceed until apprehended," as he puts it. Back in San Diego on the Friday of the week of the conference, Halder met with the hospital's 23 chief administrators, summarized for them in one hour what he had learned, and asked them to join him in forming a quality council. He asked them to make up their minds by Monday morning. All except one (who was about to retire) did join. Halder appointed a senior captain as a special assistant for patient relations and put her in a front suite near his office. He appointed a Navy commander to be TQM coordinator.

Before the end of that year, 1989, Halder brought in Harvard Community Health Plan specialists to train his top 75 senior leaders and then pushed the training on down through all of the hospital staff. The physicians came aboard willingly. By the spring of 1991, the hospital had 35 quality teams at work and some of them were making a significant difference. A maternity team, lead by a nurse who believed in Halder's phrase, "proceed until apprehended," reduced the average length of stay for childbirth without any complications from three days to more like the national average of one day. Halder says he did encounter passive resistance, but by the time he retired in 1992 to become a consultant at the Juran Institute, he figured that one third of the staff was really involved in quality.[5]

A Leader Left Behind: The Harvard Community Health Plan

The Harvard Community Health Plan, the largest HMO in New England, operates 47 clinics and contracts with a network of 50 hospitals for its inpatients. It helped spark the quality movement in medicine, then found that for itself the road to total quality was a rocky one. At the launch of the National Demonstration Project in 1987, the Harvard Plan was a leader. Don Berwick, then a Harvard Plan pediatrician and the head of its quality measurements, helped organize the project. Other institutions had to try to persuade their physicians to join the quality effort, but at the Harvard Plan it was the physicians who led it. Other institutions picked peripheral administrative problems to attack, but the Harvard Plan went straight to a clinical matter that was bothering the physicians—what seemed like excessive variation in the use of ultrasonography on pregnant women among the plan's clinics.

In 1990, the Harvard Plan formally adopted what it called "quality management" as a strategic goal for the whole organization. Project by project, team by team, the Harvard Plan began applying total quality to its processes. Organization for quality began with the creation of an executive committee at the top, then division quality councils, and finally site councils for the clinics. To avoid the use of the discredited name of "quality circles," the teams were called "quality work groups." By 1992, the Harvard Plan had some good success stories to tell. For example, the plan wanted to get the rate of female members who had mammograms up from the 62% that prevailed (already a respectable rate by national standards). Doctors were supposed to urge women patients who came in for any reason to have mammograms—but they were not urging. A team got to the root of the problem. It turned out that the doctors believed a breast examination should accompany the mammogram and they felt too rushed to conduct an examination unrelated to the patient's complaint. The clinics got around that by getting the doctor's assistant to try to sign the patient up for mammograms, blood tests, and Pap smears. A pilot test of this approach got the rate of mammograms up to 91%. The Harvard Plan was completing 30 quality projects every six months. However, quality was still a project-by-project affair. It had not become pervasive, in the view of its vice president for quality in 1992, Matt Kelliher.[6]

In the meantime, the Harvard Plan ran into the kind of leadership problems that have derailed quality drives elsewhere. While the doctors and administrators unrolled quality in the clinics and administrative offices in 1990 and 1991, the CEO, Thomas O. Pyle, a Harvard MBA who had come to the plan from the Boston Consulting Group, went off to Oxford University on a nine-month sabbatical. A top-down type of executive, he did not so much lead quality management as become persuaded to go along with it. During Pyle's absence in England, the Plan's president, Heinz Galli, a former Swissair executive and a quality enthusiast, ran the organization, pushing quality hard. On his return from England, Pyle found that the physicians had left him a long way behind. Then he received a study by the Boston Consulting Group saying that the Harvard Plan's real problem was the low productivity of its doctors. So Pyle demanded more productivity, incensing the doctors. They met 350 strong in an unprecedented meeting, disowned and vilified him, and in effect pulled off a coup d'état by threatening to resign en masse. The board sacked him.

Such turmoil at the top does not create the consistency of leadership required by total quality, and that was not the end of it. The next episode bears a resemblance to what happened at Florida Power & Light after Broadhead replaced Hudiburg (see Chapter 8). In 1992, the Harvard Plan board chose as a successor to Pyle Manuel M. Ferris, the acting chief, a former hotel manager who had run Sheraton North America and the Howard Johnson Accommodations Group. Like Broadhead, Ferris decided to cut back the quality bureaucracy and methodology. Galli returned to Switzerland. Kelliher, his protegé, left, and so did most of Kelliher's staff. (Kelliher says he was escorted out of the building the moment he announced his departure.) The new management dropped many of the accoutrements of quality, in terms of training, recognition, goals, and measures. The old team prepared an internal quality report full of indicators and had it ready for distribution at the end of 1992, but the new management did not distribute it.

Kelliher says quality management "lost a lot of momentum by virtue of the change in leadership." But his successor, Chris Holland, director of quality consulting and training, stresses instead that the plan has been reevaluated and modified to make it "less cumbersome," and "more user friendly." People at the Harvard Plan had come to feel that teams were the only way to solve problems—but some teams were spending months just writing their own charters, says Holland. Under the new simplified system, the Harvard Plan will continue to use teams, but 80% of the problems will be solved by the staff or by individuals. Holland says that the Harvard Plan is not backing away from the team approach, just no longer regarding it as the only way to manage. The various quality committees have merged into the regular management committees, and the quality data and reviews have merged into the more general management and financial reporting.

The No. 3 man at the Harvard Plan, Medical Director John M. Ludden, survived through all the turmoil and views it with a certain ironic humor. "The decrease in dependence on jargon is incredibly good," he says, although he regrets that it stopped just as he was getting the hang of it. The Harvard Plan no longer has "quality goals," he says, just goals, and instead of "quality council meetings" they just have staff meetings. However, these changes do not mean that TQM has been dropped at the Harvard Plan; rather, it has been folded into the everyday way of thinking and working. The physicians have come to like the quality approach, which is one reason they rebelled against Pyle. In a second tumultuous meeting two weeks after Pyle's dismissal, the angry doctors calmed down when they decided to use the less emotional, data-driven team processes to run the organization. The improvement of clinical practices, says Ludden, "carried on with remarkable momentum." Without pressure from the top to go by the quality book, says Ludden, "it's within the care-providing arms that you see the clearest recognition of the importance of teamwork and process improvement is continuing without a hitch."[7]

The Long Wait in the Lounge:
University of Michigan Medical Center

The University of Michigan Medical Center, a large teaching hospital in Ann Arbor, also launched its "total quality process" as part of the 1987 National Demonstration Project. This hospital has also stumbled, but consistent leadership has kept it on track. Michigan had a full burden of problems in the mid-1980s. As a teaching hospital that treated a high proportion of critically-ill patients, Michigan was bound to be expensive. But it was the most expensive hospital in Michigan and it badly needed to get the growth of costs under control.

Doctors, staff, and patients all had complaints about the way the hospital ran. Patients arriving at the hospital for admission were held up an average of 120 minutes in the admissions lounge. Patients' records did not reach the doctors in time for 5% of the scheduled appointments, and 5% of 870,000 appointments every year added up to a lot of frustrated doctors and patients. The percentage of operations not performed as scheduled because of delays, cancellations, or misscheduling ran to 13%. Patients who telephoned with questions about their accounts got a busy signal 32% of the time.[8]

The hospital picked for its 1987 demonstration project the admissions and discharge delays at the hospital, which turned out to be all part of the same mess. A quality-improvement team of nurses and representatives of housekeeping, administration, and admissions performed the flow chart–fishbone diagram–Pareto chart act. The physicians, who were among the customers who suffered from the system's failures, stood aside and said, "Let us know when you have solved the problem."

The team discovered that patients were waiting so long to be admitted mainly because their rooms were not ready.

Why were the rooms not ready?

Because too often the patients occupying the rooms were discharged late.

Why were they discharged late?

Most often because there was no one to take them home. The families had not been notified.

There were other reasons for delays too, of course. Since the hospital treated severely ill patients, many of them went directly from hospital to nursing home, but sometimes the bed in the nursing home was not ready. Or the doctor had not signed the discharge form because a lab report did not reach the ward in time for the doctor's rounds. Or some other reason. Delays in discharges hit hospitals hard, and they are all trying to reduce the length of stays. Many insurers pay a fixed amount (capitation fee) for a procedure, regardless of the length of stay.

The flow charts for the discharge–admission process revealed a complicated, disorganized chain of events marked by poor communications. Too many people intervened between the unit clerk who had the empty bed, the housekeeper who cleaned the room, and the admissions clerk trying to pacify restive patients. The process for each admission was, if not an emergency, certainly a surprise. To speed the room cleaning, housekeepers got beepers and the chain of communication was cut to the minimum. For common procedures, the patient's family now gets a printed schedule of what will happen to the patient, including the estimated date of discharge and any home care that needs to be prepared in advance. The hospital established an outreach program to nursing homes. These and many other measures reduced admission delays rapidly and dramatically, from the 120-minute average of mid-1987 to a 22-minute average by October 1988. By 1992, the hospital had cut the wait further to 10 minutes.[9]

Other projects, involving accounts receivable, billing errors, or the telephone service, for example, also achieved big gains at the outset and then slower gains later. Over four years the hospital reduced costs by $17.7 million while the incremental costs of total quality, including training, amounted to only $4 million. A good portion of these savings are repeated from year to year. The numbers do not take into account the benefits of improved care, improved employee morale, and presumably happier patients. Against an annual budget of $550 million, the savings are not exactly overwhelming. However, the savings from total quality plus a cost-cutting drive and new marketing efforts gave the Michigan hospital enough of a surplus in 1992 to pay most of its 11,000 employees a gain-sharing bonus of $2,500 in cash and set aside money to reinvest in the hospital. The hospital also reduced its regular room rates 20% in 1992 (the price of intensive care rooms remained the same) and then froze all its rates for 1993. It is no longer the most expensive hospital in Michigan.[10]

Though most of the improvement projects at Michigan were administrative, the physicians did get involved. One of the ten lessons learned from the demonstration project, according to its organizers, Berwick and Godfrey, "is that any health-care organization that begins a major TQM initiative without the involvement of physicians and physician leaders does so at its peril." They said that beginning with processes that seem purely administrative "is a formula for slow going and inevitable rework."[11] At Michigan, of the 19 teams that achieved those $17.7 million in savings, the most successful team in terms of savings achieved included physicians. The team attacked the delays, cancellations, and mis-scheduling in the operating rooms. A whole series of measures adopted by the team—such as revising the scheduling system, standardizing inventories, adding more registered nurses to the staff—reduced the proportion of operations not performed as scheduled from 13% to 3.5%. As a result, the hospital freed up beds and operating room time, allowing it to handle 13% more operations in 1988, just when it had reached its limit. For 1988 and 1989, the hospital incurred only nominal increases in the costs of operations, although they started to climb again after that.[12]

Nevertheless, the administration of the Michigan hospital has been disappointed in the participation of the doctors. Ellen Gaucher, the hospital's forthright chief operating officer and quality champion, says, "It took a long time to get the physicians to pay attention." Once they do get interested, they tend to jump to conclusions and think they have the answers before they know the questions, she says. A nurse by training and a Baldrige Award judge, Gaucher found that department heads with around 20 years' seniority were the the most resistant to total quality. As of 1992, some had not reached the stage of establishing flow charts. "Not enough department heads have set up measures," she said. "That's very depressing."[13]

"A Precarious Stage": Doctors Examine TQM

The issue of doctors' participation in total quality, and for that matter the participation of professionals in any field, is controversial. Berwick believes their resistance is exaggerated, and should be relegated to a non-issue. He agrees that it is hard to get a physician's attention. Berwick and Godfrey wrote "physicians (especially those not salaried) have not been trained to understand some of the issues of interdependency, customer focus, and process-mindedness that characterize TQM. . . . Unsalaried physicians have a great deal of trouble devoting the time to learning and team participation that TQM demands. Their beepers go off and, due to the structure of their work, they leave the room."[14] A doctor who has spent a 12-hour day with patients is not likely to have time or patience for a quality-improvement team.

Whatever the obstacles to their participation in quality may be, doctors are fact-oriented scientists who can be impressed by data. Brent C. James, the leader of quality efforts at Intermountain Health Care Incorporated in Salt Lake City, suggests that the evangelical approach often used successfully in business only puts off doctors. They see another passing fad. They reject the idea that what works in industry will work in medicine. But when quality comes to them as a natural extension of their scientific training, and when they see data, then they believe. Instead of mandating standards, says James, show them variation and the variation tends to disappear.[15]

LDS hospital, one of the 24 in the Intermountain chain, furnishes a vivid example of how effective quality methods can be when used by doctors in their clinical practices. Infections of surgical wounds are among the most troublesome and common complications that affect hospital patients. In 1985 the 1.8% rate of postoperative infections at LDS Hospital was better than the national standard (a range of 2% to 4% was acceptable), but still represented a quality failure to the hospital. A research team assigned to find ways to reduce the rate of postoperative infections narrowed its investigation to the use of antibiotics and then further focused on the time when the antibiotics were first given. It turned out that the timing was crucial. The study followed only patients who had elective surgery and met certain other conditions. Of the patients in this group who were administered antibiotics in the two hours prior to surgery, only .6% developed infections, while patients who got antibiotics earlier than that had a 1.4% rate of infection. Patients who received the antibiotics within three hours after the operation had a 3.3% rate of infection, and later than that the rate became 3.8%.[16] In 1985, when the infection rate was 1.8%, 40% of the patients in the same cohort at LDS Hospital were getting their first antibiotic in the two hours before the operation. In 1986, with 58% getting the antibiotic at the optimal time, the infection rate dropped to 0.9%, and in 1991 with 96% of the patients receiving the antibiotic at the optimal time, the infection rate had fallen to 0.4%.

Since each postoperative infection added about $14,000 to the costs of treating a patient, and the hospital avoided 50 infections in 1991, the savings that year amounted to $700,000—not to mention the lives saved and suffering avoided.[17] Although the study of postoperative infections began with a traditional research group, it moved to a total quality mode as it developed. The hospital established a team of physicians, nurses, and pharmacists and they used the flowcharts, Pareto charts, and other quality tools. The entire Intermountain chain has made it standard to administer antibiotics in the two hours prior to an operation, and hospitals elsewhere in the country are duplicating the experiment.[18]

Total quality clearly can play an important role in getting U.S. health costs under control and improving care. Hospitals are adopting TQM on a massive scale. A national survey by Northwestern University for the American Hospital Association found in 1993 that of 3,303 hospitals responding to the survey, 68.9% practiced formal TQM. However, of those using TQM, 73.4% had been at it for less than two years so the results were slim. The hospitals were trying to practice TQM with "relatively little physician involvement" as only 16.2% of the doctors had taken training and 10% had participated in teams.[19] With so much change coming in the health system, it would be easy to lose sight of TQM. It is hard to focus on process improvements when, for example, you are trying to figure out how to expand medical insurance to 39 million Americans who do not have coverage and how to pay for it, when employers and insurers are screaming for cost containment. Berwick believes that total quality in medicine has reached "a very precarious stage."[20] TQM will have to pay some rich dividends to establish itself in American hospitals.

EDUCATION

In Japan, of all places, the university is one institution that remains untouched by total quality. The big names in the quality movement in Japan are mostly university professors—Noriaki Kano, of the Science University of Tokyo, Yoshio Kondo, professor emeritus at Kyoto University, the late Kaoru Ishikawa and his successor, Hitochi Kume, of the University of Tokyo—but their teachings have had no effect on their own institutions. Japanese universities do not practice TQM. Higher education in America remained even more isolated from total quality. Academe neither practiced nor taught quality until long after much of industry became immersed in it. None of leaders of the American movement—Crosby, Deming, Feigenbaum, and Juran—came out of academe, although Deming for years taught a course at New York University and Juran served as chairman of the department of industrial engineering at the same university from 1945 to 1951.

"Although educators are among the first to write about new ideas, they are almost always the last to apply them to their own activities," writes Myron Tribus. "Schools of business are not well managed. Schools of engineering do not apply engineering methods to their own operations."[21]

Tribus was a senior vice president at Xerox, a dean of engineering at Dartmouth, and a director of the Center for Advanced Engineering at MIT. His frustrating experiences as an academic left him an enthusiastic promoter of TQM in education. Professors live in a sequestered world fenced in by what their colleagues consider academically respectable. They take almost a perverse pride in not letting the outside world influence them. One teacher I talked to just after he had been to a three-day Xerox quality seminar sniffed that "the theoretical context seemed to be rather slim, but the empirical evidence is very good." In other words it sure works, but until an academic discipline can be built around it he cannot take it seriously. Total quality does not slip readily into one discipline. Academic researchers dig themselves deeper into narrower specialties, whereas total quality is broad and breezy. It ranges over many fields and admits opinions from high and low. It is interdisciplinary, whereas academics teach, study, and write their obscure papers entirely inside one discipline.

The academic walls are beginning to crumble. Statistics offer one academically acceptable route of entry into TQM. Statistics is a bona fide discipline and it is fundamental to improving processes. Statisticians established the Institute for Productivity Through Quality at the University of Tennessee in 1981, the Center for Quality and Applied Statistics at the Rochester (New York) Institute of Technology in 1982, and the Center for Quality and Productivity Improvement at the University of Wisconsin in 1985. As the quality movement gathered momentum in the 1980s, interest in it at these and other centers and institutes picked up. The universities became aware that they were failing to teach a subject that was becoming increasingly important to their, ah . . . uhmmm . . . (gulp!) customers, the people who hire their graduates. Business schools and engineering schools became particularly anxious to be relevant and teach what was needed.

A wave of reform rolled through the business schools in the late 1980s as they became fiercely competitive and woke up to the truth that they were not teaching what employers needed their recruits to know. Curriculum reform became epidemic. By now no self-respecting business school will admit to not teaching and promoting globalism, ethics, and of course total quality. Over the years, a few academics have emerged as experts on quality. They include David A. Garvin at the Harvard Business School and Robert E. Cole of the business school at the University of California at Berkeley (and formerly of the University of Michigan). Garvin wrote *Managing Quality* in 1988 and Cole, a specialist in Japan (see Chapter 10), has written books, articles, and papers on quality since the late 1970s.[22]

Why Should a Nobel Laureate Change?
TQM Goes to Graduate School

The transition from teaching total quality on the campus to practicing it is a big one, but that has begun too, especially in the business schools. They may not be desperate, but stiff competition among schools, rising costs, and tight budgets are creating some of that "emotional experience" that forces organizations to turn to TQM. The big-name business schools such as Chicago, Harvard, and Stanford have shown varying degrees of interest, but some of the schools that have to struggle for recognition are more committed. Richard N. Rosett experienced both types of institutions, first as dean of the Chicago business school and then as dean at the College of Business at Rochester Institute of Technology. Only a handful of Chicago's 100-odd business professors are interested in practicing quality methods, says Rosett. After all, a Nobel laureate can do just about anything he wants. Why should he adapt? He likes what he has. At Rochester, Rosett finds a different attitude. The faculty has smaller horizons, and more to gain and less to lose by changing.

Rosett arrived at Rochester in July, 1990, and a month later attended a Xerox forum on quality with the usual skepticism. He came away a believer. The following summer he took the entire faculty and staff of the Rochester business college to a retreat on one of New York State's beautiful Finger Lakes to discuss the application of TQM to the college. Then with the help of IBM, Rochester got some free training before launching its TQM initiative. Both students and faculty at Rochester are starting to work as teams. In the faculty, teams for each major subject have replaced the usual academic departments. There are no departmental chairmen. For tenure, promotion, and raises, teachers will have to submit to student evaluation of their teaching (among other things, of course). Beginning with the undergraduate freshman class of 1993, students will work and study as teams for periods of a quarter or a semester. When a team is asked to solve a problem, all the members must be ready to make the presentation because any of them may be called on. Students will get a team grade (unless they have a particularly backward member, in which case they must ask for help if that member's performance is to be excluded from the team grade). The team method of learning will spread up through the undergraduate school, the graduate school, and eventually into the executive programs.

Rochester Institute's student services are all being scrutinized by teams looking for improvements to the maddening ways colleges usually work. Rochester Institute had a rule that if a student wanted to drop a course for which he has already registered, he first had to get the professor's signature, then the business school's approval, and then stand in line again where he had registered in order to withdraw. A team assigned to this problem discovered no one could remember a case of either a professor or the business school refusing permission to withdraw. So these two requirements were dropped. And instead of lining up again to withdraw, the student simply fills out a form in the student services office and hands it in. The office notifies the professor and the registrar.[23]

The University of Tennessee's College of Business Administration, another striving institute, but one with a history of teaching TQM, revised its MBA program in 1991 largely on the basis of practicing what it preaches. Professors no longer own their courses, but teach two- or three-week modules of courses in the new curriculum. Students are graded almost entirely on the basis of written and verbal reports delivered by teams. The proportion of a student's grade dependent on the team was 90% in 1993, but the school is experimenting with that to see what ratio works best. For its courses for executives, Tennessee does the same customer research that a business might do. It asks the corporations what they want their people to learn, then presents the requirements to the faculty, which puts together a team to teach what the customer wants.[24]

Student Customers: The University of Michigan

Beyond the business and engineering schools, on the campuses at large, TQM is moving along sluggishly. During the 1980s, the University of Michigan attempted the usual across-the-board cost cutting, but when it became evident that this would not be enough the university appointed a task force on costs in higher education in March, 1989, chaired by the dean of the business school, Gilbert R. Whitaker, Jr. (This effort is independent of the University of Michigan Medical Center process described earlier in the chapter, although some of what the hospital has done rubs off on the university.) The task force came back a year later with a report recommending that the university implement a more fundamental cultural change and focus on quality improvement as well as cost containment. Instead of meaning "more and better of everything," as it had, quality would have to mean searching for means of improving while also reducing costs.[25]

"Quality can be improved only by developing a deep understanding of customer needs and expectations," the report stated. "Thinking about the people we serve, and with whom we interact, as 'customers' is not normal or natural in many parts of the University. Indeed, some may find it offensive." The report names as customers the university's students, the Michigan taxpayers, the sponsors of research, and other universities that evaluate the work at Michigan. The university also has internal customers, such as the professor who depends on administrative services. The report said that those activities and resources that do not meet customer needs were candidates for "probable elimination."

Some professors did indeed find the suggestion offensive. Some also had superficial misconceptions of what total quality meant, imagining that if students requested less homework, or Fridays off you had to give in to them. Three years after the report came out, the university was moving very slowly to implement it. The chairman of the study, Gilbert Whitaker, found himself promoted to provost, which made him responsible for implementing his own report. He was succeeded as dean of the business school by B. Joseph White, a believer in total quality. The school has annual surveys of the customers (students) and the faculty, has nearly completed designing quality measures, and sends students out to work on real-life quality-improvement projects during the seven weeks they spend working in a business as part of their requirements.[26]

Outside the business school at the University of Michigan, M-Quality, as the process has been named, moves glacially. After the task force report was accepted in 1990, a design team went to work on an implementation plan, which was accepted in the summer of 1992. Then followed a year of experimentation. The Quality Council, made up of 24 of the university's most senior people, turned out not be the right body for guiding the whole project; it was too cumbersome, and too many of its members did not know enough about quality. So its function became more to educate its own members than to guide total quality, and it expanded to 45 members, including all the deans and administrative heads of the university. A new M-Quality Steering Group of eight members took over its original job.

The university appointed Robert Holmes as vice president for academic affairs and executive adviser for M-Quality. Here and there quality projects started up. The College of Literature, Science, and the Arts began flow-charting its cumbersome, complex hiring procedure, and a blue-collar team began studying injuries to employees. The faculty found much to ridicule in the university's approach. They did not see much quality in the "statements of purpose" hastily scribbled on big sheets of paper at brainstorming sessions and then copied and distributed in raw form without tidying up or even typing. They did not like what they felt were "Mickey-Mouse" activities they thought better suited to a fourth-grade audience, such as the stick-on gold stars that were meant to be put on the classrooms' chalkboards to mark the best suggestions. Instead, some of the professors put the stars on their lapels.

Robert Kahn, a prominent professor emeritus of psychology at Michigan, performed worthy service for M-Quality in a talk to the university's regents in which he defined the intellectual or academic basis for quality. It has two roots. One grew in statistical research, which produced statistical process controls. The other grew in behavioral science, which produced the ideas behind employee involvement and participative management. Happily, one of the original behavioral theorists in this line of thinking was the late Rensis Likert, who had also been a professor of psychology at Michigan. He wrote *The New Patterns of Management* in 1961 and *The Human Organization* in 1967.[27] Now the theoretical basis for total quality no longer seemed so slim. Still it will be slow going at Michigan. The university's faculty and administrators have a standing invitation to join in when they feel like it, rather than a directive to start practicing total quality now or else.

Shortening the Lines

Here and there other universities are at a similar point in moving to total quality. The Wharton School at the University of Pennsylvania began looking into total quality early in the 1980s. Then when it overhauled its curriculum at the end of the decade, it listened to the voice of the customer by going out to get the opinions of its alumni and its business clients on the educational needs of the graduates. Out of this grew a university-wide TQM effort, which was adopted in 1989 and guided by the Juran Institute. Penn set up a quality council in 1990 and launched the first four pilot teams in support areas. In 1991 the division of finance organized seven teams to improve business processes and the first teams with students were created. More teams sprouted in 1992. Unfortunately, Penn's TQM drive then lost three of its champions. Marna Whittington, the university's executive vice president and the key person in the implementation, left to join the Clinton administration, and the president and the provost announced that they were leaving too. Obviously, their replacements will have a lot to say about the deployment of quality at Penn.

John E. Murray, Jr., president of Duquesne University, convened the entire faculty on a cold Saturday morning in January 1992 and held them for five hours to listen to his quality vision for the school. Murray, a former law-school dean and an authority on contracts, announced a "continuous effort toward perfection" to make sure that "Duquesne University becomes, in substance, the leading Catholic university in America." In a preliminary statement issued to convene the meeting, he said that "total quality performance," as he called it, could be applied to any activity and has a "strong ethical mandate." He said that every activity at the university—the entire administration, the Student Government Association, the Faculty Senate, and teaching itself—should be viewed as a process which can be improved. Addressing a particular complaint of students everywhere, Murray wrote that "if registration lines are too long, they should be shortened and further shortened until *there are no registration lines.*"[28] He was cautious on how to apply TQP to the core activity of teaching. In a subsequent interview, he said that "Teaching is essentially an individual creative process. We do not wish to make anyone feel as though he or she will have to march in lockstep. That would be counterproductive." He did suggest, however, that the faculty could make teaching assignments in imaginative ways so as to put teachers where they could best be used.[29]

Fast Feedback for the Faculty

As happens at other universities, at Duquesne the business school spearheads the quality effort. The school's dean is Thomas J. Murrin, who led Westinghouse into its first attempts at productivity and quality improvements at the beginning of the 1980s when he was president of its Public Systems Company (see Chapter 1). To advise the university, he recruited another Westinghouse alumnus, Jack Fooks, who headed the company's Quality and Productivity Center. The business school initiatives include rating the professor who teaches total quality on a weekly basis. At many universities the students rate the courses and teachers at the end of the semester, but that helps only future students. However, when the students give their opinion of the teacher, the reading, and the material every week, and track the ratings, then they can get an immediate benefit.

The Graduate School of Business at the University of Chicago finds this fast feedback extremely useful. It evolved out of an unusual course, called informally the "teaching lab," in which students try to help professors improve the curriculum and their teaching. (The teaching lab itself evolved out of an earlier "laboratory course" in which students tried to help companies develop new products.) The teaching lab looked at various tools for improving teaching and found that the best was a short, fast feedback questionnaire filled out at the end of most classes or even every class. Painful as the results may be, many professors are using the questionnaires. As I have written several times in this book, some of the quality failures seemed so obvious that it is hard to understand how they had been overlooked. The questionnaires at the Chicago business school revealed that in almost every class students had problems hearing or understanding the professor, reading what he wrote on the blackboard, or understanding the visual displays. The students always wanted more concrete examples to illustrate concepts. And the professor rarely knows whether he is going too fast or too slow for the class. To make the process work properly, the professor has to react. When a class gives a clear-cut answer to the question, "What was the muddiest point?" in a lesson, the professor had better clear it up quickly.

Two of the Chicago business school professors who have worked on improving teaching, George F. Bateman and Harry V. Roberts, believe it is a mistake to concentrate improvements on the administrative side in college. Administrators are "likely to have great difficulty when they try to change rigid bureaucracies," whereas professors, although they may not be receptive to an idea that essentially comes from business, as TQM does, do have freedom to act on their own and they want to improve their teaching. Bateman, Roberts, and their students researched the literature of teaching methodology and its effect on teaching practices. The results were discouraging. Research into teaching has had little or no effect on the classroom. But TQM, they say, can have an immediate effect.[30]

Industry leaders in quality management are pushing the universities to more efforts, through grants, through partnerships between colleges and companies and through an annual TQ Forum sponsored by industry for senior university staff. At the first forum, hosted by Xerox in 1989, Motorola's Bob Galvin jolted the academics by saying, "I wonder if it's fair to ask you, as we in industry have been obliged to ask of ourselves, 'How efficient are you? Why can't you teach 50% more in a year than you're teaching now?' Not 1%."[31] Interest in the Forum has grown and the 1993 host, Motorola, had to limit attendance to 300 people. Colleges could send only their presidents, chief academic officers, and deans of business and engineering—no substitutes allowed. In 1991, Galvin surprised a meeting of corporations interested in quality by abandoning a prepared speech and announcing that his company would provide one week's worth of quality training free at Motorola University to 100 teachers and administrators from any one university if other corporations would do the same. As a result, eight corporations each donated one week's training to universities in their region in a continuing effort that became known as the "Motorola challenge."

In 1992 IBM offered eight $1-million grants to colleges to help them put TQM into their courses, to fund research in TQM, and to implement it in their own operations. The application from each college had to come jointly from its business school and its engineering school. In addition to the $1 million, each winner gets free access to a local IBM site to learn about quality there. For the eight grants, IBM was swamped with 204 applications, some from the best-known colleges in America.* Howard Wilson, director of market-driven quality at IBM, says that corporate interest in helping the universities is spurred by ignorance of TQM among the college graduates the companies hire and the cost of teaching them the subject after they are hired.[32]

An Unusual Asset in Alaska: Mt. Edgecumbe High School

If TQM were to take hold in the education system, then we would see a realignment of roles, as we see happening in business. Teachers might become managers of an education process conducted by the students. The students would learn more by doing, which is the way to retain the most of what you learn. Something like this happened in an extraordinary experiment in an unlikely place. In 1983 the Bureau of Indian Affairs closed down a boarding school for native Alaskan children situated on an 80-acre former naval base at Sitka. The state acquired the school, Mt. Edgecumbe High School, and reopened it in 1985 with high hopes and ample funding. However, its performance was disappointing. Staff morale collapsed as the teachers' union and the administration battled acrimoniously.

But the school had one unusual asset. Since Alaska lies on the Pacific Basin, all students are required to study Japanese or Chinese. And since the school wants to send students back to their villages prepared to start businesses, it stresses entrepreneurship. The school conceived the idea of selling smoked salmon to Japan and sent escorted groups of students to Japan to try to sign up customers. But the Japanese, they found, were insulted because the young entrepreneurs had not researched their customers' standards of quality. The salmon was the wrong color, had the wrong taste, and was not properly packaged for Japan. However, the students learned; by 1989 they were exporting successfully to Japan. (The business soon became too big for them to handle, and the school turned the trade over to a community business.) But the school was still troubled. Nearly half the original staff had quit.

One of the teachers, David P. Langford, was thinking of quitting when, on a visit to Arizona, he talked to McDonnell-Douglas Corporation's director of quality, who persuaded him to go back to try the total-quality approach and

---

* IBM actually chose nine winners, because one successful application came jointly from the Clark Atlanta University business school and the Southern College of Technology. The other winners: Georgia Tech, Oregon State, Penn State, Rochester Institute of Technology, the University of Houston–Clear Lake, the University of Maryland, and the University of Wisconsin.

loaded him up with materials. Langford picked his best class, started talking to the students about quality concepts and how they might fit into education, and encouraged them to use the tools of quality. These students, many of them from Alaskan villages too small to support a school of their own, took the ideas and ran with them. At first they went around the school collecting data on things like how many students were late to class, how many slept in class, how much time was spent listening to lectures and how much time doing something. As the students learned more, they raised money to visit McDonnell-Douglas, Motorola, and other companies in the lower 48 states to see what they did. Langford even became a little concerned about the independence the students showed; they wanted to take responsibility for their own education! But they were becoming extremely capable at making presentations, analyzing situations, and planning ahead.

By now, Langford's ideas were spreading through the school with the support of the principal and the superintendent of the school. Mt. Edgecumbe had several advantages: it was amply funded; it had 90 computers for 210 students; and the whole school frequently went through a "ropes course," an Outward Bound-type experience meant to build confidence and forge bonds. However, it was TQM that fixed the character of the school. Langford adapted Deming's 14 Points. For example, "abolish merit ratings" became "abolish grades." Students get either an "A" or an "incomplete." Langford developed a somewhat complex self-evaluation system for the students to use. To give students more of chance to get into a subject in depth and to do things themselves, classes were stretched to 90 minutes each.

Such a school naturally attracts attention. Among others, Myron Tribus and Donald Berwick visited Mt. Edgecumbe and were impressed. The students themselves track the school's performance by looking at what the previous four years' graduates are doing and comparing the results with other groups of Alaskans aged 20 to 24. In 1991, while about one fifth of young Alaskans were unemployed, only 2% of Mt. Edgecumbe's graduates were looking for jobs. Among the other 98% of the school's graduates, 39% were in college and 37% had jobs.[33]

Quality Grows in Brooklyn: George Westinghouse V&T

Styling himself "the Deming of education," Langford moved to Montana in 1992 to serve as a consultant to schools in the "lower 48" that want to take the quality path. Faced with reduced budgets, hostile unions, unsympathetic schools boards and superintendents, they may not easily match Mt. Edgecumbe's performance. Nevertheless, quality has made a surprising appearance in downtown Brooklyn, in New York City, at the George Westinghouse Vocational and Technical High School. The school is 75% black, 22% Hispanic. It has four white students. New York City cut its budget three years running up to 1993 and the faculty shrank by 21%. For the 1993–94 school year, no money was appropriated for chalk, erasers, or paper. Metal detectors and three security guards greet students as they arrive for classes.

Yet Westinghouse Vocational High is making a TQM effort that attracts a lot of attention. The principal, Lewis A. Rappaport, and an assistant principal, Franklin P. Schargel, got interested after they attended a quality seminar at National Westminster Bancorp in 1988. Schargel became the quality champion. Before involving the students, which only started in late 1992, the school sought to draw the demoralized teachers and the apathetic parents into the process in 1991 and early 1992. The teachers got recognition awards and the parents were pressed to join the Parent-Teachers Association and show concern for their children's performance. From a pathetic membership of 20 (with a school population of 1,700 students), the PTA grew to 211 members, and as many as 400 show up for some meetings.

The rate of total failure—students getting F's in all their courses—needed immediate attention because it was so high. Applying the basic tools of quality to the problem, a team that included administrators, teachers, parents, and students decided to focus several weapons on these students. They needed remedial training, but when could that be fitted into the schedules of students who traveled from all over New York City to get to class? The answer was to combine tutoring with lunch. All four of the school's guidance counselors were assigned to work exclusively with the failing students. The school talked to their parents to tell them why it was so important for their children to pass. In one year, the number of total failures dropped from 151 to only 11.

Schargel says that incoming students at Westinghouse do not have the basic survival skills they need for school. They do not know how to study, take notes, or make decisions. For the 1992 freshmen, he organized a three-day preschool session to teach the students these basic tools and to introduce them to total quality. Although the New York City Board of Education refused to provide funding for the session, Schargel invited 200 freshmen out of 400 and 245 showed up on the first day. On the third day, 187 still showed. In 1993 the Board of Education agreed to fund the orientation for the freshman class and to pay their subway fares. Schargel plans to introduce each successive freshman class to total quality and so involve the whole student body by 1995. Obviously, Westinghouse Vocational High has a difficult struggle ahead, but it is making progress. The school cut its dropout rate from 7.8% in 1992 to 5.3% in 1993, compared with city-wide averages of 21.9% in 1992 and 17.8% in 1993.[34]

While TQM can clearly benefit education in some respects, some of the applications seem naive—just as business seemed naive when it seized on quality circles early on as *the* answer. Unfamiliar with even the rudiments of management, many academics may fail to draw proper distinctions. John Early of the Juran Institute points out that while TQM is a well-established management technique, it has not been tested as a pedagogical technique. Learning is an individual experience, not a team experience. Harvard admits individuals, not teams. Business hires individuals, rarely teams. TQM may not work that well in the classroom.[35]

THE LAW

The practice of law in the United States of America cries out for a strong dose of total quality; it is a classic example of a poor process allowed to drift out of control: insensitive to the customers, shrouded in mystique and arcane vocabulary, wrapped in costly rituals—notably discovery—that lead slowly and expensively to settlements of little benefit to anyone except the lawyers involved. Since the whole system is defended not only by combative and intelligent lawyers but by judges and by legislators many of whom were trained as lawyers, the law has seemed almost impervious to the cries of help from corporations and the citizenry.

Like medicine, the law in America has finally reached a point beyond tolerance. When the cost of the law became a competitive drag on U.S. corporations, and the whole economy for that matter, then clients started to fight back. Richard H. Weise, Motorola's general counsel, reports in outrage that his company pays out about half of 1% of its sales to lawyers, which is about the same proportion of the gross domestic product that the whole United States spends on legal fees. Weise, who tends to the dramatic and vivid, admits he has made himself a pariah among his fellow attorneys by calling our legal system things like "broken down, lousy, non-value added." The practice of law, he says, "is redundant, wasteful, and self-serving. Lawyers do dumb things in the same dumb way. The law is rapidly becoming unaffordable. It's a quality problem and requires big changes." To explain to lawyers what he wants done, Weise published a four-pound, 1,376-page opus called *Representing the Corporate Client: Designs for Quality.*[36] (It is the heaviest volume in my small library of books about quality, which includes some other heavyweights.)

What really gives Weise's opinions weight, however, is his position as legal chief for a major corporation that demands quality not only from its own people but from its suppliers. Law departments in other TQM companies have lagged behind the rest of the company, but they are coming aboard now and insisting that the law firms they hire practice total quality too. Lawyers, of course, maintain that they have always practiced high-quality law. They are professionals, after all. But what the clients want today is high-quality law faster and cheaper. One approach, increasingly popular since the early 1980s, bypasses the legal system by going to some form of "alternative dispute resolution"; this can take a number of forms, including arbitration, negotiations, and mini-trials. Since 90% of all suits eventually conclude with a settlement anyhow, Weise argues, why not in effect come to a settlement early on? Then you do not have to shovel money into discovery and all the other rituals that precede a trial.

However, alternative dispute resolution can address only a portion of Americans' legal needs, and for the rest Weise and others look to quality improvements in the practice of law. Lawyers argue that what they do is so varied, and so special, that process improvement cannot apply to what they do. Weise avers that if you look at what lawyers do you can identify cycles and processes just as in any other activity. Things like contracts and patent applications are fairly repetitious and routine. Motorola's legal department uses what it calls "automated contract engineering." Every clause of every form of contract the company uses can be pulled separately out of a computerized data bank and combined into a customized contract. Weise likes to relate that when a senior executive came to see him to get a contract for a consultant, Weise plinked away at his computer while they talked, somewhat to the executive's annoyance. When they had finished talking Weise went over to a printer and pulled out the finished contract the executive wanted.

The Arrogance of the Profession: Corporate Counsel

Weise views high-quality law as not so much winning cases but avoiding disputes. Quality can be designed into a product at an early stage; so can dispute avoidance be designed into a product with a lawyer's early participation. Although they are not always welcome, Weise likes to have his lawyers present at the earliest meetings when a project is starting at Motorola, and then at other stages, for instance when the sales literature is prepared, so they can head off potential trouble. "Prophylactic counseling is very effective," says Weise. "That's the lawyer's greatest added value. Timing is the most important part of it." For straight cost cutting, Motorola's legal department has switched to using more in-house lawyers. Weise figures an outside lawyer costs three times as much as a corporate lawyer. Their fees are double the cost of an inside lawyer and they add another factor for the learning curve. Years ago outside lawyers got 80% of Motorola's legal business; now they get about 50%.

Texaco, which adopted total quality in 1989, gave its outside counsel guidelines in 1991 on how they were to operate. The oil company wanted real partnership with its lawyers, not the kind of distant uncommunicative relations that usually exist between lawyer and client, and it wanted the firms to submit bills its way, not their way, for easier analysis.[37]

M. Michael Grove, general counsel of Bell Communications Research, says that when his company launched its quality effort he, like other lawyers, was skeptical and so he hung back. But eventually the company prodded him into action and he found that when he tried it he liked it. The performance of the company's lawyers is rated by the inside clients in terms of timeliness, teamwork, flexibility and other criteria. The lawyers return telephone calls faster and talk more frankly with their clients, says Grove. With outside counsel, Bell Communications expects a clear understanding at the outset of a case as to what is to be done and what it will cost; then it expects regular status reports; finally it expects a detailed, understandable bill.[38]

Johnson Controls Inc., a Fortune 500 company, signed an agreement in 1993 with a large Chicago law firm, Sidley & Austin, to give the firm all its environmental business if the firm followed the Johnson TQM plan. Johnson had previously divided this business among about eight firms.[39]

Here and there law firms are responding to pressure from their corporate clients by instituting quality reforms, or perhaps by just announcing for marketing purposes that they have gone to TQM without actually doing much about it. The legal profession certainly has a sense of urgency about its own fate. Firms have gone under, associates have been turned out, even partners have lost their jobs. Lawyers are showing up at quality seminars and the New York State Bar Association is organizing a year-long series of workshops, to be conducted by the Juran Institute, to help a consortium of firms take their first steps in quality. At this writing, the American Bar Association was also organizing a national demonstration project.

T. Barton Jones has experience with two large New York firms starting off on TQM. It is not easy for them, he agrees. "The biggest barrier is the arrogance of the profession itself," he says. "Lawyers do not believe TQM applies to them; it sounds like a fad. Lawyers do not like buzzwords." So at Haight, Gardner, Poor & Havens, where Jones was a partner until 1992, they called it "Client Focused Management" and they engaged in "client service improvement projects." As they began projects, talking among themselves and with clients, they found that their problems often boiled down to poor communications with the clients which could be improved relatively easily.

At Haight, Gardner the focus fell on administrative processes. One practice that bothered clients was that when they had a closing, say on a big loan, they would get a bill for perhaps $100,000 and think that was the end of it. But months later, Haight, Gardner might deliver the final documents and another bill for perhaps $10,000. The lawyers tended to relax once the closing was over and not get the papers collected and copied until much later, running up new expenses which they sometimes had to swallow because the client objected to another bill. The lawyers assumed that 90% of the time the closing papers were delivered within 30 days, a reasonable period. But when a team reviewed the history of 65 closings they discovered that the delivery time varied from three to 360 days, and only 15% had taken less than 30 days. The process was out of control. Haight, Gardner was starting to apply the usual process tools to get at the root causes of the delays when Jones left the firm in November 1992 to join the larger firm of Winthrop, Stimson, Putnam & Roberts, names that are rich with U.S. history.

At Winthrop, Stimson it was the litigation group that wanted to use total quality to cut costs and raise efficiency. Several of the firm's most senior people went to seminars and training sessions, then assigned two partners to each of six major clients to interview them extensively about what they wanted from Winthrop, Stimson. And so one of the larger and grander old Wall Street firms, one that surely never doubted its excellence over the decades, took the first step to quality.[40]

CONCLUSIONS

- It may be more difficult to apply TQM to the professions than to manufacturing or the services, but it is worth doing and it has begun.
- What professionals do may seem to be too subtle and sophisticated to be subject to statistical process controls and other tools, but in fact, like everybody else's, much of their work lies within a system of routines and variations. The tools work as well in the professions as anywhere else.
- Doctors, teachers, and lawyers, being proud, independent people with their own concepts of excellence, need special handling. More than managers do, they need to be drawn in by examples, by test projects, by proof rather than exhortation. They cannot be commanded to join.
- In a professional organization, it is tempting to launch TQM in periph-

eral administrative activities, rather than face the difficulties that may be encountered at the heart of the organization, in clinical practice or in litigation. But this may be a mistake because it will tend to indicate to the doubting professionals that TQM really is not for them.

- Overenthusiastic or naive converts to TQM should exercise care in applying it to activities that may be beyond its competence. TQM can make the operating room more productive and safer, but it does not make the surgeon more skillful. The teacher may be partly right in scorning attempts to regard the student as a customer. The relationship should go well beyond a simple customer relatonship.

12

The Government
Did the Dinosaur Twitch?

M ore than a decade ago, in 1981, when I was researching an article on efforts to improve productivity (later to be known as quality) in government, I was surprised at how much activity there appeared to be. I was even more surprised at the volume of documentation given me to prove that it was working. I came away from each appointment with a briefcase bulging with documents to demonstrate how much the Office of Management and Budget, or the New York Sanitation Department, or the State of North Carolina, or the U.S. Navy was accomplishing. If the weight of the paperwork had been the measure of quality or productivity, then government at all levels in the United States was making extraordinary progress.

Here and there some government productivity initiatives did work and even took root. The city of Phoenix asked private contractors to compete with public collectors for garbage routes, and tied the contracts to quality as well as costs. The idea succeeded and spread to other city services. For the most part, however, these early efforts at improving quality and productivity disappeared without ever reaching the public's awareness or making politicians realize that here was a way for government to do things better.

Quality and politics do not mix well, and the U.S. government is highly politicized. Politicians focus on all the wrong things to make TQM work. They focus on issues, not process; on ideology, not the facts. Politics is impatient; quality is patient. Politics wants to make a big splash; quality takes small steps. Politics is sporadic; quality is continuous. Politicians have short-term goals limited by the next election. They know little about management, and have little reason to learn; managing well will not win them any headlines or votes. TQM is not the sort of thing that catches the attention of the press or the public. It does not make for good sound bites. The politician who talked about TQM would be written off as a bore not worth the media's attention. President Clinton, a politician who does understand TQM, complained in 1992, "As I travel the United States making campaign speeches, I am often tempted to talk about quality management. But seldom do my audiences include enough people who understand quality management for such a discussion to be productive."[1] Governor Jim Hunt of North Carolina said something similar to me in 1981 about his efforts to improve the quality and productivity of the state government: the issue was not sexy and the legislators did not understand it.

You can see two forces pulling government in opposite directions in America today. On the positive side, TQM really does have a few footholds in federal, state, and local government and is advancing by thousands of little steps, almost unnoticed by the public and the uncomprehending media. On the negative side, the worst of the political practices that make it so hard to run government well have reached the point where many Americans believe that their government simply is not working. Business has learned that organizations run best when the power is pushed downward and people are managed and inspected as little as possible, but the federal government continues to move in the other direction, micromanaging, inspecting, auditing, reviewing, and otherwise meddling.*

Congress obviously must exercise some oversight, but when senior government officials spend half or more of their time testifying on Capitol Hill, they cannot do their jobs. With its swarms of staff aides and proliferating committees sniffing for something to make their patrons look better, Congress intrudes oppressively. It passes unworkable junk legislation that has to be deciphered interminably by the courts and agencies. The administration, no matter which party is in power, is as politicized, shortsighted, and irrational as Congress. Whenever the White House changes hands, more than 3,000 jobs are vacated and filled by political appointees, compared to less than 100 each when the British, French, or German governments change hands. Appointees serve an average tenure of two years, half what it was in the 1950s.[3] They cannot provide the continuity that good government requires, or even get to learn their way around their departments in the time they allot themselves for so-called public service before taking the next step in their careers.

---

* Juran wrote 30 years ago, "Government departments have been notoriously addicted to using the same elaborate procedures for trivial matters as for important matters. But the politicians and the public press have contributed to this attitude by making headlines out of any government error, however small. So it is 'logical' for the government employee to spend $10 of public money to avoid $1 worth of personal criticism."[2]

Measuring the Wrong Things

Government does not work under the lash of competition that forced business to start transforming itself, but it does now finally have its own compulsions: debt and deficits, and the revolt of citizens fed up with bad government. Examples of bad government hit us in the face every day, whether we are in New York dealing with the insolent incompetence of the Immigration and Naturalization Service or the Motor Vehicle Bureau, or in Iowa getting the wrong answer from the Internal Revenue Service (if you can break through the busy signals), or in California reading about the shambles at HUD or in defense procurement. Poor government became even more intolerable as it continued to deteriorate while business began to show us that there are better ways. As David Osborne and Ted Gaebler point out in *Reinventing Government*, government and business are headed in opposite directions and the contrast emphasizes the poverty of government.[4] While government pulls power into the center, business decentralizes and pushes power downward. While rules drive the government, the mission drives TQM companies. Government measures the wrong things—the inputs (how many bureaucrats are assigned to change light bulbs), rather than the outputs (how many light bulbs got changed). The government usually has no way of knowing how it is performing (how many bulbs are working, how many need changing, and how many got changed). When you have the wrong measures you have the wrong incentives. Government officials are rated by seniority, by the size of their staffs, by the amount of money they spend. They rarely get credit for spending less or saving money or satisfying the customer.

The head of the General Accounting Office described how far behind management theory and practice the government has fallen. In testifying before a Senate committee in 1993, Charles A. Bowsher, who bears the title of Comptroller General of the United States, said:

"The hierarchical, centralized bureaucracies designed in the 1930s and 1940s simply do not function as well in the rapidly changing, knowledge-intensive society and economy of the 1990s. The kind of government that developed during this period, with its reliance on rules, regulations, hierarchical chains of command, and direct provision of services, worked well in a stable environment. It accomplished great things in its time. But today it is a dinosaur. For example, the Department of Agriculture has an extensive and costly field structure of

11,000 field offices, many of which date from the 1930s—before modern transportation systems, computers, and universal telephone coverage facilitated communications.''[5]

Government is not the same as business. It has different goals and motivations and that is obviously as it should be. Business is judged by its profits; government by the political, social, and economic goals it chooses and to what extent it achieves them. However, the fundamental ideas of TQM—teamwork, pushing power downward, substituting responsibility for inspection, and the methodical, continuous search for improvement—are as applicable to government as to business. As Bowsher points out, the way government works today is out of tune with technology, communications, education, and management theory. It does not fit the way most Americans see themselves, or their work, or their relations with others.

''A Strong Negative Role'': Government vs. Quality

The government way not only contrasts with the business way, it actually handicaps business. Government has drifted so far out of tune with the economy that it has become one of the chief obstacles to making America more competitive. McDonnell-Douglas may believe in TQM and practice it as best it can, but it is a defense contractor and so has to follow the Defense Department rules. In 1985 alone, McDonnell-Douglas endured 6,000 separate government audits, which means three new audits started every hour.[6] A. Blanton Godfrey, CEO of the Juran Institute, has testified that U.S. competitiveness would progress if only the government would play a neutral role rather than the ''strong negative role'' it plays now in improving quality. He said,

> ''Not only do far too many government agencies still buy solely on low price rather than on low cost or high value [i.e., without taking into account quality, reliability, or operating and maintenance costs], they pass laws requiring others to do the same. They ignore past performance and proven ability when awarding contracts, preferring to base new business relationships on promises in bids. They fail to build long-term relationships with suppliers, choosing instead to incur the enormous costs of yearly contracts and renegotiations. They will rely on bureaucratic detailed specifications and requirements enforced through wasteful and costly inspections rather than working together with suppliers to meet actual needs on partnership bases.''[7]

In spite of the lack of leaders in government who favored total quality, or were even acquainted with it, some efforts to promote total quality began in government as early as the 1970s and in the late 1980s began spreading rapidly through the bureaucracy. Without leadership support at first, these were mostly tentative and insecure efforts, but they reached remarkably many places in government. The General Accounting Office learned in a survey of 2,800 military and civilian agencies in 1992 that 68% of them had some level of TQM activity. Fewer than 1% of these TQM activities had started before 1985, and 74% were born in the 1990s. Therefore most of the agencies were in the start-up stage or beginning to implement TQM. However, about 15% of the units who tried it said they had already achieved significant results and 3% believed it had become ingrained in the organization.[8]

At the top level of government the Office of Management and Budget (OMB) has promoted quality improvement since the early 1980s, but the effort has been so low-keyed as to be invisible to the public and even to much of the government. The OMB took charge and, like many corporations, began by thinking of productivity improvement. It wanted to use instruments like the Civil Service Reform Act of 1978, which allowed the government to reward exceptional senior administrators with bonuses of $20,000. In practice, however, the bonuses were simply handed out in lieu of the raises that Congress refused to vote. By 1987, OMB saw that its productivity drive was having no effect and it invited companies such as Ford and Corning to come in and explain what they were doing. Then OMB sent out a task force to visit the better-run companies. OMB got the message that the practices and principles practiced by these companies added up to TQM and could be applied to government.

In 1988, OMB converted its productivity-improvement effort to a quality-driven effort, created two annual quality awards for performance in government (the Presidential Award for Quality and the Quality Improvement Prototype Award), and helped establish the Federal Quality Institute. Two years later, OMB transferred its own quality staff to the Institute.[9] The Institute, which is self-supporting, runs seminars and conferences for government workers, provides consulting services, puts out a newsletter and other publications, and produces a list of quality contractors for the government offices to use. The quality push in government is not mandatory, but the Institute is there to prod and encourage. "They don't have to talk to us," says Tina Sung, one of the Institute's original staffers, "but they do now because it is such a hot topic. Our role is advocacy and education about quality."[10]

What was lacking all along in Washington was a top-level advocate of quality. President Reagan showed no interest beyond the occasional award ceremony, nor did President Bush. Some enthusiasts achieved fairly high office. Thomas Murrin, formerly of Westinghouse, and now of Duquesne (see Chapter 11) served some frustrating years as Under Secretary of Commerce, and David Kearns, Xerox's champion of quality, had a brief spell as Deputy Secretary of Education in the Bush Administration.

Grass-Roots Quality

With the election of Bill Clinton to the presidency, America acquired a genuine total-quality convert at the summit of government. The President's introduction to total quality came through a grass-roots movement that began to spread through the United States in the 1980s and caught fire in the 1990s. Community-wide quality groups now exist in about 200 U.S. towns and cities. They enlist schools, colleges, businesses, hospitals, local government, and civic organizations to promote TQM through training, conferences, and consulting. The number of councils had grown gradually and more or less spontaneously through the 1980s in places such as Philadelphia; Kingsport, Tennessee; Madison, Wisconsin; and Erie, Pennsylvania; there were a total of about 100 in mid-1992. In the next year, by mid-1993, the number doubled.[11]

Four umbrella groups pull the councils together into networks. Myron Tribus (see Chapter 11) founded the first umbrella organization, the Community Quality Coalition, in 1980 and the small city of Lawrence, Massachusetts created the first center in the same year. The other three umbrella groups, the World Center for Community Excellence, the Community Quality Council Committee of the American Society for Quality Control, and the Community Quality Council Leaders' Group, were all formed in 1992, the year the growth of councils took off.

President Clinton recalls that he recognized the potential of quality management in state government at the first celebration in 1988 of what was called Quality First Community Initiative in Batesville, Arkansas. The initiative council, the first of 22 in Arkansas, was created with the help of a major local business, the Arkansas Eastman Company, a specialty chemical producer. The company's quality director, Asa Whitaker, invited then-Governor Clinton to be its first luncheon speaker. For once Clinton arrived early, and so he accidentally got to hear presentations by local quality teams about their projects before he gave his own speech. What he heard appealed to him intellectually and suited his style, so he asked Whitaker for more information. Clinton devoured the reading material Whitaker gave him, talked to his CEO friends about quality, and invited quality experts to stop by. One of them, Tribus, reports that Clinton caught on to TQM quickly. A TQ task force already existed, established by the Arkansas Industrial Development Commission in 1986 to promote quality in industry.

Now Clinton borrowed Whitaker from Arkansas Eastman to help launch TQM in the state government. He called it the Quality Management Process and started with five state agencies, and the governor's office. Clinton himself presided over a cabinet team. The process spread to 11 agencies and then to 34 agencies over a two-year period. In 1991 10,000 state employees (of a total of 32,000) attended quality orientation sessions and 4,000 took training, based on Juran Institute manuals, on the tools of quality. The 200 projects completed by 1993 included a reduction in the processing time it takes to renew an auto registration by mail from two or three weeks to two or three days. The average wait in the state revenue offices where drivers go to renew their licenses dropped from 60 minutes to 15 minutes. One team saved $27,000 a year on the cost of postage in schools, another $87,000 on the purchase of footwear for prison inmates. After Clinton left for Washington, his successor as governor, Jim Guy Tucker, issued an executive order directing all state agencies to practice TQM. He commissioned a team to recommend a standard curriculum that could be used statewide to train public employees.[12]

Clinton arrived in Washington armed with the ideas in *Reinventing Government*, the influential best-seller by David Osborne and Ted Gaebler.[13] Although the main ideological thrust of the book is that the entrepreneurial spirit can transform the government, many of the specifics in the book come straight out of the TQM lexicon. Osborne and Gaebler would empower the civil servant (and the citizen), change the performance measures of government, focus on the needs of the citizen (customer) rather than the politician and bureaucrat, decentralize, and change the role of top management to "steering rather than rowing." The authors find TQM lacking when applied to government, since it was developed primarily for industry. The additions to TQM that they advocate include a reliance on market mechanisms and the injection of competition into government monopolies. Clinton also brought to his cabinet two members who know and like TQM, Labor Secretary Robert Reich and Health Secretary Donna Shalala, who presided over quality improvement at the University of Wisconsin while she was chancellor there.

In March 1993 the President announced a National Performance Review "of every single government agency and service". He commissioned Vice

President Al Gore to run a six-month study with a staff of 200 government specialists. He also asked the government departments to review their own operations. "We intend to redesign, to reinvent, to reinvigorate the entire national government," said President Clinton. Somewhat prematurely, he added, "When I was the governor of Arkansas, our state became the first in the nation to institute a government-wide total quality management program. And I can tell you, it works. It isn't easy, it isn't quick."[14] To those remarks, Gore added the ringing words: "Mark this date: President Clinton is starting a revolution in government." Gore then set about gathering suggestions by telephone and mail and by holding town hall meetings in government departments, soliciting and telling horror stories about government. His favorite, adapted from *Reinventing Government*, tells of the trap that catches dirt and oil in steam lines. When the trap fails, it leaks about $50 worth of steam a week. A federal worker reported that when he suggested replacing some leaky traps he was told the procurement office had decided to pile up all the orders for steam traps for a year and then buy in bulk at a discount. By waiting, the office got $10 off each $100 trap. But a trap that had been leaking for a year had already wasted $2,500 worth of government steam.[15]

Whether all the other demands of government and the pressures of politics will allow President Clinton to push TQM at the federal level as he did in Arkansas is questionable. The National Performance Review produced by Gore contains much of the language and philosophy of TQM. It embraces the view that we have to look at how government does things as much as what it does. Whatever policies the government chooses become irrelevant if the government has broken down. As the review says, "If the car won't run, it hardly matters where we point it; it won't get there."[16] The review is full of hopeful ideas and upbeat examples, but does it create a priority issue or is it a winning political theme? TQM could furnish the answer to some of our government problems. Assuming the cost of poor quality in government is at least as much as the 20% to 30% of sales that corporations have found—and if anything it is likely to be more than that as a percentage of the budget—then TQM could certainly help reduce the deficit and improve government services.

Memories of the fate of President Carter's plan to reform government, the Grace Commission Report, and other attempts to remake the federal government tend to squelch any optimism about President Clinton's initiative. Changing the way government works is a monumental task compared to merely changing, say, General Motors. But here and there the attempt does show some promise.

THE IRS

For reasons that may be obscure to the ordinary taxpayer, the Internal Revenue Service has long had a reputation in government as being one of the best-run federal agencies. Then in 1985 the IRS suffered what Alvin H. Kolak, until recently assistant to the commissioner for quality, calls "a significant emotional event"—the sort of thing that set corporations off on the quest for quality. The IRS started up an untested computer system in Philadelphia which "brought us to our knees as an agency." Files disappeared, taxpayers did not get their refunds, or got refunds they were not entitled to, errors piled on errors. An outpouring of legislation also plagued the IRS. Congress passed more than 100 new tax laws in the 1980s; these required new forms, new instructions, new software, new training. The public, savvier about taxes and finances than in the past and more demanding of good service, grew less tolerant of the IRS's slips. "All of this caused us to rethink," says Kolak, as well it might.[17]

With the help of the Juran Institute, beginning in 1986 the IRS developed the closest thing the government has to total quality in a large agency. Juran taught the IRS management the theory and practice of quality, how to identify problems, how to proceed systematically on a diagnostic journey to get at the root cause, and to resist the temptation to go straight from problem to solution.

The IRS has some advantages over other government agencies in implementing TQM. It has less politics and more continuity. Only the commissioner is a political appointee, and although the terms of the previous three commissioners averaged only 28 months, they were all committed to quality. The Clinton administration commissioner, Margaret Milner Richardson, a Washington lawyer, also supports TQM. The IRS benefits from good relations with its union, the National Treasury Employees Union, which agreed in 1987 to a new relationship based on cooperation rather than confrontation.[18] The mass-production work of the IRS lends itself readily to quality improvement. The IRS is mostly a vast paper and data factory. Its 120,000 employees processed 204 million returns in 1992 and collected $1.12 trillion in revenues.[19] For all these reasons the IRS is more responsive to TQ remedies, relatively speaking, than other parts of the government.

The IRS also has monumental problems to solve, including appalling working conditions, low morale, antiquated equipment, and shocking error rates. After a visit to the IRS center in Andover, Massachusetts, in 1990

Money magazine reported that it had found 3,400 employees laboring "in a dreary, largely windowless space the size of five football fields. Mail clerks, who begin the processing of returns, sit at paper-shuffling nightmares called Tingle tables (after the IRS employee who designed them in the mid-1960s). Each clerk confronts 18 bins, stacked three high, into which he or she is expected to sort 265 returns and related documents an hour. To combat this mind-numbing work, many clerks wear headsets tuned to their favorite rock station. The roof leaks so strategically that during heavy rainfalls employees have to position wastebaskets on top of their computers to prevent them from being drowned. Supplies are so limited that if you need a stapler, you may have to barter your calculator with another worker for it." Andover had the highest error rate of all the IRS centers.[20]

Even as Andover struggled with its Dickensian conditions, the IRS had started to improve. After reaching that important agreement with the union in 1987, the Service began to form teams to tackle its mass of problems. By 1992, some 1,000 improvement teams had finished their projects and hundreds more were at work. Savings at that point totaled more than $300 million, according to Kolak. Many of the savings came from a lot of little improvements, but one idea, from the Austin, Texas office on a better way to find nonfilers, held the promise of saving billions.[21]

The IRS showcase can be found at Ogden, Utah, the IRS's largest center. Ogden's 5,700 employees handle 26 million tax returns a year. Under Robert Wenzel, who became director of the center in 1986, Ogden formed teams to break bottlenecks and improve morale. Employees who write to taxpayers now sign letters personally and include their telephone numbers. With the addition of a sense of responsibility or ownership, letters issued from Ogden became more accurate. The proportion of outgoing letters containing an error fell from a shameful 40% in 1986 to below 8% in 1990. Instead of requiring an average of four contacts with a taxpayer to resolve a dispute, it now takes only two.[22] The Ogden center tested a number of steps in the IRS's modernization program, including the automated "underreporter" system. With this system, the IRS will be able to spot differences between the income a taxpayer reports and what their employees or other sources of income report by computer rather than by the laborious manual comparison of batches of documents. The Ogden center won the Presidential Award for Quality in 1992, becoming the first civilian agency to win the top quality prize in government. Previous winners of the award, established in 1989, were Navy and Air Force units.[23]

Giving the Right Answer

The IRS's struggles to transform itself resulted in an unusual document for a government agency, a strategic plan to carry the IRS into the 21st century. The plan states three objectives: to increase voluntary taxpayer compliance (be a friendlier IRS); to reduce the burden on taxpayers (simplify the returns), and to "improve quality-driven productivity and customer satisfaction," which is just what an enlightened corporation might say. To achieve these objectives, the IRS has five strategies. The first is called "Compliance 2000," to increase compliance by helping and educating taxpayers, by simplifying the regulations and procedures, and by tightening enforcement. The second is to practice "total quality" by using a systems and cross-functional approach, by reducing errors, developing measurements, and identifying the customers' needs. The third is "tax systems modernization," principally by spending $8.3 billion to replace the agency's hodgepodge of old computers; today only 2% of the data stored by the IRS is electronic; the rest is still on paper. The modernization plan includes the purchase of 50,000 workstations and 3,000 minicomputers, which AT&T will furnish. (The fourth and fifth strategies relate to diversity and ethics, which seem to have more to do with social responsibility than with the performance of the agency.)[24]

After all this, how is the IRS doing? Well, it is improving, somewhat. The General Accounting Office entitled one of its frequent reports on the agency, "IRS's 1992 Filing Season Was Successful but Not Without Problems." Taxpayers calling the IRS got the correct answer to their questions 88% of the time in 1992, compared to 84% in 1991 and a big improvement over 1989, when the poor taxpayer got the correct answer only 63% of the time. On the other hand, it was harder to get through to ask your question. While the IRS picked up 58% of the calls in 1989, it answered only 33% in 1992. (Perhaps that is because it took longer to give the correct answer than the wrong one: the IRS had more tax "assistors," as they are called, in 1992 and tried to assign more experienced people to the job.) The GAO found that 45% of the taxpayers who received checks for earned income credits (for low-income families with children) were not entitled to them, creating an estimated loss of $175 million. The mailing of forms to taxpayers slowed in 1992 and necessary forms were less likely to be available in IRS offices. Accounts receivable, money that the IRS has not collected (largely because of weak collection procedures) increased in 1992 by $7.5 billion to $70.9 billion.

On the positive side, the IRS performed well in delivering refunds, which is certainly one way to the taxpayer's heart. Nine out of the ten service centers sent the correct refunds 98% of the time, and all ten met the goal of averaging 40 days or less to get the refunds out. Many taxpayers found it easier to file their taxes by using the new "EZ" forms and by filing electronically. The number of returns filed electronically jumped to 11 million in 1992, up from 7.6 million in 1991.[25] The IRS has made a start.

AIR MOBILITY COMMAND

The military have contributed more to the advancement of quality concepts in America than one might imagine. The Pentagon is not solely devoted to cost overruns and procurement fiascos. During World War II, the Army and the Navy sponsored the first significant use of modern quality methods based on the statistical controls created by Walter Shewhart at AT&T in the 1920s (see Chapter 1). Shewhart and Deming served on a committee that developed the American War Standards requiring World War II military contractors to use statistical controls to assure the quality of the weapons they built. These wartime standards were the basis for the quality standards developed since. The people trained in statistical methods all over the United States by the War Department came together in several groups and societies which later merged to become the American Society for Quality Control, formed in 1946.[26] Soon after World War II, it was the U.S. Army that first began teaching statistical quality control to the Japanese. While the Japanese absorbed the lesson, American manufacturers were themselves so busy satisfying the huge postwar demand for goods that they forgot all about quality assurance. As Juran says, "Quality always goes down during shortages."[27]

With their strong traditions, their insistence on obedience, and their top-down command structures the armed forces would seem to be barren ground for the TQM philosophy. However, the military do have attributes favorable to the TQM philosophy that business lacks. The military stress leadership. The whole focus of officers' training is on leadership. A civilian can go all the way through college, on to business school, and then into corporate life without being taught anything at all about leadership. Most leaders in business today have studied finance, accounting, marketing, personnel administration, and management, but not leadership. Business schools belatedly woke up to the need to teach leadership in the 1980s. The leadership that the military learn consists of much more than how to bark out a command—a modern officer rarely gives a direct order. Good leadership means having a vision, setting an example, caring for the people you lead. These are things that the military learn, and they are needed in a TQM organization.

Lifetime education is another advantage the military have over business. Some corporations, such as IBM and Motorola, require managers to take annual or at least frequent courses, but most provide no training at all for their employees beyond sending a few of the anointed to executive training at prestigious business schools for a few weeks. The military, on the other hand, send their rising officers off to get large periodic doses of education at universities and institutions like the war colleges. As they climb through the ranks, they learn more about the larger world outside the military—and TQM is one of the things they learn about today.

If the military had an emotional event comparable to the Japanese invasion of the auto market, it was earlier: the disastrous era of Robert McNamara's tenure as secretary of defense combined with the Vietnam War. Overcentralized micro-management and obsessive standardization, plus a bad war, left the military of the 1970s demoralized, poorly equipped, and poorly maintained. The gut processes of the military, like procurement and maintainance, had become bureaucratic monsters. Thoughtful officers began looking for ways out of the mess. Like industry, they spotted quality circles early on. Had you visited the Norfolk Naval Shipyard or the Watervliet Arsenal in New York, where they made big guns, in 1980 you would have found quality circles looking for ways to save money. As Osborn and Gaebler relate in *Reinventing Government*, Lieutenant General W. L. Creech became an Air Force hero by getting rid of the McNamara legacy after he took over the decrepit Tactical Air Command in 1978. He pushed authority downward in the command, gave his people authority, started using measurements, and promoted morale boosters such as recognition and a general sprucing up of the facilities. By the time he retired in 1984, more planes were ready to fly, fewer planes were crashing, pilots were getting more time in the air, and spare parts were readily available.[28]

Let the Pilot Decide

Like most organizations, military and otherwise, the Air Force operated by the old "give-no-quarter, only-by-the-book, I-gotcha-now" inspection philosophy of quality. Gradually that began to change. In 1980, the Air Force changed its terminology from "quality control" to "quality assurance," a recognition that quality inspection alone could not achieve excellence—it came more from motivated, well-trained people.[29] In bits and pieces, in various units and installations, and at the Pentagon, TQM ideas began to take hold in the Air Force and the other services.

A few weeks after taking command of the Air Mobility Command (then known as the Military Airlift Command) in 1989, General Hansford T. Johnson was conferring with his staff when a question came up about a MAC plane that had cut short a flight to Bangkok. It was a C-141 (the military equivalent of a Boeing 707) on a round-the-world embassy mission. When it got to India it ran into Air Force regulations about crew time. An air crew's working day is limited to 14 hours, and if preparation for the mission takes two hours, time in the air is limited to 12 hours. This crew's air time would have exceeded the 14-hour limit had the plane continued to Bangkok, so the pilot radioed headquarters for permission to exceed the limit, as regulations required him to do. The two-star general whose waiver was needed could not be found, and the plane stayed on the ground. When Johnson heard this he asked whether a pilot who knew his crew's condition, his plane's condition, the local weather, and the priority of the mission really had to wait on the decision of a general halfway around the world who knew none of these things. When told that was so, Johnson declared that henceforth the pilot would make the decision. When an officer spluttered that he could not do that, Johnson said he just had. That was how total quality made its appearance in the Air Mobility Command, a force of 80,000 responsible for moving military passengers and cargoes around the world.[30]

At headquarters at Scott Air Force Base in Illinois, Johnson called in his new inspector general, Brigadier General (then Colonel) Donald E. Loranger, and told him he was in charge of "Action Eagle." The mystified Loranger asked what that might be and Johnson replied vaguely that it had to do with empowerment, trusting others, and a new way of working. Loranger found an officer who had been studying total quality, Lieutenant Colonel John E. Hayden, and read the material he had assembled. He attended a seminar at the Federal Quality Institute. Juran and others came to help design a process. During the course of 1990, AMC unrolled its Quality Plan with a clattering of new military nomenclature, such as QETs (Quality Enhancement Teams) and QVs (Quality Visits).

On August 2, 1990 Iraq invaded Kuwait and five days later President Bush deployed American forces for Operation Desert Shield, starting the largest airlift in American history. The 20 most senior officers at AMC were scheduled to take quality training for three days beginning August 11. Since AMC (still known as MAC at that time) was responsible for the airlift and was in a pandemonium organizing the flights to support Desert Shield, everyone in the command assumed that Johnson would cancel the training. He did not. In the middle of a war, he and his generals and colonels sat through eight hours of training each day for three days. "A lot of people were incredulous," Loranger recalls, but Johnson's decision sent a strong message through the command: If a four-star general takes quality this seriously, we should too. The decision sent out a second message: the working stiffs at AMC were capable of running an airlift. They did not need a four-star general hovering over them all the time. (Obviously Johnson and his senior managers did not isolate themselves for the whole three days. They made themselves available during breaks and put in hours of work after the training sessions finished each day.)[31]

AMC launched the airlift with its traditional measure of getting as much into the air as possible. It looked at departures rather than deliveries. With all the men and supplies pouring out of bases all over the United States, huge bottlenecks developed at the staging bases in Spain and Germany and at the unloading points in Riyadh and Dhahran. Crews sat for hours waiting for refueling, sometimes putting in more than 30 hours on duty. At the bases in Spain and Germany as many as 30 planes could be waiting for servicing. By pushing authority to control the flow of aircraft down from the States to the base in Ramstein and empowering Ramstein to hold aircraft Stateside, AMC steadied the traffic flow and the unloadings in Saudi Arabia picked up. Using regular process-improvement tools, a team in the States improved the approach to loading the planes. Teams coordinating with the "customers," the units in Saudi Arabia, learned how to make up the cargoes so they could be most easily digested at the other end, and then passed the word back to the units that were delivering materiel to the Stateside airfields. Loranger figures that the improvements increased MAC's airlift capacity by 20%. At one point AMC was going to ask for more aircraft, in addition to its own and the 200 commercial airliners it had requisitioned from the civil reserve fleet, but the improvements in the airlift made this unnecessary.[32]

The Empowered Airman

As the Desert Shield airlift built up, AMC also turned its attention to the maintenance mechanics at home. Like almost everybody else, AMC had the traditional inspect-and-blame approach to management. When an airman-mechanic finished a job on a plane, the line chief would come by to check the work and sign off, and maybe an inspector would follow to check him too. Often, if the line chief trusted the mechanic, he would sign the write-up without bothering to get out of his truck. Late in 1990, AMC pulled in some of those line chiefs and inspectors—the very people who might perceive that TQM would cost them their jobs—and set them up as a team at headquarters to study what was wrong with the current process and figure out how to improve it. What they came up with was a new approach that eliminated

much of the inspection and gave the mechanics themselves, once they were
certified in a particular maintenance job, the power to sign the write-up.
After testing that approach successfully at Altus Air Force Base in Okla-
homa for the first six months of 1991, AMC adopted it for the whole
command. The idea is that once a mechanic shows he can do a certain job,
then he could be trusted to do it right.[33]

As happens in other institutions, a change in command at AMC in 1993
signaled a check on the progress of total quality. The four generals who had
driven TQM in the command left for retirement or other assignments, and
Johnson was replaced by General Robert Fogleman, a disciple of Creech's
but not a quality fanatic. In the macho tradition of the Air Force, an outgoing
commander clears the base before his successor arrives. Thus Loranger did
not get a chance to pass on his enthusiasm for TQM to his successor.

In his next assignment, as commander of the 435th Airlift Wing at Rhine/
Main, Brigadier General Donald Loranger found himself in charge of the
airlift to Bosnia. He saw how much the Air Force was changing. In earlier
days, he would have been ordered to fly the airlift and then told in detail how
to do it. Now he was given the mission and allowed to figure out how to do
it with his staff.

Touring the base one day he found an Air Policeman studying a new
training book he had to master to get a promotion. It was an introduction to
TQM. Another day he found out that a captain and three senior enlisted men,
loadmasters and riggers, had been tossing packages of MREs—the so-called
meals-ready-to-eat that the military inflict on their people in the field—from
the top of the control tower. Here was a spontaneous team trying to solve a
problem. The wing was parachuting containers of MREs into Bosnia. These
containers each weighed 1,800 pounds and hit the ground at 55 m.p.h., so
they were too lethal to drop directly on villages. But shrinking perimeters
left little space outside the villages for the drops. The team had gone to
fundamentals and had seen that the problem was not how to drop a container
weighing nearly a ton safely on a village but how to get food to the villagers.
The airmen were dropping individual packets of MREs off the tower to test
their speed and damage inflicted. The packets landed relatively undamaged
and at a maximum speed of 58 m.p.h. Weighing only 1.2 pounds each, they
would not be lethal; the impact would hurt a person about as much as a
softball. So the idea proved sound—but how do you shovel hundreds of
packages of MREs out of a plane fast enough to make the drop? The team
devised a carton with a lanyard that remains attached to the plane. The carton
is pushed overboard and when the lanyard draws tight, it explodes, and 480
MREs tumble out. During the summer of 1993, U.S. aircraft delivered 555

tons of MREs to places like Mostar by this method. On one run, an aircraft can drop 6,700 MREs on an area 1,800 yards long by 700 yards wide. The Pentagon was impressed enough with this delivery method to contract for a new ration pack designed specifically for a free-fall delivery.[34]

Policies Instead of Rules

Back at Scott Air Force Base in Illinois, the word "quality" is not heard as often as it was. But mechanics can still sign off on their own work. More important now than what happens at AMC, the whole Air Force is moving toward total quality. Previously, individual units were able to adopt TQM (AMC was the first operational command to do so). Under General Merrill A. McPeak, the chief of staff and a quality enthusiast, the Air Force formed a quality council of top officers, including McPeak, that met six times in 1992 to discuss how to achieve what they are calling the "Quality Air Force." The results are becoming apparent. For example, since the Air Force is to be governed now by policy rather than detailed rules, 1,500 regulations covering 35,000 pages have been boiled down to 155 more general policy directives that tell Air Force people what to do but not exactly how to do it. The Air Force has established a Quality Center at Maxwell Air Force Base, Alabama, with a staff of 50 to train instructors who will work throughout the service.[35]

The other armed services have their quality initiatives too, although the Air Force has probably gone farther than the Navy, and the Navy farther than the Army. A summary of what they are doing would probably become repetitive. However, it is worth noting what the Chief of Naval Operations, Admiral Frank B. Kelso, II, wrote in the *Proceedings of the U.S. Naval Institute* in 1992. He said that the "drawdown" and restructuring of the military means that the Navy,

> simply cannot continue with business as usual. That is the single most important reason total quality leadership (TQL) is such a high priority. TQL is not a fad. In fact it is critical to the operational success of the Navy in the years ahead. . . . Every job—every process—in the Navy must be examined in light of its contribution to the overall effectiveness of the Navy as a whole. TQL is the blueprint we will use to improve the Navy's processes.

Kelso cited the Navy's own success stories with TQL in Desert Storm and elsewhere. For example, he said, the Naval Air Warfare Center in Indianapolis applied quality tools to speed the flow of Walleye missiles to the Middle East and cut production time from an average of 123 days to 29 days. TQL master trainers were taking courses so they could provide Navy-wide instruction. The top 800 officers and civilian executives in the Navy had already attended week-long seminars. Kelso reported that the Navy had just mailed out a new *Navy Policy Book* that he hoped would be a catalyst for improvement. He agreed that in the short run TQL increased the workload in commands that had tried it, but he concluded resoundingly, "In the long run, it will decrease our reliance on inspections, lower our accident rate, improve our efficiency by reducing repetitive and unproductive work, and upgrade our quality of life. It will take time and hard work, but we will have a Navy built on the concept of total quality leadership."[36]

MADISON, WISCONSIN

Madison, a state capital with an experimental turn of mind, is a hotbed of quality activism today. It has been home to the Progressive Party and other movements ahead of, or outside, the mainstream. A small lakeside city, Madison harbors in pleasant proximity the University of Wisconsin, the state government, and, of course, the city government. They and many local businesses are all pursuing total quality at varying levels of intensity. One of the leading consulting firms in the field of TQM, Joiner Associates Incorporated, a subscriber to the Deming philosophy, has its offices in Madison. The city government got involved in 1983 when an audit revealed the wretched condition of the city's motor vehicle pool. The state government took its first step in 1984 when the revenue department assigned a team to clean up the backlog in tax delinquency notices. The university established its Center for Quality and Productivity Improvement in 1985 under William G. Hunter, a prominent statistician and a Deming disciple. He died the following year and was succeeded by the cofounder of the center, George E. P. Box, a British statistician.

All these activities in Madison acquired a focal point in 1985 with the establishment of one of the early local councils, the Madison Area Quality Improvement Network or MAQIN. The organization drew its membership from colleges and schools, the city and the state government, health organizations, local businesses, labor unions, and the local offices of some national corporations and federal agencies. MAQIN sponsors workshops, seminars, an annual conference, provides information, puts out a newsletter, and does all the good things such organizations usually do. As quality has spread through government and business in Madison, MAQIN's membership has grown, reaching a total of 229 organizations in 1993. Even so, as MAQIN's executive director Barbara Hummel points out, few of Madison's 195,000 citizens are aware of the existence of TQM.[37]

The state's press releases boast of Governor Tommy G. Thompson's commitment to TQM in the state government and refers to the state as the "capital of quality." In fact, though Thompson does talk about total quality and listen sympathetically to those who are seeking it, the state has no overall drive or policy to promote TQM. A state quality council that existed in the 1980s petered out for lack of leadership. Nevertheless, half a dozen state agencies have started quality efforts, notably the department of revenue and the division of motor vehicles. In the legislature, Sue A. Rohan, who has served both on the Madison city council and in the state assembly and as president of MAQIN, found some demand for the quality skills she offered. She served as a facilitator for the Democratic caucus and other groups in the legislature, helping them apply quality tools to make their meetings and other activities more productive and open. She could not keep up with the demand for her services as a consultant in the legislature, she says. But the leadership did not buy her ideas, and Rohan left the legislature to work on the university's quality plans.[38]

The Quick Response: State Government

The Wisconsin department of revenue lends itself particularly well to TQM solutions for the same reasons that the IRS does. It is a mass-production factory processing enormous quantities of paper. W. Michael Ley, a Madison consultant today, was state secretary of revenue in 1984 when he had a lunch with several of the local quality enthusiasts and "got excited very quickly," as he puts it. He passed some literature around his staff and got help with training from Hunter and his students at the university. The department had a big backlog of delinquency notices to process, so Levy formed a team to break it. Instead of coming back with the usual bureaucratic answer that more money and people would be needed, the team used quality tools to pick the process apart. Often the notices could not be typed up because the handwriting on the backup interoffice memos was illegible. Every notice was marked "Rush," so none was rushed. The team's suggestions cut the backlog to an acceptable level of three or four days' worth. However, two other pilot projects started by Ley did not produce good results. His immediate successor as secretary had little interest in TQM, but some of the permanent employees worked unobtrusively to keep it alive.[39]

When current secretary Mark D. Bugher assumed office in 1988 he found "an ember of interest" left, in the bureau of alcohol and excise taxes. He could see no activity elsewhere in the state government, and no overall endorsement of TQM. He liked the quality approach, at least the portions of it that encourage using employees at all levels and data-gathering for making decisions. He says he does not have much tolerance for "group think and seminars." Bugher decided to give quality a high profile in the revenue department, so he appointed a quality improvement coordinator and picked a particularly hot issue: the speed of refunds. Taxpayers want their refunds fast, but the workload at tax time makes that difficult to achieve. In Wisconsin, 70% of the state's 2.4 million taxpayers are entitled to refunds, but 68% of them file in the last two weeks—and expect their refunds right away. Bugher found that the department's performance was slipping. The department was six to eight weeks slower with its refunds than the IRS, which is the standard the public uses.

Bugher and his staff put together a team to develop a quick refund system. The team consisted of 20 people, more than is usually considered ideal, but this one had to cross the lines between many bureaus. It did not include any of the department's top managers. The team took a year to come up with a solution. Its data gathering showed that only 10% of the returns had errors in them, but all the refunds were held up while all the returns were checked thoroughly for errors. The team suggested that the system be designed for the 90% who get their returns right, rather than the 10% who make a mistake. That was one of the ideas included in the quick-refund plan. The returns are checked only for the basics of name, address, and Social Security number, and then the refund goes out. The errors are cleared up later. In the first year, the department sent 456,000 refunds out within the targeted two weeks, and by 1992 760,000 taxpayers got their quick refunds.[40]

One thing motorists hate is standing in line to renew their registrations. They get even madder when they see the clerk attending their line saunter off to take a break. When the Wisconsin Division of Motor Vehicles put this annoyance at the top of its list of problems to be tackled by its quality initiative, it discovered that the clerks were not taking breaks at all but going into the back room to check vehicle identification numbers against the list of stolen cars, as required by law. When a manager asked how many stolen cars were recovered that way, no one could remember a single instance. The division got the legislature to change the law, and stopped checking. The division also introduced phone-in registration renewal. Drivers pay with their credit cards and get their new stickers in two or three days. The division studied how to make those hideous license photos more attractive, and suggests a retake if the first picture does not turn out well. When motorists complained that the offices closed too early, and the state legislature threatened to legislate late hours, the division asked its employees to figure out new schedules. For the state workers, who had assumed that the workday would forever end at 4:30 P.M., the experience was traumatic, but they figured out new staggered hours, starting and ending later, varying them in different cities depending on the patterns of demand they found. Division Administrator Roger D. Cross came out of banking in 1991 to take over the division with "the usual prejudices against state government." But when he found out what quality processes could accomplish, he saw the job as "the opportunity of a lifetime."[41]

Going for the Low Sticker Price: City Government

The city of Madison presents a singularly interesting case of quality and government, probably the most interesting in the United States. Unlike the state of Wisconsin, the city has a quality initiative championed by its top elected leaders, its mayors. They have pushed the initiative throughout the city government. They have kept the initiative going (with ups and downs) for ten years, sustaining it through elections, political uproars, and the succession of rival politicians.

Just after he was elected mayor of Madison in 1983, L. Joseph Sensenbrenner, the state's 34-year-old deputy attorney general, welcomed Deming at the start of a two-day seminar in the city and stayed on to listen to part of it himself. The concepts of quality intrigued him and a tight budget was forcing him to seek new solutions, so he looked around for a pilot project to see if the principles could be applied to government (which Deming doubted at the time). As it happened Sensenbrenner had just received a depressing audit on the abysmal state of the First Street municipal garage, which cares for the city's squad cars, dump trucks, refuse packers, and road scrapers. The city had given up preventive maintenance of its vehicles 20 years earlier as an economy move, so 75% of the cases brought to the garage were breakdowns; only 25% of the vehicles came in for regular maintenance. (In a well-run garage, the ratios are the reverse.) Vehicles spent an average of nine days in the garage before they were once more fit for use. Spare parts traveled through a 24-step process with multiple controls.

Sensenbrenner suppressed the urge to raise hell, and instead moved slowly over the next two years to take a quality approach to improving the system. He brought in some trainers from the Joiner group, enlisted the support of the union president, and set up teams to look for the causes of the garage's failures.

Repairs were slow, the mechanics and parts people reported, because they could not stock enough parts for so many types of vehicles. In a fleet of 765, the city had accumulated 440 different types, makes, and models of vehicles.

Why was that?

The parts purchaser said central purchasing insisted that the city buy the vehicle with the lowest sticker price at the time of purchase.

Why?

Because the city comptroller insisted.

Why?

Because that was the city attorney's policy.

It turned out that the city attorney had no such policy. As long as the city got the proper warranties and parts guarantees, it could buy compatible vehicles even when they were not the cheapest available.

Garage employees figured out how to reduce the 24 steps for purchasing parts to three. Mechanics rode with police and found that while they were tuning the cars for high-speed chases, the cars in fact spent most of their time idling. They got drivers of city vehicles to start using check sheets to report the condition of their vehicles. Average turnaround time in the garage dropped from nine to three days.

When Sensenbrenner first went before the city council and the board of estimate to request a modest $5,000 for training, he did not mention pilot projects or TQM. Sensibly, he talked instead of savings and improved performance. For every $1 spent on preventive maintenance the city would save $7—and could send seven more vehicles out in a snowstorm.[42]

David Couper had been police chief of Madison for 10 years when Sensenbrenner was elected mayor.* Couper, an ex-Marine, describes himself in those days as belonging to "the kick-ass and take-names school of management which permeates our culture, even our families." His officers still carried a reputation they acquired in the 1960s as a force of right-wing hippie-bashers. Couper ordered them to be nice to the citizenry but to no one's surprise that did not work. Today he says, "Policing is not failing because of a lack of ideas, but because we want the police to give us a sensitive and democratic service but we are not willing to treat police officers that way."

Early in the Sensenbrenner administration, Couper went to a session on quality. He walked out in disgust before it was over. "I wasn't going to take that crap," he says. "God forbid that we should treat people with a sense of decency in the workplace." However, his deputy chief started reading books

---

* The relatively restricted powers of the mayor do not include hiring and firing department heads.

about quality and passed them on to Couper. What caught his interest were not the regular quality textbooks, but business books about companies that were achieving excellence. Couper, who has graduate degrees in sociology and criminology, says he needed the intellectual basis for changing his mind which these books provided. He began to see how TQM might transform the police force to what he wanted it to be.

The Criminal as Customer: The Madison Police

Together with a group of officers he identified as progressive, Couper established an elected council of officers to work out a mission statement for the police. It would concentrate on peacekeeping rather than crime prevention. Couper established in 1986 an experimental police district on the South Side of Madison where the officers elected their own captains and lieutenants from a list of qualified candidates. Policemen began patrolling the streets on foot, showing up at neighborhood meetings, and knocking on doors to find out what was bothering people. The police in the district set their own schedules. They learned that most of the overtime was put in by officers answering emergency calls near the end of their shifts. But a high percentage of those calls were not real emergencies; they were for barking dogs and such matters. So the precinct decided if a barking-dog-type emergency call came in 45 minutes before the end of a shift, the dispatcher would put it on a "B" list to be answered by the next shift. Overtime hours in that district dropped to one fifth of what they were in the rest of the Madison police. While burglaries in Madison went up 15% from 1986 to 1989, they dropped 28% in the experimental district.

Many of Couper's initiatives went beyond the experimental district. In low-income neighborhoods the police began working as teams with firemen, social welfare workers, and health and building inspectors. They all look out for each other's problems. If a police officer sees a violation the building inspector should know about, he tells the inspector. The Madison police now hire more people with college degrees, more older people, more minorities, and more women—more than 25% of the officers today are women. The recruits are chosen partly for their aptitude for teamwork and collaboration.

Any quality process is incomplete unless it knows its customers, so the Madison police survey their customers, including the people they arrest. For every 35th case, the police send out a survey to the victims, the witnesses, and the alleged perpetrators to find out what they think of the service. A sampling of these surveys in the fall of 1992 supported a point Couper makes that "what drives people nuts is not burglaries but barking dogs and

loud parties. Noise is the Number One urban problem in the United States.''
In the old days people would talk to their neighbors about a problem like
that. Today they call 911. The Madison police are trying to teach people how
to take care themselves of matters that are less than emergencies.[43]

Doug Kratsch, a solid Madison citizen who is vice president of the South
Central Federation of Labor (AFL-CIO) of Wisconsin and who has served
on the city council and as chairman of the public safety review board, finds
Madison's police much improved. ''They were brutal,'' he says. ''The tenor
has changed. The police are now respected. I think we now have the best
police department in the U.S. A Los Angeles situation is inconceivable
here.'' Relations between the police and its union, once dreadful, are now
good.[44]

By 1989 Sensenbrenner was coming to the end of his third term. He had
established quality processes fairly securely in six city departments: Community Services, Data Processing, Health, Madison Metro (the municipal
bus company), Police, and Streets. Sensenbrenner had hired Tom Mosgaller,
a one-time organizer for the community activist, Saul Alinsky, as a city
coordinator for quality and installed him in the mayor's suite of offices. In
1987 Sensenbrenner had offered pay raises to the five department heads he
thought were contributing the most to total quality, including Couper, and he
was astonished when they all turned him down. They apparently were so
imbued with quality concepts that they said singling out individuals for
rewards was not right.

But after three terms, Sensenbrenner's popularity had slipped. He was not
very adept politically and many of the city's bureaucrats resented his efforts
to push quality. Some of his associates felt he was poor at making decisions,
allowing the quality process to substitute for making up his mind. In the
elections that year he faced another Democrat,* Paul Soglin, who had already served as mayor in the 1970s. TQM did not become an issue in the
election, which was fought mainly over a plan, backed by Sensenbrenner, to
build a convention center.

Soglin won, and Madison got the sort of mayor you might expect in a city
with its reformist background. Soglin wears a flamboyantly droopy mustache and is a former student radical, ex-treasurer of the Student Nonviolent
Coordinating Committee, arrested three times, veteran of the Chicago riots
of 1968. He still considers himself part of the left, he says, but has a different
view of the world. Today he is a popular and acceptable Democrat, a bit of
a cowboy in politics, with a personal style.

* In Madison, mayoral candidates do not run on party tickets.

At first it seemed as if TQM might disappear with Soglin's election. He came to office with a chip on his shoulder about it. On his way out, Sensenbrenner had given those raises to the five department heads who he thought had helped the most, and this time the raises were accepted. Soglin resented that. He says, "I give Sensenbrenner a lot of credit for starting quality, but it was done in a way that created tremendous resistance and backlash. I am still dealing with that. It was perceived as hypocrisy. If you wanted a larger share of the budget you called it a quality project even if you had no data to back that up." He had a meeting with Deming and Myron Tribus that went badly, he says, because they would not admit that any mistakes had been made. He did not get along with Couper. He threw Mosgaller, the quality coordinator, out of the mayor's office and exiled him to share quarters with the animal-control officer.

However, Soglin found that quality would not go away. Mosgaller refers to this period as the "catacomb experience." The departments that had quality processes continued to develop them. Soglin found that TQM had a logic that he liked, and the idea of pushing responsibility down into the community appealed to him. He was thinking deeply about how to get the city's 2,500 employees and 195,000 inhabitants to work better together. He says now that "the ideas intrigued me a lot—despite the efforts of Deming and Tribus to convince me." He got over the resentments that he brought with him from the election. He began talking to Mosgaller, and "the more I talked to him the more I embraced quality." He brought Mosgaller back from the catacombs with enhanced responsibilities for training as well as quality. He made total quality a goal for the entire city government. By 1993, the Planning and Development department had joined the other six city departments that had chosen TQM. The Fire Department, which had resisted before, started some team projects and the city began training all employees.[45]

Soglin's acceptance of TQM, curiously, alienated some of his old friends of the left. "The problem with political correctness is they want to define me out of the left," he says. "Some say I have sold out, but I think the left should embrace TQ." It does give politics a different color. It undermines the prevalent idea that you ought to get what you want by confrontation. Where would that leave Saul Alinsky's movement? Or most other movements and lobbies?

But total quality could go beyond changing style and tone and basically change the orientation of politics and government. So much of government today is based on finding needs and problems and then figuring out what to do about them. It is an attitude that focuses on weaknesses, thereby encouraging the discovery of more weaknesses needing attention. Government expands the failures of society. TQ provides a way of looking in the other direction to find the strengths in a community—not what the politicians think they are but what the people in the community think they are—and encouraging them. Rather than throwing our energies away on an inexhaustible supply of problems, why not find out what we can do well, do it, and see what happens then to our problems? In this respect, Madison is far ahead of almost all other political entities in America. Sensenbrenner and Soglin have started an interesting journey.

CONCLUSIONS

The proposition that total quality can make government work better as it has made business work better is not yet fully proven in the United States or anywhere else. However, these conclusions can be drawn:

- The tools and principles of TQM appear to be as applicable to many aspects of government as they are to other human activities.
- If the road to quality is long and hard in business, it is longer and harder in government.
- The public is unlikely to get excited about total quality, and politicians are unlikely to win any votes by advocating it.
- The short-term, ideological, confrontational, personalized nature of politics all works against quality.
- On the other hand, the sheer size and uncontrollability of government allows total quality to survive here and there and reemerge even when the people at the top are indifferent or hostile.
- In view of the sad state of government, of the size of public debt, the growth of spending, the inefficiency of service—in short, the general incompetence we suffer in our public services and servants—we should at least continue to give total quality a try.

Conclusion

A fter 13 years' exposure to the concepts of quality improvement—assuming that 1980 can be set down as the beginning of the movement in the United States—then what have we accomplished and where do we stand? Have we learned a new way of working that produces better products and services economically and makes working more congenial? Or have we simply been indulging in another of those fads that afflict the business community regularly and that regularly disappoint the exaggerated expectations that they raise? If we are doing the right thing, then what must we do to sustain it and to do it better? If we are doing the wrong thing, then what should we do next?

The evidence tells us that even if Total Quality Management has disappointed many businesses and has not been accepted by many others, it is at the least being tested on a vast scale. As we have seen in this book, not only is TQM prevalent in large manufacturing companies and, by necessity, among their suppliers, it is also widespread among smaller manufacturers and in service industries. Its use is growing in education, the professions, and government. After a relatively slow diffusion of TQM in the 1980s, the pace of growth picked up in the 1990s. Since most of the organizations practicing TQM started it recently, it is too early to know whether they will succeed broadly. Certainly there has been widespread disappointment among many of the entrants. However, for those who started early and did it right, TQM has proven that it can produce spectacular results here in America, with American managers and American workers. That success is not enough to assure its permanent acceptance. The faith, enthusiasm, and hero worship among the quality boffins may blind them to several large obstacles:

- After 13 years, indifference to TQM remains widespread in the United States, and those who are aware of it are frequently skeptical or critical.
- TQM has already survived well beyond the normal span of American management's patience with new ideas. Signals of restlessness and the search for something new are already evident.

• The spread of TQM clashes directly with another force driving American executives: the tough if not ruthless determination of some to cut people and plants and replace them with cheaper temporary and contract labor. Just when we need more trust, management breaks the implicit social contract between corporation and employee.

Fatally Flawed? TQM on the Carpet

Tom Peters, never shy with his opinions, has already predicted the coming death of TQM. He wrote in his newsletter in 1992: "TQM is flawed. The Baldrige is flawed. Or so I used to think. Now I think they're *fatally* flawed. Prediction: Twenty years from now, when the history is written of the epic transformation of American business during the 1980s and 1990s, TQM won't even get a footnote (though maybe a couple of laughs)."[1] Thus Peters, whose *In Search of Excellence* started many executives on the path to quality, leaves his fans behind and goes on to his new discovery, quality in Germany. In truth, what Peters was really condemning was the excesses of TQM, the "bureaucratic bull" that has attended some efforts that are all charts, graphs, meetings, and procedures, with but little empowerment or results.

Another line of criticism takes some of the extremes of TQM and sets them up as straw men. An article in *The New Republic* by Leon Wieseltier, the magazine's literary editor, overintellectualized the implications of TQM to a bizarre degree. Does not TQM include the word "total," "one of the most sinister adjectives in the language"? Furthermore, does not TQM foster "the cult of leadership"? Put the two together, mix in some of Deming's more messianic statements, argue that they form the core of the Clintons' philosophy, and before you know it, gosh, you are looking at the birth of a totalitarian state. Wieseltier sees in Vice President Gore's National Performance Review "an orgy of TQM."[2]

Rather than an orgy, what we might get, if we are lucky, is a few morsels of better government here and there. It is hard to imagine today the whole government smothered in a righteous crusade for total quality. Wieseltier misinterprets much of what TQM stands for. It believes in leaders, certainly, but not the authoritarian dictators that he seems to fear. The leaders of quality organizations show the way by example, by commitment, and by constancy of purpose, not by dominating. On the contrary, it is a basic principle of TQM that the leader should delegate power down through the organization. TQM is democratic, not totalitarian.

Of course, the spokesmen for total quality tend to generate suspicion or derision because they do sometimes act like members of a cult, carry their hero worship too far, and obscure their thinking with too much jargon and too much alphabet soup.* In his last book, Deming contributed to the tone of righteous crusade. He speaks of the government agencies that require quarterly reports as "evil forces" (because they encourage short-term thinking and planning) and he writes of the individual transformed by "profound knowledge" so that he perceives "new meaning to his life, to events, to numbers, to interactions between people."[3]

With some big exceptions, the media have provided more of a forum for the critics of TQM than for its supporters. The NBC White Paper of 1980 had enormous influence in introducing Americans to the potential of total quality, and *Business Week, Fortune, Industry Week, Training* and *USA Today* cover total quality with interest. However, for the most part the media mix indifference with an occasional stab. A lead article in *The Wall Street Journal* in 1993, for example, reported a decade after the fact that quality circles were going out of style, but neglected to say that other forms of teamwork and participation have taken root in much of U.S. business.[4] Of course, it is the duty of journalists to be skeptical, and when confronted with something that promises to be uplifting their skepticism turns to cynicism and derision. When TQM invades the newsroom, then we will know that it has been accepted. A number of publications have approached total quality tentatively and with caution. At my own alma mater, Time Inc., attempts to introduce quality thinking were met mostly with derision, at least on the editorial side, although the books division in Alexandria, Virginia, is applying TQM ideas to speed and streamline the editing process. At *The New York Times* a retreat to talk about radical change along the lines of TQM turned bitterly contentious.[5] At this writing, *USA Today* is planning its TQM ap-

*Ron Zemke, the senior editor of *Training* magazine, a witty and sympathetic observer of quality enthusiasts in action, wrote this description of a corporate meeting (he was kind enough not to identify the company): "The auditorium lights grow dim. A diffusion of sunrise hues washes languidly across a sweep of rear-projection screens. From beneath the stage level, rising in single file like a septet of hunter's moons, come the seven letters of the sacred rite: Q-U-A-L-I-T-Y. With the weighty dignity of Biblical prophets—or is it more the cosmetic self-assurance of Radio City Music Hall chorines?—the imperial-purple letters take up in turn their proper spots against a field now of blazing gold. As the 'Y' glides into place, the cello strains fade to a whisper. From banks of loudspeakers hidden in the dim reaches of the cavernous room, a rich baritone voice rumbles forth, dripping with Old Testament portent. Thrice it speaks, intoning the Word of Words: Quality. Quality! QUALITY! The auditorium plunges into velvet blackness. Four beats of silence. Then: 'At International GeoWidgets Inc., we are committed to world-class total quality!' The air explodes with light and sound, and the audience is plunged into a multi-media hell: Trumpets blare, trombones boom, cymbals clash, frantic white strobe lights induce nausea in the weak . . . (Ron Zemke, "Faith, Hope, and TQM," *Training* [January 1992], p. 8)

proach and a number of other dailies, including the Madison and Milwaukee papers, already have their quality improvement plans in place.

The Same Old Story: Reengineering

Quality takes time but the American businessman wants results now. TQM has enjoyed an unusually long run for a business theory. It is meant to last forever, of course. But inevitably business theorists are looking for something new, something that will catch the attention of executives sick of hearing about quality and the Japanese, or perhaps disappointed with the results of their attempts at creating TQM. Should we seek salvation instead in the "virtual corporation," a network of companies pared down to their core competencies which bring together the skills needed for a specific product or project and then dissolve to be replaced by another network?

Or should we "reengineer"? Reengineering captured first place among business fads in 1993 with the success of a best-seller, *Reengineering The Corporation*, by Michael Hammer and James Champy. The book is billed as "a manifesto for business revolution." The alternative to reengineering, say the authors of the book, "is for corporate America to close its doors and go out of business. The choice is that simple and that stark."[6] The excitement puzzles some of the business professors and consultants I have talked to, because much of reengineering theory sounds remarkably like TQM. One of the prize cases the authors cite to validate reengineering is that same tale of the improvement of Ford's method of paying vendors that Juran has been citing as an example of total quality (see Chapter 5). The authors admit that reengineering and TQM share common themes, but say the two approaches differ fundamentally because TQM seeks the incremental improvement of existing processes whereas reengineering achieves breakthroughs by discarding existing processes and replacing them with new ones. As we have seen in this book, TQM does in fact achieve breakthroughs and massive, rapid change. Juran points out that successful companies "undertake quality improvement at a revolutionary pace."[7] The approach is different in that TQM assumes that existing processes can be improved, whereas reengineering puts aside the existing processes and starts from scratch. TQM is hard on an organization; reengineering is even harder. With TQM you have a chance to bring the organization along and win support; with reengineering you throw the organization into a new format and hope the support will follow. The tools used in reengineering are almost the same as the tools used in TQM.

"Flipped Upside Down": Reorganization

Since many companies have not achieved that revolutionary pace with their versions of TQM, be they halfhearted or wholehearted, they may look for ways of tweaking it. In 1991, four years after he had become chairman of Aluminum Company of America (Alcoa) and started the company along the road to continuous improvement, Paul O'Neill announced a major reorganization to the company's executives assembled from around the world. "Continuous improvement is exactly the right idea if you are the world leader in everything you do," O'Neill said. "It is a terrible idea if you are lagging the world leadership benchmark. It is probably a disastrous idea if you are far behind the world standard. In too many cases we fall in the second and third categories. In those cases we need rapid, quantum-leap improvement."[8]

To free the company to make those quantum leaps, O'Neill "flipped the organization upside down," as the company's senior vice president for quality, Thomas Carter, puts it.[9] The new structure became an inverted triangle with the 22 business units along the broad top and the chairman at the point at the bottom. It takes a leap of faith to believe that today's munificently paid CEOs really see themselves at the bottom of an organization, but O'Neill, at least, is an exceptional chairman. O'Neill eliminated the two layers of management (the president and the group vice presidents) that separated him from the the business unit presidents, who now became fully responsible for the performance of their businesses. The corporate staff would help them, adjudicate among them, and set corporate goals and policy, but would no longer tell them what to do, how to do it, or inspect them. To prod Alcoa people, every employee's pay, from the factory floor to the chairman's office, has a variable portion, the portion rising with the employee's rank. Half of the variable pay depends on company earnings and the other half on indicators such as quality and safety that each unit can choose for itself.

With their new freedom and incentives, the business units were to shoot for "quantum leaps" in areas where Alcoa's performance most needed improvement. Specifically, within two years they were to close 80% of the gap between Alcoa and the world leaders in 190 areas as determined by benchmarking. The targets chosen would be attacked by high-level or cross-functional teams or whatever resources seem most appropriate for a particular problem. O'Neill's action was interpreted in some places as an abandonment of the company's quality improvement process. In fact, Alcoa's regular quality improvement activities continued in other areas where progress on the order of 10% or less a year was acceptable.[10]

The 190 targets Alcoa picked for special treatment included safety, inventories, long-term debt, the cost of converting alumina into aluminum ingots, and lengthening "pot" life. Alumina is converted to aluminum in carbon-lined steel "pots" by a process invented by Alcoa more than 100 years ago. Pot life is a critical cost factor; to Alcoa's embarrassment, the life of its own pots was below the industry average. By applying quality techniques Alcoa cut its premature pot-lining failures from 100 in 1990 to 24 in 1992. Alcoa hit 31 of its 190 targets by the end of 1992, a year earlier than planned, and expected to achieve costs reductions of $400 million in 1993.[11] While other companies have achieved similar rapid breakthroughs by applying TQM without "reengineering," in Alcoa's case, the reorganization presumably heightened the power of the quality techniques.

In Japan, the maturing of TQM and of the economy itself (which is growing more slowly) provokes some interesting revisionist thinking. The resentment overseas of Japan's aggressive marketing and the desire for a more comfortable life at home may together weaken Japan's single-minded pursuit of better quality in its export products. Akio Morita, the head of Sony, called on Japanese businessmen to change their ways after a trip to Europe where he encountered criticism that obviously shook him. He wrote in 1992 that "Japanese companies should be aware that European and American tolerance for Japanese business practices is reaching their [*sic*] limits. . . . Japanese companies should realize that they will no longer be allowed to continue their single-minded pursuit of economic efficiency and success in the market."

Morita said that Japanese companies pay their employees less, work them longer hours, pay less money to their stockholders, give less to charity, and make their suppliers more subservient than Western companies. The Japanese worked an average of 2,159 hours in the year 1989, compared to 1,957 hours for Americans and 1,638 for Germans. (The Japanese government already promotes the 1,800-hour working year.) Japanese corporations paid out on average 30% of their profits in dividends, compared to 54% in the United States and 66% in Britain in 1990. The Japanese gave .33% of their pretax profits to charity in 1989, versus 1.82% for the Americans. Morita told Japanese employers to ease up by giving their people shorter hours and longer vacations. He urged companies to pay their workers and stockholders more, to treat suppliers more as equals, to give more to their communities, and show more concern for the environment.[12]

Though Morita did not address the matter of quality directly, the things he urges, some of which are already coming to Japan, would in the long run slow the pace of quality improvement in Japan. For example, the Japanese now think in terms of balancing the advantages of just-in-time deliveries with the environmental damage they may cause (see Chapter 5). Yoshinori Iizuka, a young associate professor in the engineering faculty at the University of Tokyo, sees a number of changes coming, including the possible slowing of the rate of improvement. He believes that Japanese thinking about quality should refocus and is doing so. Japan needs to integrate its marketing more into TQM (as many U.S. companies have done) and to focus on the quality of its software (as U.S. companies are doing). *Hoshin* or strategic quality planning needs to be "enriched" to divorce it sharply from annual objectives. It needs to be pointed at the big policy issues facing a company. Iizuka believes Japan needs a new comprehensive textbook about quality, expanding on Ishikawa's works, which are too limited in scope to cover quality as it has evolved.[13] In the meantime, in the view of Noriaki Kano, the passion for improving quality in Japan has cooled, and in the decades ahead Japan's rate of progress will likely be slower than in the past.[14]

Sustaining enthusiasm for TQM in companies that have practiced it for some time becomes a problem as the years go by, more in Japan now than in America simply because Japan started earlier. The tension of straining to reach formidable stretch goals, of constant improving, is bound to lead to a relapse at some point. Success easily becomes complacency. Yotaro Kobayashi, having led Fuji Xerox to a Deming Prize in Japan in 1980, found that the company slumped as the 1980s rolled along. TQM practices became bureauractic and the company lost its edge as younger employees, with no experience of the company's brush with collapse in the 1970s, moved in. Kobayashi introduced what he called the New Work Way in 1988 as an addition, not a substitution, for TQM. Instead of just asking the "five whys" now, Fuji Xerox people are encouraged to ask "Why not?" and take a risk. "We are trying to increase the element of individuality and make it a little more fun and less mechanical," says Kobayashi.[15]

A series of crises, beginning with the postwar chaos, drove Japan over the years. But now with its success and prosperity, Japan does not have the same stimulus. As Kano has said, the crisis of (quality in) Japan is that it there is no crisis. But to Milliken President Tom Malone sustainability is an important issue. Malone does not think stimulation by crisis will work for long, at least not in the United States. He says, "In this country, I believe if we try to drive just on survivability over a long period of time, people will finally say, 'Well, I'm going to go to another company or another industry where there's not such a crisis.' '' The key to sustaining extraodinarily high levels of improvement in America, Malone argues, is leaders who will delegate where appropriate to empower people and then make it stimulating, exciting, and even fun. "What we've got to do," says Malone, "is build on our culture and our culture is one of competition, team success and recognition and achievement, individual recognition after that and applause, applause, applause for those teams that win."[16]

Losing the Cook with the Recipe: Employee Turnover

What should most concern TQM practitioners today is the basic conflict between the need for trust and openness in a TQM company and the thrust of American business to cut people, plants, offices, and whole divisions ruthlessly. Corporations cannot on one hand tell people they are highly valued and on the other treat them as expendable, especially when the CEOs pay themselves munificently. To put it another way, as a headline in *Business Week* did, corporations are "talking marriage and thinking one-night stand."[17] They cannot force out hundreds of thousands of workers, blue-collar and white-collar, as they have done in the last decade and continue to do, without weakening the social contract that presumably existed between company and worker. If you are going to spend many years, or perhaps your whole working life, with one company you are concerned for its welfare and responsive to its pleas. But if you have seen your fellow workers pushed out the door, and if you think that might happen to you at any time, or if you are inclined to skip from company to company, then why should you be ready to give the company everything you have and put your trust in the boss? The wretched level of morale in many parts of IBM has handicapped its market-driven quality efforts. The extreme hostility between labor and management at Caterpillar has certainly hurt its efforts to be more competitive.

A new quality policy, when introduced to employees, is almost inevitably accompanied by the promise that no one will lose his or her job as a result of it. The promise is often meant sincerely, and to the extent that the company uses attrition rather than layoffs the downsizing is relatively painless. However, the efficiencies of TQM are so enormous that inevitably jobs will be lost, whether now or later, on a big scale. If Ford reduces its accounts payable department from 600 to fewer than 200 people, and repeats that operation in many other departments, and if hundreds of other corporations do the same, then clearly TQM has contributed to unemployment. In a time of growth it might not have mattered so much but today, with so much overcapacity hanging over the economy, it does matter. Eventually we will all benefit from the more competitive enterprises created by TQM, but today unemployment and the threat of it create a conflict between employees and management that handicaps TQM.

Robert Cole, the Berkeley scholar, analyzes in a new study the damage to continuous improvement caused by the transience and shallowness of the ties today between employer and employee.[18] He points out that the average annual job turnover rate in the United States is 9.6% (but up to 70% in the motel business and up to 100% in auto sales). Corporations are hiring a growing number of contingent workers, by which Cole means temporary, part-time, and contract workers. Contingents now amount to 25% of the labor force. In the literature on quality improvement, Cole writes, "these practices are typically treated as though they were totally unrelated to the achievement of quality objectives." Companies "loudly declare their support for quality improvement while continuing to reward policies that work against quality improvement."

A high rate of turnover hurts, Cole writes, because employees' memories are repositories of an organization's operational knowledge and trust; sometimes one person is the sole repository of key knowledge. When that person leaves, "it is like losing the cook with the recipe." He continues, "trust is even more problematic than knowledge since it invariably rests with individuals and is based on reliability of performance built up over time. It cannot be 'documented' and thereby passed on to the next incumbent." The lowest-paid workers, such as bank tellers and fast-food restaurant workers, are often at the crucial point of contact with the customer—and they have the highest rates of turnover. When a new employee replaces a knowledgeable employee the "probability of quality failure and customer defection" increases. "There is a subtlety in the job knowledge required for producing high and continually improving quality of products and services," Cole continues. "At the management level it is particularly important to know how to get things done and this requires an intimate knowledge of the politics of an organization." Rapid promotions and transfers can have "devastating" effects on quality because people are likely to cause "greater variation in performance" when they are new to a job and "further disruption when they leave." Contingent workers are less likely to reach the high level of performance of permanent workers and are unlikely to acquire "the depth of intimate knowledge of core internal employees."

We can hope that downsizing on a massive scale will come to an end at some point and lead to more comfortable relations between management and employees. But the use of more contingent labor and the view of many executives that employees are an expense that can be cut will remain a major obstacle to the success of total quality in America.

THE IMPACT OF A DOZEN YEARS

In spite of the criticism, the obstacles, the difficulties, and the many failures and disappointments, quality improvement has, in the dozen or so years since Americans began taking it seriously, had an enormous impact on the way we work and run our businesses and other organizations. TQM may be replaced by some other approach to management. Certainly it will evolve. Those who have succeeded at TQM do not see it as a static set of methods, but as a family of activities with the overarching goal of satisfying the customer. Successful companies keep refining and adding to their quality policies. It is hard to imagine abandoning what has been accomplished and going back to where we were in 1980. Think about how we used to work and how we work today, at least in those companies that are well along in quality improvement:[19]

- We know now that we can achieve quality improvements on a speed and scale that we could not have imagined before. Achieving improvements at a revolutionary pace has become simply good management at the more successful companies.
- We see that close partnerships between suppliers and their customers are preferable to the distant, adversarial relations that were the norm. Corporations collaborate with their suppliers to an extraordinary degree, allowing them access to their premises and computers, accepting shipments without inspection, and making long-term deals with the suppliers that are willing to improve.
- We recognize that employees should be trained continually. Skilled employees are critical to achieving a competitive advantage and are not just another cost. Some companies are giving every employee more than 100 hours of training a year.
- We accept the idea of working in teams. After stumbling at first over quality circles, the team approach succeeded widely and at some companies is now the standard way to tackle big projects like developing new products. The more comfortable we become with teams, the more we move towards fully self-directed work teams that make important decisions about their own work.
- We understand more about the kind of information necessary to run an

organization and how to use it. The need to measure quality activities forced us to develop new measures, to find out what the really important measures are, and to use the results to guide our actions.

- We have learned that it is not enough to design a good product; you must at the same time design the process to produce that product. In fact, Japanese companies spend two thirds of their R&D money on the process and one third on the product. If you do not have a superior process, the competitive advantage of a new product will not last. The process can make the product competitive by adding speed and cutting costs.

- We have finally begun to listen to customers and to understand their needs. An almost obsessive attention to the customer gives the whole company a focus it lacked before. For customers, the experience can be a delight.

- We have seen that benchmarking, one of the most popular tools of total quality, is better than being secretive and pretending we know all the answers. Comparing yourself to the best, or judging yourself by the standards of the Baldrige Award or other such measures, is remarkably refreshing and invigorating.

- We have learned the value of strategic quality management as an umbrella for the all the elements of TQM: to give a company a clear idea of where it is going, what are the key things it must do to get there, how each person's efforts must fit those goals, and how well the company is achieving its goals.

- We have found out that the CEO does not need to be a cowboy, a real tough guy, or a buccaneer. There is a better way to run a company. It means real leadership—by example, by concern, by consistency, by commitment.

These are not small accomplishments. We are creating a new way to work and it is better. America is a much tougher competitor than it was in 1980.

Notes

Introduction

1. This account of the accident is taken from National Transportation Safety Board, *Railroad Accident Report, Derailment of Southern Pacific Transportation Company Freight Train on May 12, 1989 and Subsequent Rupture of Calnev Petroleum Pipeline on May 26, 1989, San Bernardino, California* and from interviews with Southern Pacific executives.
2. Interview with Lloyd Simpson, Vice President of Quality, Southern Pacific Transportation Co., July 1, 1992.
3. Subcommittee on Oversight and Investigations, Committee on Energy And Commerce, U.S. House of Representatives, *The Bork-Shiley Heart Valve: "Earn as You Learn"* (Washington, DC: U.S. Government Printing Office, 1990), pp. 45–46.
4. Pfizer, Inc. press releases.
5. Subcommittee on Oversight and Investigations, *op. cit.*, p. 4.
6. Report of The Presidential Commission on The Space Shuttle *Challenger* Accident.
7. *The New York Times,* "A New Heave in Tax Tug-of-War" (Dec. 8, 1992), p. D1.
8. Craig Walter, Corporate Quality Director, Hewlett-Packard Co., interview with the author, August 20, 1992.
9. Information on the 1940 Lincoln Contintental was obtained by the author on a visit to the Henry Ford Museum in 1976.
10. James R. Houghton, Chairman, Corning Glass Works, speech, Oct. 13, 1987.
11. Craig Barrett, executive vice president, Intel Corporation, interview with the author, August 25, 1992.
12. The Gallup Organization, *Quality: Executive Priority or Afterthought?* (Milwaukee: American Society for Quality Control, 1989); Arthur D. Little Inc., press release, March 24, 1992; Ernst & Young and the American Quality Foundation, *Best Practices Report,* 1992.
13. Delta Consulting Group, "Ten Years After: Learning About Total Quality Management" (New York: 1993); Development Dimensions International, Quality & Productivity Management Association; "TQM: Forging Ahead or Falling Behind?" *IndustryWeek* (April, 1993).

14. Joseph M. Juran, "A Look Back—10 Years of Impro," speech to the Impro conference, Chicago, Nov. 13, 1992.
15. B. Joseph White, dean of the Business School, University of Michigan, interview with the author, February 21, 1992.
16. Kaoru Ishikawa, *What Is Total Quality Control? The Japanese Way* (Englewood Cliffs, NJ: Prentice-Hall, Inc., 1985), pp. 29–34.
17. Juran, *op. cit.*
18. Robert D. Buzzell & Bradley T. Gale, *The PIMS Principles* (New York: The Free Press, 1987), p. 7.
19. *Business Week*, "Betting to Win on the Baldie Winners" (October 18, 1993), p. 8.
20. Newport News Shipyard public relations department.

Chapter 1: The Beginning

1. J. M. Juran, *Quality Control Handbook*, 1st ed. (New York: McGraw-Hill, 1951), p. 34.
2. Roger Milliken, chairman of Milliken & Co., interview with the author, August 12, 1992.
3. Robert W. Galvin, chairman of the executive committee of the board of directors, Motorola Inc., interview with the author, July 30, 1992.
4. A. Blanton Godfrey, "The History and Evolution of Quality in AT&T," *AT&T Technical Journal* (March–April, 1986).
5. Barrett Tillman, *Hellcat: The F6F in World War II.* (Annapolis, Maryland, Naval Institute Press, 1979), pp. 6–30.
6. Kenneth Hopper, "Quality, Japan, and the U.S.: The First Chapter," *Quality Progress* (September, 1985); Kenneth Hopper, "Creating Japan's New Industrial Management: The Americans as Teachers," *Human Resource Management* (Summer 1982).
7. Noriaki Kano, professor at the Science University of Tokyo, interview with the author, October 6, 1992.
8. Thomas J. Murrin, Dean, School of Business & Administration at Duquesne University, interview with the author, June 3, 1992, as well as earlier interviews with Murrin and other Westinghouse executives.
9. David T. Kearns and David A. Nadler, *Prophets in the Dark: How Xerox Reinvented Itself and Beat Back the Japanese* (New York: HarperCollins, 1992), pp. 134–135.
10. Joseph M. Juran, "Made in U.S.A.: A Renaissance in Quality," *Harvard Business Review* (July–August 1993).
11. Yotaro Kobayashi, chairman of Fuji-Xerox, interview with the author, October 16, 1992.
12. Frank Pipp, retired director of manufacturing, Xerox Corp., interview with the author, March 17, 1992.
13. Richard W. Anderson, manager, Data Systems Division, Hewlett-Packard Co., speech on March 25, 1980.

14. Katsumi Yoshimoto, quality manager, Hewlett-Packard Asia Pacific, interview with the author, October 7, 1992.
15. John A. Young, president & CEO, Hewlett-Packard Co., interview with the author, August 20, 1992.
16. Irving Bluestone, Walter Reuther Library, Wayne State University, interview with the author, March 30, 1992.
17. Harvard Business School, *Transformation at Ford*, Case Study #9-390-083 (revised November 11, 1991), p. 6.
18. Alton F. Doody and Ron Bingaman, *Reinventing the Wheels: Ford's Spectacular Comeback* (Cambridge, MA: Ballinger Publishing Co., 1988), pp. 31–32.
19. James Bakken, former director of quality, Ford Motor Company, interview with the author, April 2, 1992.
20. Jeremy Main, "Detroit's Cars Really Are Getting Better," *Fortune* (February 2, 1987), p. 90.
21. Harvard Business School, *op. cit.*, p. 5.
22. Harbour & Associates, Inc., *The Harbour Report, A Decade Later, Competitive Assessment of the North American Auto Industry, 1979–1989*. Most of the numbers in the preceding three paragraphs are drawn from the Harbour Report.
23. Don Ephlin, former vice president, United Auto Workers, interview with the author, May 18, 1992.
24. *Harvard Business Review*, *op. cit.*, pp. 8–13.
25. Bakken interview. Also, the author followed W. Edwards Deming around on some of his early visits to Detroit.
26. Galvin interview.
27. *New York Times*, "The Japanese Way at Quasar," October 16, 1981.
28. Milliken & Co. quality seminar, August 12, 1992, Spartanburg, SC.
29. Roger Milliken, chairman, Milliken & Co., interview with the author, August 12, 1992.
30. Delta Consulting Group, *op. cit.*, p. 11.
31. C. Robert Kidder, chairman, Duracell International Inc., interview with the author, April 13, 1992.
32. Hudiburg, John J., *Winning With Quality: The FPL Story* (White Plains, NY, Quality Resources, 1991), p. 13.
33. Marshall McDonald, president, FPL Group Inc., speech to the Juran Institute's Fourth Annual Conference on Quality Improvement, October 9, 1986.
34. W. Kent Sterett, former director of the Quality Improvement Department at FPL, interview with the author, June 8, 1988.
35. Harvard Business School, *op. cit.*, p. 9.
36. Ray Stata, chairman, Analog Devices, interview with the author, May 29, 1992.
37. Phillip M. Scanlan, vice president, Corporate Quality Office, AT&T, interview with the author, January 7, 1993.
38. Jeremy Main, "How to Win the Baldrige Award," *Fortune* (April 23, 1990), p. 67.
39. Robert Peixotto, vice president, total quality management, L. L. Bean, interview with the author, September 16, 1992.

Chapter 2: The Leaders

1. Galvin interview.
2. Bakken interview
3. Graef S. Crystal, "How Much CEOs Really Make," *Fortune* (June 17, 1991), p. 72.
4. Eizo Watanabe, counsellor to the Japanese Union of Scientists and Engineers, interview with the author, October 15, 1992.
5. Takashi Hara, general manager in charge of research and planning, Takenaka Corp., interview with the author, October 14, 1992.
6. Dan Ciampa, president, Rath & Strong, interview with the author, May 18, 1992; also Dan Ciampa, *Total Quality* (Reading, MA: Addison-Wesley Publishing Company, 1992), pp. 115–119.
7. Mike Walsh, "The Processes and Principles of Tenneco," undelivered speech distributed April, 1992.
8. James A. Hagen, chairman of Consolidated Rail Corp., interview with the author, October 27, 1992.
9. This section on Milliken is based on the author's interviews with Roger Milliken and Thomas J. Malone, the president, and on a Milliken & Co. quality seminar, in Spartanburg, SC, August 12–13, 1992.
10. Analog Devices Inc., *Annual Report*, 1991.
11. The section on Analog Devices is based mainly on the author's interviews with Ray Stata, chairman of Analog Devices, on October 30, 1985 and May 29, 1992, and with Arthur M. Schneiderman, Vice President of Quality and Productivity at Analog Devices, on May 29, 1992 and January 19, 1993. Mr. Schneiderman is now an independent consultant.
12. Kidder interview.
13. Jeremy Main, "The Curmudgeon Who Talks Tough on Quality," *Fortune* (June 25, 1984), p. 78.
14. Charles Clough, chairman, Nashua Corp., interview with the author, September 23, 1992, and Lloyd S. Nelson, retired director of statistical methods, Nashua Corp., letter to the author, May 29, 1992.
15. Robert Geiger, manager, tape division, Nashua Corporation, interview with the author, January 10, 1993.
16. Young interview.
17. Galvin interview.
18. John J. Hudiburg, former chairman, Florida Power & Light Company, telephone interview with the author, January 15, 1993; also see Hudiburg's *Winning With Quality*, pp. 162–168.

Chapter 3: The People

1. Frederick Winslow Taylor, *The Principles of Scientific Management* (New York, Harper & Brothers, 1911), pp. 13, 33, 86–95.
2. Jeremy Main, "Ford's Drive for Quality," *Fortune* (April 18, 1983), p. 62.

3. Søren Bisgaard, Center for Quality and Productivity Improvement, University of Wisconsin–Madison, interview with the author, September 15, 1992.
4. Harvard Business School, *Transformation at Ford*, Case Study #9-390-083 (revised November 11, 1991), p. 11.
5. Douglas McGregor, *The Human Side of Enterprise* (New York: McGraw-Hill Book Company, 1960), Chapters 3 and 4.
6. Keith Lawrence, associate director, Global Product Supply, Procter & Gamble, telephone interview with the author, January 26, 1993.
7. Edward E. Lawler, III, and Susan A. Mohrman, "Quality Circles: A Self-Destruct Approach?" unpublished article, School of Business Administration, University of Southern California, 1984.
8. McGregor, *op. cit.*, p. 124.
9. Donald Dewar, president, QCI International, telephone conversation with the author, March 16, 1993.
10. Jeremy Main, "Westinghouse's Cultural Revolution," *Fortune* (June 15, 1981), p. 74.
11. J. M. Juran, *Juran on Leadership for Quality: An Executive Handbook* (New York: The Free Press, 1989), pp. 285–287.
12. Junji Noguchi, Executive Director, Japanese Union of Scientists and Engineers, interview with the author, October 15, 1992.
13. J. M. Juran, and Frank M. Gryna, eds., *Juran's Quality Control Handbook*, 4th ed. (New York: McGraw-Hill Book Company, 1988), p. 10.
14. Shigeyoshi Takashi, chief engineer, Reliability and Quality Control Division, NEC Corporation, interview with the author, October 16, 1992.
15. Tadashi Matsuma, chief engineer, Quality Control Office, Saitama factory, Honda Motor Company, Ltd., interview with the author, October 14, 1992.
16. Kenichi Ohmae, McKinsey & Co., "Quality Control Circles: They Work and They Don't Work," *Wall Street Journal* (March 29, 1982).
17. Edward E. Lawler III, director, Center for Effective Organizations, Graduate School of Business Administration, University of Southern California, telephone interview with the author, December 11, 1992.
18. James B. O'Connor, ex-president of UAW Local 974 and service representative for central Illinois, telephone interview with the author, February 2, 1993.
19. Murrin interview.
20. David B. Luther, senior vice president, corporate director–quality, Corning Inc., speech to the Japanese Management Association, October 13, 1992.
21. Kidder interview.
22. Noguchi and Lawler interviews.
23. Edward E. Lawler, III, Susan Albers Mohrman, and Gerald E. Ledford, Jr., *Employee Involvement and Total Quality Management* (San Francisco: Jossey-Bass Publishers, 1992), pp. 27, 29, 116.
24. International Association of Machinists and Aerospace Workers, White Paper on Team Concept Programs, October 1990.
25. Donald L. Dewar, "National Labor Relations Board vs. Teams," *Quality Digest* (May 1993), p. 60.

26. Ephlin interview.
27. The account of what happened at Buick City is based on interviews with Tim Lee, plant manager; JR Mays of the UAW; Russ Cook, shop committee member for UAW Local 599; and other managers and employees, on September 25, 1992. I also drew on "Buick City: From Bottom to No. 1," *Automotive News* (December 18, 1989) and "The Halloween Party," *Road & Track* (February, 1984).
28. Harvard Business School, *FP&L's Quality Improvement Program,* Case Study #9-688-043 (revised August 8, 1990), p. 6.
29. Philip Anschutz, chairman, Southern Pacific Transportation Company, speech to the Juran Institute Impro 91 conference, October 29, 1991.
30. Carl James, general chairman, Brotherhood of Locomotive Engineers, Denver Rio Grande Western, remarks at a meeting of the Southern Pacific Transportation Company Labor-Management Advisory Committee, July 1, 1992.
31. Galvin interview.
32. Ralph Ponce de Leon, vice president and corporate director, supply and environmental management, Motorola Inc., interview with the author, July 29, 1992.
33. Background and nonattributable interview.
34. Stata interview.
35. Bakken interview.
36. Miscellaneous Xerox documents.
37. Motorola memo to the author, April 7, 1993.
38. A. Blanton Godfrey, chairman and CEO, Juran Institute, Inc., testimony before the Subcommittee on Technology and Competitiveness of the House Committee on Science, Space, and Technology, February 5, 1992.
39. Tom Griffth, manager, purchasing support and development, Honda of North America, interview with the author, September 24, 1992.
40. Galvin interview.
41. David B. Luther, senior vice president, corporate director–quality, Corning Glass Works, interview with the author, November 11, 1992.
42. Michael Bennett, president, UAW Local 1853, interview with the author, October 28, 1992.
43. Winston H. Chen, chairman and co-CEO, Solectron Corporation, interview with the author, August 26, 1992.
44. William Wiggenhorn, "Motorola U: When Training Becomes an Education," *Harvard Business Review* (July–August 1990), p. 71. Wiggenhorn is Motorola's vice president for training and education and president of Motorola University.
45. *Ibid.*
46. John Rampey, vice president and director of human relations, Milliken & Company, interview with the author, August 13, 1992.
47. Galvin interview.
48. Kearns and Nadler, *op. cit.,* pp. 201–217.
49. Nelson interview.

50. Peixotto interview.
51. William W. Barnard, vice president, Juran Institute Inc., interview with the author, November 20, 1992.
52. *Training* magazine, July, 1992.
53. W. Edwards Deming, *Out of the Crisis* (Cambridge, MA: The MIT Press, 1991), p. 102.
54. James Paulsen, director of quality, Ford Motor Co., interview with the author, May 21, 1992.
55. Clough interview.
56. Peter R. Scholtes, Joiner Associates Inc., interview with the author, September 17, 1992.
57. John F. Early, Vice President, Juran Institute, interview with the author, March 22, 1993.
58. Ernst & Young and the American Quality Foundation, "Automobile Industry Report," "Banking Industry Report," "Computer Industry Report," "Health Care Industry Report," *International Quality Study*, 1992.
59. Bennett interview.
60. Thomas L. Carter, senior vice president, quality, training and education, Aluminum Company of America (Alcoa), interview with the author, November 12, 1992.
61. Charles R. LaMantia, president and CEO, Arthur D. Little Inc., interview with the author, March 26, 1992.
62. James McIngvale, owner, Gallery Furniture Store, Dallas, TX, telephone interview with the author on February 2, 1993.
63. Patrick C. Bowie, vice president, quality, Milliken & Company, interview with the author, August 12, 1992.
64. Malone interview.

Chapter 4: The Customers

1. Galvin interview.
2. John Marous, former chairman, Westinghouse Electric Corp., interview with the author, June 4, 1992.
3. Walter Wriston, former chairman of Citibank, phone conversation with the author on December 7, 1992.
4. "Conversation with John Akers," *Think*, (No. 1, 1989), p. 13.
5. Pipp interview.
6. L. L. Bean section is based on interviews with Robert Peixotto, vice president for total quality management, September 16, 1992, and Bob Olive, administrative manager of distribution, May 29, 1992, and visits to the company offices in Freeport and Portland, ME.
7. Hara interview.
8. Ishikawa, *op. cit.*, pp. 107–108.
9. Harvard Business School, *Honda Motor Company and Honda of America (A)*, Case Study #9-390-111 (Revised January 2, 1991), p. 3.

10. Taiichi Ohno, *Toyota Production System* (Cambridge, MA, Productivity Press, 1988, first published in Japan 1978), pp. xiv, 26.
11. Bowie interview.
12. Thomas N. Kennedy, vice president, quality, Solectron Corporation, interview with the author on August 26, 1992.
13. Michael Brassard, director of research, GOAL/QPC, interviews with the author on March 24, 1992, and February 2, 1992.
14. Doody and Bingaman, *op. cit.*, pp. 48–56; and John Risk, director of car and truck body engineering, North American Automotive Operations, Ford Motor Company, interview with the author May 18, 1992.
15. Philip Condit, executive vice president of Boeing Commercial Airplane Group and general manager of the 777 program, and other Boeing officials, during a visit to Renton, WA, Jan. 7–10, 1992. Condit has since become president of Boeing.
16. Harvard Business School, *Ford Motor Company, Dealer Sales and Service*, Case Study #39-690-030 (1989, Revised February 2, 1992).
17. Texaco sources.
18. "Saturns and Such," *The New York Times*, August 29, 1993.
19. C. Warren Neel, dean of the business school, University of Tennessee, interview with the author, December 3, 1992.
20. Marty Raymond, manager, training and strategic implementation, sales, service and marketing, Saturn Corporation, interview with the author, October 28, 1992.
21. Thomas J. Zimbrick, general manager, Saturn of Madison, WI, interview with the author, September 17, 1992. The material on Saturn is also based on visits to Saturn, in Spring Hill, TN, and the Zimbrick dealership in Madison, as well as an interview with Richard LeFauve, president of Saturn, on October 28, 1992.
22. J. D. Power and Associates, *The Saturn Way*, September, 1992.
23. J. D. Power and Associates, *The Power Report (1992 New Car Initial Quality Study)*, June 1992.
24. Susumu Uchikawa, director and member of the board, production control logistics, Toyota Motor Corporation, interview with the author, October 13, 1992.
25. LeFauve interview.
26. Hiroyuki Yoshino, president, Honda of America Manufacturing, Inc., speech in Traverse City, MI, August 7, 1991.
27. Tadashi Matsuda, chief engineer, quality control office, Saitama factory, Honda Motor Company, Ltd., interview with the author on October 14, 1992.
28. Yoshimoto interview.
29. David B. Luther, senior vice president and corporate director–quality, Corning Inc., speech to the Japanese Management Association, October 13, 1992.
30. These views were obtained from executives or employees who asked not to be identified.

Chapter 5: The Tools

1. Matsuda interview.
2. Professor Hitochi Kume, faculty of engineering, University of Tokyo, interview with the author, October 6, 1992.
3. Joseph DeFeo, vice president, Juran Institute, interview with the author, May 13, 1992.
4. James L. Broadhead, chairman, FPL Group, in a letter to employees, May 15, 1990. (Courtesy of Ron Zemke, editor, *Training* magazine).
5. C. K. Prahalad, Business School, University of Michigan, interview with the author, March 31, 1992.
6. J. M. Juran, *op. cit.,* pp. 16.25–26.
7. GOAL/QPC, *The Memory Jogger* (Methuen, MA: GOAL/QPC, 1988), pp. 51–57.
8. Juran Institute, *On Quality Improvement,* Workbook (Wilton, CT: Juran Institute Inc., 1989).
9. W. Edwards Deming, *op. cit.,* p. 910; Lloyd S. Nelson, interview, 1984.
10. Nelson interview.
11. Janice Ceridwen (Ventana Corporation), "Using Quality's Tools: What's Working Well," *The Journal for Quality and Participation* (March, 1992).
12. Kaoru Ishikawa, *Guide to Quality Control* (White Plains, NY: Quality Resources, 1990).
13. GOAL/QPC, *op. cit.*
14. *Quality Improvement Tools:* Workbook Set (Wilton, CT: Juran Institute, 1989).
15. AT&T, *The Statistical Quality Control Handbook* (Knoxville, TN: SPC Press Inc., 1985).
16. Clough interview.
17. Ohno, *op. cit.,* p. 17.
18. Donald Wadanse, chief, division of research management, National Capital Parks/Central, telephone conversation with the author, April 14, 1993.
19. Scherkenbach, William W., *Deming's Road to Continual Improvement* (Knoxville, TN: SPC Press, 1991), pp. 61–81.
20. J. M. Juran, *Managerial Breakthrough* (New York: McGraw-Hill Book Co., 1964), pp. 1–17.
21. Ohno, *op. cit.,* pp. 24–42.
22. Jeremy Main, "The Trouble With Managing Japanese-Style," *Fortune* (April 2, 1984), p. 14.
23. Deming, *op. cit.,* p. 45.
24. James P. Womack, Daniel T. Jones, and Daniel Roos, *The Machine That Changed the World* (New York: HarperCollins, 1991), p. 161.
25. Walter interview.
26. Young interview.
27. William G. Martin, manufacturing manager, and Kent Stockwell, quality department manager, Hewlett-Packard, Corvallis division, interview with the author, August 19, 1992.

28. Kume, Matsuda, Takashi, and Yoshimoto interviews and interview with Yoshio Kondo, professor emeritus, Kyoto University, with the author, October 5, 1992.
29. Ohno, *op. cit.*, pp. 25–26.
30. Robert C. Camp, *Benchmarking* (Milwaukee: ASQC Quality Press, 1989).
31. Risk interview.
32. J. M. Juran, chairman (retired), Juran Institute Inc., talk to Milliken & Company seminar, May 15, 1992.
33. Ernst & Young, *op. cit.*
34. Robert C. Camp, manager of benchmarking, Xerox Corporation, interview with the author, May 6, 1992.
35. Kobayashi interview.
36. Carl H. Arendt, communications manager, Productivity and Quality Center, Westinghouse Electric Corp., interview with the author, June 3, 1992.
37. For the Boeing material I have drawn on John Newhouse, *The Sporty Game* (New York: Alfred A. Knopf, 1985), pp. 161–172, and my own notes taken on a visit to Renton, Washington, January 7–10, 1992.
38. For this sketch of some extremely arcane matters I am indebted to Madhav S. Phadke and others at Bell Labs, whose works I have read and whom I interviewed in 1988, but they should not be held responsible for what I have written.
39. Steven C. Wheelwright and Kim B. Clark, *Revolutionizing Product Development* (New York: The Free Press, 1992), pp. 234–236.
40. Martin interview.
41. Young interview.
42. Aleta Holub, vice president and manager, quality assurance, The First National Bank of Chicago, interview with the author on July 31, 1992; also First National Bank of Chicago's *Quality Performance Chart Book*, 9th ed. (July–December 1989).
43. H. Thomas Johnson, *Relevance Regained* (New York: The Free Press, 1992), pp. 1–32.
44. Stata interviews.
45. Marous interview.
46. Motorola, *The Six Steps to Six Sigma* (undated document).
47. Paul Noakes, vice president and director of external quality programs, Motorola Inc., interview with the author, July 30, 1992.
48. Stephen B. Schwartz, senior vice president, quality, IBM, August 31, 1992. Mr. Schwartz has since retired.
49. Hagen interview and David M. LeVan, senior vice president, operations, Conrail, interview with the author, October 27, 1992.
50. Schneiderman interviews.
51. Luther interview; and David Luther, "Advanced TQM: Measurements, Missteps, and Progress Through Key Result Indicators at Corning," *National Productivity Review*, Winter 1992/93.
52. IBM communication to the author, March 19, 1993.
53. U.S. Department of Commerce press release, January 10, 1992.

Chapter 6: The Automakers

1. J. D. Power and Associates, *The Power Report (1992 New Car Initial Quality Study)*, June, 1992.
2. "A New Way to Figure Reliability," *Consumer Reports* (April, 1993), p. 234.
3. Alex Taylor, "Can GM Remodel Itself?" *Fortune* (January 13, 1992), and "U.S. Cars Come Back" *Fortune* (November 16, 1992).
4. Harbour & Associates, Inc., *The Harbour Report, A Decade Later, Competitive Assessment of the North American Auto Industry, 1979–1989.*
5. Economic Strategy Institute, *The Future of the Auto Industry: It Can Compete, Can It Survive?* (Washington, DC: 1992). p. iii.
6. Womack, *op. cit.*; Keller, Maryann, *Rude Awakening* (New York: Harper Perennial, 1990), and Richard Tanner Pascale, *Managing on the Edge* (New York: Touchstone, 1991).
7. Bakken interview.
8. Pascale, *op. cit.*, pp. 132–133.
9. More detailed accounts of this chimney-breaking can be found in the Harvard Business School study, *The Transformation at Ford, op. cit.*, and in Pascale's *Managing on the Edge, op. cit.*, Chapter Five.
10. This paragraph is based mostly on interview by the author on May 18, 1992, with John Risk, program manager of the Taurus project and later director of car and truck body manufacturing for Ford's North American Automotive Operations.
11. Doody and Bingaman, *op. cit.*, p. 63.
12. "The Taurus: Big Sales, Big Repairs," *The New York Times* (June 19, 1988).
13. *The Harbour Report, 1989–92*, pp. 45–51.
14. Paulsen interview.
15. Michael Oblak, plant chairman, Wayne I.S.A. Stamping Plant, Local 900 UAW, interview with the author, May 20, 1992.
16. *The Harbour Report, 1989–1992*, pp. 13 and 15.
17. *The Wall Street Journal*, "Ford's Strong Sales Raise Agonizing Issue of Additional Plants" (October 26, 1988), and "Ford Thunderbird Setbacks Dim Luster of Car of Year" (February 7, 1989).
18. Lee A. Iacocca, chairman, Chrysler Corporation, speech at Jefferson Assembly Plant, Detroit, August 6, 1980.
19. The Maritz (formerly Rogers) surveys, the most exhaustive of the quality surveys, are made for the private use of industry and Maritz does not publish the results. However the automakers sometimes leak the findings, at least when they are not unfavorable. I cannot confirm these findings, but they fit with the results of other surveys.
20. Keller, *op. cit.*, p. 204
21. "A Surge at Chrysler," *Business Week* (November 9, 1992), p. 88.
22. This account of Chrysler's revival is taken mostly from secondary sources, including "Chrysler Hits the Road Again," *Industry Week* (October 19, 1992), p. 68; "Can Iacocca Fix Chrysler—Again," *Fortune* (April 8. 1991), p. 50 and

"U.S. Cars Come Back," *Fortune* (November 16, 1992), p. 52; "The Viper Is Already a Winner for Chrysler," *Business Week* (November 4, 1991), p. 36, and "Surge at Chrysler," *Business Week* (November 9, 1992), p. 88. *Consumer Reports* (April 1993), p. 220, recommended the LH cars.

23. Keller, *op. cit.,* has an excellent account of the reorganization, pp. 99–123.
24. William W. Scherkenbach, group director, statistics and process improvement methods, BOC Group, General Motors, interview with the author, April 1, 1992. (Scherkenbach has since become an independent consultant.)
25. Keller, *op. cit.,* pp. 171–172.
26. Womack, *op. cit.,* pp. 104–109.
27. "How G.M. Is Losing Its Hold on the Crucial Family Sedan," *The New York Times* (March 7, 1993), D-5.
28. *The Harbour Report, 1989–1992.* pp. 37–47.
29. "Cadillac Seville," *Car and Driver* (May, 1991), p. 97.
30. Charles Stridde, people systems team leader, Saturn Corp., interview with the author, October 28, 1992.
31. Bennett interview.
32. LeFauve interview.
33. J. D. Power, *The Saturn Way, op. cit.*
34. The preceding paragraphs on GM are based on a wide variety of published sources and my own interviewing in the auto industry.
35. G. Richard Wagoner Jr., executive vice president, General Motors Corporation, speech to auto industry briefing, Traverse City, Michigan, August 6, 1993.
36. "GM Tightens the Screws," *Business Week* (June 22, 1992), p. 30.
37. John Jacobson, steel industry analyst, The WEFA Group, telephone conversation with the author, April 22, 1993.
38. Most of the information on the steel industry comes from my interviews with Bakken, cited earlier, and with Gerald S. Hartman, a steel industry consultant, of State College, Pennsylvania, interviewed on June 5, 1992.
39. Abraham H. Maslow, *Motivation and Personality* (New York: Harper & Brothers, 1954).
40. David E. Cole, director, Office for the Study of Automotive Transportation, University of Michigan, interview with the author, April 2, 1992.
41. Kenichi Yamamoto, chairman (now retired), Mazda Motor Corporation, speech in Traverse City, Michigan, August 6, 1986.
42. Thomas Gorcyca, customer quality research, Ford Motor Co., telephone conversation with the author, April 15, 1993.

Chapter 7: The Pacesetters

1. Motorola Corporation, "The Six Steps to Six Sigma," undated company document.
2. Pascale, *op. cit.,* p. 232.
3. The account of what happened to the 68040 is based on the author's interviews

with John Young, then CEO of HP, and with Robert Weinberger, marketing manager for HP's workstations systems group, on September 4, 1992, and with Jack Browne, director of marketing for Motorola's 68000 division, on January 20, 1993.

4. "Framework for Our Objectives," *Measure* (July, 1989), p. 22. *Measure* is a Hewlett-Packard in-house publication.
5. Pascale, *op. cit.*, pp. 230 and 232.
6. Much of the material on Hewlett-Packard comes from managers who prefer to remain anonymous.
7. The MIT Commission on Industrial Productivity, *Working Papers*, Vol. 2. (Cambridge, MA: The MIT Press, 1989), pp. 31–32.
8. Bob King, *Hoshin Planning, The Developmental Approach.* (Methuen, MA: GOAL/QPC, 1989).
9. Young interview.
10. Walter interview.
11. John Young, letter to *Electronic Business*, August 5, 1991.
12. John Young speech, Syracuse University, October 16, 1991.
13. MIT Commission on Industrial Productivity, *op. cit.*, pp. 57–58, 71.
14. Milliken & Co. quality seminar, August 13, 1992. Much of what follows comes from that seminar and unless otherwise indicated is the source of my information.
15. MIT Commission on Industrial Productivity, *op. cit.*, p. 62.
16. *Ibid.*, p. 63.
17. Patrick Bowie, vice president, quality, Milliken & Company, interview with the author on August 12, 1993.
18. Roger Milliken, telephone interview on February 5, 1990.
19. Bowie interview.
20. William Wiggenhorn, "Creating Your Own Quality Definition," *The Conference Board Report*, No. 963, 1991.
21. Wiggenhorn, *op. cit.*
22. Galvin interview.
23. Brenda Sumberg, director for quality, Motorola University, telephone conversation with the author, September 20, 1991.
24. "Motorola Illustrates How an Aged Giant Can Remain Vibrant," *The Wall Street Journal* (December 9, 1992).
25. Noakes interview.
26. The account of Operation Bandit is derived from Motorola documents, from a telephone conversation on May 28, 1993, with Russell Strobel, resource manager, Paging Products Group, Motorola, and from the Harvard Business School, *Motorola, Inc.: Bandit Pager Project*, Case Study #9-690-043 (1989; revised June 28, 1991).
27. Gerry G. Link, vice president and director of quality, Pan American Cellular Subscriber Group, Motorola, interview with the author, July 29, 1992.
28. John Gervasio, manager of reliability engineering, Pan American Cellular Subscriber Group, Motorola Inc., interview with the author, July 29, 1992.

29. Wiggenhorn, *The Conference Board Report*, No. 963.
30. Galvin interview.
31. Noakes interview.
32. Kearns, *op. cit.*
33. *Ibid.*, p. 229. (Most of this paragraph is based on the Kearns book.)
34. Xerox Corporation, *Leadership Through Quality* (Corporate booklet published 1990).
35. Jeremy Main, "How to Win the Baldrige Award," *Fortune* (April 23, 1990), p. 67.
36. Terry Wirth, Buyers Laboratory Inc., telephone conservation with the author, October 7, 1993.
37. B. Alex Henderson and Jack W. Murphy, "Xerox Corp. Company Update" Prudential Securities Inc. (December 3, 1992).
38. Barrett interview.
39. Intel Corporation, "1991 Malcolm Baldrige Award Application," pp. 3–4.
40. Jeremy Main, "Battling Your Own Bureaucracy," *Fortune* (June 15, 1981), p. 54.
41. Intel Corporation, *op. cit.*, pp. 5, 24.
42. "Inside Intel," *Business Week* (June 1, 1992), p. 86.
43. "Pentium Power," *PC Magazine* (April 27, 1993), p. 112.
44. Pascale, *op. cit.*, pp. 68–70.

Chapter 8: The Fumblers

1. Thomas J. Watson, Jr., and Peter Petre, *Father, Son & Co.: My Life at IBM and Beyond.* (New York: Bantam Books, 1990), p. 302.
2. Stephen B. Schwartz, senior vice president, market-driven quality, IBM, interview with the author, August 31, 1992. Schwartz has since retired. Much of the IBM material in this chapter comes from half a dozen retired IBM executives who dealt with quality over the last 15 years, most of whom spoke not for attribution. Unless I attribute information to a specific source, as I have done with Steve Schwartz, the reader may assume that my information comes from these retired executives.
3. James Riley, vice president, Juran Institute, Inc., interview with the author, March 12, 1992.
4. "A Think Special Report: Market-driven!" *Think*, No. 1, 1989, p. 3. (*Think* is an IBM house organ and, as such, terminally upbeat. However, it prints far more substance than most corporate house organs and it is very helpful in reconstructing the chronology of IBM's efforts.)
5. *Ibid.*
6. "More Than Just Problems;" *Think*, No. 1, 1990, p. 9.
7. "On Market-Driven Quality;" *Think*. No. 4, 1990, p. 26.
8. Letter from the chairman and "What's Next for IBM?" *Think*, No. 1, 1990, inside cover, p. 2.

9. Larry Osterwise, director, market-driven quality, IBM, talk to Benchmarking Week '92, American Quality and Productivity Center, Dallas, May 6, 1992. Osterwise has since succeeded Steve Schwartz as head of quality for IBM.
10. Roy Bauer, Emilio Collar, and Victor Tang, *The Silverlake Project, Transformation at IBM* (New York: Oxford University Press, 1992). This account of Silverlake is taken mostly from the book, but also from interviews with Tom Furey and Victor Tang, both of the Santa Teresa Laboratories, on August 20 and August 25, 1992, respectively, as well as the Stephen Schwartz interview.
11. Osterwise, Dallas talk.
12. Tang interview.
13. Furey, Tang interviews.
14. Nelson interview.
15. Nashua Corp., *1991 Annual Report*.
16. Nelson letter to the author.
17. James Brian Quinn, Buchanan professor of management, Amos Tuck School of Business Administration, Dartmouth College, telephone conversation, May 14, 1993.
18. Geiger interview.
19. Clough interview.
20. McDonald speech.
21. Sterett 1988 interview.
22. This account of FPL's quality efforts is taken from interviews with Kent Sterett, and from several FPL documents, notably *Summary Description of FPL's Quality Improvement Program* (1989), and Harvard Business School case #9-688-043, *Florida Power & Light's Quality Improvement Program* (1987), and several speeches by FPL managers.
23. Most of this account of the prize process is taken from Hudiburg, *op. cit.*, pp. 130–168.
24. Florida Public Service Commission, Docket No. 900478-EI, May 9, 1991.
25. James L. Broadhead, chairman of the FPL Group, letters to the employees, May 15, 1990, and June 19, 1990 (Courtesy of Ron Zemke, editor, *Training* magazine.)
26. Joseph D. Jenkins, director, electric and gas division, Florida Public Service Commission, phone conversation with the author, January 15, 1993, plus other facsimile communications.
27. Florida Public Service Commission (Consumer Affairs Division), *1992 Consumer Complaint Activity Report* (Tallahassee, 1993).
28. Florida Public Service Commission, *Summary of Electric Inspections and Variances—1986 to 1992.*
29. Hudiburg interview.
30. A. Blanton Godfrey, "At the Cutting Edge of Quality," speech to the U.S. Chamber of Commerce Quality Learning Series, February 26, 1993.
31. Ronald Henkoff, "This Cat is Acting Like a Tiger," *Fortune*, (December 19, 1988), p. 69.
32. The author visited the KK plant in 1990.

33. "Strife Between UAW And Caterpillar Blights Promising Labor Idea," *The Wall Street Journal* (November 23, 1992).
34. O'Connor interview.
35. Charles Elwyn, manager, Business Center H, Caterpillar Inc., note to employees, August 6, 1992. "Tractors", in Cat talk as used here, refers to any heavy equipment such as excavators, wheel loaders, and agricultural tractors.

Chapter 9: The Railroaders

1. Conrail's billing errors were reported in "Conrail Puts Quality up Front," *Railway Age*, June, 1992, p. 27. Southern Pacific reported its customer satisfaction ratings in "SP Management Systems Overview" issued early in 1993 (undated). The rest of the preceding paragraphs come from many interviews and written sources, some of which are referred to below.
2. Information provided by David Seybolt, manager, locomotive reliability, General Electric Transportation Systems, September 24, 1993.
3. Robert J. Scanlon, director of quality and reliability engineering, Southern Pacific Rail Corporation, speech to Juran Institute's Impro Conference, October 29, 1991.
4. Anthony Hatch, PaineWebber, report on Consolidated Rail, May 28, 1992.
5. Andrew Kupfer, "An Outsider Fires up a Railroad," *Fortune* (December 18, 1989), p. 133; and John Huey, "Mike Walsh Takes on Brain Cancer," *Fortune* (February 22, 1993), p. 76.
6. The performance data comes from two Union Pacific documents, *UPdate*, a management newsletter (June, 1992), and *A Quality Partnership* (undated).
7. John T. Bielan, vice president, continuous quality improvement, Consolidated Rail Corp., interview with the author, October 28, 1992.
8. Hagen interview.
9. Bielan interview.
10. David M. LeVan, senior vice president–operations, Consolidated Rail Corp., interview with the author, Oct. 27, 1992. (LeVan has since been appointed executive vice president of Conrail.)
11. Hatch, *op. cit.*
12. Southern Pacific Lines, *Key Performance Indicators, June 1992* (known as the "red book" inside the company).
13. Raland H. Berry, chief mechanical officer, Southern Pacific Lines, during a tour of SP's Burnham locomotive shop, July 2, 1992.
14. Edward Kammerer, vice president, Juran Institute, interviews June 25, 1992, and April 21, 1993. At the time, Kammerer was vice president for marketing (chemicals) at Southern Pacific.
15. Philip Anschutz, chairman, Southern Pacific Rail Corp., interview with the author, July 2, 1992.
16. Anschutz speech.
17. This account of the first year of SP's quality efforts comes from previously cited speeches by Anschutz and Scanlon, interviews with Anschutz, Sterett, and other

SP officials, and from the company's "red book" of key performance indicators.

18. Berry interview and tour of Burnham Shops.
19. Based on a visit by the author to the customer services center on June 30, 1992, with Dennis Jacobson, managing director of customer service, Southern Pacific Lines.
20. Southern Pacific Lines, *Key Performance Indicators*, June 1992, pp. 6, 8, 9.
21. Southern Pacific Lines, *SP Management System Overview*, undated document issued early in 1993.
22. William G. Ditoro, director, national inventory, Nabisco Foods Group, talk at Juran Impro Conference 1992, November 13, 1992.
23. John Badger, director, transportation and distribution services, Olin Chemicals, Olin Corp., interviews with the author, July 17, 1992 and April 13, 1993.
24. Southern Pacific Rail Corporation, *Prospectus*, August 10, 1993, p. 12.

Chapter 10: The Services

1. National Institute of Standards and Technology, press release NIST 92-17, August 10, 1992.
2. Frederick E. Reichheld and W. Earl Sasser, Jr., "Zero Defections: Quality Comes to Services," *Harvard Business Review* (September–October 1990), pp. 105–111.
3. Leonard L. Berry and Linda R Cooper, "Competing With Time-Saving Service," *Business* (April–June 1990), pp. 3–7.
4. Linda Cooper and Beth Summers, *Getting Started In Quality*, First National Bank of Chicago, 1990, p. 1.
5. Jeremy Main, "Service Without a Snarl," *Fortune* (March 23, 1981), p. 58.
6. Holub interview.
7. The preceding three paragraphs are based mostly on the Holub interview and the author's attendance at a performance review on November 13, 1992.
8. The description of First Chicago's community banking is based on an interview with Linda R. Cooper, head, consumer affairs department, The First National Bank of Chicago, on July 31, 1992, as well as Cooper & Summers, *op. cit.*, and Berry & Cooper, *op. cit.*
9. The description of Banc One's quality process comes mainly from an interview with Charles A. Aubrey, vice president, Juran Institute, on July 13, 1992. Aubrey was formerly Banc One's vice president for quality.
10. Banc One Wisconsin material is based on interviews with Fred Cullen, CEO of Banc One Wisconsin, and Shari Michael-Kenney, quality director, on September 18, 1992. Cullen has since become chief financial officer of the parent Banc One Corp. in Columbus, Ohio.
11. Robert E. Cole, letter to John Garamendi, insurance commissioner, state of California, February 29, 1992.
12. Thomas Clarkson, vice president, corporate quality, Allstate Insurance Company, telephone conversation on January 29, 1993, and Lev Landa, Landamatics International Inc., interview on March 18, 1992.

13. "The Best (And Worst) Airlines," *Consumer Reports*, (July 1991), p. 462.
14. "Southwest Airlines Is A Rare Air Carrier: It Still Makes Money," *The Wall Street Journal* (October 26, 1992).
15. Brent D. Bowen and Dean E. Headley, *The Airline Quality Report 1993*. (Wichita, KS: National Institute for Aviation Research, Wichita State University, 1993.)
16. The material on Midwest Express comes from interviews with Tim Hoeksema, chairman and CEO, and Daniel Sweeney, director of passenger services, on September 18, 1992.
17. Laurence C. Seifert, vice president, engineering, manufacturing, and production planning, AT&T. Speech to Juran Institute's 1987 Impro Conference, Chicago, November 9, 1987.
18. Scanlan interview. Much but by no means all of the material on AT&T comes from him.
19. James W. Zachman, division manager, quality management, AT&T, talk to the Juran Institute's 1990 Impro Conference, October 28, 1990.
20. Brian R. Churm, engineering manager, AT&T Network Software Center, speech to Juran Institute's 1990 Impro Conference, October 29, 1990.
21. Ellen Bravo, district manager, quality public relations, AT&T, letter dated June 10, 1993.
22. Universal Card Services data comes from a summary of UCS's Baldrige Award application and from other company sources.

Chapter 11: The Professions

1. Donald M. Berwick, A. Blanton Godfrey, & Jane Roessner, *Curing Health Care*. (San Francisco: Jossey-Bass Inc., 1990), pp. 7–8.
2. Gregory F. Binns and John F. Early, "Hospital Care: Frontiers in Managing Quality," *Juran Report No. 10* (Autumn 1989), pp. 18–31.
3. Brent C. James, "How Do You Involve Physicians in TQM?" *Journal for Quality and Participation* (January–February 1991), pp. 42–47.
4. Berwick, Godfrey & Roessner, *op. cit.*, pp. 24–25. Most of this account of the National Demonstration Project is taken from their book.
5. Rear Admiral Robert B. Halder, senior vice president, Juran Institute, interview with the author on July 17, 1992.
6. Matt Kelliher, vice president of quality, Harvard Community Health Plan, interview with the author March 24, 1992. Kelliher has since moved to Massachusetts Blue Cross/Blue Shield.
7. The account of what happened at the Harvard Plan came from interviews or telephone conversations with Matt Kelliher, vice president of quality, Harvard Community Health Plan, March 24, 1992 and June 11, 1993; by the latter date he had moved to Massachusetts Blue Cross; Chris Holland, director of quality consulting and training at Harvard Community Health Plan, June 11, 1993; and Dr. John M. Ludden, medical director, June 22, 1993. Other sources who prefer not be quoted also contributed.

8. University of Michigan Medical Center, "Costs, Benefits, and Return From UMMC Total Quality Process: July 1987 Through June 1991" (February 26, 1992), also interviews with hospital officials.
9. Richard J. Coffey, director of management systems, University of Michigan Hospitals, interviews with the author, March 31 and May 20, 1992.
10. Richard J. Coffey, telephone conversation, June 7, 1993.
11. A. Blanton Godfrey, Donald M. Berwick, and Jane Roessner, "Can Quality Management Really Work in Health Care?" *Quality Progress* (April, 1992), p. 23.
12. University of Michigan Medical Center, *op. cit.*, pp. 43–44.
13. Ellen J. Gaucher, chief operating officer, University of Michigan Hospitals, interview with the author, March 31, 1992.
14. Godfrey et al., *op. cit.*, p. 25.
15. Brent C. James, "TQM and Clinical Medicine," *Frontiers of Health Services Management* (Summer, 1991), pp. 42–46
16. David C. Classen et al., "The Timing of Prophylactic Administration of Antibiotics and the Risk of Surgical-Wound Infection," *The New England Journal of Medicine* (January 30, 1992), p. 281.
17. Brent C. James, "Quality Improvement in the Hospital: Managing Clinical Processes," *The Internist* (March 1993), pp. 11-13.
18. David C. Classen, LDS Hospital, Salt Lake City, telephone conversation with the author, June 23, 1993.
19. Robin R. Gillies, Stephen M. Shortell, et al., "National Survey of Hospital Quality Improvement Activities," *Hospitals & Health Networks*, December 5, 1993, and "Improving Quality Improvement Methods," *Hospitals & Health Networks*, January 5, 1994.
20. Donald M. Berwick, president, Institute for Healthcare Improvement, telephone conversation with the author, June 15, 1993.
21. Myron Tribus, "Total Quality Management in Schools of Business and of Engineering." (Unpublished paper written in 1991.)
22. David A. Garvin, *op. cit.*
23. Richard N. Rosett, dean, School of Business, Rochester Institute of Technology, telephone conversation with the author, July 7, 1993.
24. Michael Stahl, associate dean, School of Business Administration, University of Tennessee, telephone conversation, July 7, 1993.
25. The University of Michigan, "Enhancing Quality in an Era of Resource Constraints: Report of the Task Force on Costs in Higher Education" (1990), pp. 1, 16–17.
26. White interview.
27. Robert Holmes, vice president for academic affairs and executive director for M-Quality, University of Michigan, telephone conversation with the author, June 17, 1993.
28. John E. Murray, Jr., "Total Quality Performance at Duquesne University." (Undated document).
29. "Total Quality Performance," *Duquesne University Record* (Spring 1992), p. 9.

30. George R. Bateman and Harry V. Roberts, "TQM For Professors and Students," unpublished paper in the Graduate School of Business, University of Chicago, dated February 1993.
31. *Ibid.*
32. Howard Wilson, director, Market Driven Quality, IBM, telephone conversation with the author, July 13, 1993.
33. The material on Mt. Edgecumbe High School comes from a variety of sources, including interviews with David Langford and Myron Tribus; speeches and articles by Langford; Myron Tribus's *Quality First: Selected Papers on Quality & Productivity Improvement* (Alexandria, VA: National Institute for Engineering Management & Systems, 1992), pp. 293–304; and "Why Are We Here?" *Focus in Change* (Fall 1992). *Focus in Change* is a quarterly publication of the National Center for Effective Schools Research & Development in Madison, Wisconsin.
34. Franklin P. Schargel, assistant principal, George Westinghouse Vocational & Technical High School, interview with Patricia Langan on October 5, 1992. Schargel also provided documentation and other telephone interviews.
35. John Early, vice president, Juran Institute, interview with the author, March 22, 1993.
36. Richard H. Weise, *Representing the Corporate Client: Designs for Quality.* (Englewood Cliffs, NJ, Prentice-Hall Law & Business, 1991). The author interviewed Weise on July 30, 1992.
37. Rick Pfizenmayer, assistant general counsel, Texaco Inc., interview with G. Howland Blackiston, president, Juran Institute, July 18, 1992.
38. N. Michael Grove, vice president and general counsel, Bell Communications Research, interview with G. Howland Blackiston, president, Juran Institute, July 20, 1992.
39. "Sidley gets with the TQM Program," *The American Lawyer* (May 23, 1993), p. 23.
40. T. Barton Jones, partner, Winthrop, Stimson, Putnam & Roberts, telephone interview, June 17, 1993. (Also interviewed by Howland Blackiston, July 18, 1992.)

Chapter 12: The Government

1. Clinton, Bill, "Putting People First," *Journal for Quality and Participation,* (October/November 1992), p. 10.
2. J. M. Juran, *Managerial Breakthrough* (New York: McGraw-Hill, 1964), p. 128 fn.
3. David Kirkpatrick, "It's Simply Not Working," *Fortune* (November 19, 1990), p. 194.
4. David Osborne and Ted Gaebler, *Reinventing Government.* (New York: Penguin Books, 1993).
5. Charles A. Bowsher, Comptroller General of the United States, "Improving

Government," statement to the Senate Committee on Government Affairs, March 11, 1993.

6. "Doing More With Less in the Public Sector," *Quality Progress* (July 1987), p. 20.

7. A. Blanton Godfrey testimony, *op. cit.*

8. General Accounting Office, "Quality Management: Survey of Federal Organizations," October 1, 1992.

9. Don G. Mizaur, "Is Quality Government Possible?" *Looking Ahead* (October 1992).

10. Tina Sung, senior quality executive, Federal Quality Institute, interview with Pat Langan, October 16, 1992.

11. James H. Brown, quality manager, Tennessee Valley Authority, telephone conversation, July 2, 1993; and "Four Major Community Quality Groups—A Basic Simplified Guide," *Community Link Newsletter*, Vol. 3, No. 2, 1993. Brown is also president of the Community Quality Coalition.

12. Melanie Kennedy, Arkansas state quality coordinator; Jan Partain, quality management program, Arkansas Industrial Development Commission; and Asa Whitaker, quality manager, Arkansas Eastman Co., telephone conversations July, 1993. Also the Myron Tribus interview and Bill Clinton, "Putting People First," *op. cit.*

13. Osborne and Gaebler, *op. cit.*

14. Bill Clinton, speech, March 3, 1993.

15. "Gore Gets Earful of Bureaucratic Horror Stories As He Shapes a Plan to 'Reinvent' Government," *The Wall Street Journal* (June 23, 1993.)

16. National Performance Review, *Creating a Government That Works Better & Costs Less* (Washington, DC: U.S. Government Printing Office, 1993), p. 2.

17. Alvin H. Kolak, assistant to the commissioner (quality), Internal Revenue Service, interview with Patricia Langan, October 15, 1992.

18. Kolak interview.

19. Internal Revenue Service, *1992 Annual Report*, pp. 3–4.

20. Joseph S. Coyle (with Elizabeth M. MacDonald and Robert Wool), "Four Basic Letters Can Help You to Win When the IRS Demands Extra Money from You That It Doesn't Deserve," *Money,* (April 1990), p. 87.

21. Internal Revenue Service, *1992 Annual Report*.

22. Kirkpatrick, *op. cit.*

23. IRS and Federal Quality Institute press releases.

24. Internal Revenue Service, *1991 Annual Report*, *1992 Annual Report*, and *Strategic Business Plan FY 1993 and Beyond* (revised September 1992).

25. General Accounting Office, *Tax Administration: IRS' 1992 Filing Season Was Successful but Not Without Problems* (Washington, DC: U.S. Government Printing Office, September 1992); IRS, *1992 Annual Report*.

26. Carol Krismann, *Quality Control, An Annotated Bibliography* (White Plains, NY: Quality Resources, 1990) p. xvi.

27. J. M. Juran, *Quality Control Handbook,* p. 35G.4.

28. Osborn and Gaebler, *op. cit.*, pp. 255–259.

29. Major General John M. Nowak, Deputy Chief of Staff for Logistics and Engineering, Military Airlift Command, U.S. Air Force, speech to 1991 Juran Impro Conference, October 28, 1991.
30. Brigadier General Donald E. Loranger, Inspector General, Air Mobility Command, U.S. Air Force, interview with the author, November 13, 1992.
31. Loranger interview.
32. Loranger interview; Lieutenant General Vernon J. Kondra, deputy chief of staff, AMC, speech to 1991 Juran Impro Conference, October 28, 1991.
33. Loranger interview and Nowak speech.
34. Loranger, telephone conversations with the author, April 1 and September 1, 1993.
35. "USAF Using TQM to Exploit Scaled-Back Forces," *Aviation Week & Space Technology* (February 15, 1993).
36. Admiral Frank B. Kelso, II, Chief of Naval Operations, U.S. Navy, "Building a Better Navy," *Proceeding of the U.S. Naval Institute* (August 1992), pp. 9–10.
37. Barbara Hummel, executive director, Madison Area Quality Improvement Network, interview with the author, September 15, 1992.
38. Sue A. Rohan, continuous improvement consultant University of Wisconsin Systems, interview with the author, September 17, 1992.
39. W. Michael Ley, vice president, David M. Griffith & Associates Ltd., interview with the author, September 16, 1992.
40. Mark D. Bugher, state revenue secretary, Wisconsin, interview with the author, September 14, 1992; also Forward Wisconsin news release dated February 24, 1992.
41. Roger D. Cross, administrator, Division of Motor Vehicles, Wisconsin, interview with the author, September 17, 1992.
42. L. Joseph Sensenbrenner, Sensenbrenner & Associates, interview with with author, September 14, 1992; Sensenbrenner, "Quality Comes to City Hall," *Harvard Business Review* (March–April 1991), pp. 64–75; Roger Goodwin, Street Superintendent, Public Works Department, Madison, WI, interview with the author, September 16, 1992.
43. David Couper, chief of police, Madison, WI, interview with the author, September 16, 1992; also Sensenbrenner, "Quality Comes to City Hall," *op. cit.*
44. Doug Kratsch, University of Wisconsin Hospital, vice president, South Central Federation of Labor of Wisconsin, interview with the author, September 15, 1992.
45. Paul Soglin, mayor of Madison, WI, interview with the author, September 14, 1992; Tom Mosgaller, city coordinator, Madison, WI, interview with the author, September 15, 1992, and several telephone conversations in 1993.

Conclusion

1. Tom Peters, "Burn That Article, Quick!" *Update* (Spring 1992).
2. Leon Wieseltier, "Total Quality Meaning," *The New Republic* (July 19 & 26, 1993), pp. 16–26.

3. W. Edwards Deming, *The New Economics* (Cambridge, MA: Massachusetts Institute of Technology Center for Advanced Engineering Study, 1993), pp. 25, 95.
4. "Some Manufacturers Drop Efforts to Adopt Japanese Techniques," *The Wall Street Journal*, (May 7, 1993), p. 1.
5. Ken Auletta, "Opening Up The Times," *The New Yorker* (June 28, 1993), pp. 55–70.
6. Michael Hammer and James Champy, *Reengineering The Corporation.* (New York: HarperBusiness, 1993), p. 1 (and *passim*).
7. J. M. Juran, "A Look Back—10 Years of Impro," speech to Juran Impro Conference, 1992.
8. Paul H. O'Neill, chairman and CEO, Aluminum Company of America, speech in Pittsburgh, August 9, 1991.
9. Carter interview.
10. Carter interview.
11. "Paul O'Neill, True Innovation, True Value, True Leadership," *Industry Week* (April 19, 1993), p. 24.
12. Akio Morita, "A Critical Moment for Japanese Management," *Bungei Shunju*, January 10, 1992.
13. Yoshinori Iizuka, associate professor, faculty of engineering, University of Tokyo, interview with the author, October 5, 1992.
14. Kano interview.
15. Kobayashi interview.
16. Malone interview.
17. "Talking Marriage and Thinking One-Night Stand," *Business Week* (October 18, 1993), p. 16.
18. Robert E. Cole, "Learning from Learning Theory: Implications for Quality Improvement of Turnover, Use of Contingent Workers and Job Rotation Policies," *Quality Management Journal* (Fall 1993).
19. For these conclusions I am indebted to A. Blanton Godfrey, CEO of the Juran Institute, who outlined them in his speech to the Juran Impro conference on November 13, 1993 and in subsequent speeches.

Bibliography

Books

AT&T, *The Statistical Quality Control Handbook*. Knoxville, TN: SPC Press Inc., 1985.

Bauer, Roy, Emilio Collar, and Victor Tang. *The Silverlake Project, Transformation at IBM*. New York: Oxford University Press, 1992.

Berwick, Donald M., A. Blanton Godfrey, and Jane Roessner. *Curing Health Care*. San Francisco: Jossey-Bass Inc., 1990.

Buzzell, Robert D., and Bradley T. Gale. *The PIMS Principles*. New York: The Free Press, 1987.

Brassard, Michael. *The Memory Jogger Plus+*. Methuen, MA: GOAL/QPC, 1989.

Camp, Robert C. *Benchmarking*. Milwaukee: ASQC Quality Press, 1989.

Ciampa, Dan. *Total Quality*. Reading, MA: Addison-Wesley Publishing Company, 1992.

Crosby, Philip B. *Quality Is Free*. New York: McGraw-Hill Book Company, 1979.

Deming, W. Edwards. *Out of the Crisis*. Cambridge, MA: Massachusetts Institute of Technology Center for Advanced Engineering Study, 1982.

Deming, W. Edwards. *The New Economics*. Cambridge, MA: Massachusetts Institute of Technology Center for Advanced Engineering Study, 1993.

Doody, Alton F., and Ron Bingaman. *Reinventing the Wheels: Ford's Spectacular Comeback*. Cambridge, MA: Ballinger Publishing Co., 1988.

Feigenbaum, Armand V. *Total Quality Control*. 3rd ed., rev. New York: McGraw-Hill, 1991.

Garvin, David A. *Managing Quality*. New York: The Free Press, 1988.

GOAL/QPC. *The Memory Jogger*. Methuen, MA: GOAL/QPC, 1988.

Hammer, Michael, and James Champy. *Reengineering The Corporation*. New York: HarperBusiness, 1993.

Hudiburg, John H. *Winning With Quality: The FPL Story*. White Plains, NY: Quality Resources, 1991.

Ishikawa, Kaoru. *Guide to Quality Control*. White Plains, NY: Quality Resources, 1990.

Ishikawa, Kaoru. *What is Total Quality Control?* Englewood Cliffs, NJ: Prentice-Hall, Inc., 1985.

Johnson, H. Thomas. *Relevance Regained*. New York: The Free Press, 1992.

Juran Institute. *Quality Improvement Tools:* Workbook Set. Wilton, CT: 1989.

Juran, J. M. *Quality-Control Handbook,* 1st ed. New York: McGraw-Hill Book Co., 1951.

Juran, J. M. *Managerial Breakthrough*. New York: McGraw-Hill Book Co., 1964.

Juran, J. M. *Juran on Leadership for Quality: An Executive Handbook*. New York: The Free Press, 1989.

Juran, J. M., Frank M. Gryna, eds. *Juran's Quality Control Handbook,* 4th ed. New York: McGraw-Hill Book Co., 1988.

Kearns, David T., and David A. Nadler. *Prophets in The Dark: How Xerox Reinvented Itself and Beat Back the Japanese*. New York: HarperCollins, 1992.

Keller, Maryann. *Rude Awakening*. New York: Harper Perennial, 1990.

King, Bob. *Hoshin Planning, The Developmental Approach*. Methuen, MA: GOAL/QPC, 1989.

Krismann, Carol. *Quality Control, An Annotated Bibliography*. White Plains, NY: Quality Resources, 1990.

Lawler, Edward E., III, Susan Albers Mohrman, and Gerald E. Ledford, Jr. *Employee Involvement and Total Quality Management*. San Francisco, Jossey-Bass Publishers, 1992.

Likert, Rensis. *New Patterns of Management*. New York: McGraw-Hill Book Co., 1961.

Likert, Rensis. *The Human Organization*. New York: McGraw-Hill Book Co., 1967.

Maslow, Abraham H. *Motivation and Personality*. New York: Harper & Brothers, 1954.

McGregor, Douglas. *The Human Side of Enterprise*. New York: McGraw-Hill Book Co., 1960.

Newhouse, John. *The Sporty Game*. New York: Alfred A. Knopf, 1985.

Ohno, Taiichi. *Toyota Production System*. Cambridge, MA: Productivity Press, 1988. First published in Japan, 1978.

Osborne, David, and Ted Gaebler. *Reinventing Government*. New York: Penguin Books, 1993.

Pascale, Richard Tanner. *Managing on the Edge*. New York: Touchstone, 1991.

Peters, Thomas J., and Robert H. Waterman, Jr. *In Search of Excellence*. New York: Warner Books Paperback, 1984.

Scherkenbach, William W. *Deming's Road to Continual Improvement*. Knoxville, TN: SPC Press, 1991.

Taylor, Frederick Winslow. *The Principles of Scientific Management*. New York: Harper & Brothers, 1911.

Tichy, Noel M., and Mary Anne Devanna. *The Transformational Leader*. New York: John Wiley & Sons, 1986.

Tillman, Barrett. *Hellcat: The F6F in World War II*. Annapolis, MD: Naval Institute Press, 1979.

Tribus, Myron. *Quality First: Selected Papers on Quality & Productivity Improvement*. Alexandria, VA: National Institute for Engineering Management & Systems, 1992.

Watson, Thomas J., Jr., and Peter Petre. *Father, Son & Co.: My Life at IBM and Beyond*. New York: Bantam Books, 1990.

Weise, Richard H. *Representing the Corporate Client: Designs for Quality*. Englewood Cliffs, NJ: Prentice-Hall Law & Business, 1991.

Wheelwright, Steven C., and Kim B. Clark. *Revolutionizing Product Development*. New York: The Free Press, 1992.

Womack, James P., Daniel T. Jones, and Daniel Roos. *The Machine That Changed the World*. New York: HarperCollins, 1991.

Articles

The American Lawyer, "Sidley gets with TQM Program" (May 23, 1993): 23.

Auletta, Ken. "Opening Up The Times." *The New Yorker* (June 28, 1993): 55–70.

Automotive News, "Buick City: From Bottom to No. 1" (December 18, 1989).

Aviation Week & Space Technology, "USAF Using TQM to Exploit Scaled-Back Forces" (February 15, 1993): 59.

Berry, Leonard L., and Linda R. Cooper. "Competing With Time-Saving Service." *Business* (April–June 1990): 3–7.

Brown, James H. "Four Major Community Quality Groups—A Basic Simplified Guide." *Community Link Newsletter* (Vol. 3, No. 2, 1993).

Business Week. "GM Tightens the Screws" (June 22, 1992): 30.

Business Week. "The Viper Is Already a Winner for Chrysler" (November 4, 1991): 36.

Business Week. "Inside Intel" (June 1, 1992): 86.

Business Week. "A Surge at Chrysler" (November 19, 1992): 88.

Business Week. "U.S. Cars Come Back" (November 16, 1992): 52.

Business Week. "Betting to win on the Baldie Winners" (October 18, 1993): 8.

Business Week. "Talking Marriage and Thinking One-Night-Stand" (October 18, 1993): 16.

Car and Driver, "Cadillac Seville" (May 1991): 97.

Ceridwen, Janice, Ventana Corporation. "Using Quality's Tools: What's Working Well." *The Journal for Quality And Participation* (March 1992): 92.

Classen, David C., et al. "The Timing of Prophylactic Administration of Antibiotics and the Risk of Surgical-Wound Infection." *The New England Journal of Medicine* (January 30, 1992): 281.

Clinton, Bill. "Putting People First." *Journal for Quality and Participation* (October/November 1992): 10.

Cole, Robert E. "Learning from Learning Theory: Implications for Quality Improvement of Turnover, Use of Contingent Workers and Job Rotation Policies." *Quality Management Journal* (Fall 1993).

Consumer Reports. "A New Way to Figure Reliability" (April 1993): 234.

Consumer Reports. "The Best (and Worst) Airlines" (July 1991): 462.

Consumer Reports. "The 1993 Cars" (April 1993): 220.

Coyle, Joseph S. with Elizabeth M. MacDonald and Robert Wool. "Four Basic Letters Can Help You to Win When the IRS Demands Extra Money from You That It Doesn't Deserve." *Money* (April 1990): 87.

Crystal, Graef S. "How Much CEOs Really Make." *Fortune* (June 17, 1991): 72.

Dewar, Donald L. "National Labor Relations Board vs. Teams." *Quality Digest,* (May 1993).

Duquesne University Record. "Total Quality Performance" (Spring 1992): 9.

Focus in Change. "Why Are We Here?" (Fall 1992). *Focus in Change* is a quarterly publication of the National Center for Effective Schools Research & Development in Madison, Wisconsin.

Gillies, Robin R., Stephen M. Shortell, *et al.* "National Survey of Hospital Quality Improvement Activities." *Hospitals & Health Networks* (December 5, 1993) and "Improving Quality Improvement Methods." *Hospitals & Health Networks* (January 5, 1994).

Godfrey, A. Blanton. "The History and Evolution of Quality in AT&T." *AT&T Technical Journal* (March–April 1986): 9.

Godfrey, A. Blanton, Donald M. Berwick, and Jane Roessner. "Can Quality Management Really Work in Health Care?" *Quality Progress* (April 1992): 23.

Henkoff, Ronald. "This Cat is Acting Like a Tiger." *Fortune* (December 19, 1988): 69.

Hopper, Kenneth. "Quality, Japan, and the U.S.: The First Chapter." *Quality Progress* (September 1985): 34.

Hopper, Kenneth. "Creating Japan's New Industrial Management: The Americans as Teachers." *Human Resource Management* (Summer 1982): 13.

Huey, John. "Mike Walsh Takes on Brain Cancer," *Fortune* (February 22, 1993): 76.

Industry Week. "Chrysler Hits the Road Again" (October 19, 1992): 68.

Industry Week. "Paul O'Neill, True Innovations, True Values, True Leadership" (April 19, 1993): 24.

James, Brent C. "How Do You Involve Physicians in TQM?" *Journal for Quality and Participation* (January–February 1991): 42.

James, Brent C. "TQM and Clinical Medicine." *Frontiers of Health Services Management* (Summer 1991): 42.

James, Brent C. "Quality Improvement in the Hospital: Managing Clinical Processes." *The Internist* (March 1993): 11.

Juran, J. M. "Made in U.S.A.: A Renaissance in Quality." *Harvard Business Review* (July–August, 1993): 42.

Kelso, Admiral Frank B., II, Chief of Naval Operations, U.S. Navy. "Building a Better Navy." *Proceedings of the U.S. Naval Institute* (August 1992): 9.

Kirkpatrick, David. "It's Simply Not Working." *Fortune* (November 19, 1990): 179.

Kupfer, Andrew. "An Outsider Fires up a Railroad." *Fortune* (December 18, 1989): 133.

Luther, David. "Advanced TQM: Measurements, Missteps, and Progress Through Key Result Indicators at Corning." *National Productivity Review* (Winter 1992/93): 23.

Main, Jeremy. "Service Without a Snarl." *Fortune* (March 23, 1981): 58.

Main, Jeremy. "Battling Your Own Bureaucracy." *Fortune* (June 15, 1981): 54.

Main, Jeremy. "Westinghouse's Cultural Revolution." *Fortune* (June 15, 1981): 74.

Main, Jeremy. "Ford's Drive for Quality." *Fortune* (April 18, 1983): 62.

Main, Jeremy. "The Trouble with Managing Japanese Style." *Fortune* (April 2, 1984): 14.

Main, Jeremy. "The Curmudgeon Who Talks Tough on Quality." *Fortune* (June 25, 1984): 78.

Main, Jeremy. "A Chipmaker Who Beats the Business Cycle." *Fortune* (December 23, 1985): 78.

Main, Jeremy. "Detroit's Cars Really Are Getting Better." *Fortune* (February 2, 1987): 90.

Main, Jeremy. "How to Win the Baldrige Award." *Fortune* (April 23, 1990): 67.

Measure, "Framework for Our Objectives" (July, 1989): 22. *Measure* is a Hewlett-Packard in-house publication.

Mizaur, Don G. "Is Quality Government Possible?" *Looking Ahead* (October 1992): 1.

Morita, Akio. "A Critical Moment for Japanese Management." *Bungei Shunju* (January 10, 1992).

The New York Times. "The Japanese Way at Quasar" (October 16, 1981).

The New York Times. "The Taurus: Big Sales, Big Repairs" (June 19, 1988).

The New York Times. "U.S. Steelmakers Staging Comeback on World Market" (March 31, 1992): A1.

The New York Times. "A New Heave in the Tax Tug-of-War" (December 8, 1992): D1.

The New York Times. "How G.M. Is Losing Its Hold on the Crucial Family Sedan" (March 7, 1993): D5.

The New York Times. "Saturns and Such" (August 29, 1993).

Ohmae, Kenichi, McKinsey & Co. "Quality Control Circles: They Work and They Don't Work." *Wall Street Journal* (March 29, 1982).

PC Magazine. "Pentium Power." (April 27, 1993): 112.

Peters, Tom. "Burn That Article, Quick!" *Update* (Spring 1992): 3.

Quality Progress. "Doing More with Less in the Public Sector" (July 1987): 20.

Railroad Age. "Conrail Puts Quality up Front" (June 1992): 27.

Road & Track. "The Halloween Party" (February 1984): 60.

Reichheld, Frederick E., and W. Earl Sasser, Jr. "Zero Defections: Quality Comes to Services." *Harvard Business Review* (September–October 1990): 105–111.

Sensenbrenner, L. Joseph. "Quality Comes to City Hall." *Harvard Business Review* (March–April 1991): 64–75.

Stata, Ray. "Organizational Learning—The Key to Management Innovation." *Sloan Management Review* (Spring 1989): 63.

Taylor, Alex. "Can GM Remodel Itself?" *Fortune* (January 13, 1992): 26.

Taylor, Alex. "U.S. Cars Come Back." *Fortune* (November 16, 1992): 52.

Taylor, Alex. "Can Iacocca Fix Chrysler—Again?" *Fortune* (April 8, 1991): 50.

Think. "Conversation with John Akers" (No. 1, 1989): 13.

Think. "A *Think* Special Report: Market-Driven" (No. 1, 1989): 14.

Think. "Letter from the Chairman" (No. 1, 1990): inside front cover.

Think. "What's Next for IBM?" (No. 1, 1990): 2.

Think. "More Than Just Problems" (No. 1, 1990): 9.

Think. "On Market-Driven Quality" (No. 4, 1990): 26.

The Wall Street Journal. "Ford's Strong Sales Raise Agonizing Issue of Additional Plants" (October 26, 1988).

The Wall Street Journal. "Ford Thunderbird Setbacks Dim Luster of Car of Year" (February 7, 1989).

The Wall Street Journal. "Southwest Airlines Is A Rare Air Carrier: It Still Makes Money" (October 26, 1992).

The Wall Street Journal. "Strife Between UAW And Caterpillar Blights Promising Labor Idea" (November 23, 1992).

The Wall Street Journal. "Motorola Illustrates How an Aged Giant Can Remain Vibrant" (December 9, 1992).

The Wall Street Journal. "Some Manufacturers Drop Efforts to Adopt Japanese Techniques" (May 7, 1993): 1.

The Wall Street Journal. "Gore Gets Earful of Bureaucratic Horror Stories As He Shapes a Plan to 'Reinvent' Government" (June 23, 1993).

Wieseltier, Leon. "Total Quality Meaning." *The New Republic* (July 19 and 26, 1993): 16–26.

Wiggenhorn, A. William. "Motorola U: When Training Becomes an Education." *Harvard Business Review* (July–August 1990): 71. Wiggenhorn is Motorola's vice president for training and education and president of Motorola University.

Wiggenhorn, A. William. "Creating Your Own Quality Definition." *The Conference Board Report,* No. 963, 1991.

Zemke, Ron. "Faith, Hope And TQM." *Training* (January 1992): 8.

Documents

Analog Devices Inc., *Annual Report* (1991).

Bateman, George R., and Harry V. Roberts. "TQM For Professors and Students." Paper in the Graduate School of Business, University of Chicago, February 1993.

Binns, Gregory S., and John F. Early. "Hospital Care: Frontiers in Managing Quality." *Juran Report,* Autumn 1989.

Bowen, Brent D., and Dean E. Headley. *The Airline Quality Report 1993.* Wichita, KS: National Institute for Aviation Research, Wichita State University, 1993.

Bowsher, Charles A., Comptroller General of the United States, "Improving Government," statement to the Senate Committee on Government Affairs, March 11, 1993. 103d Congress, 1st Session.

Bravo, Ellen, district manager, quality public relations, AT&T. Letter to the author, June 10, 1993.

Broadhead, James L., chairman, FPL Group. Letters to employees, May 5, 1990 and June 19, 1990.

Cole, Robert E. Letter to John Garamendi, insurance commissioner, state of California, February 29, 1992.

Cooper, Linda, and Beth Summers. *Getting Started In Quality,* First National Bank of Chicago, 1990.

Delta Consulting Group. "Ten Years After: Learning About Total Quality Management." New York, 1993.

Development Dimensions International, Quality & Productivity Management Association and *IndustryWeek.* "TQM: Forging Ahead or Falling Behind?" 1993.

Economic Strategy Institute, *The Future of the Auto Industry: It Can Compete, Can It Survive?* Washington, DC: 1992.

Elwyn, Charles, manager, Business Center H, Caterpillar Inc. Note to employees, August 6, 1992.

Ernst & Young and the American Quality Foundation. "Automobile Industry Report," "Banking Industry Report," "Computer Industry Report," and "Health Care Industry Report." All in *International Quality Study,* 1992.

First National Bank of Chicago. *Quality Performance Chart Books,* 9th ed. July–December 1989.

Florida Power & Light Co. *Summary Description of FPL's Quality Improvement Program,* 1989.

Florida Public Service Commission. Docket. No. 900478-EI, May 9, 1991.

Florida Public Service Commission, Consumer Affairs Division. *1992 Consumer Complaint Activity Report.* Tallahassee, 1993.

Florida Public Service Commission. *Summary of Electric Inspections and Variances—1986 to 1992,* Tallahassee, 1993.

The Gallup Organization. *Quality: Executive Priority or Afterthought?* Milwaukee, American Society for Quality Control, 1989.

General Accounting Office. *Quality Management: Survey of Federal Organizations.* Washington, DC: U.S. Government Printing Office, October 1, 1992.

General Accounting Office. *Tax Administration: IRS' 1992 Filing Season Was Successful but Not Without Problems.* Washington, DC: U.S. Government Printing Office, September 1992.

Godfrey, A. Blanton, chairman and CEO, Juran Institute, Inc. Testimony before the Subcommittee on Technology and Competitiveness of the House Committee on Science, Space, and Technology, February 5, 1992. 102d Congress, 2d Session.

Harbour & Associates, Inc. *The Harbour Report, A Decade Later: Competitive Assessment of the North American Auto Industry, 1979–1989.* Troy, MI, 1990.

Harbour & Associates, Inc. *The Harbour Report: Competitive Assessment of the North American Automotive Industry, 1989–1992.* Troy, MI, 1993.

Harvard Business School. *Florida Power & Light's Quality Improvement Program.* Case Study #9-688-043, 1987, revised August 8, 1990.

Harvard Business School. *Ford Motor Company, Dealer Sales and Service.* Case Study #39-690-030, 1989, revised February 2, 1992.

Harvard Business School. *Honda Motor Company and Honda of America (A).* Case Study #9-390-111, 1989, revised January 2, 1991.

Harvard Business School. *Motorola, Inc.: Bandit Pager Project.* Case Study #9-690-043, 1989, revised June 28, 1991.

Harvard Business School. *Transformation at Ford.* Case Study #9-390-083, 1989, revised November 11, 1991.

Hatch, Anthony, PaineWebber. Report on Consolidated Rail, May 28, 1992.

Henderson, B. Alex and Jack W. Murphy. "Xerox Corp. Company Update," Prudential Securities Inc., December 3, 1992.

Intel Corp. *1991 Malcolm Baldrige Award Application.*

Internal Revenue Service. *1991 Annual Report.* Washington, DC: U.S. Government Printing Office, 1992.

Internal Revenue Service. *1992 Annual Report.* Washington, DC: U.S. Government Printing Office, 1993.

Internal Revenue Service. *Strategic Business Plan FY 1993 and Beyond.* Washington, DC: U.S. Government Printing Office, 1992, revised September 1992.

International Association of Machinists and Aerospace Workers. *White Paper on Team Concept Programs,* October 1990.

Juran Institute, Inc. *On Quality Improvement,* Workbook. Wilton, CT: 1989.

Lawler, Edward E., III, and Susan A. Mohrman. "Quality Circles: A Self-Destruct Approach?" Paper at School of Business Administration, University of Southern California, 1984.

The MIT Commission on Industrial Productivity. *Working Papers,* Vol. 2. Cambridge, MA: The MIT Press, 1989.

Motorola memo to the author, April 7, 1993.

Motorola. *The Six Steps to Six Sigma.* Undated.

Murray, John E., Jr. "Total Quality Performance at Duquesne University." Undated.

Nashua Corp. *1991 Annual Report.*

National Institute of Standards and Technology. Press release NIST 92-17, August 10, 1992.

National Performance Review. *Creating a Government That Works Better & Costs Less.* Washington, DC: U. S Government Printing Office, 1993.

National Transportation Safety Board. *Railroad Accident Report, Derailment of Southern Pacific Transportation Company Freight Train on May 12, 1989 and Subsequent Rupture of Calnev Petroleum Pipeline on May 25, 1989, San Ber-*

nardino, California. Springfield, VA: National Technical Information Service, 1990.

Nelson, Lloyd S., retired director of statistical methods, Nashua Corporation. Letter to the author, May 29, 1992.

Power, J. D., and Associates. *The Power Report (1992 New Car Initial Quality Study)*, June 1992.

Power, J. D., and Associates. *The Saturn Way.* September, 1992.

Report of the Presidential Commission on the Space Shuttle Challenger Accident. Washington, DC: U.S. Government Printing Office, 1986.

Southern Pacific Lines. *Key Performance Indicators, June 1992.*

Southern Pacific Lines. *SP Management System Overview.* Undated; issued in early 1993.

Southern Pacific Rail Corporation. *Prospectus.* August 10, 1993.

Subcommittee on Oversight and Investigations, Committee on Energy and Commerce, U.S. House of Representatives, *The Bjork-Shiley Heart Valve: "Earn as You Learn."* Washington, DC: U.S. Government Printing Office, 1990. 101st Congress, 2d Session.

Tribus, Myron. "Total Quality Management in Schools of Business and of Engineering." Unpublished paper written in 1991.

Union Pacific Railroad. *UPdate* (management newsletter). June 1992.

Union Pacific Railroad. *A Quality Partnership.* Undated.

U.S. Department of Commerce press release, January 10, 1992.

The University of Michigan Task Force, Gilbert R. Whitaker, Jr., Chair. "Enhancing Quality in an Era of Resource Constraints: Report of the Task Force on Costs in Higher Education," 1990.

University of Michigan Medical Center. "Costs, Benefits, and Return From UMMC Total Quality Process: July 1987 Through June 1991," February 26, 1992.

Xerox Corp. *Leadership Through Quality.* Corporate booklet. 1990.

John Young letter to *Electronic Business,* August 5, 1991.

Interviews

Note: All interviews were with the author unless otherwise noted.

Philip Anschutz, chairman, Southern Pacific Rail Corp., July 2, 1992.

Carl H. Arendt, communications manager, Productivity and Quality Center, Westinghouse Electric Corp., June 3, 1992.

Charles A. Aubrey, vice president, Juran Institute, Inc., and former vice president for quality at Banc One in Columbus, Ohio, July 13, 1992.

John Badger, director, transportation and distribution services, Olin Chemicals, Olin Corp., July 17, 1992 and April 13, 1992.

James Bakken, former director of quality, Ford Motor Co., April 2, 1992.

William W. Barnard, vice president, Juran Institute, Inc., November 20, 1992.

Craig Barrett, executive vice president, Intel Corp., August 25, 1992.

Michael Bennett, president, UAW Local 1853, October 28, 1992.

Raland H. Berry, chief mechanical officer, Southern Pacific Lines, July 2, 1992.

Donald M. Berwick, president, Institute for Healthcare Improvement, telephone conversation, June 15, 1993.

John T. Bielan, vice president, continuous quality improvement, Consolidated Rail Corp., October 28, 1992.

Søren Bisgaard, Center for Quality and Productivity Improvement, University of Wisconsin–Madison, September 15, 1992.

Irving Bluestone, Walter Reuther Library, Wayne State University, March 30, 1992.

Patrick C. Bowie, vice president, quality, Milliken & Co., August 12, 1992.

Michael Brassard, director of research, GOAL/QPC, March 24, 1992.

James H. Brown, quality manager, Tennessee Valley Authority, telephone conversation July 2, 1993. Brown is also president of the Community Quality Coalition.

Jack Browne, director of marketing for Motorola's 68000 division, January 20, 1993.

Mark D. Bugher, revenue secretary, state of Wisconsin, September 14, 1992.

Robert C. Camp, manager of benchmarking, Xerox Corp., May 6, 1992.

Thomas L. Carter, senior vice president, quality, training and education, Aluminum Co. of America, November 12, 1992.

Winston H. Chen, chairman and CEO, Solectron Corp., August 26, 1992.

Dan Ciampa, president, Rath & Strong, May 18, 1992.

Thomas Clarkson, vice president, corporate quality, Allstate Insurance Co., telephone conversation on January 29, 1993.

David C. Classen, LDS Hospital, Salt Lake City, telephone conversation June 23, 1993.

Charles Clough, chairman, Nashua Corp., September 23, 1993.

Richard J. Coffey, director of management systems, University of Michigan Hospitals, interviews March 31 and May 20, 1992, telephone conversation June 7, 1993.

David E. Cole, director, Office for the Study of Automotive Transportation, University of Michigan, April 2, 1992.

Philip Condit, president of Boeing Co., January 7, 1992.

Russ Cook, shop committee member, UAW Local 599, Buick City, September 25, 1992.

Linda R. Cooper, head of the consumer affairs department, The First National Bank of Chicago, July 31, 1992,

David Couper, chief of police, Madison, September 16, 1992.

Roger D. Cross, administrator, Division of Motor Vehicles, Wisconsin, September 17, 1992.

Fred Cullen, CEO of Banc One Wisconsin, September 18, 1992. Cullen has since become chief financial officer of the parent Banc One in Columbus.

Joseph DeFeo, vice president, Juran Institute, Inc., May 13, 1992.

Donald Dewar, president, QCI International, telephone conversation with the author March 16, 1993.

John F. Early, vice president, Juran Institute, Inc., March 22, 1993.

Don Ephlin, former vice president, United Auto Workers, May 18, 1992.

Tom Furey, general manager, IBM Santa Teresa Laboratory, August 20, 1992.

Robert W. Galvin, chairman of the executive committee of the board of directors, Motorola Inc., July 30, 1992.

Ellen J. Gaucher, chief operating officer, University of Michigan Hospitals, March 31, 1992.

Robert Geiger, manager, tape division, Nashua Corp., January 10, 1993.

John Gervasio, manager of reliability engineering, Pan American Cellular Subscriber Group, Motorola Inc., July 29, 1992.

Roger Goodwin, Street Superintendent, Public Works Department, Madison, September 16, 1992.

Thomas Gorcyca, customer quality research, Ford Motor Co. telephone conversation April 15, 1993.

Tom Griffith, manager, purchasing support and development, Honda of North America, September 24, 1992.

N. Michael Grove, vice president and general counsel, Bell Communications Research, interview with G. Howland Blackiston, president, Juran Institute, Inc., July 20, 1992.

James A. Hagen, chairman, Consolidated Rail Corp., October 27, 1992.

Rear Admiral Robert B. Halder, senior vice president, Juran Institute, Inc., July 17, 1992.

Takashi Hara, general manager in charge of research and planning, Takenaka Corp., October 14, 1992.

Gerald S. Hartman, steel-industry consultant, State College, Pennsylvania, June 5, 1992.

Tim Hoeksema, chairman and CEO, Midwest Express Airlines, September 18, 1992.

Chris Holland, director of quality consulting and training, Harvard Community Health Plan, telephone conversation June 11, 1993.

Robert Holmes, vice president for academic affairs and executive director for M-Quality, University of Michigan, telephone conversation, June 17, 1993.

Aleta Holub, vice president and manager, quality assurance, Global Corporate Bank, The First National Bank of Chicago, July 31, 1992.

John J. Hudiburg, former chairman, Florida Power & Light Co., telephone interview, January 15, 1993.

Barbara Hummel, executive director, Madison Area Quality Improvement Network, September 15, 1992.

Yoshinori Iizuka, associate professor, faculty of engineering, University of Tokyo, October 5, 1992.

Dennis Jacobson, managing director of customer service, Southern Pacific Lines, June 30, 1992.

John Jacobson, steel industry analyst, The WEFA Group, telephone conversation, April 22, 1993.

Joseph D. Jenkins, director, electric and gas division, Florida Public Service Commission, telephone conversation, January 15, 1993.

T. Barton Jones, partner, Winthrop, Stimson, Putnam & Roberts, telephone conversation June 17, 1993. Also interviewed by Howland Blackiston, July 18, 1992.

Edward Kammerer, vice president, Juran Institute, Inc., June 25, 1992, and April 21, 1993. Kammerer previously was vice president for marketing (chemicals) at Southern Pacific.

Noriaki Kano, professor, Science University of Tokyo, October 6, 1992.

Matt Kelliher, vice president for quality, Harvard Community Health Plan, March 24, 1992. Telephone conversation June 11, 1993. Kelliher has since moved to Massachusetts Blue Cross/Blue Shield.

Melanie Kennedy, quality coordinator, state of Arkansas, telephone conversations, July and September, 1993.

Thomas N. Kennedy, vice president for quality, Solectron Corp., August 26, 1992.

C. Robert Kidder, chairman, Duracell International Inc., April 13, 1992.

Yotaro Kobayashi, chairman of Fuji-Xerox, October 16, 1992.

Alvin H. Kolak, assistant to the commissioner (quality), Internal Revenue Service, interview with Patricia Langan, October 15, 1992.

Yoshio Kondo, professor emeritus, Kyoto University, October 5, 1992.

Doug Kratsch, University of Wisconsin Hospital, vice president, South Central Federation of Labor of Wisconsin, September 15, 1992.

Professor Hitochi Kume, faculty of engineering, University of Tokyo, October 6, 1992.

Charles R. LaMantia, president and CEO, Arthur D. Little Inc., March 26, 1992.

Lev Landa, Landamatics International Inc., March 18, 1992.

David P. Langford, Langford Quality Education, telephone interview, December 11, 1992 with Patricia Langan and subsequent calls.

Edward E. Lawler, III, director, Center for Effective Organizations, Graduate School of Business Administration, University of Southern California, telephone interview, December 11, 1992.

Keith Lawrence, associate director, Global Product Supply, Procter & Gamble, telephone interview, January 26, 1993.

Tim Lee, plant manager, Buick City, September 25, 1992.

Richard LeFauve, president of Saturn Corporation, October 28, 1992.

David M. LeVan, senior vice president–operations, Conrail, October 27, 1992.

W. Michael Ley, vice president, David M. Griffith & Associates Ltd., September 16, 1992.

Gerry G. Link, vice president and director of quality, Pan American Cellular Subscriber Group, Motorola, July 29, 1992.

Brigadier General Donald E. Loranger, Inspector General, Air Mobility Command, U.S. Air Force, November 13, 1992., and telephone conversation April 1, 1993.

Dr. John M. Ludden, medical director, Harvard Community Health Plan, telephone conversation, June 22, 1993.

David B. Luther, senior vice president, corporate director–quality, Corning Glass Work, November 11, 1992.

Thomas J. Malone, president, Milliken & Co., August 29, 1992.

John Marous, retired chairman, Westinghouse Electric Corp., June 4, 1992.

William G. Martin, manufacturing manager, and Kent Stockwell, quality department manager, Hewlett-Packard, Corvallis, OR division, August 19, 1992.

Tadashi Matsuda, chief engineer, Quality Control Office, Saitama factory, Honda Motor Co., Ltd., October 14, 1992.

JR Mays, organizational development coordinator, UAW, Buick City plant, September 25, 1992.

James McIngvale, owner of the Gallery Furniture Store, Dallas, by telephone, February 2, 1993.

Shari Michael-Kenney, quality director, Banc One Wisconsin, September 18, 1992.

Roger Milliken, CEO, Milliken & Co., August 12, 1992, and by telephone February 5, 1990.

Tom Mosgaller, city coordinator, Madison, September 15, 1992.

Thomas J. Murrin, dean, School of Business & Administration, Duquesne University, June 3, 1992.

C. Warren Neel, dean of the business school, University of Tennessee, December 3, 1992.

Lloyd S. Nelson, director of statistical methods, Nashua Corp. (retired), May 28, 1992, and other occasions beginning in 1992.

Paul Noakes, vice president and director of external quality programs, Motorola Inc., July 30, 1992

Junji Noguchi, executive director, Japanese Union of Scientists and Engineers, October 15, 1992.

Michael Oblak, plant chairman, Wayne I.S.A. Stamping Plant, Local 900 UAW, May 20, 1992.

James B. O'Connor, ex-president of UAW Local 974 and service representative for central Illinois, by telephone, February 2, 1993.

Bob Olive, administrative manager of distribution, L. L. Bean, May 29, 1992.

Jan Partain, quality management program, Arkansas Industrial Development Commission, telephone conversation, June 30, 1993.

Madhav S. Phadke, supervisor, network performance, Bell Laboratories, June 10, 1988.

James Paulsen, director of quality, Ford Motor Co., May 21, 1992.

Robert Peixotto, vice president, total quality management, L. L. Bean, September 16, 1992.

Rick Pfizenmayer, assistant general counsel, Texaco Inc., interview with G. Howland Blackiston, president, Juran Institute, Inc., July 18, 1992.

Frank Pipp, retired director of manufacturing, Xerox Corp., March 17, 1992.

Ralph Ponce de Leon, vice president and corporate director, supply and environmental management, Motorola Inc., July 29, 1992.

C. K. Prahalad, Business School, University of Michigan, March 31, 1992.

James Brian Quinn, Buchanan professor of management, Amos Tuck School of Business Administration, Dartmouth College, telephone conversation, May 14, 1993.

John Rampey, vice president and director of human relations, Milliken & Co., August 13, 1992.

Marty Raymond, manager, training and strategic implementation, sales, service and marketing, Saturn Corp., October 28, 1992.

James Riley, vice president, Juran Institute, Inc., March 12, 1992.

John Risk, director of car and truck body engineering, North American Automotive Operations, Ford Motor Co., May 18, 1992.

Sue A. Rohan, continuous improvement consultant, University of Wisconsin system, interview with the author, September 17, 1992.

Richard N. Rosett, dean, School of Business, Rochester Institute of Technology, telephone conversation, July 7, 1993.

Phillip M. Scanlan, vice president, Corporate Quality Office, AT&T, January 7, 1993.

Franklin P. Schargel, assistant principal, George Westinghouse Vocational and Technical High School, interview with Patricia Langan, October 5, 1992.

Arthur M. Schneiderman, Vice President of Quality and Productivity at Analog Devices, on May 29, 1992 and January 19 and March 2, 1993. Mr. Schneiderman is now an independent consultant.

William W. Scherkenbach, group director, statistics and process improvement methods, BOC Group, General Motors, April 1, 1992. Scherkenbach has since become an independent consultant.

Peter R. Scholtes, Joiner Associates Inc., September 17, 1992.

Stephen B. Schwartz, senior vice president, quality, IBM, August 31, 1992. Mr. Schwartz has since retired.

L. Joseph Sensenbrenner, Sensenbrenner & Associates, September 14, 1992.

David Seybolt, manager, locomotive reliability, General Electric Transportation Systems, telephone conversation, September 24, 1993.

Lloyd Simpson, vice president of quality, Southern Pacific Transportation Co., July 1, 1992.

Paul Soglin, mayor of Madison, September 14, 1992.

Michael Stahl, associate dean, School of Business Administration, University of Tennessee, telephone conversation, July 7, 1993.

Ray Stata, chairman of Analog Devices, May 29, 1992 and October 30, 1985.

W. Kent Sterett, as director, Quality Improvement Department, Florida Power & Light Co., June 6, 1988; as executive vice president of Southern Pacific Transportation Co., August 24, 1992.

Charles Stridde, people systems team leader, Saturn Corp., October 28, 1992.

Russell Strobel, resource manager, Paging Products Group, Motorola Corp., telephone conversation on May 28, 1993.

Brenda Sumberg, director for quality, Motorola University, telephone conversation, September 20, 1991.

Tina Sung, senior quality executive, Federal Quality Institute, interview with Pat Langan, October 16, 1992.

Daniel Sweeney, director of passenger services, Midwest Express Airlines, September 18, 1992.

Shigeyoshi Takashi, chief engineer, Reliability and Quality Control Division, NEC Corp., October 16, 1992.

Victor Tang, director, strategy, planning, and quality programming systems, IBM, San Jose, California, August 25, 1992.

Susumu Uchikawa, director, production control logistics, member of the board, Toyota Motor Corp., October 13, 1992.

Donald Wadanse, chief, division of research management, National Capital Parks/ Central, telephone conversation, April 14, 1993.

Craig Walter, corporate quality director, Hewlett-Packard Co., August 20, 1992.

Eizo Watanabe, counselor to the Japanese Union of Scientists and Engineers, October 15, 1992.

Robert Weinberger, marketing manager, workstations systems group, Hewlett-Packard Co., September 4, 1992.

Richard H. Weise, senior vice president and general counsel, Motorola Corp., July 30, 1992.

Asa Whitaker, quality manager, Arkansas Eastman Co., telephone conversation, July 1, 1993.

B. Joseph White, dean, Business School, University of Michigan, February 21, 1992, plus several telephone conversations.

Howard Wilson, director, Market Driven Quality, IBM, telephone conversation, July 13, 1993.

Terry Wirth, Buyers Laboratory Inc., telephone conversation, October 7, 1993.

Walter Wriston, former chairman, Citicorp, telephone conversation, December 7, 1992.

Katsumi Yoshimoto, quality manager, Hewlett-Packard Asia Pacific, October 7, 1992.

John A. Young, president and CEO, Hewlett-Packard Co., August 20, 1992.

Thomas J. Zimbrick, General Manager, Saturn of Madison, Wisconsin, September 17, 1992.

Speeches

Richard W. Anderson, manager, Data Systems Division, Hewlett-Packard Co., speech to the Electronics Industry Association of Japan, Washington, DC, March 25, 1980.

Philip Anschutz, chairman, Southern Pacific Transportation Co., speech to the Juran 1991 Impro Conference, October 30, 1991.

Bill Clinton, remarks at the White House, March 3, 1993.

Brian R. Churm, engineering manager, AT&T Network Software Center, speech to Juran 1990 Impro Conference, October 29, 1990.

William G. Ditoro, director, national inventory, Nabisco Foods Group, talk to Juran 1992 Impro Conference, November 13, 1992.

A. Blanton Godfrey, CEO, Juran Institute, Inc., speech to the Juran 1992 Impro Conference, November 13, 1992.

A. Blanton Godfrey, "At the Cutting Edge of Quality," speech to the U.S. Chamber of Commerce Quality Learning Series, February 26, 1993.

James R. Houghton, chairman, Corning Inc., speech to the National Quality Forum III, New York, October 13, 1987.

Lee A. Iacocca, chairman, Chrysler Corp., speech at Jefferson Assembly Plant, Detroit, August 6, 1980.

Carl James, general chairman, Brotherhood of Locomotive Engineers, Denver Rio Grande Western, remarks at a meeting of the Southern Pacific Transportation Co. Labor-Management Advisory Committee, July 1, 1992.

J. M. Juran, chairman, Juran Institute, Inc., retired, talk to Milliken & Co. seminar, May 15, 1992.

J. M. Juran, "A Look Back—10 Years of Impro," speech to 1992 Juran Impro Conference, Chicago, November 13, 1992.

Lieutenant General Vernon J. Kondra, deputy chief of staff, AMC, speech to 1991 Juran Impro Conference, Atlanta, October 28, 1991.

David B. Luther, senior vice president, corporate director–quality, Corning Inc., speech to the Japanese Management Association, October 13, 1992.

Marshall McDonald, president, FPL Group Inc., speech to the Juran Institute's fourth annual conference on quality improvement, Chicago, October 9, 1986.

Roger Milliken, chairman of Milliken & Co., speech accepting the Baldrige Award, November 2, 1989.

Major General John M. Nowak, Deputy Chief of Staff for Logistics and Engineering, Military Airlift Command, U.S. Air Force, speech to 1991 Juran Impro Conference, October 28, 1991.

Paul H. O'Neill, chairman and CEO, Aluminum Co. of America, speech to corporate management in Pittsburgh, August 9, 1991.

Larry Osterwise, director, market-driven quality, IBM, talk to Benchmarking Week '92, American Quality and Productivity Center, Dallas, TX, May 6, 1992.

Robert A. Scanlon, director of quality and reliability engineering, Southern Pacific Transportation Co., speech to 1991 Juran Impro Conference, Atlanta, October 29, 1991.

Laurence C. Seifert, vice president for engineering, manufacturing, and production planning, AT&T. Speech to 1987 Juran Impro Conference, Chicago, November 9, 1987.

G. Richard Wagoner, Jr., executive vice president, General Motors Corp., speech to auto industry briefing, Traverse City, Michigan, August 6, 1993.

Mike Walsh, *The Processes and Principles of Tenneco*, undelivered speech distributed in April, 1992.

Kenichi Yamamoto, chairman (since retired), Mazda Motor Corp., speech to auto industry briefing in Traverse City, Michigan, August 6, 1986.

Hiroyuki Yoshino, President, Honda of America Manufacturing, Inc., speech to auto industry briefing in Traverse City, Michigan, August 7, 1991.

John Young, CEO of Hewlett-Packard Co., speech at Syracuse University, October 16, 1991.

James W. Zachman, division manager, quality management, AT&T, talk to the 1990 Juran Institute Impro Conference, Atlanta, October 28, 1990.

Acknowledgments

O ne of the gratifying things about investigating the evolution of total quality management is that the people who practice it cannot stop telling the world what they have discovered. Sometimes that becomes a handicap, because their enthusiasm becomes a little overpowering. But for the most part it means that the sources for such research are extremely generous in giving their time and sharing their knowledge. It is part of the quality ethic to be open and honest and I was a beneficiary.

I am particularly indebted to the Juran Institute in Wilton, Connecticut, which offered me the expertise of its consultants and funded my research without ever trying to impose its views on me. I should especially mention the president, Howland Blackiston; he was the project's shepherd, and, along with John Early, a vice president, he slogged through the first manuscript and gave me many helpful suggestions. The chairman emeritus, Joseph Juran, and the current chairman, Blanton Godfrey, shared some exceptional insights. Theresa Amaral, Chuck Aubrey, Bill Barnard, Joe De-Feo, Rick Dmytrow, Al Endres, Bob Halder, Dick Harshbarger, Marcia Heath, Bob Hoogstoel, Ed Kammerer, Gabe Pall, Joan Pinck, Jim Riley, Pete Robustelli, Judy Schalick, Frank Tedesco, Frank Troha, and Bob Wilson, all of the Juran Institute, made a big contribution to whatever virtues this book may have. They shared their knowledge and opened doors that might otherwise have remained closed to me.

The heart of this book lies in the many interviews granted me by CEOs, current or recent, who were extremely generous with their time and frank in their talk. My interviews with Bob Galvin of Motorola and John Young of Hewlett-Packard, both statesmen among businessmen, were especially rewarding. I also want to thank these CEOs: Phil Anschutz of Southern Pacific, Winston Chen of Solectron, Charles Clough of Nashua, Fred Cullen of Banc One (Wisconsin), Jim Hagen of Conrail, Tim Hoeksema of Midwest Express, Bob Kidder of Duracell, Tony Kobayashi of Fuji-Xerox, John

Marous of Westinghouse (retired), Roger Milliken of Milliken & Co. (as well as Milliken's company president, Tom Malone), and Ray Stata of Analog Devices.

Other senior executives who were most helpful included Craig Barrett, executive vice president of Intel; Skip LeFauve, the president of Saturn; David Luther, senior vice president of Corning; Kent Sterett, executive vice president of Southern Pacific; and Stephen Schwartz, a senior vice president at IBM until recently.

I am indebted to Lloyd Nelson, formerly of Nashua, for good advice and good suggestions, as well as for vetting portions of the manuscript. Special thanks also go to Carl Arendt of Westinghouse, Margot Brown of Motorola, Richard Coffey of the University of Michigan Hospitals, Bob Cole of the University of California at Berkeley, David Cole of the University of Michigan, Susan Crocker of Hewlett-Packard, Barbara Hummel of MAQIN in Madison, General Donald Loranger and Colonel "Jocko" Hayden of the U.S. Air Force, Tom Murrin of the School of Business & Administration at Duquesne, Warren Neel and Mike Stahl of the University of Tennessee College of Business Administration, Frank Pipp and John Kelsch of Xerox, the late John Rampey of Milliken, Art Schneiderman, formerly of Analog Devices, Tina Sung of the Federal Quality Institute, Joe White of the University of Michigan business school, Ron Zemke of *Training* magazine, and many, many others.

In Japan, Junji Noguchi and Eizo Watanabe of the Japanese Union of Scientists and Engineers, Hitoshi Kume and Yoshinori Iizuka of the faculty of engineering at the University of Tokyo, Noriaki Kano of the Science University of Tokyo, Yoshio Kondo of Kyoto University (emeritus), Masayuki Yokoyama of the Japan Productivity Center, and Yoshinao Nakada of Bell Labs in Japan generously contributed to my education in quality. The representatives of Toyota, Honda, Takenaka, NEC, Yokogawa Hewlett-Packard opened my eyes to much that I did not know. Without the help of Cindy Kano of *Fortune's* Tokyo office I could never have made the contacts and arranged the rewarding schedule that greeted me in Tokyo.

My former colleague at *Fortune*, Pat Langan, contributed very useful research from Washington and New York. Over the years, successive managing editors of *Fortune*, Bill Rukeyser and Marshall Loeb, and executive editor Allan Demaree, encouraged my interest in total quality and helped me lay the groundwork for this book. My friend and colleague Roy Rowan spurred me on to do it. My editor at The Free Press, Bob Wallace, proved patient, wise—and most encouraging.

As is usual in these cases, my family endured. My wife, Patricia, not only put up with my mental and physical absences but performed heroic labor transcribing many interviews and reading copy for content and errors. My children and grandchildren got less of my time and attention than they deserve.

I add the customary disclaimer that whatever faults the book has are entirely my own doing.

J. M.

Index